CUTOVER CAPITALISM

HISTORIES OF CAPITALISM AND THE ENVIRONMENT
Bart Elmore, Series Editor

Cutover Capitalism: The Industrialization of the Northern Forest
Jason L. Newton

Rogues in the Postcolony: Narrating Extraction and Itinerancy in India
Stacey Balkan

CUTOVER CAPITALISM

The Industrialization of the Northern Forest

JASON L. NEWTON

WEST VIRGINIA UNIVERSITY PRESS
MORGANTOWN

First edition published 2024 by West Virginia University Press
Printed in the United States of America

ISBN 978-1-959000-29-7 (paperback) / 978-1-959000-30-3 (ebook)

Library of Congress Cataloging-in-Publication Data

Names: Newton, Jason L., 1986– author.
Title: Cutover capitalism : the industrialization of the northern forest / Jason L. Newton.
Description: Morgantown : West Virginia University Press, 2024. | Series: Histories of capitalism and the environment | Includes bibliographical references and index. | Identifiers: LCCN 2024009296 | ISBN 9781959000297 (paperback) | ISBN 9781959000303 (ebook)
Subjects: LCSH: Loggers—United States. | Logging—United States.
Classification: LCC HD8039.L92 U565 2024 | DDC 333.75/150973—dc23/eng/20240514
LC record available at https://lccn.loc.gov/2024009296

Book and cover design by Than Saffel / WVU Press.
Cover image: Winslow Homer, *The Woodcutter*, 1891.
Artefact / Alamy Stock Photo

To my grandfather

CONTENTS

LIST OF ILLUSTRATIONS

Figures drawn from statewide data as opposed to just data from Northern Forest counties have the word "statewide" in the title or caption.

ACKNOWLEDGMENTS

This has been a very long project and a culmination of my personal and professional influences to date. For that reason, there are countless people, institutions, places, and things I would like to thank but won't be able to here. Among the people who have been the greatest help is Andrew W. Cohen, who has been a role model and inspiration. He has given me constructive earnest advice and has trusted my creative process.

I must thank other influential teachers, including Donald Little, Brian Freeland, Myriam Ibarra, Laurie Marhoefer, Andrew Lippman, Carol Faulkner, Gladys McCormick, John Roger Sharp, Ralph Ketcham, and finally Robert Wilson, who first piqued my interest in environmental history. My colleagues in graduate school, Elissa Michelle Isenberg, Mark Dragoni, Sravani Biswas, Namhee Lee, Lei Zhang, Adam Parsons, Paul Andrew Arras, Thomas A. Guiler, Alexandra Marie Elias, Yoshina Hurgobin, Lex Jing Lu, Judd David Olshan, Robert John Clines, Will Murphy, Jesse Hysell, Silas Webb, and Molly Jessup, were vital sources of advice and reflection. I am especially thankful for my friendship with Philip D. Erenrich, who provided advice and conversation that inspired several chapters.

I was supported by many of the faculty at Cornell University, including Louis Hyman, Ileen Devult, Verónica Martínez-Matsuda, and Aaron Sacks, among others. Not all teaching takes place in a classroom, and I must thank the following people who were never formally teachers of mine but who were nonetheless inspiring advisers: Don Mitchell, Thomas Andrews, Richard Judd, and Graeme Wynn. At the University of North Carolina at Charlotte, I was well received by many faculty who immediately supported this work, including Tina Schull, Mark Wilson, Peter J. Ferdinando, Carol Higham, and Gregory Mixon, among others. Few history books would be possible without the support of libraries, librarians, and archivists. Particularly helpful for my research were Jamie Rice at the Maine Historical Society, Desirée Butterfield-Nagy at the

University of Maine library, and Pauleena MacDougall and Katrina Wynn at the Northeast Archives of Folklore and Oral History.

The fellowships and grants that I received for research and writing were supportive in two ways. The first is obvious—they allowed me to get to archives and gave me time to write. Second, each award I won helped me feel like a historian, giving me confidence during periods of self-doubt. The Maxwell School of Citizenship and Public Affairs at Syracuse University was an essential source of funding, as was Cornell University and the University of North Carolina at Charlotte. The New England Regional Fellowship Consortium, managed by the Massachusetts Historical Society, kickstarted this research but there were several other sources of funding that made this book possible, including the Anna K. and Mary E. Cunningham Research Residencies in New York State History and Culture, the Weston A. Cate Jr. Fellowship, the Alfred D. Bell Jr. Travel Grant, the Alfred D. Chandler Jr. Travel Fellowship, and the World Wood Day Foundation research grant.

My family was a constant source of support, but more than anything, they helped me build the skills needed to complete this book and stoked my curiosity at a young age. My wife, Krysten Reilly, has been consistently supportive and has ensured that I did not get lost in this work. Finally, I thank the snow and trees.

INTRODUCTION

Most summers when I was a kid, my family drove our 1986 Chrysler LeBaron past a twelve-foot-tall wooden, chainsaw-carved lumberjack statue on our way to our late grandfather's vacation home in Tupper Lake, in the heart of New York State's Adirondack State Park (figure 0.1). My grandparents were born in this village, moved away for work as adults, and later bought this cabin. As my family drove from our urban downstate home into the forest, the roads became narrow, and the smell of wood smoke wafted through the vents. At camp, we made our own campfires, swam in the lake, and hiked up mountain trails that revealed views of a great forest dotted with little communities.

Down the street from the lumberjack statue, we saw the old Oval Wood Dish Company factory, crumbling and in disrepair. Closed for production since 1964, it was once a hub of manufacturing that transformed forest resources into disposable wooden plates and cutlery. To feed its machines and the mills across the Adirondacks, thousands of workers were mobilized to cut, transport, and process wood. This industry once brought prosperity to the region.[1]

The shuttered factory symbolized larger problems in the village. Even as a child I recognized the poverty in Tupper Lake. The permanent residents did not live in stylized rustic cabins like our vacation home but in small houses or trailers. The lack of streetlights, plumbing, and a local hospital, quaint features for vacationers, were signs of a depressed rural economy. In the 1990s and early 2000s, only four Adirondack counties had a poverty rate below 15 percent, and Franklin County, where Tupper Lake is located, was the fourth poorest county in the state with about one in five residents considered impoverished.[2] For me, these childhood trips were early lessons not only in environmental history but also in inequality.[3]

The economic troubles and forest landscape of Tupper Lake were both juxtaposed in my mind with the lumberjack statue. The lumberjack figure

Figure 0.1. Tupper Lake lumberjack statue, 2023 (Photo by Susan Riley)

and references to it were found all over Tupper Lake. The Lumberjack Inn on Main Street served stacks of pancakes, local shops sell books with tales (some true, some fictional) from the old lumber camps, the baseball teams' mascot was the timberjacks (later it changed its name to the riverpigs, a reference to log drive workers), and the high school's mascot is the lumberjack. Tourists can buy lumberjack T-shirts and hoodies at the local gas stations, and every summer there is a Woodsmen's Day festival that draws crowds to watch amateur athletes reenact the work of the old lumberjacks.

I had a family connection to these workers and their environment. My great-grandparents were Adirondack lumberjacks who immigrated from Québec in the 1900s. By the 1930s the wood products industry in Tupper Lake was in decline, and in the 1950s my grandparents moved downstate for jobs because of the lack of opportunities.

In college I traveled across the Northeast and saw many communities that reminded me of Tupper Lake. I also saw more lumberjack statues, all of which emphasize the size and power of these workers. It made sense that locals would have pride in this history. Lumber was the second most valuable commodity in the United States in 1860. By 1869 the Northeast was the center of production for forest products.[4] New York and Maine remained among the top eleven lumber producing states from 1839 to 1940.[5] The people in Tupper Lake understood their place in this history. There was deeper meaning in the symbolism of the lumberjack—but what was that meaning? Was it a memorial to organized labor, or was it a commemoration of something else? The forests, the statues, this industry, and the present economic stagnation inspired me to look deeper into regional history.

The economic stagnation provoked a congressional investigation in 1990 that would give a coherency to the region. This investigation, *The Northern Forest Lands Study of New England and New York*, examined the economic conditions in this thirty-million-acre bioregion that stretched from the Atlantic coast of Maine to the western edge of the Adirondacks in New York (figure 0.2). Twenty-seven counties were included in the region. In Maine: Aroostook, Franklin, Penobscot, Piscataquis, Somerset, Hancock, Oxford, Washington. In New Hampshire: Coos. In New York: Clinton, Essex, Franklin, Fulton, Hamilton, Herkimer, Jefferson, Lewis, Oneida, Oswego, St. Lawrence, Warren. Finally, in Vermont: Caledonia, Essex, Franklin, Lamoille, Orleans, and Washington. Vivacious and diverse forests covered somewhere from 77 to 90 percent of the land. Trees define and unite the region.[6]

When I began my research, I planned to write a labor history. I hoped to uncover instances of resistance and union organization that would fit the Northern Forest into the larger narrative of United States labor history. I found little evidence of organizing here compared to other US industries and other lumbering regions. The first important instance happened in 1924 when the Industrial Workers of the World (IWW) tried and failed to organize loggers in Greenville, ME.[7] IWW organizers found that "there was no labor movement"

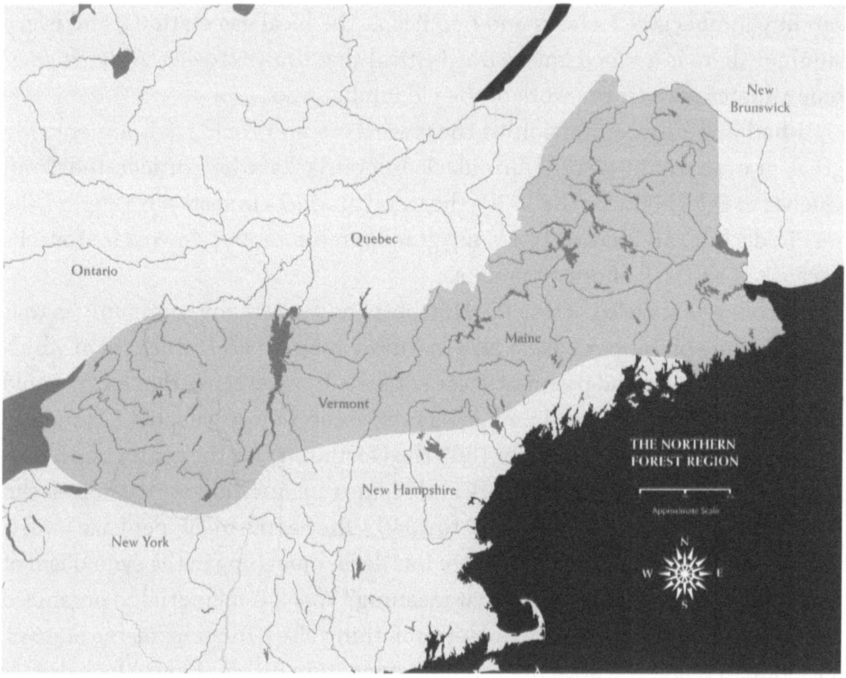

Figure 0.2. Northern Forest map (Created by the Northern Forest Center, Concord, NH)

in the Northern Forest and workers were difficult to rally.[8] The first successful organization attempt happened in 1955 with Brown Company woodcutters in New Hampshire. The union did not last long, nor did it spread.[9] There were no other examples until 1975, when the Maine Woodsmen Association was founded, largely to oppose immigrant Canadian loggers and truckers from entering the country.[10]

After discovering the lack of organization, I shifted my focus to why loggers in the Northeast didn't rebel against industrial capitalism with the same ferocity of notoriously radical western lumberjacks or Northeastern factory workers.[11] The scope of the study needed to widen. Instead of researching organizers or union records, I needed to explore what made forest product production in the Northern Forest unique. I needed to explain how value was created there, and how this history of value creation was different than the history of value creation in other regions. My focus became all-encompassing, a study of both human and nonhuman nature. This is a labor history of a forest.

Cutover Capitalism

This book describes the connected ways in which capitalism worked on and through human and nonhuman forms of nature. My definition of capitalism is modern, simple, and undoubtedly contestable: Capitalism happens when and wherever powerful parts of economic and government structures, along with popular social, familial, intellectual, and cultural norms, align to prioritize the indefinite and rapid growth of private capital. This alignment can cause interdependencies locally, within nation-states, and globally, making it difficult for stakeholders to abandon or alter the desire for growth. A vital but not essential part of capitalism is making the smallest amount of capital produce the greatest returns in the shortest period of time with the least risk. In capitalism, the support for the accumulation of private capital often takes preference over the use of capital for improving general social welfare, even though such improvements may occur.

When capitalism becomes hegemonic, human and nonhuman nature can become types of capital used to grow capital. Thus, this definition contrasts with definitions of capital that consider labor distinct from it. Within these conditions, the use of capital changes over time. *Cutover Capitalism* explains changes in how human and nonhuman capital were used to generate returns.[12]

More specifically, this book shows that capitalism depends on shifting the target of value creation from nonhuman nature to humanity-as-nature. The initial colonial and early American endeavors in forest product creation had been a time of great prosperity for producers and investors due to the bounty of high-value forest products produced by forest ecologies over time. Starting in the 1850s, however, in the face of diminishing returns from a cutover forest landscape, the owners of land and productive property shifted their search for value from the most obvious forms of natural resources into the labor process, using environmental forces to further the extraction of value from human bodies—native, migrant, and immigrant. The Schumpeterian sees the shift in the target of value creation to the human body as stagnation in entrepreneurship or a lack of technological innovation, but it was not that; it was the profit motive working perfectly.[13] If bodies could work harder and produce more with minimal inputs this was progress, at least from the perspective of those who sought returns on capital. An important goal of this book is to provide a new synthesis of the history of body, labor, and environment. In this study the lines between the working body and nonhuman nature are obscured because capitalism has historically obscured them. Unlike other studies of environment, work, body, nature, or food the focus in this work is metabolism—digestion, cellular respiration, and muscle action. This is, in part, an intimate and internal history of the body as a system and force.[14]

Why else is this book necessary? This book tells a mostly untold story of a region and a community of people as they underwent an historic transition to industrial modes of production. Over time this transition fundamentally changed the way that generations of people experienced quotidian reality. Another reason is that, with a few exceptions, popular and academic understandings of the shift to fossil fuel-powered production depict it as a shift toward labor-saving technology. Historians and businesspeople have assumed that economies before industrialization—what historian Tony Wrigley called "organic economies"—were inflexible and fundamentally limited, while fossil fuel economies were expansive and dynamic.[15] Perhaps this is true in long enough timescales and at the level of the nation or the globe, but this is not always true at the level of the region, sector, firm, or working family. In this book, the term *organic* will be used in the way that Wrigley intended. It refers to economies that draw their power from energy flows like water, wind, and muscle power rather than from energy stocks, most importantly fossil fuels. This book applies the idea of an organic economy to a specific industry at a specific place and time. This level of analysis is important because industrialization happens at the level of the firm expanding out geographically through competition. Prime movers in the Northern Forest forest products industry during the period under consideration were mostly organic, drawing their power from muscles and water, but they were still industrializing.

Andreas Malm's brilliant work *Fossil Capital: The Rise of Steam Power and the Roots of Global Warming* has challenged the standard narrative of industrialization by showing that a major motivation for the shift to fossil fuel–powered production in English cotton mills was not necessarily the limits of the organic economy, but instead the desire on the part of managers, inventors, and investors to gain more control over human bodies. Malm's point was made earlier by anarchist theorist Murray Bookchin who wrote in his *Post-Scarcity Anarchism* that "the notion that man must dominate nature emerges directly from the domination of man by man."[16] Unfortunately, *Cutover Capitalism* shows that no labor process, be it advanced or primitive, industrial or preindustrial, is inherently freedom-inducing or exploitative; it is instead the context of the social and political relations of a society that determine those latter properties of production. Nevertheless, it is difficult to imagine a future free from exploitation unless we understand how coupled the exploitation of human and nonhuman nature have been. This research implies that, for a system of production to be ethical, a primary goal of that system must be sustainability, at the level of the worker, the firm, the region, the sector, the nation, and the globe. Sustainability here refers to both local and global ecosystems but also to the human body and mind, not in the abstract aggregate but at a personal level. Here again a lineage of radical scholars and reformers were more succinct in their many permutations of the phrase, "From each according to his ability, to each according to his needs," a phase ultimately popularized by Karl Marx.[17]

Cutover Capitalism as Historic Process

Forest products production provides an ideal example of how capitalism works on people and environments through time. Fundamentally, the forest products business has historically depended on mixing productive labor with productive land, the latter often a result of hundreds of years of ecological activity. In the early seventeenth century, European powers were drawn to the Northern Forest because of the wealth created by forest ecology. Trees stored a tremendous amount of energy drawn mostly from the sun, energy that could be released for warmth, light, and fuel for industrial processes.[18] They sequestered carbon from the atmosphere, shaping it into a lignin matrix creating a pliable, durable, and endlessly versatile building material. Wood provided chemicals such as potash, tar, turpentine, tannin, and cellulose for paper.[19] Nearly everything that seventeenth-, eighteenth-, and nineteenth-century Euro-Americans used daily was made of wood.[20] It served the functions that both plastic and metal served in the second half of the twentieth century and now.[21]

In the age of sail, the most valuable of the New World trees were mature hemlock, oak, spruce, fir, and white pine, which were used to make masts and spars for European ships. A mature white pine might sell for £100 in eighteenth-century Britain, a small fortune. Over two thousand trees twenty inches in DBH (diameter at breast height) were required for the largest warships.[22] Without some source of mature trees, European exploration and colonization would have halted. These trees, their abundance, or the lack of them, moved people across oceans in the process of colonization.[23]

By the seventeenth century, there were no virgin forests in England and there was a growing perception of a wood shortage.[24] The wood could grow again but pasture for sheep or fields for grain promised a quicker return than waiting a hundred or more years for merchantable timber to grow.[25] By contrast, when Europeans arrived in America, New England was about 95 percent forested, with perhaps three-quarters of a million trees at least three inches DBH in every ten square miles of forest. There was large valuable ship-timber on coastal islands, close to shores, and along riversides. These trees were coveted because they could be felled directly into the water or near to it and water was the quickest and cheapest way to transport these commodities.[26]

Many histories of colonial extraction highlight exotic commodities like spices or tea, but there were few resources in colonial America whose basic functions were new to Europeans or Euro-Americans. Trees for masts and spars could be obtained in Baltic ports, for example, but by 1652 the Anglo-Dutch War limited their availability in England.[27] Later, when American loggers moved west, they often looked for species that functioned like the white pine they found in the Northern Forest.[28]

Exploring new forests was lucrative because mature trees were numerous and easy to extract. When settler-colonists claimed to have discovered virgin nature on the "frontier," Euro-American law and morality gave them dominion over it, no matter the form. Humans had the right to treat nonhuman things as capital. When new forms of nature or natural processes were discovered whether by frontiersmen, scientists, or labor managers, they could be commoditized. The idea of discovery is a misnomer, however. The process of discovery has historically been a process of privatizing common goods or appropriating private property. This is clear from the massive dispossession of Native American land that was labeled by colonial contemporaries as exploration or discovery, as the western European common law doctrines of discovery laws made explicit. Alternatively, discovery could be the process of using the labor of things deemed to be nature in new ways to generate returns. This latter type of discovery will be the subject of this book but it's important to understand its connection to discovery in the colonial sense.

When Europeans discovered new forests to extract from in America, they did so simply to overcome resistance to the extraction of forest resources at home.[29] Resistance has three connected meanings. It means mechanical resistance, like the force that meets and resists an axe blade as it cuts into a tree, or the force that slows a lumber cart on a rough road. It also means the act of humans fighting against unwanted impositions on their wants, needs, and desires, like the resistance of Native Americans against European encroachments or the resistance of workers against bosses. Finally, resistance is synonymous with economic cost, a concept that often encompasses the other two types of resistance. The economic notion of time preferences means time itself is a type of resistance. These forms of resistance to extraction made it cheaper to obtain forest products by conquest in America than to produce them in Europe, even though transatlantic voyages were some of the most expensive endeavors of the early modern world.[30] The work of the Northern Forest ecology—the relationships between all the living and nonliving parts of the forest, which allowed some trees to reach healthy maturity—did a type of work that provided settler-colonists with forest products *cheaply*, with less resistance than faced at home. Increasingly, social scientists and humanists are beginning to see the drive for cheapness as a global historical phenomenon essential to the development of capitalism.[31]

Professional woodworkers arrived in New England around 1628, and by 1645 masts were being exported. The seventeenth and eighteenth centuries were bonanza periods for producers of forest products. Forest products were, by tonnage, over half of all total exports. In 1675 New Hampshire and Maine mills were producing 13.5 million board feet of white pine a year, worth between £13,500 to £27,000. Individuals like merchant Sir William Warren amassed over £35,000 worth of masts, harnessing the value that ecologies and time built. These forests were not endless as the colonial imagination hoped they were. As early as 1690, there was a shortage of mast pines along rivers in colonial New England. By 1750, reports from the inland region of Exeter, NH, showed a scarcity of large pines. These cutover spaces were absent of the most easily accessible sources of value, but sources of value hide even in the most barren lands, as this study shows.[32]

After extraction, the easily accessible forest wealth along the Atlantic seaboard would grow and become valuable again, but instead of waiting and facing this resistance, settler-colonists moved west and north looking for cheaper resources produced by ecology and time, expropriating more land from Native Americans.[33] In New England, prices paid for forest products rose in relation to how distant they were from markets, increasing the incentives to seek them out.[34] Frontiers to the west and north were not Eden-like. Indigenous people, the land, animals, and forbidding winter weather resisted colonizers' drive for cheapness, but there were still pockets of valuable resources, unguarded and relatively cheap. From the perspective of colonists or capitalists, resistance and cheapness are what made moving to new frontiers—new spaces—valuable.[35]

Ecologies, time, and the desire for cheapness created the conditions for the "cut and run" lumbering that continued in the United States well into the twentieth century. Cut and run lumbering was the chronic pattern whereby investors funded the cutting of valuable trees from a lightly settled region and then sold or abandoned the land to move to new, more mature tracts of timber.[36] The threat of forest fires and the opening of new "free" western land meant waiting to cut was unwise.[37] The general western movement of cut and run lumbering characterized what forest historians David Smith and later Thomas Cox called "the logging frontier" or "the lumberman's frontier."[38]

As American lumberers moved westward, they moved forward in time, approaching the forests of the western Lake States—Michigan, Minnesota, and Wisconsin—and the far West, with improved technologies and organizational structures that quickened extraction and made it more profitable.[39] Using money made from the work of ecologies, time, and labor in earlier frontiers, lumbermen in the Pacific Northwest dumped capital into the forest and sought large and immediate returns from the abundant gigantic redwoods and Douglas fir. They used high capital technologies like logging railroads and steam-powered winches. They employed a new type of labor, a mostly mobile class of young men, often called hoboes, who were not attached to farm or family. Large investments were warranted because the value created by time and ecology was more than equally large. This was another bonanza and fortunes accumulated quickly.[40]

Here again, when the most valuable lumber was cut, once-profitable spaces were often abandoned. Again, given time, human economic value creation resumed. The cut and run heuristic, one that continues to influence historians of forest product production, obscures how profit continues to be made on cutover land. If we think of frontiers existing in geographic space in a finite world, the continued progression of all frontiers is uncertain. Marginal spaces, places that are used up, places where nonhuman nature no longer yields its value to humans easily, provides a better model for how economic value was created.[41] These are places like the Dust Bowl, the Rust Belt, the Berkeley mine waste pit in Butte, MT, or forest lands that lumbermen call *cutover*.[42] Some writers have labeled this type of value creation in marginal spaces "disaster capitalism," or "salvage capitalism" and they associate it with ruptures and discontinuities. The cutover capitalism described in this book depicts value creation on marginal or disrupted lands as a defining part of healthy capitalism.[43]

How was value created in cutover spaces? The methods of extraction changed.[44] As opposed to relying on time, ecology, and the appropriation of land and resources, capital used improved labor processes to squeeze value from what remained on the land. These new processes could be the result of scientific investigation, or the implementation of some new technological advancement. Perhaps more often they were small adjustments in production that were not chronicled in the entrepreneur-focused history of technology of the past.[45]

Value creation continued in cutover spaces by opening frontiers in the labor process; in other words by rearranging or "improving" how people worked with human and nonhuman nature. Apart from the Northern Forest, an example of this can be found during World War II, when the United States freed itself from dependence on colonized land through the synthetics revolution—"chemistry for colonies," as Daniel Immerwahr phrased it. But Immerwahr did not see this as freedom from dependence on natural resources. To get the sought-after rubber that the United States needed, the government ceased to look to the labor of farmers, plants, chemists, and industrial facilities but instead used petroleum, different chemists, and different industrial facilities to achieve the same ends. The labor process changed and became more "efficient."[46] Fossil fuel–powered machines were near panaceas for extraction in all types of cutover spaces. Another path that capital took was the opposite. Instead of using non-human nature to greater effect, capital could make bodies the focus of value creation.[47] Most commonly, there was a mix of these two methods: improved technology and an increased intensity of work.

For example, as the lumbermen's frontier advanced westward in the 1910s and 1920s, there was another type of logger who made a living on cutover tracts.[48] The IWW called these operators "gyppo loggers" because one strategy they used to cut costs was "gypping" workers out of pay, the word deriving from a degrading term for Romani people (often referred to as "gypsies").[49] "Gyppos" worked through contracts or piece work and relied on the cheap labor of the family unit, women in particular.[50] As small entrepreneurs, they pushed themselves harder than wage workers to make a profit. They also employed new, experimental, and therefore risky low-capital technology like modified tractors.[51]

Most importantly for continued profit-making, these small, ad hoc units of production stifled labor organization, which would have ended "gypping," the ultimate source of value here. Referring to "gyppos," a contributor to the IWW's *Industrial Worker* wrote in 1922, "this is no doubt the principal reason, if not the sole reason, why the organization [the IWW] has not progressed faster in the last couple of years."[52] All the characteristics of production that defined "gyppo" logging were exactly what made value creation in these marginal lands possible. Nearly all of the strategies used by the "gyppo" loggers were employed in the cutover Northern Forest, but most took a different form. When resources were scarce, unions weak, and regulation minimal, all producers were either "gyppos" or "gypped." Sometimes they were both.

The idea that human bodies could be the impetus for capital growth was well understood by Fredrick Winslow Taylor, the father of "scientific management."[53] Taylor began his seminal work, *The Principles of Scientific Management*, not with the factory but with the forest: "We can see our forest vanishing, our water-powers going to waste, our soil being carried by floods into the sea; and the end of our coal and our iron is in sight." He saw the connection between scarcity of natural resources and the need to use bodies efficiently.[54] When

Taylor figured out how to get more work out of a body in an hour, he made a natural discovery that could be capitalized on. Under Taylorism, millions of working bodies became targets of extraction, as if they were trees in an expanse of old growth forest. Industrialization was, as historian Edmund Russell argued, "a biological as well as a mechanical process."[55]

More than just capitalism, this book focuses on industrialization in capitalism. Historical debates over industrialization are vast and there is no attempt to summarize them here. Instead, this book depends on Jonathan Levy's definition in *Ages of American Capitalism: A History of the United States*. Levy argues that industrialization was increased investment in intermediate capital goods allowing for "capital deepening," whereby "there is more productive capital in the hands of the same workers." Historiographically, the standard example is the factory or mill where workers had access to more precise and powerful machinery powered by running water then fossil fuels.[56] Machines and their power sources have been the fixation of the older literature on accelerating productivity during industrialization. When looking at rural laborers the situation is different. High-capital, specialized machines entered isolated rural areas later than cities or places well connected to infrastructure. Rural areas still industrialized even in the absence of these machines.

Cutover Capitalism claims that human metabolic capital (not human capital, which typically refers to skill, training, or other production knowledge) can be deepened if bodies are pushed to consistently exceed expectations. This could be achieved by the lash, as the new literature on slavery exemplifies, but also by market forces. In the Northern Forest, metabolic capital deepening was accompanied by environmental capital deepening. The new history of slavery is again instructive as the increased labor discipline on the plantation in the early nineteenth century was accompanied by improved cotton cultivars.

There is an obvious problem with correlating the improved productivity of cotton production with new cotton cultivars alone, however. If the cotton plant was more productive one might assume that slaves would have worked less over time. This is a ridiculous conclusion because the imperative created by capitalism and chattel slavery means that slaves would continue to be pushed to work harder regardless of how productive the cotton was. New management systems accelerated production by systematically torturing workers, what Edward Baptist called "the whipping machine." This idea of productive advancement does not fit neatly into historians' or economists' understanding of change over time, which is why the new history of slavery is so contentious and important.[57]

There were no whipping machines in the Northern Forest, but the market pressures of the jobbing system described in the chapters below served a similar (not the same, however) disciplinary function. There was also no equivalent to new cotton cultivars in the Northern Forest. Trees did not get more productive over time. In the Northern Forest the forest environment was, however, used in new ways, not necessarily by improving the trees, but other subtler manipulations. Together, metabolic and environmental capital deepening mimicked industrialization via high-capital, fossil fuel-powered machinery.

Industrialization as conceived by historians and economists in the past had the goal of creating value using less labor and resources, but pecuniary gain did not necessitate either. New production methods could put a greater strain on human and nonhuman nature. Workers sweating on the job found ways to complete their work faster and cheaper, even if it broke their bodies. From the perspective of capital when production was cheap and profit generated, "advancements" were being made.

Cheapness is an essential concept in Northern Forest production. Jason Moore and Raj Patel have led the way in explaining how this drive for cheapness motivated capitalism as a historical force.[58] To Moore, capitalism is the search for "Cheap Nature." Cheap nature, Moore argued, is the idea of "use-values produced with below-average value-composition. In systematic terms, cheap nature is produced when the interlocking agencies of capital, science and empire . . . succeed in releasing new sources of free or low-cost human and extra-human natures for capital."[59] Cheap nature relied on the externalization of costs, the transfers of goods and services from human and nonhuman nature to humans in exchanges that took place outside of the "cash nexus": exchanges with improper or no compensation for one or more parties. In competitive markets, Moore argued, "capital pays for only one set of costs [exchange-values], and works strenuously to keep all other costs [typically the work of nature] off the books."[60] Cheap nature is a useful way of describing the type of nature that is the focus of this book. Negative externalities are essential to capitalism, and they linked human labor and nonhuman nature.

This book further qualifies the concept of externalities in three ways. (1) Some economists would say a cost is externalized only if a human third party is injured. This book considers damages to nonhuman nature as an injury even when these damages have no direct or indirect effect on a human. (2) This book considers work that regularly interferes with the maintenance of healthy human metabolic homeostasis, such as wages that are below the cost of living, to be an externalized cost. Stolen wages are not externalized because the law internalized these costs, ideally but not always.

(3) Finally, this book posits that there are parts of the human body or patterns of human behavior—metabolic homeostasis and addiction, for example—that a person has no or only partial control over. When work is so rigorous that it damages metabolic homeostasis or mental well-being as a requirement of the job, it is externalizing the cost of production onto a natural entity, the body.

Cutover Capitalism in the Northern Forest

The historic process of cutover capitalism described above operates similarly in different places and different times. The bonanza period of forest products production in the Northern Forest was winding down between 1833 and 1857. At this time, the number of logs cut each year increased but the volume of wood procured decreased by about half.[61] Not coincidentally, this was a period of rapid depopulation and underinvestment in the Northern Forest.[62] This was not the end of forest product production. Capital focused on cutting smaller, less valuable trees—namely spruce, second-growth pine, or niche forest products from isolated tracts.[63] By 1870, improved paper-making technology opened markets for small trees of a variety of species. Around 1900 there was a boom in cutting pulp wood to make paper, which could be done in cutover, second- or third-growth forests. The paper industry in Maine grew 157 percent in the first decade of the twentieth century.[64]

Even though technology created new markets, cutting small trees for lumber, niche products, or pulp presented a problem. Each tree was worth less compared to the large trees of the past, though they "require[d] about as much effort to fell" and transport according to several reports from workers and foremen.[65] Without abundant, highly valuable resources, lumbermen had to figure out ways to improve the labor process, making production of less valuable resources cheaper.

This could be achieved by using high-capital technologies like railroads and the new steam-powered logging machines that were utilized in the forests of the West as early as 1880.[66] The tight margins caused by production on cutover lands meant that investing in high-capital technology was unwise.[67] Into the 1950s in the Northern Forest, depending on the size of the operation, most trees were still felled by crosscut saws or axes, hauled by horse, and transported to mills via rivers.[68] Without high-capital technological improvements, extracting value from cutover land required getting more value from the nature that remained in, or could be coaxed cheaply into, the woods. Bodies needed to be used in the same callous ways as other natural resources.

As the Epilogue argues, the lumberjack statues discussed above speak to the idea that these workers became imbedded in nature through production.

The history of the Northern Forest shows that industrial capitalism was not always a "metabolic rift" that alienated people from natural cycles as Karl Marx and John Bellamy Foster argued. Industrialization actually further imbedded people into these cycles. This is demonstrated in this book but is also evident from the process of anthropomorphic climate change that has embedded all production into the global carbon cycle, a natural process that most humans in the past could justifiably ignore.[69]

The chapters that follow will guide the reader through capital's hunt for cheap nature in the cutover lands of the Northern Forest. The manifestations of this hunt were not always obvious and, in hindsight, were not always even a real factor of production, as will become clear in the last chapter on race management.

Part 1, "The Working Frontier Forest," is a natural and social history of the Northern Forest before and during the end of the white pine bonanza. Before any people arrived in the region, the forest was working and struggling and coincidentally creating things that people would find tremendously valuable. It was also creating the conditions for eventual environmental capital deepening. The first chapter narrates this type of work and these struggles. Chapter 2 explains the preindustrial lumber production methods of forest farmers and immigrant Canadian workers from roughly 1850 to 1870, the time white pine was becoming scarce. By settling and living in the Northern Forest, inhabitants acquired "woodskills" that would become a form of cheap nature investors would rely on as production scaled up. Chapter 3 describes how workers transitioned from small-scale production for subsistence to production mediated by systematic contractual relationships with mill and landowners beginning roughly around the period of the transition from white pine to spruce and second-growth trees, ca. 1860–1895. This hypercompetitive business environment continued to mediate production until the second half of the twentieth century. This business environment also facilitated the exploitation of workers' bodies while obstructing solidarity, both key components of cutover capitalism. For the forest products industry to be efficient, products needed to aggregate in an organized way. The interlude explains how regional waterways served this function.

Part 2, "The Rise of Industrial Capitalism," focuses on capital deepening and its effects. Chapter 4 explains how the utilization of a low-cost source of power—seasonal change—made the movement of forest products quick and cheap. Between roughly 1870 and 1920, two distinct historical trajectories emerged in production that would be crucial for defining class. Operations that sped up their work using these new methods became industrial, as did their workers, distinguishing themselves from other operations that remained dependent on agrarian extractive methods.

These chapters show that the condition of both urban factory workers and rural workers were, in many ways, the same: these were classes pushed to increase the rate of production in ways that were damaging to body and mind. In the Northern Forest, labor management took the traditional form of the walking boss, but the more common and more formidable manager was the pressure of the market, which was imposed on workers through a contracting system.

Industrial production had to be taxing on bodies. Using a 1904 USDA food study of loggers in Maine among other sources, chapter 5 argues that workers' metabolisms became another form of cheap nature that allowed the cutover land to remain productive. Chapter 6 describes rituals of consumption and production in the Northern Forest between roughly 1890 and 1950 that gave structure and coherence to this new class of workers, structure that diminished absenteeism.

In cutover regions, the nature inside working bodies sustained profitability, but some of these bodies were also racialized. Scientific racial taxonomies placed the bodies of immigrant French-Canadian workers in a category between humanity and exploitable nonhuman nature, leading to especially inhumane treatment of this group. Though the racialization of French-Canadian immigrant workers began as early as the 1850s, immigrant workers became the most important way extraction remained profitable after the New Deal, as chapter 7 shows.

Around the 1950s, the effective use of fossil fuels in production along with a neoliberal management style nearly destroyed the forest products industry in the Northern Forest. The Epilogue describes how the hardships of deindustrialization enticed Northern Forest residents to draw value from the collective memory of the extractive industries. These memories, embodied in local history and memorials, extolled the connections between land and labor that cutover capitalism created.

Cutover capitalism depended on the seemingly endless search for cheap nature. Much of that value was created by the work of forest ecology through time. These are the subjects of the following chapter.

Part 1

THE WORKING FOREST

CHAPTER 1

THE WORK OF TREES

In the middle of December 2021, a giant fell. Tree 103, in Elder's Grove in the Upper St. Regis region of the Adirondacks, crashed to the forest floor with the force of several sticks of dynamite. This was not human caused; no humans were around to hear it fall. It was discovered by a hiker, likely many days or weeks after the crash. The death was the result of advanced age and wind. This 165-foot white pine was perhaps the tallest tree in New York, but its home was unremarkable. To find Elder's Grove, you pull off a two-lane road into a roadside cutout that leads to an unmarked trail. This will take you under power lines and hopefully to an unmarked herd-path, and from there, into the Grove. Tree 103 was about a half a mile from the road. If you are as unprepared as I was when I first sought out Elder's Grove, you probably won't find any of the other two dozen giant white pines there. If you do find the trees, as I did on my second attempt, you will be entering a tract of forest that has been untouched by the search for cheap nature for over four hundred years. The trees here were too big for the primitive human- and water-powered sawmills of the colonial period and the early republic, and they were too far from water to be used as ship masts. Elder's Grove was also in a unique spot. It was located on a property line, so loggers might not have known who owned the land. Trees like 103 were the jewels of the Northern Forest. These massive trees moved European ships to American shores.[1]

Giants like Tree 103 were common in the Northern Forest into the 1850s, making the forest comparable to the much-admired wildernesses of the West. In his book *The Maine Woods*, Henry David Thoreau wrote, "we have advanced by leaps to the Pacific and left many a lesser Oregon and California unexplored behind us."[2] In the Northern Forest, trees large and small worked together and struggled among themselves and against the harsh environment, a struggle that has produced very valuable things. This chapter explores the conditions that Tree 103 and millions of other trees worked in. Most of this content covers prehistory before the arrival of any humans, Indigenous or European. In doing so this chapter explains the metabolic processes that are at the core of value creation in cutover capitalism.

Work and Place

The Northern Forest environment produces an abundance of living things, but it is not an easy place to live. Glaciation and other erosion built rolling hills and mountains and dug out spaces that would become the lakes, rivers, and ponds that characterize the land. Half of New England is 1,000 or more feet above sea level, but the White, Green, and Adirondack mountains are significantly higher.[3] The Northern Forest contains all of the highest peaks in each state—which are, from west to east, Mount Marcy in New York (5,344 ft), Mount Mansfield in Vermont (4,393 ft), Mount Washington in New Hampshire (6,288 ft), and Katahdin in Maine (5,268 ft). Mount Washington is the highest point in the Northeast.[4]

Time, flora, fires, hurricanes, ice storms, and other factors helped to create three soil regions in the Northern Forest that trees took advantage of and changed.[5] The Tug Hill Plateau in New York has moderate terrain with glacial till derived from sandstone and is well drained in hilly areas. The Northeastern Mountains are rugged with shallow, stony soil that is typically well drained, and lower slopes have glacial till and fragipan. The Northern Uplands have varying hilly terrain "with a thin mantle of till" and higher hills with well-drained soils.[6]

When the glaciers receded 12,000 years ago, they exposed rocky, nutrient-poor soil. The Northern Forest was then a tundra. Places where there are sun and soil, however, trees will try to colonize. About 10,000 years ago, spruce and fir, adapted to the harsh, nutrient-poor soil, settled the land, first in the low-lying areas and southern latitudes, but slowly creeping into the Northern Forest. Nine thousand to 7,000 years ago, the weather warmed. Spruce populations declined and pine and oaks grew to predominate. In cooler climatic periods, hemlock, yellow birch, and beech established themselves. Hemlock declined 5,400 years ago. The cause of this decline is a mystery, but by sampling mud in the bottom of regional lakes, scientists have determined that there was a great dendrological event, one not caused by humans but one that was internal to this ecosystem. The hemlock eventually recovered and is a noticeable part of the Northern Forest today. Spruce also made a resurgence in the last 1,000 years. Forests change and migrate. They don't do this as a group; instead, they move as individual pioneers into areas they are suited to. Once settled, however, they form strong bonds and have internal conflicts, all of which are imperative for their survival.[7]

The first pioneer trees that ventured into the Northern Forest had one main antagonist: cold weather. Low pressure systems "from the South Atlantic, Gulf region, and Pacific Northwest" converged on the Northern Forest. These systems dragged with them cold Canadian air, circulating over the Gulf of St. Lawrence valley and Hudson Bay. Mountainous terrain obstructs the air currents and as the air rises up it "cools as it expands under the decreasing atmospheric pressure."[8] There is a three- to five-degree temperature drop for every 1,000 feet of elevation gain. This cold means that the tree line in the White Mountains is at 4,500 feet, one of the lowest in the world at this latitude. Research suggests that "ice storms are more common in this region than any forested region of the globe." Mount Washington specifically has some of the worst winter weather in the world with subzero, hurricane-force winds blowing throughout the year. The mountain claims human victims nearly every year, and there have been perhaps 169 deaths in New Hampshire's Presidential Range since 1849. Conditions here are deadly to most types of life, including plants. Blowing ice crystals strip trees' foliage and bark.[9]

Even outside of high-altitude regions, the Northern Forest receives a prodigious amount of snow and cold weather. Lake Ontario to the west of the Adirondacks creates lake-effect snow, a type of weather found in only eight inland water bodies on the globe.[10] These immense precipitation events occur when cold air moves across the relatively warm waters of large lakes, picking up water vapor. The water vapor moves up in altitude and freezes. In the Northern Forest, the frozen vapor moves leeward, piles up on itself at Tug Hill, and is released quickly in the Adirondacks and areas west.

To the east, the Gulf of St. Lawrence, the Bay of Fundy, and Massachusetts Bay create similar ocean or bay effect snowstorms that affect Maine, New Hampshire, and Vermont, and which can reach into the Adirondacks. The Northern Forest receives between four and six snowstorms a year with six inches of snow accumulation over a 24- to 48-hour period. For comparison, the areas around New York City and Washington, DC, receive less than 1.5 inches during storms.[11]

The region does provide some gifts to plant life, namely moisture. Precipitation in the Northern Forest is between eighty-eight and fifty inches annually, evenly distributed throughout the year. When air currents rise up mountains and cool, they release stored moisture. For every one thousand feet of elevation gain, precipitation levels increase around eight inches per year; therefore, higher elevation areas can get double the amount of precipitation compared to lowlands.[12] Coniferous trees, which keep their needles all year, are adept at grabbing water from the clouds as they pass through the foliage, making these forest types especially moist. Traveling through the Maine woods in 1846, Thoreau commented that the ground was "wet and spongy . . . [even] in the driest part of a dry season."[13] However, there are dangers associated with the moisture. This water runs down mountains into rivers and streams creating powerful torrents, especially in spring after the snow melts. Rushing water erodes soil, destroying plants and washing away nutrient-rich soil that is vital for trees' health and structure.

The valleys and ravines of the Northern Forest are also forbidding. Lowland temperatures here are similar to Anchorage, AK, and the soil remains frigid for a majority of the year.[14] The snowpack is deep and long-lasting. There is a high frequency of cloudy days, almost as many as in the Olympic Peninsula. At night, the ground loses the heat that it absorbed during the day. This "radiational cooling" lowers the temperature of the air, which then sinks. Compared to surrounding hillsides, these lowland "frost pockets" are fifteen to twenty degrees lower and retain snow longer into the spring (all temperatures in this book are in Fahrenheit).[15]

Life's Labor

Humans were reluctant to settle permanently in the Northern Forest, and even most animals avoided high-altitude areas, but spruce and fir trees were more adventurous. They lived, worked, and struggled in landscapes humans avoided all the while growing value for humans to eventually discover and extract. Fir trees are one of the few varieties in the Northern Forest that actually have greater rates of photosynthesis at low temperatures and high elevations. But as Tree 103 demonstrates, wind is a deadly force across the Northern Forest. Trees also had to contend with fungal spores that search out and infect abrasions in bark. Fungus takes advantage of wind damage to limbs and trunks to slowly drain the life from the trees. Cold wind can also rob trees of their water by evaporation.

Conifers adapted to these conditions. The low surface area of conifer needles means they are less susceptible to desiccation compared to broadleaf trees. With a few exceptions, conifers don't drop foliage in winter. They are able to begin photosynthesis earlier in the spring when compared to deciduous trees, converting sun into carbohydrates by mid-March when broadleaves are just beginning to bud. This adaptation also allows them to conserve energy and nutrients by not growing new photosynthesizing apparatus each year. Because of erosion on mountains, these highland trees don't get as many nutrients from the soil, but they don't need as many. Finally, many Northern Forest conifer species have cold tolerances well below the lowest temperatures in the region. Some hemlock, cedar, pine, spruce, and fir can survive temperatures of negative seventy-five degrees.[16]

Yet even hardy fir and spruce had a difficult time extending their range into the very high elevation of the subalpine regions. Moving 1,000 feet higher is equivalent to moving hundreds of miles north. In the midst of winter here, all moisture freezes and can't be absorbed by tree roots. The air moisture crystallizes, covering the landscape in rime ice. Needles of ice push out of the freezing ground, eroding topsoil and heaving seeds and plant sprouts, often killing them. Expanding ice can exert forces of 150 tons per square foot, shattering rocks and creating craggy boulder fields. By midwinter, snow and ice can accumulate up to twenty inches thick on trees, weighing them down with as much as 1,300 pounds of extra material. Here, decay is retarded and nutrients cycle into new life slowly.[17]

The spruce and fir that ventured into these subalpine zones were warped, gnarled, and dwarfed. Their unique shapes define the area's krummholz forests. Here, trees huddled tightly together, grew behind rocks or in recesses to escape the powerful wind and blowing ice. They also reacted to weather in real time, as periods of very cold temperatures triggered extra cold resistance. There is evidence that trees that grow in these climates are more adapted to freezing temperatures than members of the same species that grow in temperate climates.[18]

Trees have a number of ways of resisting these stresses. Conifer trees fight fungi by releasing chemicals into the air to kill spores before they land. This is part of what gives conifer forests their characteristic smell.[19] Trees find strength in numbers. Their combined branches and foliage dissipate the power of the wind. Recent research has also shown that trees can aid one another through extensive underground networks of mycelia, or fungus, which allow trees to communicate about dangers and share nutrients.[20]

The trees' constant struggle against the elements left marks on the landscape. Most remarkable are "fir waves" or "wave regenerated forests," alternating strips of dead, mature, and developing trees that from a distance look like stripes extending across mountainsides.[21] When one tree dies, is defoliated, or loses limbs, tall, healthy upwind trees are exposed to more stress. Waves of death move forward in the direction of the wind, about three to ten feet per year, but something remarkable happens in the wake of death. New fir begins to grow, now with ample sunlight and decaying matter provided by windblown material. Shaded from wind by mature downwind fir, the young trees grow rapidly in high numbers.[22] From beneath the canopy, moving downwind, these new firs grow progressively taller until they poke their terminal ends out of the "wind-shade" and begin the process of slow death-by-wind.[23]

These fir waves are in a near steady state equilibrium, subject to drastic change only after infrequent large disturbances such as human activity, a hurricane, or a typhoon. In these high-stress environments, the trees only live for sixty to seventy years, around the time of human lifespans. And within the fir waves, the entire progression of the life of a fir tree, from sapling to dying tree, is expressed in a 200-foot space.[24]

Fir waves are found nowhere else in the world except for a few mountains in Japan and Argentina. This unique phenomenon, along with the krummholz forests, shows how hardy these trees are, how readily they adapt, and most importantly, their constant resistance to forces that try to destroy them. This also shows the forest's fecundity. Death in the Northern Forest is followed by wellsprings of life, and the communities surge toward metabolic productivity.[25]

Of course, there are trees other than conifers in the Northern Forest. Conifers are not unique in their adaptability to cold, nutrient-poor landscapes—birch, aspen, and alders can also prosper here. The Northern Forest is situated between the boreal forests of Canada and the temperate deciduous forests in the south. Ten thousand years ago, as the spruce and fir were finding a foothold in the Northern Forest, hardy "pioneer" broadleaves were establishing themselves further south.[26] As the climate oscillated, tree species would compete with each other over territory in battles that are best viewed over geological time scales.

The battle lines moved north and south as well as up and down mountains, with pioneer hardwoods and coniferous species taking the advantage in colder areas, and other broadleaves in warmer regions.[27] Nine thousand years ago, oak, maple, ash, hemlock, and white pine gained a foothold in the Northern Forest. Two thousand years ago the climate was sufficiently warm in places for beech, sugar maple, and yellow birch.[28]

During these ongoing territorial battles, tracts of forest of varying levels of diversity reach a point where the canopy was dominated by a species or a community of species that were shade tolerant. These trees reproduced in their own canopy. Nutrients, for the most part, recycled from dead plant matter back into living. Between eight thousand and one thousand years ago, the Northern Forest became home to a number of diverse forest types that in some ways resemble the forest that settler-colonists encountered: "northern hardwoods (beech-birch-maple), spruce-fir, red-white pine, aspen-birch, elm-ash-red maple, and oak-hickory."[29] These forests would, in human timescales, seem stable or even timeless. In these places—unlike in fir wave forests—pine, spruce, hemlock, and oak could live hundreds of years.[30] It was in one of these stable old-growth regions that Tree 103 was born and died. And it was trees like Tree 103 that colonizing Europeans put a high monetary value on.

Forest Wealth

Felled trees, young or mature, were economically valuable to eighteenth- and early nineteenth-century Euro-Americans for four primary reasons: fuel, the strength and pliability of their fibers for tools and building material, their chemical compositions, and their unique shape. Important chemicals produced from American felled trees in the colonial period into the nineteenth century were carbon in the form of charcoal, potassium-carbonate in the form of potash and pearl ash, and tannins for leathermaking. Other chemicals like wood alcohol and cellulose for paper production would not become important until later in the nineteenth century. A few tree species stood out for their importance in the development of the Euro-American economy, however, because of their value as commodities.[31]

Conifers were hardy, pioneering species but they were also agreeable to humans. Infused with resin, the trees were rot resistant. They were called softwoods because they were less dense than hardwoods and easily worked by tools. This also meant they floated for longer periods of time before becoming waterlogged as compared with hardwoods, making them easier to move by water.

Mature, straight, white pine, reaching perhaps as tall as two hundred feet lured settler-colonists. The wood from white pine is light, durable, and easy to work. As was discussed in the introduction, they were used for ship masts and spars, but also for lumber. When colonial Euro-American lumbermen probed the interior of the Northern Forest they were looking for these large pines and often did not disturb other trees. By the nineteenth century, the Connecticut River valley forests had as much as 22 percent mature white pine. Parts of northern and eastern Maine may have had 15 to 30 percent white pine. The Northern Forest more generally was 2 to 5 percent white pine.[32]

Trees like Tree 103 towered above neighboring maple, birch, and cedar, making them easy prey for lumberers. They grew well in "swamps, river valleys, side slopes, sand plains . . . dry, rocky ridges" and regenerate in small canopy gaps after selective cutting.[33] After forest fires, blowdowns, ice storms, or after cultivated land was abandoned, white pine quickly regenerated and thrived with the lack of other mature trees to compete against. In these disturbed forests, these trees established themselves in dense, evenly aged stands, perfect for the needs of the pulp industry that would develop after 1880. By

1900, hundreds of billions of board feet of white pine had been logged out of American forests.[34]

Though hemlocks experienced a mysterious dieback in the ancient forests of America, by the time of colonization they were a domineering part of the landscape. Hemlock require abundant water and so are often found in valleys and the wet northern slopes of mountains. They rivaled only the white pine in terms of size and girth. The wood was used for spars, masts, planks, railroad ties, plank roads, lumber, fuel, and pulp. In the late eighteenth century, it was discovered that the bark contained high amounts of tannin that could be used to make leather. Thereafter the trees were often cut and stripped of their valuable bark while the rest of the log was left in the woods.[35]

Like white pine, red and black spruce were "easy to plane, with medium strength and a straight, close grain."[36] Though not as tall as white pine, they could reach 100 feet tall. Spruce is a resilient species growing in areas that people don't often settle. They thrive high in the mountains, though at altitudes of about 1,200 feet or higher, fir is likely to outcompete them. Spruce also grow in areas with a lot of water such as bogs, where the lack of decomposition and sphagnum moss can create soil pH levels as low as 3.8. They are adept at storing water during periods of drought, meaning they can be found in dry areas. Thirsty spruce are such prodigious drinkers that they sometimes burst or crack their engorged trunks.[37] The spruce and fir woodlands of the Northern Forest will actually make their own environment less hospitable to other trees as the needle litter acidifies soil over time. Spruce withstand temperatures as low as negative eighty degrees. After spruce and fir are killed by fire, windthrow, or old age, they are usually replaced by more fir and spruce, which can create a climax community that regenerates within its own canopy for multiple generations.[38] The edges of these communities moved with climate changes as individual species took advantage of colder or warmer temperatures.[39]

Scientists' best evidence from pollen records indicates that spruce thrived during early Euro-American colonization. The trees did not grow where Native and Euro-Americans liked to live and, as land was cleared and white pine was harvested, spruce could grow in the canopy gaps.[40] After 1850, Euro-American loggers began to depend on this spruce. As a result, some spruce logs cut for paper in the 1900s were large, mature trees that were two hundred years old or older.[41]

The swamp-loving, rot-resistant tamarack had many uses. Native Americans used it in canoe making. It could be used for lumber and pulp. One of the most valuable parts of the tree was where the roots become the trunk as this formed the perfect shape for boat knees. Red and white cedar were coveted for building material, shingle making, and railroad ties. Because roofing material was almost always in demand in colonial and nineteenth-century America, low capital, ad hoc shingle manufacturing was sometimes a more worthwhile venture than long log harvesting. When railroads finally came to the region, they brought a nearly unquenchable thirst for hand-hewn or machine-made cedar and tamarack ties.[42]

Because hardwoods did not float as well as softwoods, they were difficult to transport in frontier regions like the Northern Forest. They were the local fuel source, however, as no conifer gave off as much heat as broadleaves.[43] Oak was prized for barrel staves, ship timbers, and, before people understood that hemlocks had tannins, for leathermaking.[44] Old American oaks rivaled hemlock and white pine for their size and height. Some grew up to one hundred feet.[45] Other hardwoods were ideal for building material, tools, and fuel, and the chemicals in the wood could be extracted on rudimentary farm facilities.

The trees listed above were valuable as commodities but only because they existed in spaces where they were allowed to work and struggle until they reached maturity. Metabolic action is essential for value creation in capitalism, but trees take time to grow. It was valuable to move spatially to where value had already developed, places like the Northern Forest, and especially Elder's Grove, even if tremendous expense was required to reach these isolated locations. Time preference, the desire for returns sooner rather than later, meant that the expenses of moving to isolated places were worth it compared to the cost of waiting for trees to grow again.

Trees were not commodities, they had to become them. This happened through the actions and thoughts of humans. For people who made their homes in the Northern Forest, both Indigenous and non-Indigenous alike, there were thousands of uses for the hundreds of different species of trees in the woods and most of these were for providing the necessities of life. The culture and habits of people in the Northern Forest were built on wood. The next chapter discusses the Euro-Americans who used the trees to make a living and the conditions under which trees became commodities.

CHAPTER 2

COMMON LABOR, COMMON LANDS

John Conklin was a drunk and a gambler, habits he picked up working as a seaman during the first few decades of the Republic. These habits brought debt and near-constant movement from job to job across the Northeast. In 1845, at the age of thirteen, John's son Henry Conklin and his family moved to "the frontier post" of Wilmurt in the Adirondack Mountains and began clearing land.[1] This work left little time for school for Henry but over time he became very familiar with the woods. The family was poor, as Conklin's autobiography, *Through "Poverty's Vale": A Hardscrabble Boyhood in Upstate New York, 1832–1862*, makes clear. In poverty, Henry gained valuable assets: woodskill—the art of surviving, navigating, and making value from the forest with little capital input. For instance, when not working in the fields Henry was working or playing in the woods. When his older brother John Jr. "had nothing else to do he would tinker away by the great blazing fire for hours making or repairing a sled." Henry would race his brothers and neighbors in chopping contests or in wooden shingle making and packing, a practice called shingle weaving.[2]

Materials drawn from the woods could help them survive and build wealth. From a young age, Henry Conklin could make new axe handles when one broke and hang the bit to fit his preferences.[3] Skill and power in the woods gained one respect in his community. As he grew older, Conklin became a *woodsman*, a term that described both a generalist farmer-logger and laborer and a term that would later be one of many words used to describe an industrial wage-working logger.

Words like woodsmen and farmer-logger are important; the former is a historically accurate term and the latter a modern term used mostly by historians. Both terms describe pre-industrial nonspecialists who maintained consistent connection to the means of basic subsistence. Having not specialized they were not maximally efficient at either farming or logging. Similarly, there were farmer-fishers, farmer-miners, farmer shoemakers. The skills necessary to industrialize a business or a sector were not created ex nihilo but needed to be brought into modernity, whether guided or forced by markets.

Henry was not just a farmer-logger or a woodsman. Like his brother, neighbors, and even the Canadian immigrants that traveled to the Northern Forest that will be discussed later in the chapter, Conklin had many different professions. He farmed, made shingles, cut "four-foot wood," and sometimes just "tramped" about, hunting and foraging. He had no desperate drive to work, as the forest almost always provided Henry with options, either something to eat, an opportunity to make something to sell, or an opportunity to take a waged job. Sometimes Henry worked on land he or his family owned, sometimes on a neighbor's land, an employer's land, or on land that no one had claimed, at least no one he knew personally. Much of the great forest that surrounded Conklin was, formally and not so formally, a vast commons open to all.

Through working and living here, settlers like Conklin came to know their environment better than any other Euro-Americans. This skill and knowledge allowed them to build valuable human capital, which could be used to make trees into commodities.[4] This type of preindustrial subsistence-based resource harvesting prepared Conklin for work in operations of larger scale and intensity. These larger operations in fact depended on the woodskills of people like Conklin. It was workers like him who would use knowledge and skill to set the standards for the industry and build the early infrastructure that would make later lumbering possible. This chapter explores how these people came to know the forest through work in the period before and up to the exhaustion of the mature white pine and the transition to cutting spruce as the major cash commodity between roughly the 1850s to the 1870s. Conklin, after all, lived a life that was not so different from many frontier farmers of the colonial period. This chapter explains what the forest provided Euro-Americans, what these people added to the ecosystems, and the laws and customs that they used to organize their survival and production. For Conklin and other Euro-Americans, the forest was both an adversary and an ally, but ultimately the forest was in charge.

Laboring Life

The first people who came to the Northern Forest between twelve thousand to thirteen thousand years ago were not seeking to create commodities or make farms.[5] Perhaps because of this there were likely few permanent Native

American settlements in the interior of the Northern Forest. However, there were two Native American groups who utilized the region's resources and considered the region a part of their homeland: the Iroquois to the west of Lake Champlain and the Algonquians to the east. As many as twenty thousand native peoples might have lived on the outskirts and along the region's major waterways.[6] The Algonquians and Iroquois hunted, gathered, and took mineral and forest resources from the interior. They cleared trees to ready land for their agriculture, to promote nut production, for ease of movement, and to promote game habitat. They girdled trees, cutting a ring in the bark around the trees, which killed them slowly. They also burnt the forest regularly.[7] Indigenous forestry activities quickened with the introduction of European steel trade axes. For longhouses, palisades, and dugout canoes, the Iroquois and Algonquins harvested both juvenile and mature trees. Their largest seagoing vessels, made of tulip, one of the tallest trees in North America, were up to sixty feet long and could carry thirty to sixty passengers. Native effects on the ecosystem's interior were limited, though undoubtably intentional, as the Iroquois and Algonquians were active foresters.[8]

For the Indigenous and Euro-Americans alike, the ability to reliably grow corn was a sign of an area's suitability for habitation, and corn did not grow in many parts of the Northern Forest.[9] The growing season could be as short as eighty days a year, which limited the decomposition of organic matter. Coniferous leaf litter acidified large portions of the soil. For domesticated flora, every 1,000-foot change in elevation is equivalent to a 500-mile move north.[10] The Northern Forest had limited agricultural potential.

Initial European contact with Native Americans killed perhaps around 95 percent of the latter group. This Great Dying of the Indigenous was an imperialist event but also an ecological one. Trees, white pine especially, began to grow on the land that was abandoned due to the Great Dying.[11] A recent study suggests that trees' land grab after the Great Dying may have sequestered enough CO_2 out of the atmosphere between 1500 and 1600 to have an effect on global temperatures, though the size of the effect is debatable. This regrowth from death created immense value that Euro-Americans like the Conklins would eventually harvest.[12] If we assume a mature white pine produces 1,000 board feet of lumber, from colonial contact to 1872 it is estimated that more than 200 billion board feet of white pine was removed from the region.[13]

Like small-scale agriculture, preindustrial wood harvesting depended on uncertain natural energy flows. One of these flows was the draft animals that moved forest products. According to historian Ann Norton Greene, oxen "were used whenever people needed cheap power, but not speed, in regions with subsistence agriculture, little commerce and poor roads, and for jobs requiring very grueling draft work."[14] They cost about half of what draft horses did, and they "would haul some awful loads." When they were hurt on the job or past their usefulness, they could be slaughtered for meat.[15] They were, however, slow, stubborn, and could overheat easily. Oxen required more work to be shoed than horses but needed less grooming, less rigging, and could "stand rougher treatment." If moving away from the farm for production, farmer-loggers could cut hay on common lands. Importantly, oxen could be released in the off-season to forage and then corralled again for work in the winter.[16]

Settlers like the Conklins used these draft animals to produce forest products from their homes, but the most lucrative trees were quickly used up. To harvest large trees and specialty products, settlers moved deeper into the woods and built temporary structures. Harvesting firewood, or taking on a small contract for tan bark, hop poles, or shingles required only hand tools, and no elaborate facilities were needed. Draft animals were only brought into the woods once or twice to haul out the product. In these cases, temporary shacks or shanties were built from bark, mud, hay, leaves, sticks, moss, and small logs; underbrush might be used for walls and roofs.[17] Even hollow logs could be used as habitation. Frontier workers sometimes slept in the open in the winter with a large fire, spruce-bough bedding, and a buffalo robe.[18]

In the early 1850s, Conklin worked for wages in the "lumber woods" for the first time cutting and hauling saw logs of twelve feet or longer.[19] Saw logs, masts, or spars were long and heavy, so draft animals were required at all times. When animals were brought into the woods, new structures, more tools, supplies, and fodder needed to be hauled in. The more draft animals needed, the more workers and capital were required and the larger the camp grew.[20] Building substantial log cabins was one of the many skills that defined woodsmen. It was even a form of employment. "Set-up" men traveled from county to county helping pioneering farmers build log houses and barns.[21] Logging camps were built quickly and cheaply using hand tools, forest products, and sometimes no metal at all, not even nails. These were crude one-room buildings with dirt floors and an open fire pit for warmth and cooking.[22] The log-walls were rarely peeled or peeled only on the inside. Mud, dung, clay, hay, oakum, or moss was used to chink gaps in the logs. They were dark, with few windows. Roofing materials were kept in place with wooden pegs, or poles laid across them. Shingles, doors, and other panels were made with a froe and mallet in the woods. There was little upkeep, and camps degraded as workers lived inside.[23] Oxen hovels were built in the same way, but according to author and logger John S. Springer, were higher quality, built with floors to keep hooves dry.[24] Despite their primitive look, these log camps were important sites in the development of industrial production. They were specialized; distant and distinct from the farm.

Winter Work

Until the second half of the twentieth century, forest product production of any significant scale was a winter activity. In the Northern Forest, snow covered the ground from three to five months a year. The regularity of the cold weather increased in the high altitudes of the Green, White, and Adirondack Mountains where more snow fell annually and where it stayed on the ground longer. Forest cover provided shade that also lengthened the life of the snowpack. Using the winter as an aid to commerce was innovative because in colonial America, cold was a detriment to Euro-Americans' survival.[25] The colony of Sagadahoc in Maine failed partly because of the cold climate.[26] Cold slowed or stopped photosynthesis, the driver of the economy. Wages declined and prices increased. There was a regular, seasonal increase in poverty. It was common for people to take low-wage work in factories simply for the benefit of the warmth.[27]

By mid-nineteenth century, as Northern Forest denizens became more reliant on markets, they needed to make the cold productive.[28] Winter could be a great boon to production because snow and ice were slick, and friction was the universal impediment to commerce. In the warmer months, roads were muddy and ill-repaired.[29] Besides reducing friction, the cold weather froze wet ground, and filled potholes and ruts with snow and ice. Good winter conditions allowed a 1,500-pound load to pass on roads that would typically only hold 500 pounds. Two horses could suddenly move a ton of material forty miles, a feat not possible at other times. Some estimated that in winter one draft animal could haul the load of five.[30] The records of five stores in Windham and Windsor, VT, show that between 1813 and 1843 nearly all hauling of loads weighing between one and two tons took place between October and April. In addition, the cold cooled workers and animals so they could work more intensively.[31]

By the early nineteenth century, Americans had developed a number of ways to work with winter. They drew weighted rollers over roads to compact the snow into slick surfaces. Continuous tracks of white snow roads have high albedo factor, reflecting up to 95 percent of the sunlight and maintaining frozen thoroughfares during warmer weather.[32] Snow fences were erected to prevent drifts from obstructing roads. In 1785, Bostonians were urged to plant trees to block wind and preserve the "useful snow." Urbanites actually resisted the early suggestions to spread salt on roads to eliminate snow and ice.[33]

In the winter, the Northern Forest's 2.5 to 3 million acres of wetlands, 68,515 miles of rivers and streams, and 16,285 lakes and ponds became slick, completely flat, and obstacle free, creating highways of commerce.[34] Before trains, moving things on frozen water was often the quickest way to move across land, but it could be dangerous. John Springer's team broke through the ice on his way to camp in Maine in the 1840s. Luckily, his crew had devised a system for recovering oxen, so they only lost some of their hay.[35] The advantages of winter outweighed the disadvantages to many. New York farmer Hector St. John de Crèvecœur wrote that in upstate New York, "the constancy of this serenely cold weather is one of the greatest blessings which seldom fails us."[36] Maine surveyor Moses Greenleaf wrote in 1829: "The uniform continuance of the snow in the forest is calculated upon, with a degree of certainty which is seldom disappointed; and the steady cold winters of the interior . . . furnish . . . means of subsistence and wealth . . . which are denied to those of regions which boast a milder climate."[37]

Winter weather changed nearly all aspects of work. Snow decreased the chances of forest fires. It impeded bugs like mosquitoes and blackflies that limited work in hot weather. Most importantly, it shifted labor away from farms. Because of the planting and harvest seasons, labor demand and wages grew to their highest annual levels in the hinterland around June and then again in October. Workers were so expensive during this time that American canal-building companies, an industry dependent on warm, penetrable soil, decided to import cheap labor from Ireland rather than pay high wages to native farm workers. As Greenleaf pointed out, in the winter in Maine, "a large part of the farmers, released from the agricultural labors of summer, employ themselves and their teams in cutting and transporting the timber of the forests to the banks of the streams and rivers."[38]

Flows of Commerce

As Greenleaf knew, understanding water and particularly its state-change—its transformation from a solid, to a liquid, and to a vapor—was vital to understanding production in the United States. Water's transformation to steam at 212 degrees dictated the rhythm of industrialization in manufactories across the world starting in the second half of the nineteenth-century. In lumbering, water's transformation to ice at thirty-two degrees dictated the rhythm of production. When it froze, starting in December, cutting and hauling took place on slick snow roads. When ice started to melt in March and April, the state-change released tremendous energy in rivers and streams, which was used to move logs to the mills.[39]

Being able to use buoyancy and the power of the rivers was a great benefit to farmer-loggers and legally they could use the gifts that flowing water provided for free. In the first half of the nineteenth century, an older "first in time, first in right" riparian law gave exclusive use of some waterways to certain parties. This was eventually replaced by a "reasonable use" doctrine. Reasonable use meant upriver parties only had the right to alter the "natural flow" of a river in ways that would not inhibit other river users. Rivers became "public highways," aquatic commons. Though land around the rivers could be owned, the "flow," the movement of the water, could not. This idea was at least as old as Roman law and an important part of English common law.[40] This gave rivers some advantages over manmade canals and even technologically "advanced" infrastructure like railroads or steamboats.[41]

Since colonial times, logs were conjoined into large rafts to be moved long distances on water.[42] Some species of trees floated well, others did not, but making rafts of different types of lumber allowed all species to move efficiently.[43] These rafts were sometimes used to float other forest products, commodities, and even animals downriver.[44] New York's legislators declared almost all major waterways in the Adirondacks legally navigable between 1818 and 1867; they were designated legal highways for commerce. Commissioners were given franchise and paid to make improvements to allow for better driving of rafts down river.[45]

There were many problems with moving commodities in this way. Large rafts could only be moved on wide waterways, limiting the geographic area that could be logged. Even the large rivers in the Northeast were less than perfect conduits. Boulders, sandbars, and shallows obstructed rafts.[46] Constructing rafts was a time-consuming process done by skilled specialists who charged for their services. Each raft was guided to market by workers, adding labor time to the cost of transportation. Finally, rafts often needed to be broken up and the logs scaled individually to determine the volume of the wood. They then needed to be reassembled for further transport.[47]

As the largest valuable hemlock, oak, and pine were lumbered, small producers began cutting less expensive, smaller species used for lumber, shingles, clapboards, and various other products.[48] Along small, sparsely populated tributaries, logs meant for these purposes were floated individually to larger rivers where they could then be rafted or sometimes floated right to the mill. Booms, or "long sticks of timber fastened together end to end and moored to objects on shore or to piling or cribs in the stream" were used to collect logs, direct their movement, and prevent them from jamming.[49] Early American log drivers were like shepherds moving on foot along the shore or in boats called bateaus, driving logs.[50] This was a labor-intensive process but when dealing with a large volume of logs on smaller tributaries it was cheaper than rafting.

Initially, special charter corporations were created by states to ensure that river driving would not congest the rivers and other users could have access to the flow. This worked as long as the scale of cutting remained small. As the scale of cutting increased in the spruce era of logging, driving intensified conflict and confusion on the rivers, and this began to subvert the speed, efficiency, and equity that rivers were meant to provide. For example, at the end of the drive each operator who floated logs on a stream had to use boats and crews to pick their logs out of the mass of logs held by the boom near the mill. The task was like solving a giant floating jigsaw puzzle. Operators worked day and night, keeping large fires blazing at the shore for light.[51]

Large-scale river driving also clearly violated the reasonable use doctrine. Reflecting common thoughts on river use at the time, a law passed in 1806 forbade driving individual logs on New York's Salmon River, demanding all logs be transported in rafts so as not to obstruct other riparian users. When large-scale lumbering first began on the upper Penobscot River in Maine around 1828, all logs had to be rafted as well.[52]

Driving logs individually was much quicker and easier, yet for the river drive to become equitable and less labor-intensive, the natural flow of these rivers needed to be further improved. More dams would need to be built, shallows would need to be dredged, boulders blasted, and wing booms constructed.[53] Any of these improvements, even if they could be conducted legally, created a free rider problem because once they were made no one could be restricted from using them. This was not always true of dams or booms, for which the builder could charge fees for passage if they had franchise. To solve the free rider problem and fix the problem of separating logs at the end of the drive, many states gave franchise to monopoly companies on specific high-traffic tributaries. These companies were also typically given the right to drive all logs on the river.[54] This main drive was often called the "union" or "company" drive. In some cases, the law declared these monopoly companies were not held responsible for property damage caused by their improvements or by the drive.[55]

These rivers and these monopoly driving companies were one of the few organized systems that gave cohesion to forest product production. Farmer-loggers like Conklin could drive their logs short distances on small streams, or even draw them by oxen to the larger rivers like the Hudson, Connecticut, or Penobscot where the drive was taken over by monopoly companies. These were common carriers, charging all users a set rate based on how many logs they had in stream. On some particularly long waterways, a river might be divided into multiple union drives, each section being handled by a different monopoly.[56] Driving and improvement companies meant that by mid-century, rafting was almost completely replaced by the quicker and more efficient process of driving logs downriver individually.

The Organization of Labor

River driving companies were one of the few complex systems of cooperation in the Northern Forest. The settling and "improving" of forest land was the affair of individuals and families. Like the Iroquois and Algonquians, European settler-colonists thought the interior of the Northern Forest was uninhabitable. Forays were made to extract the value that the Great Dying, ecologies, and time had grown there, but settlement was rare. In disturbed areas, successional spruce and fir can grow densely, obstructing nearly all the sunlight and obstructing transportation. Old forest was likewise hard to navigate, with thick tangles of deadfall, and pits and root mounts from toppled trees. Old growth was seen as ugly and hostile, a "wrath of savage vegetation," as one adventurer put it.[57]

Up until approximately 1800, most settlements clung to the coast and river valleys.[58] Revolutionary War veterans were given free Adirondack land grants, yet few chose to settle there. Some settlements had reached the west side of the Adirondacks by 1840 but much of the interior of the Northern Forest remained sparsely settled.[59] Travel writer Joel Tyler Headley wrote about the Adirondacks that, "I would like to see this desolate country settled; but it never will be till the west is all occupied. . . . *Crowding* may drive farmers here, but no gentler means. . . . It is awfully rough, cold, and forbidding country [emphasis in the original]."[60] By 1850, 10 percent of land in Maine, 37 percent in Vermont, and 45 percent in New Hampshire had been cleared for farming.[61]

Pushed by ungentle means, or perhaps entrepreneurial drive, some did settle the land. As early as the Revolution, in southeastern New England there was little land available for the sons of landowners to inherit. They would need to move to a city and work for wages or rent land that was increasing in price every year. The ability to make a farm from this forbidding land was a way to build an estate and a reputation, and gain certain citizenship privileges.[62] Far from state police powers, families like the Conklins squatted on unclaimed forest land.[63] In 1786, Founding Father Benjamin Rush said forest settlers were "generally a man who has out-lived his credit or fortune in the cultivated parts of the State." Rush continues, "his first object is to build a small cabin of rough logs for himself and his family. The floor . . . is of earth, the roof of split logs . . . A coarser building adjoining this cabin affords a shelter to a cow and a pair of poor horses. The labor of erecting these buildings is succeeded by killing the trees on a few acres of ground near his cabin."[64] By 1800, much of the arable land near water sources had been cleared and inhabited in this way.[65] The more desperate who settled inland did so on higher elevation "hill farms" that would come to characterize the region.[66] These were plots with "shallow soil, poor drainage and short growing seasons" and could only support farmers for a short period of time.[67] For these settlers, trees and the life that they supported provided the means to survive, but it was also their prerogative to destroy them. These farmer-loggers had an antagonistic but intimate relationship with the forest.

Despite the antagonism, farmer-loggers and trees had something in common: the pursuit of sunlight. To farmers, trees had negative value. They were impediments to the rays of sunlight that people wanted to shine into the few windows of their cabins and, more importantly, onto their crops. Destroying the trees was hard, energy-intensive work. Fire was best for this task. Settler-colonists burnt more Northern Forest land than Native Americans ever had and at a more rapid pace. Learning from Native Americans, Euro-Americans also girdled trees. No farmer could completely avoid the daunting labor of cutting portions of the forest with an axe. After burning, girdling, or cutting, settlers could plant corn around the stumps, which, depending on the tree, could take from five to twenty years to rot. Rock removal was a constant problem.[68] In 1841 it took two men and a yoke of oxen twenty days to clear three acres of stumps, though by 1850 there were simple machines that helped in the process. Five to ten acres a year was the maximum two people could cultivate.[69]

Still, settlers could only regularly expect yields of root crops and hay.[70] There was little capital invested in agriculture in the Northern Forest. Farmer-loggers often used primitive wooden tools and ineffective farming methods.[71] During his visit to Maine, Thoreau mentioned that isolated Northern Forest farmer George McCauslin "grew oats, grass and potatoes . . . but he raised also, a few carrots and turnips and 'a little corn for the hens,' for this was all he dared risk, for fear that it would not ripen. Melons, squash, sweet-corn, beans, tomatoes and many other vegetables, could not be ripened there."[72] Potatoes and turnips, mashed and boiled then added to dough, stretched store-bought flour. Needles from trees, spruce in particular, were boiled for tea and to flavor beer. It was not unheard of for farmers to abandon agriculture and turn to foraging in the woods.[73] Conklin regularly left the farm to gather sweet fern, sage, honey, butternuts, walnuts, wild leeks, cowslips, adder tongues, and the many varieties of berries, along with hunting rabbits and deer, and catching fish.[74]

Northern Forest diets were universally lacking in fruits and vegetables, and preserved pickles, jellies, and jams were vital sources of nutrition.[75] Besides salt pork and game, meat was rare. Before refrigeration it rarely made sense to slaughter an entire animal. It was not until 1965 that rural meat consumption matched urban meat consumption in the United States. When there were abundant calories, the diets were monotonous: day after day of boiled cornmeal, homegrown buckwheat pancakes, or potatoes with salt. Up until the 1870s, rural diets were seasonal and limited by geography. In the 1830s, a married couple in Barnet, VT, celebrating their sixtieth wedding anniversary, claimed they had never bought any meat, flour or sugar from a store in their entire married life.[76]

State governments had little incentive to build infrastructure because of the small, scattered population.[77] For example, the Morrison family found a "beautiful tract" in northeastern Maine in 1861 on which they built "an extensive farm . . . twenty miles from a single neighbor." They had no access to markets and, as one Maine official explained, "they manifest commendable patience and contentment in their situation and cheer themselves with the hope and expectation that the Canadian government . . . will soon make a road through to the St. John settlements."[78] It was only in the 1870s and 1880s that railroads began to probe interior regions. By 1870, New Hampshire and Maine had 900 miles of rail. In northern Maine, however, the ratio of railroad miles to square miles of land was one to 3,000.[79]

By 1850, there were 876,021 people living in the Northern Forest. Interior settlers remained self-sufficient and only lightly touched by markets into the 1840s and 1850s. Many, like the Conklins, were poor, and regularly on the edge of starvation. These were marginal lands inhabited by marginal people.[80]

These marginal people had woodskill, however, and this made them essential to capital. Thoreau found that some of these rural workers had a type of knowledge that was only gained from experience in the wild: "The deeper you penetrate into the woods," he wrote, "the more intelligent, and, in one sense, less countrified do you find the inhabitants."[81] Thoreau's colleague Ralph Waldo Emerson agreed. In his poem "The Adirondacs: A Journal" he refers to his woodsmen guides as "doctors of the wilderness."[82]

To families like the Conklins, the axe was more important than the plow. This tool became extensions of their limbs. Maine logger Harry Dyer remembered that "some of them old fellows that used an axe all their life could . . . They're wonderful what they can do with an axe. . . . Just like your pen."[83] From 1805 to 1905, axes represented between 7 and 10 percent of equipment costs for Vermont farmers, one of the outlays that had the least variation over time.[84]

Adjacent to the woods, with skilled labor at hand, forest farms became manufactories of many products.[85] A short list includes shingles, boxboards, clapboards, cordwood, tanbark, washboards, firkins, pails, bowls, chairs, bedsteads, ladders, potash, railroad ties, barrel staves, laths, planks, tool handles, posts, pulp wood, fiddle butts, canoes, sleds, shoe pegs, spools, clothes pins, toothpicks, wooden bootjacks, shoe last blocks, ship knees, hop poles, spruce oil, countless types of folk-art, and consumables like maple sugar and spruce gum.[86] Firewood was always in demand. Americans built large fires, the average family consuming thirteen to fourteen cords a year, and firewood prices increased as rapidly as the trees receded. A cord, or 128 cubic feet of cut, stacked wood, increased in value 3.2 times from 1830 to 1880 in Vermont. As wood in settled southern areas was cut, urban Northeasterners looked to the Northern Forest as a source of fuel.[87]

The labor process was divided in these forest workshops. Children did smaller tasks while adults concentrated on complex and difficult jobs. On Edwin Walker's farmstead in Maine in the 1870s, Walker's son Daniel often missed school to help his father with log clearing, brush work, and making roads so that it would be easier to get products back to the farm. In one instance, Daniel had neighbor boys over to play and Edwin recruited them all to help cut and haul elm tops.[88]

Knowledge and ability in the woods allowed farmer-loggers like Conklin to quickly adapt to changing markets. When a sounding board mill put out calls for spruce in the southern Adirondacks, New York state agents had a hard time keeping residents from cutting on state lands. Lumberman S. D. Warren mailed hundreds of postcards to farmer-loggers near his mills when he wanted to buy wood.[89] When Massachusetts merchant Shepard Cary announced to residents in Aroostook, ME, that he would buy all the shingles they could make, farmer-loggers abandoned their farms for the cedar swamps.[90] As the railroad sluggishly advanced North, it created demand for lumber for trusses, ties for the tracks, and huge quantities of fuel wood. Into the 1880s, the rail lines around Concord, NH, consumed about 70,000 cords annually.[91] This need for wood meant that some early farmer-loggers moved out of poverty, amassing land, skills, knowledge, capital, and reputation.[92]

Outsiders saw farmer-loggers' willingness to abandon farming for the forest as a sign of inferiority, however. In 1848, the Boston and Eastern Mill and Land Company wrote of Machias, ME, that "It is not the *fashion* in that section of the state for the People to cultivate the land . . . the consequence is the population generally are poor and will so remain until they change [emphasis in the original]."[93] Still these people should not be considered strictly loggers.

"Participation in the trade was often sporadic," historical geographer Graeme Wynn found, explaining that "Individuals might join a lumbering venture one year and not the next . . . [or a] farmer might spend a week or two in the woods between tasks."[94] Maine labor historian Charles Scontras summarized the situation well: "So extensive was the lumbering experience for many Maine farmers, that it is difficult to determine . . . whether farming was a handmaid to lumbering, or lumbering a handmaid to farming."[95] For this reason, workers would have looked like farmers. Their clothes were the same type of clothes worn on the farm in the winter: multiple layers of homemade wool underclothes, pants, sweaters, hats, mittens, and socks. At this point, much of the laboring population in the Northern Forest had no visually distinct class identity.[96]

This was the position of Conklin and hundreds across the Northern Forest: a mixed farmer, a category or class that is difficult for those existing in highly specialized economies to imagine. The northeast was full of these jacks-of-all-trades.[97] Work was abundant and land was cheap; it typically only took a year or two of work to buy 100 acres.[98] When Henry Conklin moved out of his parents' house and began his own farmstead, he continued to rely heavily on the wood resources around him. Though he considered himself a farmer, in 1879 the value of wood products sold or consumed by Conklin was $250, or 12.3 percent of the value of his entire estate.[99]

Visitors from the North

The Conklins moved from the south into the Northern Forest, but others came from the north. Many of these migrants spoke another language—French—were devoutly Catholic and had different customs. From 1850 to 1930, about one million French-Canadian people migrated to the United States, and though most went to urban mill towns and cities, not all chose that path. They were pushed by rapid population growth, a shortage of arable agricultural land, and slow industrial development in their home country. To the Americans in the Northern Forest, these strange people from the north became part of the forest and they would become essential to its industrialization.[100]

Like native-born farmer-loggers, rural French-Canadian settlers were adept woodsmen. Fur trading, a popular occupation of eighteenth- and early-nineteenth-century French Canadians, involved close contact with the forest. When the trade died down in the 1830s, these voyageurs, many of whom had been farmer-loggers before trading, settled back into their former routines. Some who came to the Northern Forest had first been part of Canadian "colonizing" on barren Canadian wilderness lands, which was sponsored by government agencies or the clergy.[101] Even though French Canadians had built the same skill-base as many American frontier farmers, a misinformed understanding of Québec affected how Americans viewed these foreigners for more than a hundred years. They were seen as primitive, even compared to Northern Forest squatters like Conklin. Some Americans saw them as innately suited to the Northern Forest.[102]

Consider the example of French-Canadian woodchopper and post maker Alex Therien, who often visited Henry David Thoreau in the forest around Walden Pond. Dressed in homespun cloth, "a more simple and natural man it would be hard to find," Thoreau wrote. He lived in a log house in the woods and admitted to Thoreau that if he could live off hunting alone, he would. To Thoreau, he was almost indistinguishable from the trees he worked among. "In physical endurance and contentment," Thoreau wrote, "he was cousin to the pine and the rock. I asked him once if he was not sometimes tired at night, after working all day; and he answered 'Gorrappit, I never was tired in my life.'" Thoreau wrote that "in him the animal man chiefly was developed." He was a skillful woodsman capable of making more posts in a day than the average person. When chopping a tree, his cuts were clean, level, and close to the ground, and his cordwood was piled correctly. To Therien, pleasure and work were the same thing. "I can enjoy myself well enough here chopping," he reportedly said. "I want no better sport."[103]

Springer repeated Thoreau's sentiments, arguing that the Acadians of Madawaska were "demi-savages," were "remarkable for the simplicity of their manners and their fealty to their employers," and that they "retain all the marked characteristics of the French peasantry" of Europe.[104] The *Bath Sentinel* of Maine reported they were "a peculiar people, distinct in tastes, habits and aspirations from the Anglo-Saxon race."[105] In Alexis de Tocqueville's works, including "Two Weeks in the Wilderness," the French settlers are "carefree," "cheerful" men of "instinct" who submit to "life in the wild." "He clings to the land," De Tocqueville wrote, "and rips from the life in the wild everything he can snatch from it."[106]

Henry W. Longfellow's wildly popular epic poem *Evangeline, A Tale of Acadie* helped spread these French Canadian stereotypes. In *Evangeline*, the idyllic "forest primeval" of Acadia was the birthplace and a safe haven for the French who were forcefully expelled by the British.[107] Americans and British Canadians alike depicted French-Canadian agriculture as backwards, leading to their lack of social and economic advancement. Parts of Québec practiced communal agriculture, which saved many Canadians from the desperate poverty common in forest communities described above. Yet this farming was seen as a relic of a medieval past.[108] To a largely Protestant American literati, the French-Canadian simpleminded primitivism was partially caused by their devout Catholicism, which kept them dumb and stripped them of individual initiative.[109]

Another part of the American opinion of French Canadians stemmed from the belief that there was widespread blood connection between the French and Native Americans.[110] This idea was furthered by James Fennimore Cooper's *Leatherstocking Tales* and midcentury nonfiction works by Zadok Cramer, Francis Parkman, and George Bancroft. According to Parkman, "the French became savages" in early North America.[111] "Hundreds [of French settlers] betook themselves to the forest, never more to return," Parkman wrote in *The Conspiracy of Pontiac* (1851). After his stay at Walden, Thoreau visited Therien's homeland and wrote *A Yankee in Canada*. He found that, like the Indians, "the French . . . had become savage."[112] This connection partially explained their oft-reported "swarthy" complexion and why they could stand near-starvation conditions with no sign of distress. Observing winter poor relief, the *Québec Mercury* reported in 1855 that French Canadians "proudly conceal any amount of privation with a sort of Indian stoicism."[113]

Though French Canadians became part of the Northern Forest landscape by the 1850s, they were not the preferred inhabitants. In 1864, the Maine Board of Agriculture recommended to the legislator that they should take measures "for the encouragement of immigration from Europe, and especially from its northern portions." The Board wanted "farm laborers, farmers, and working men from the countries of Northern Europe, as the Swedes, the Norwegians and the Danes, who are well known as among the steadiest, most reliable, and most industrious and honest of the European races."[114] The state followed through and sent an agent to Sweden to get colonists for land set aside in Aroostook.[115]

Business before Industry

Though there were nascent racial divisions in the Northern Forest, there were also hints of collective identity. The *Maine Farmer* reported on a group of poor farmer-loggers living in Rangeley Lake, ME, who lived primarily off stolen trees. They were, the periodical reported, a "rough, tough, hardy and hawbucking . . . group."[116] Conklin wrote of a neighboring family with nine children who were "poor like ourselves" and "lived mostly by making shingles from year to year."[117] Along the Aroostook and Fish Rivers there were "'wretchedly poor' settlers" who, when "joined together . . . make a small quantity [of saw logs] . . . which they get hauled by some person with a team, they being so destitute."[118]

Though poor, when several families cooperated, they could produce commodities in large quantities with little or no outside capital investment. Northern Forest residents drew on the colonial New England tradition of the "logging bee," where residents gathered in a celebratory atmosphere to draw wood from communal lots for public use.[119] These were times for overindulgence in food and alcohol. Working, consuming alcohol, and celebration could happen simultaneously in the same space and time. There was often no need for hard lines between work and leisure, a topic that will be discussed more in chapter 6.

Tools, draft animals, sleds, lumber camps, and nearly everything that was needed for small- or medium-sized forest product operations could be drawn from the farm or made in the woods. Collectivizing to build capital was important because these areas often lacked access to credit or banks. The county seat of Holton in Aroostook County, ME, remained without a savings bank until 1872.[120] These workers' skills could also help build roads, improve rivers, create dams, and their cabins and barns were rest-havens for recreationalists and timber speculators.

Subsistence-based agricultural norms seamlessly mixed with emerging market-based norms. Farmer-loggers did not fixate on profit when running their own operations or when working for wages. Historian Béatrice Craig found that many operators in these early years worked to make "a living rather than a profit."[121] Work, leisure, family, and God were all connected, and constant hard work not only provided necessities, but also improved the family's earthly and heavenly reputation. For these reasons, if they had access to credit, they "seamlessly borrowed for land, crop seeds and [for consumer items like] hats for church," as historian Louis Hyman wrote, showing little separation between the finances of business and life.[122] This was especially important in logging, where producers couldn't eat what they made. Benefits from forest product production came only after the product was sold or traded, typically six to nine months after the work began. Loans had to cover everything that an operation, and the families connected to it, needed or wanted for the season. Profits or surplus were invested back into the businesses, which were also the families. Accounts with suppliers and wage workers, often recorded in personal ledgers or memory, might run open for multiple seasons. IOU notes were common currency; foodstuffs and forest products were collateral, reserves, and remuneration.[123]

Cutting the Commons

Informality extended even into property rights. Farmer-loggers produced on their own land, on others' land under agreements, and on land where they did not have permission to cut. The country was land-rich and labor-short, so incentives were needed to attract people and capital to the land. Squatting was accepted in common and written law. Generations of Northern Forest residents had grown accustomed to two types of common forest resource pools. The first was "inner" commons of public pastures, woods lots, church lots, and school lots. Those more isolated settlers had access to the second type, a vast "outer" commons of unsettled forest.[124]

When towns were planned in the Northern Forest, they often included inner common fields and forest managed by the settlers.[125] A law passed in 1784 required that each township carved out of the wild lands in what would become Maine set aside 680 acres for these purposes. By 1788, each township had about 960 acres of public land.[126] Sometimes the common lands were for the church or for poor relief. Sometimes they were meant to support public schools. Often the poor could forage, hunt, and take forest products there. Grants, leases, or rights to strip timber from certain lots were allowed, with the proceeds of the grant going to the town or village for use in poor relief or for other uses.[127] The resources were sometimes tied to local communities and not to be extracted away. In 1679, the township of Hartford disallowed exporting of boards, timbers, and planks.[128] A 1772 New York act forbade transporting firewood from the Northern Forest into Albany or the Manor of Rensselaerswycke.[129]

English common law often considered rugged mountainous regions, swamps, and other places that were difficult to reach or survey, as outer commons, open to use and not necessarily controlled by the community.[130] Glebe Mountain, Government's Mountain, and parts of Mt. Ascutney in Vermont were all commons. Though not legally recognized, the same held true for remote land that was legally private property. In the second half of the eighteenth century, land in the Northern Forest began to accumulate in the hands of wealthy proprietors who could afford to pay for large parcels. Ira Allen's Onion River Company eventually acquired 300,000 acres of land in Vermont; John C. Jones was granted 48,160 acres of Maine by the General Court of Massachusetts. Beginning in 1793, William Bingham began buying land in Maine from the state of Massachusetts and he would eventually own over two million acres.[131] The scale of these purchases made property rights difficult to police. The forest was too immense and tangled, too prolific and fecund for subsistence uses to be exposed or prevented.[132]

For settlers like Conklin, taking food, firewood, or other necessities from unimproved land, regardless of its owner, was socially acceptable, as was taking wood products to sell or trade, if that activity was necessary for a family's survival.[133] A New York State agent commented that "Generations have made their living by lumbering where ever they please and the most preeminent men in town, the very pillars of the church have a rather queer view about stealing timber."[134] Historian Karl Jacoby called this the "law of the woods."[135]

Starving Times

The law of the woods was essential for survival in this harsh climate. The long winters aided production, as mentioned above, but winter also created deadly problems. Plants die or minimize photosynthesis to reserve their energy in the winter. This annual decrease in energy travels up trophic levels, affecting all creatures. Calories in general became scarce. This is one of the reasons why many mammals hibernate. Winters here were "starving times."[136] Forest product production was energy intensive, however, and required a superabundance of calories.

As described above, the Northern Forest had limited agricultural prospects even during warmer months. By mid-century, Northern Forest farmers were facing western competition in commodity crops and so were incentivized to abandon subsistence farming to plant whatever could be sold at the highest price, namely potatoes, oats, and hay. But fluctuating market prices and railroad monopolies meant cash profits were rare. Farmers took on more debt.[137] They spent more time growing their cash crops and less time fishing, hunting, gardening, and foraging, activities necessary for proper health.[138] This was the position of farmers across the United States, and there is evidence that the height of farmers was decreasing between 1830 and 1890, an indication of declining health.[139] While some poor farmers went hungry, woodsmen with access to outside credit could bring in consistent supplies of high energy food to the woods.[140]

The task of keeping workers and animals fed became an important part of any forest products operation. In 1837 a company agent for the Boston and Eastern Company wrote to headquarters in Boston in distress, "I have . . . to request . . . that you send *immediately* something for us to eat. One of the saws has stopped for no other reason than the want of provision[s] . . . [and] there is none about here that could be bought if there was money to buy it with [emphasis in the original]."[141] Throughout the opening years of their operations there were constant requests for pork, flour, corn, hay, and oats. Cary Brothers Lumber Company found similar circumstances in St. John, New Brunswick, in 1849.[142] When the food situation got desperate loggers ate their oxen.[143]

Machias was close to the ocean, and Boston and Eastern was eventually able to establish regular shipments of pork, corn, and flour. As operations moved further inland, supplying camps became more difficult. Operators used waterways whenever possible, employing flat-bottomed "horseboats," some of which were "a hundred feet long . . . capable of carrying 200 barrels of pork, molasses and flour." Supplies often had to be taken overland, so operators hired woodsmen to make roads. In Aroostook, ME, the Cary Brothers built a road "from L'Isle to Depot Stream to a small tributary of the . . . Black River" to supply their camps. By the 1850s, this route, known as the "California Road," was so important to commerce that the state began to fund its maintenance. Still, frozen rivers and lakes were often the most efficient route inland.[144]

Dedicated lumberers vertically integrated, starting their own farms.[145] Locations for these farms were chosen carefully to maximize yields and allow for easy transportation to camps. Lumberman Eben S. Coe's Chamberlain Farm in Piscataquis County, ME, was called a "little seaport in the wilderness," because it was tucked conveniently between Chamberlain Lake and Indian Pond. Built on a south-facing slope, the area was dryer and the snow melted quicker than the surrounding land. Coe's half dozen farm workers planted 600 acres of potatoes, oats, and hay. They raised cattle, horses, and hogs for their camps or to sell to those local woodsmen they worked with.[146] The Cary Brother's "Depot" was a similar but smaller operation located in the "rich alluvial soil" of Seven Islands, ME.[147]

Given the dearth of calories in the Northern Forest winter, desperate farmer-loggers accepted partial payment in food, though this was common in other industries and places.[148] Into the 1870s, contracts to cut wood might stipulate allotments of sugar, tea, or tobacco provided by the financing party. Workers could be rewarded for good work with increased or special rations.[149] Boston and Eastern Company agent Daniel Hammond wrote to the company for $5,000 in goods "to pay labor for lumbering, driving logs, sawing" and at the end of a season they rewarded workers with "½ bbls Flour & 3 bbls apples . . . for faithful services at moderate wages."[150]

Operators and workers alike saw little discrepancy between payment in kind, in cash, or even a return exchange of hours worked. Historian Béatrice Craig found that merchants in the upper St. John's Valley in the late 1850s and early 1860s paid between 25 and 42 percent of debts with things other than cash.[151] Northern Forest farmer and laborer Peter G. Morrill built up an account of $21.97 in 1849 at Chamberlain Farm, mainly for multiple nights of room and board for himself and his animals. He paid part of this debt in small increments of cash: $1.50 on December 25th, $4.50 sometime in January, $1.00 on March 24, and the remaining amount he paid through trade and work. This system worked well at a time and place where nearly everyone had labor to give and nearly everyone could use an extra pair of hands occasionally.[152] In these small camps people might work three to five months without cash payment, as long as they were fed. Most forest products operators comingled old agrarian and new industrial methods of remuneration, as exemplified by the Boston and Eastern Company policy to keep "on hand a Supply of Provision[s] of leading articles, from which our laborers can have anything they may choose to take [on credit], it being known and distinctly understood *that no man will be hired except for Cash at the close of each month* [emphasis in the original]." Even on paydays, it was common to pay workers in scrip or check that needed to be cashed "downriver" when logs were sold.[153] The Cary Brothers operation in Aroostook, ME, specifically had workers come downriver to more settled areas to be paid. Shepard Cary wrote to an associate, "I notice that Holman has request[ed] you send him 400 dollars, 200 to pay a man off at Fish River. I should have thought that his man might at least have come to Houlton for money. It is rather poor business for us to send money to pay men off at Fish River. You must hold [Holman] tight for money or he will pay every loafer off he has before he gets [in]."[154]

For an investor, capitalizing an operation was as simple as importing high-calorie food into the woods expecting that forest products would flow out. Pork, the ubiquitous meat of the rural poor, was the primary protein. Pigs could prosper in harsh conditions. When left to forage on their own they could increase their weight 150 percent in eight months.[155] Those who did not raise pigs secured salt-cured pork. Raw salt pork was also sliced thin on hardtack and served for breakfast, lunch, and dinner.[156] As Springer wrote, "from these gross simples the hungry woodsman makes many a delicious meal."[157] Farmer-loggers rarely slaughtered a cow because it would be too much meat for a family. However, when many families joined together for logging, beef could be justified. If supply routes were well constructed, beef could be brought in. In 1850, 317 pounds of fresh beef were toted into Chamberlain Farm from 105 miles away.[158] Salt cod was a staple, and game meat was popular. When eating with a camp of loggers, Thoreau wrote that, for the loggers, "our moose-meat was oftenest called for."[159]

Dried beans were one of the few vegetable foods that could survive the long trip into remote areas. The idea of putting pork and molasses, the other universal flavoring agent in rural America, into a pot of beans as they cooked was a natural extension of the pork-centric rural American culinary tradition. The resulting baked beans were sweet, savory, fatty, mushy, fiber rich, and quick and easy to eat. All these qualities meant they were quickly converted into energy.[160]

Those with close affiliations with area farms also had access to potatoes, turnips, beets, carrots, rutabagas, parsnips, onions, and apples.[161] Some canned items were available in America from 1850 onward, but until the 1870s and 1880s, canned food were high-priced specialty items like lobster and oysters, along with some fruits and vegetables. Until the 1880s, when canning technology improved, these items were expensive and sometimes unsafe for consumption.[162] Dishes with elaborate preparation methods were not a regular part of Northern Forest diets until late in the nineteenth century. Thoreau recalls that loggers coming out of camp desired "cakes and pies, and such sweet things, which are there almost unknown."[163] Regardless of what was on the menu, the diets of loggers were coveted during harsh Northern Forest winters. Workers' neighbors, relatives, and even strangers traveled the long distance into camps just for the lavish meals. A barrel of pork was stolen from the Cary Brothers by a boatman who was transporting their goods.[164]

Included in these shipments of food were likely some less essential items like alcohol and tobacco. Tobacco was the "ultimate article of consumption," in the Northern Forest. Loggers chewed and smoked the leaves to an excess.[165] It was common for French-Canadian workers to grow tobacco in their farm gardens and bring it to camp.

Before 1840, workers commonly drank at work.[166] Alcohol was the cure-all of choice. Consumption increased in rural communities when people got together. Harvest times, political events, militia musters, and different types of working "bees" spurred "communal binges." Akin to these market celebrations were the celebrations that historically accompanied the end of a fur-trading voyage in French-Canadian and American frontier cultures.[167] Communal bingeing took place when workers left camp for pay downriver. In a city like Bangor, "unwatered rum" could be bought for three cents a glass.[168]

By 1832, temperance efforts were beginning in Northern Forest camps, but before then, "so strong was the conviction that men could not work in the water [on the log drive] without 'spirits,'" that one temperance advocate "had great difficulty in employing the first crew of men to drive on the river on temperance principles." That year, when a drive was attempted on the St. Croix River of Maine without alcohol, workers were "forced to acknowledge, when they came downriver, that they had never succeeded so well before."[169] The state of Maine passed an early statewide prohibition in 1851, followed by Vermont in 1852, New York in 1854, and New Hampshire in 1855. Following the milieu, alcohol was nearly universally banned in large forest products camps, though there is some disagreement about this.[170]

Waste People and Waste Land

Despite the vital economic purpose that the Conklins and other Northern Forest farmer-loggers served, some outsiders disdained these producers, arguing that their poverty stemmed from their refusal to accept either full-time agricultural or full-time wage work. Their hunting, foraging, plodding oxen teams, primitive tools, rundown cabins, communal binges, and homespun clothes were signs of their inability to "advance." The word squatter was pejorative, denoting vagrancy and idleness. Working in the wilderness was only supposed to be the first step in the process of civilizing the land, not a life-long career.[171] Benjamin Rush wrote that "From a review of the three different species of settlers, it appears, that there are certain regular stages which mark the progress from the savage to civilized life. The first settler is nearly related to an Indian in his manners—In the second, the Indian manners are more diluted: It is in the third species of settlers only, that we behold civilization completed—It is to the third species of settlers only, that it is proper to apply the term of *farmers* [emphasis in the original]."[172]

In Canada as in the Northern Forest, farmer-loggers were depicted as "the most depraved and dissipated set of villains on earth." Large landholders in Maine complained about their "indolence."[173] One Canadian newspaper reported about loggers that "they contracted habit something similar to the gypsies, spent their winter in the woods and their summer lounging about the towns." Visitors found that the loggers' lifestyle led to "prodigality, thoughtlessness of future wants, profaneness, irreligion, inordinate drinking, and other ruinous habits." [174] Likely because of the negative stigma associated with logging, most farmer-loggers identified as farmers regardless of how much time they spent in the woods.

Joel Tyler Headley encapsulated the mid-century urban middle-class opinion of Northern Forest people. In the 1840s, Headley went to the Adirondacks to recover from an "attack on the brain" caused by a stressful career as a writer in New York City. His opinions of the people of the area were published in his books, *The Adirondack: Or, Life in the Woods* and *Letters from the Backwoods and the Adirondac.*[175] Headley observed that Adirondackers lusted after easy-to-access natural resources and thus "not a man here supports himself from his farm. . . . Some of the best men have left, and those that remain depend on the money (some seven hundred dollars) furnished by the State for the making of roads, to buy their provisions with." To Headley, backwoodsmen lived off the unearned fruits of the woods. He commented that the Adirondacks needed "enterprising settlers—men who go to build their fortunes, not to save themselves from starvation; who take pride in cultivating society, and have some ambition." He also criticized the backwoodsmen for their lack of desire for contact with civilization. Visiting a hunter's cabin, he was surprised to see "no books, not the sign of a paper, however old." Backwoodsmen's work blinded them to progress, the future, and worldly events, good and bad. "They have their troubles," Headley wrote, "but they are born and die in the bosom of the forest." "Theirs," he continued, was "a life of toil and ignorance."[176]

Headley and his contemporaries believed in the inevitability of progress. The lack of cultivation in the Adirondacks was the reason that much of it was considered "neglected waste," as Headley wrote, and those within it were waste people. Backwoods people were people of the past and they would progress forward eventually as the land was improved. If Northern Forest people did not progress, they would die out like Native Americans supposedly had.[177] Some of Headley's associates suggested it would take a century to make the Adirondacks habitable, though he thought it would only be sixty or seventy years.[178]

Cutover but Regrowing: The Forest Wins

Despite the opinions of urban vacationers, Northern Forest occupants were opportunists looking to advance by squatting on the land or harvesting resources. This was difficult. The forest didn't acquiesce to humans. Settlers hacked at, burned, and girdled trees but before the 1870s their early efforts were puny compared to the fecundity of the forest. The tool that could have completed the task cheaply—fire—was too unwieldy to be deployed on a large scale.[179] In fact, humans created an advantage for the forest. Flames and axes delivered sunlight to young trees, a resource they typically had to struggle for. Most settlers found it difficult to keep their field clear of new forest growth. Fresh growth took over fields and even grew into the crude log structures the frontier settlers built.[180]

For these reasons, outmigration of humans began as early as the 1820s as the Erie Canal opened up western farm and forest land to settlement. In 1849, with the reports of gold in California, the pace of outmigration quickened.[181] Midwestern boosters traveled to the Northern Forest, enticing young people with the promise of fertile ground in Iowa and Nebraska for as low as $3.00 an acre. Others moved to the factories of southern New England and New York where manufacturing wages were rising by the year.[182]

Railroads and western land provided cheap grain for sheep, cow, and horse feed, which meant Northern Foresters could stop clearing land for feed, and let it regrow.[183] A farmer in Vermont wrote that "reclaiming by the plow is impossible and what little vegetation there is seems hardly worth the

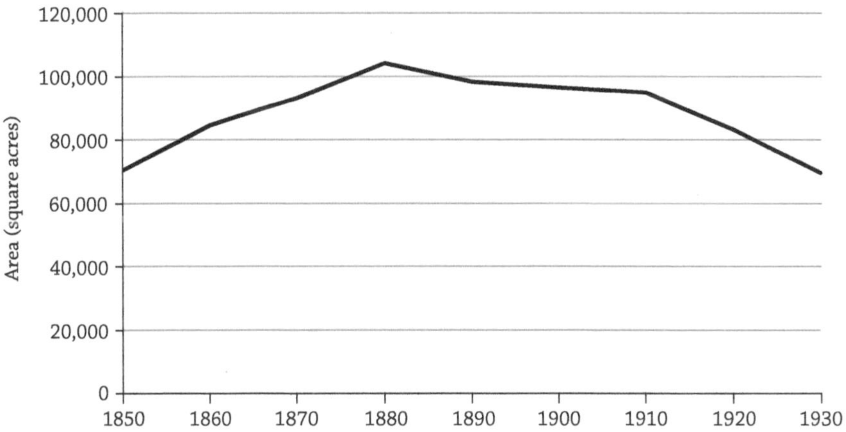

Figure 2.1. Total farms, Northern Forest (Social Explorer Dataset, custom, 1850–1950, for Aroostook, Franklin, Hancock, Oxford, Penobscot, Piscataquis, Somerset, and Washington Counties in Maine; Coos County, New Hampshire; Clinton, Essex, Franklin, Fulton, Hamilton, Herkimer, Jefferson, Lewis, Oneida, Oswego, St. Lawrence, and Warren Counties, New York; Caledonia, Essex, Franklin, Lamoille, Orleans, and Washington Counties, Vermont, census 1850 to 1950, based on data from US Census Bureau, compiled, edited, and verified by Social Explorer)

necessary effort of the stock to obtain it. . . . There is but one use that can be made of such land . . . that is to let it grow up to forest. It was once covered with timber and time will so cover it again."[184] Around 1880, the number of farms in the Northern Forest peaked and farm values tended to decrease over time (figure 2.1). The total value of farmland and farm buildings in Vermont dropped from $111 million in 1870 to $83 million by 1900.[185] By 1890, Maine had 3,300 abandoned farms encompassing 254,000 acres.[186]

By this time logging capital was not as interested in the forest as it had been. Most large trees were cleared from about three miles around major waterways, where transportation by water and ice had made extraction cheap. Capital's focus moved to larger trees growing on the banks of Lake Ontario, Erie, Huron, Michigan, and Superior. In 1849, the Northeast was producing half the nation's lumber, but by 1880, it was no longer self-sufficient in its wood supply. The forest was cutover.[187]

Just as with the Great Dying of the Indigenous, when people left the land, the trees went to work and forest cover rose quickly (figure 2.2). Settlement had its lightest effect on the interior. The soil had not been dried out on a large scale, watersheds were generally healthy or mildly altered, and even in disturbed areas, carbon and nitrogen levels were recovering.[188]

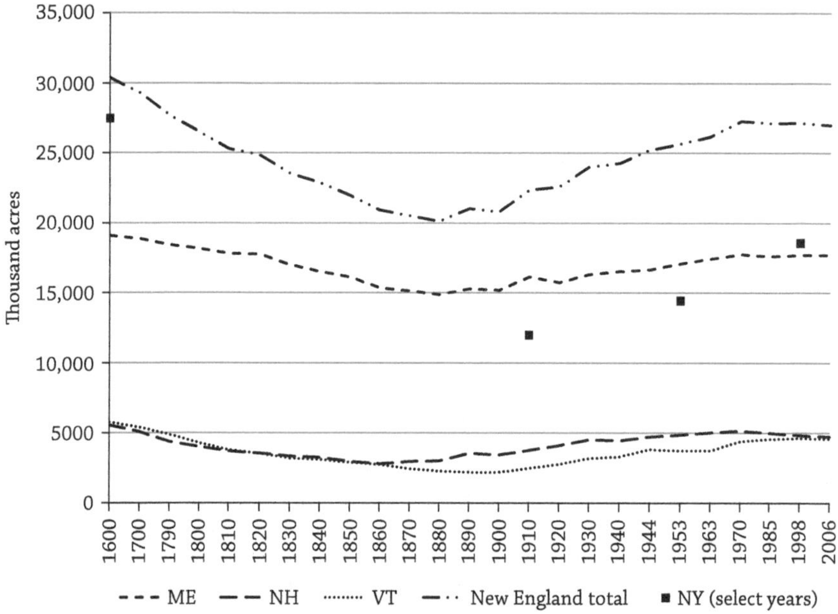

Figure 2.2. Forest cover, statewide (D. Foster and E. Gould, "Forest Change and Human Populations in New England, 1650–2006," Harvard Forest Data Archive: HF013, 2003, accessed April 14, 2017, http://harvardforest.fas.harvard.edu/harvard-forest-data-archive; Lloyd C. Irland, *The Northeast's Changing Forests* [Petersham, MA: Distributed by Harvard University Press for Harvard Forest, 1999], 4)

To understand how the forest worked in the absence of people it is important to understand succession, or "the orderly replacement over time of one species or association of species (the community) by another, as a result of competitive [and cooperative] interaction between them for limited site resources."[189] As was explained in the first chapter, forests, like people, colonize. The first successional wave on disturbed land was composed of pioneer species: paper and gray birch, aspen, pin cherry and, in some cases, white pine. In the timescale of trees, these pioneer species were mobile, producing annually a multitude of lightweight seeds that spread easily.[190] In the colonization process, trees can act individually, particularly these pioneering species, but they can also work together. In a setting like the Northern Forest, where wind is the most common and deadly threat, density of the foliage created by groups of trees dissipated the wind by as much as 40 percent. Through root systems, aided by a mutualistic relationship with fungi, trees can share resources like carbohydrates, nitrogen, or carbon.[191] Pioneering and mutualistic, these forests reclaimed the land.

The period between 1870 and 1900 was one of massive regeneration.[192] Abandoned farms often grew into valuable tracts of second growth white pine, a species that grew to outcompete the other pioneers. When the interior of the Northern Forest was cut by lumberers, it was often done selectively. For example, one of the largest landowners in Maine at mid-nineteenth century, Eben Coe, never let any of his contractors cut a tree smaller than sixteen inches DBH.[193] The selective cutting of old white pine in old forests in the winter would have mimicked the natural death of the tree. The opened canopy gaps exposed the forest floor to valuable sunlight. Because nearly all large-scale nineteenth-century forest product production was done in the winter, it did not compact the soil, so seeds could take root and grow. Upon the death of large mother trees, the smaller offspring took advantage of the gap. In 50 to 150 years these trees were mature and of sufficient size for planks and lumber.[194] In higher altitudes, paper birch might have been the quickest to take advantage of canopy gaps but red spruce and balsam fir both grew faster than birch and replaced it. Human disturbance did have some negative effects on forest growth. Second growth trees can grow in dense stands full of thin trees that grow up to reach the sun as opposed to building girth. Successive forests also tend to lack the biodiversity and genetic variability of older climax forests. This means they are vulnerable to ice storms, disease, and insects.[195]

In this cutover forest, lumbering and farming did not become irrelevant. Regardless of ecological or market conditions, forests almost always have their highest value in the present, partly because of the possibilities of future damage to the trees from fire, wind, disease, or trespass.[196] There was also a tradition of working in the woods that locals found hard to quit. The forests' fecundity assured there would be jobs cutting wood throughout the nineteenth and twentieth centuries. Moreover, there were still old forests in difficult to reach places. The most lucrative years for saw log production in the Northern Forest would actually be in the first decade of the twentieth century.[197] On the whole, however, the trees that were left were smaller and more difficult to harvest. As environmental historian Richard Judd argued, "the era of free goods in the upper Northeast was over."[198] Those who remained would have to work harder and in new ways to wrest value from the cutover land.

CHAPTER 3

A CHANCE

In autumn 1863, in northwestern Maine, farmer-logger Abner Toothaker sent a letter to the estate of wealthy landowners Eben S. Coe and David Pingree. This letter asked for a "chance" on their land. Toothaker got his chance and that winter organized neighbors, relatives, and perhaps some hired workers to cut 9,813 saw logs that he owned and would sell to support his farm. Working like this, farming in the spring, summer, and fall, cutting in the winter, Abner did well for himself. In 1860s, his farm was worth $4,500, putting him in the top quarter of farmers in all the Northern Forest.[1]

Almost thirty years later, in the winter of 1891, Abner's grandson, Lincoln, also made his way into the woods, to the Black Cat lumber camp near Rangeley, ME. Unlike his grandfather, Lincoln owned none of the logs he helped cut on this chance but instead made a daily wage. Through letters to his wife, Lincoln expressed a strong desire to leave the forest. He wrote that he was "homesick" and that he missed his wife, new baby and younger siblings. At times he felt like a "state prisoner." "I want to see you so bad," he wrote his wife, "it is only the mighty dollar that keeps me in this forsaken place."[2]

The Toothaker story shows that to write a labor history of a forest we must also see the forest environment as a business environment, a space where work was done, and class performed. This chapter describes this business environment, the factors that made up the opportunities for and limitations on the firms in the Northern Forest. It shows that the business environment changed from the time Abner was cutting, a time described in the last chapter, to the time Lincoln was cutting. This business environment, like all business environments, was a product of the natural environment. In the Northern Forest, this was a cutover forest environment.[3]

The most important change that firms had to reckon with was enclosure, a historical phenomenon that diminished producers' ability to use the land for survival. Facing more limited choices in production compared to previous generations, Northern Forest producers blended familiar regional agrarian norms with an emerging industrial and corporate order. Small-scale firms did not surrender completely to large corporate structures. Instead, they jobbed or contracted with financiers, landowners, and mills, maintaining control of production, a choice that was important to their identity as farmers. This arrangement limited producers' ability to collaborate with others in their class, however.[4]

Together, the cutover landscape and enclosure created a new competitive business environment focused on production and profit rather than survival. In this environment, farmer-loggers needed a competitive edge to get a chance, so they specialized. This chapter explains the slow process of specialization that farmer-loggers made in this period, roughly between the time that Abner and Lincoln Toothaker were working in the woods. Specialization wasn't cheap. It required woodsmen to increase their reliance on financiers, mills, and landowners, and they often got into debt. They ended up in a "sweated" production matrix wherein what meager profit could be attained by working in the forest came directly from the sweat of the workers—people and animals alike. What today is called labor flexibility or the "gig economy" was not a characteristic of capitalism that emerged after the New Deal. Instead, it was a condition that was dependent on the constructed and natural environment of business, regardless of the period of time.[5]

A business environment characterized by small firms in vigorous competition is what economists call a "market economy." Market economies are characterized by decentralization, but the forest itself, namely the geography and topography, pressed order and hierarchies out of disorder and competition, thus blurring the boundaries of the firm. Though decentralized from a legal perspective, centralization emerged through logistical processes of moving products but also due to natural conditions, as the interlude that follows this chapter makes clear.[6]

The Toothaker family clearly understood the legal, economic, and natural barriers that determined their success, and this is evident by their use of the word *chance.* In the 1910s logging expert Clement Bryant defined the term chance as "the ease or difficulty with which a particular logging operation . . . can be conducted" or simply as "a logging unit." In common usage, the word is synonymous with luck, referring to the luck entailed in getting a business opportunity in the first place and the luck necessary for a firm to succeed.[7] In a concise way, the word explains the Northern Forest business environment wherein small firms dealt with limited resources, cutthroat competition, and thousands of variables, both constructed and natural. Perhaps industry insiders understood that a chance was all Northern Forest producers really had; their merits only got them so far.

Closing the Commons

The Northern Forest business environment was shaped by the interactions between people and nonhuman nature. These interactions were themselves shaped by law, which created incentives and penalties. Generations of Northern Forest residents had grown accustomed to legal and informal rules governing their use of common forest resources, both inner forest commons and the outer commons.[8]

Access to the inner commons was the first to legally dissipate. After the Revolutionary War, the separation of church and state made ministerial or parsonage lands difficult to justify. These lands were often ceded to the clergy and ceased to serve public functions. School lots were sold by municipal governments to pay for the construction and running of the schools, though sometimes they were leased, rented, or run as communal farms or woodlots. In Danville, NH, the town leased common lots and auctioned cutting rights in 1810, 1828, and 1834. Even individual trees could be purchased.[9]

These changes meant that common lands concentrated in the hands of those who could afford it, often those who had been in the communities the longest. For example, John Wittemore bought a 100-acre farm near St. Albans, VT, in 1821. Through farming and raising cattle on common pastures he was able to buy or lease more common lands that municipalities were selling. By 1835, he had accumulated 250 acres.[10]

Until roughly the 1870s, municipal authorities proved unable to control what happened in the great outer common forests that lay outside their surveillance. Here the "law of the woods" described in the last chapter continued. Even when governments did have the ability to surveil the outer commons, they did not consider densely forested, poorly drained, mountainous, or otherwise "waste" land worth the costs of policing.

Transferring land to private parties transferred the burden of policing. Political forces in the United States, particularly Whigs and the political parties that branched off from them, believed privatization—a price per acre on all forest land—would increase the economic utility of waste lands. In the first half of the nineteenth century, state and federal policy sought to avoid making the government into a land manager. Classical economics held that government ownership of land distorted market prices. In this view the forests belonged to "the people," not the state. Due to lack of knowledge of the land, and an abundance of land in relation to capital and labor, the land often sold at the state-imposed minimum rate but in large parcels for large amounts of money.[11]

In 1850, the state of Maine embarked on a massive enclosure of the forests, hiring agents to sell timber and grazing rights until the land could be sold or incorporated into towns.[12] In 1874, the Coe family, on whose land the Toothakers worked, were already large landholders. That year they bought 20,227 additional acres of land in Northern Maine for $0.35 an acre. By the end of Coe's life, his shared landholdings totaled nearly a million acres.[13] Coe and other private landowners did police their property, often hiring agents drawn from the community to do surveillance.

Similar privatization and consolidation efforts were happening across the Northern Forest. In 1880, the New Hampshire Land Company, an organization run by out-of-staters, bought 240,000 acres of mountain land, and hired a cadre of professionals to ward off trespassers. This type of consolidation included arable land and the tracts of merchantable timber which had been out of reach of previous generations of colonial and American loggers.[14] The sales also included "waste land" like swamps and steep mountains that had served as outer commons in the past. Large landholders were exempt from improvement taxes, and they discouraged any use of land that they thought would devalue known or undiscovered natural resources. They allowed people to access their land, but for a price.[15]

The term *stumpage*, which came into popular use by 1835, identified the price required to access forest resources, namely standing timber. Land with merchantable forest products close to water or other transportation infrastructure had high stumpage costs, while isolated tracts, tracts with sparse or unhealthy trees, cutover land, or tracts on difficult topography had low stumpage costs.[16] Maps drawn up by private landholders, or sometimes state agencies, listed stumpage prices on top of other natural features, signifying the primacy of market price in determining land-use potentials. Stumpage on the Coe/Pingree lands that the Toothakers worked on ranged from $1.00 to $5.00 per thousand board feet of surveyed timber.[17]

On common lands where the "law of the woods" was respected by residents and municipal authorities, tracts of forest that were seen as unmerchantable, along with forests on mountainsides, dead and dying timber, swamps, and marshes, were places where farmers like Henry Conklin might go to make a few thousand shingles for sale and use. The labor invested in cutting and transporting these forest products was thought to be equal to or greater than their value. Stumpage put a price on all types of forest resources, high value and low, eliminating the tradition of common land use.

As common land was moving into private hands, a nascent conservation mentality was forming in the American mind. After the Civil War, more middle-class Americans began traveling to the Northern Forest not for settlement but for sport. These "sports" demanded access to wilderness.[18] In 1864, Vermonter George Perkins Marsh convinced many Americans that forests were more than just spaces for recreation. Forests, Marsh argued in his influential book *Man and Nature*, preserved the nation's health by preserving watersheds and providing sustainable resources for future generations. To Marsh, all humans, and by implication loggers specifically, were "essentially a destructive power."[19]

Though tourists were drawn to the forest for its natural setting, most were unfamiliar with Northern Forest ecology and the forest's regenerative capabilities. Large tanneries in the Adirondacks were stripping bark from 1,000 acres worth of hemlock per year between 1850 and 1890, with perhaps a million and a half acres stripped in total. Between 200,000 and 250,000 acres were cleared by iron producers to make the charcoal that fueled Adirondack forges.[20] The clearcutting that was being done by farmers for their fields, as well as for potash, charcoal, and later, pulp wood, shocked vacationers and sportsmen, who became convinced that parts of the Northeast should remain wilderness rather than places of work. They lobbied state and federal governments to prohibit local access to land and water for resource extraction. Motivated by this conservationist impulse, state and federal agencies joined private landowners in increased surveillance and control of the forests.[21]

Just as forests were regrowing on abandoned Northern Forest land, many powerful American institutions became obsessed with formally controlling forest resources. Before 1870, sustainable forestry was not practiced systematically on a large scale in the United States.[22] In 1875, forestry professionals formed the American Forestry Association. In 1876, Congress commissioned a special agency to study quickly vanishing American forest resources. This study led to the creation of the Division of Forestry in 1881, followed by the 1891 Forestry Reserve Act that created federal forest reserves. By 1894, there were 17.5 million acres of national forests that required an army of technocrats to protect it from fires, to manage it for recreation, grazing, and in some cases, to "produce the forest tree crop."[23] The 1897 Organic Act affirmed the congress's desire for managed forest lands indefinitely. By 1900, Yale, Cornell, and Biltmore were giving instruction in forestry, training hundreds of students to observe and protect public and private forests. In 1905, the Department of the Interior transferred control of the forest reserves to the Department of Agriculture for further regulation, and the US Forest Service was systematically regulating and observing both public and private forest land under the leadership of Gifford Pinchot.[24]

States also began forest conservation efforts around this time. In 1872, New York State authorized Verplanck Colvin to survey the area that would later become the Adirondack Park. Between 1885 and 1894, New York formally created the park by establishing the "blue line" around a six-million-acre area of northern New York, vowing that the land that came under state purview would be "forever kept as wild forest lands." Thereafter the state began to collect back taxes, remove squatters, and increase their surveillance of the forest. They hired agents to collect penalties, seize stolen logs, and even arrest persistent trespassers. In 1891, Maine replaced its informal system of "land agents" with a formal forest commission. In 1901, Edgar E. Ring, a timberland owner, was elected as forest commissioner in Maine. He ensured that Maine's forest land and surveillance of it would remain mostly in private hands. Vermont created a Forest Commission in 1905, followed by New Hampshire in 1910.[25] The 1911 Weeks Act "allowed the creation of National Forests in the East."[26] By 1916, "Vermont claimed 12,000 acres; . . . [and] New Hampshire, 9,100 [acres] of protected forest lands." In 1918, the 434,000-acre White Mountain National Forest was created. Apart from the 30,000 acres of the White Mountain National Forest that lay in Maine, the state had no large tracts of land under state control until the 1920s.

Within a sixty-year period, America went from having no professional or governmental organization managing forest land to having several private, state, and federal organizations that determined who could use the trees.[27] While the total amount of federal landownership in the Northeast was small compared to other parts of the country, the conservation and tourism mentalities at local and national levels materially changed how locals could use forest resources.

Through privatization and conservation, much of the inner and outer communal forest land was closed. This increased operating costs and risks for farmer-loggers. Cutting on private land without permission resulted in a trespassing fee or even arrest. Most often, when Coe dealt with trespassing it was because a party to whom he had given permission to cut had taken trees outside of their contracted area. A small mistake in determining the location of invisible lines in the forest could be costly. Coe charged increased stumpage after the trespass occurred, sometimes double market value. Trespassing could be ruinous for a small operator like Abner Toothaker who, in the 1863–64 cutting season, invested more than the value of his entire estate in stumpage. Trespass diminished the logger's reputation, reducing the possibility of getting a chance next season. Because of these harsh repercussions, recorded trespassing on the Coe/Pingree land was rare, with only about 3,328 trees and 175 cords of illegal wood cut between 1863 and 1930.[28]

The situation was similar on government conservation lands. Despite the "forever wild" agenda of the Adirondack park's creators, part of a state agent's work was to report on and consider "land values" to assess them for taxation and to penalize trespassers.[29] To do this they assigned a price per acre to conserved state lands that was similar to stumpage. Punishments for trespassing included fines but also possible jail time. Only desperate people continued to cut on state land. In 1884, a state agent in New York found about 2,750 hop poles—by definition small immature trees—cut from state lands manufactured by poor men "of large families" who owned "nothing but an old horse or two and possibly a cow."[30] Another state agent operating around Plattsburgh, NY, in 1884 found that "Charles Garrous, John Garrous, Constance Agony, & Lewis Ano, have been cutting small quantities of green timber [on state land] for fuel. . . . These men are occupants of such land & are poor, having been partially supported by the town in the past. They have no means of paying damages, but I believe a term of imprisonment would have [a] wholesome effect in preventing further trespass by them & others."[31]

These enclosures, both for privatization and conservation, were conducted by governments to bring order and stability to a complex natural and business environment.[32] It is no coincidence that formal surveys also determined, on private property and public property, the existence and value of timber. The goals of state conservationists meshed with those of large mill and landowners, all of whom "shared a concern for limiting inefficient uses of the environment." This type of efficiency did not account for the scattered populations of forest-dwelling locals. Referring to the development of the professional association of sportsmen guides that formed in the Adirondack following enclosure, Jacoby found that, "conservation inevitably magnified the importance of wage labor."[33] This was true of privatization of forest lands as well.[34]

The way enclosures did this was by increasing the startup costs of firms. As a young son of a farmer, Lincoln Toothaker likely had no capital to pay stumpage fees, which increased due to conservation and privatization. Stumpage ranged from $1.25 to $4 per acre on Maine spruce tracts between 1866 and 1900. After 1900, there was what the USDA called "a steady and remarkable increase" in stumpage, with averages in the period up to 1922 being $8.25 but with periods where stumpage on spruce was as high as $12. Stumpage for second-growth white pine in New Hampshire increased from $5 in 1900 to about $14 in 1921. Central New England had some of the highest stumpage for softwood in the United States.[35] Conservation likewise increased stumpage by taking large tracts off the market. Between 1897 and 1901, northern New York timber land values doubled. Lakeside land, desired by loggers and vacationers because of water access, was bought by the state at the beginning of the century for $7 an acre, and by 1910 it was worth $35 an acre.[36] Enclosure meant that someone in Lincoln's position could not build wealth as a sole proprietor utilizing common land, as many in the past had done. He instead worked for wages on private land.

Reasons to Persist

Facing a situation like Lincoln's, many of those farmer-loggers in the Northern Forest moved to cities or out west, but there was a cultural aversion among rural men to completely abandoning the country life. Aware of the outmigration in the Northern Forest, the *New England Farmer* asked, "what is to be done? Shall we engage in manufactures and . . . put our labor in equal competition with the pauper labor of Europe?" After describing the debauch of the city, Reverend Silas McKeen wrote in 1857, "far better is it for our youth to breathe the pure air and enjoy the salutary moral influences of their native State than to be brought into contact with such masses of putrefaction."[37] Walt Whitman argued that manual labor jobs were healthier than other occupations, writing, "Carpenters, masons, farmers, laborers, men at work on the shipping, and all at active out-door occupations, of course have a fair share of exercise already . . . By reason of it, we see that fine state of health which characterizes hunters, lumbermen, raftsmen, and sailors on shipboard." It was thought that healthy professions were those that allowed men to enter into "that combat with Nature [and] fight hand-to-hand with the very earth, air, and sea." Whitman chastised the urbanite, writing that, "so long as you give up your own self-control and allow yourself to be a victim to all these pestiferous little gratifications that are offered to you in the city, so long will you present a marked contrast to the noble physique of the lumberman and hunter."[38]

This pull to the farm and the outdoor life only strengthened as the century progressed. In 1872, the Maine Board of Agriculture wrote that "farm youth sees only the dazzling, gaudy side of city life . . . they do not see the numberless pitfalls of city life into which they [might] sink, nor the terribleness of the wreck to both body and soul of the great majority of unfortunate young men who are thus deceived." Two years later, the New Hampshire-based *Farmers' Cabinet* was more direct: "In cities, your children denigrate."[39] H. W. Foster wrote in the *Independent* magazine in 1900, "It is generally conceded that the country-bred boy has made for himself a strong record. Necessity, difficulties, effort, struggle, are essential factors in maintaining a vigorous stock." Through his constant struggle with nature, however, the "country-bred boy" gained "fearlessness, pluck, self-reliance, activity, responsibility, patience, endurance [and] judgment. . . . Upon the farm, labor is dignified; to rich and poor alike it is honorable. . . . For his labor . . . [the farmer] is rewarded with strength of body."[40] Henry C. Merwin urged Americans to "leave the office. . . . Consult the teamster, the farmer, the woodchopper, the shepherd, or the drover. You will find him . . . healthy in mind . . . free from fad, [and] strong in natural impulses. . . . From his loins, and not from those of the dilettante, will spring the man of the future."[41]

Sweating in the Woods

Though there was a cultural pressure to remain in the country, those who did were in precarious positions. In Vermont, between 1850 and 1900, the rate of real earnings with board was on average 15 percent lower than a market basket of goods and services. This deficiency rose to 30 percent during the Civil War and remained above 19 percent until 1880.[42] Though Lincoln worked for wages, for many it made more sense to take on debt for stumpage and equipment and ask for a chance to cut. Spurred by changes in the natural environment, a mixed industrial class of proletarian and petty bourgeois emerged.

To increase their chances of success, farmer-loggers specialized to survive. Some specialized in agriculture, often hay or potatoes.[43] Some invested more of their meager capital and their more abundant labor time into forest product production. Investors or landowners didn't have to coax workers into the woods, they were now desperate for opportunities. On the Coe/Pingree lands where the Toothakers worked, small producers, or sole proprietors, made most of the saw logs in the second half of the nineteenth century. Corporate influence was nearly nonexistent on the Coe/Pingree land until the season of 1900. Sole proprietors lost ground in terms of output in 1910, but by 1920 they were again producing almost as many logs as the companies were (figure 3.1). In 1899, farmers in Northern Forest states cut $3,073,549 more wood products than businesses did, or about 61 percent of the wood harvested. This is a much higher portion than in the Great Lakes states or the West (figure 3.2).[44] Between 1909 and 1919, the average value of forest products cut on reporting Northern Forest state farms increased 130 percent. It declined between 1919 and 1929, but only by 24.6 percent. In 1930, one of the first years with reliable numbers, there were 1,249 farms that made 50 percent or more of their income from forest products, about 1.57 percent of the 79,585 reporting Northern Forest farms.[45] By that time, as a percentage of the source of

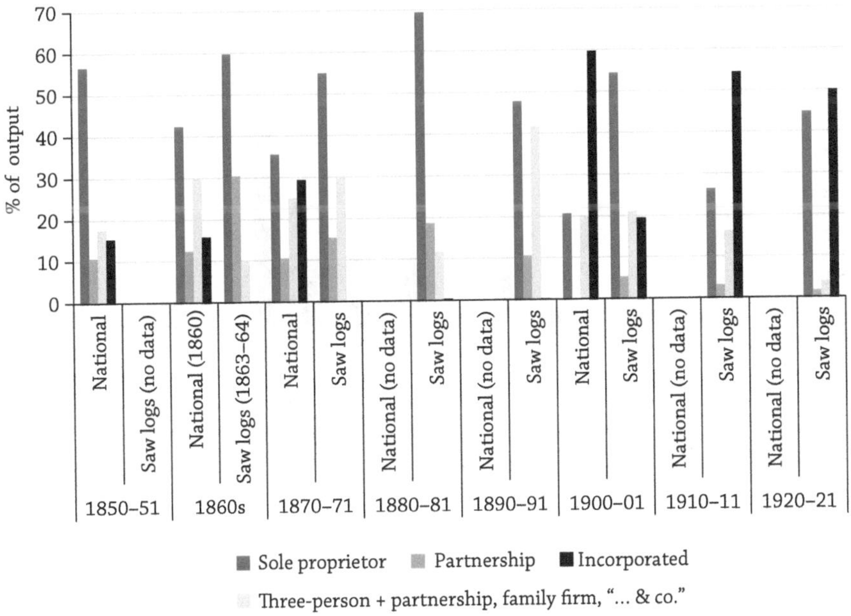

Figure 3.1. Softwood saw log output on the Coe/Pingree Lands by business form vs. total output of all US industry by business form (select years) ("Coe Family Papers," Logging operations, vol. 3, 1890–91, Special Collections, Raymond H. Fogler Library, University of Maine, Orono, ME; Jeremy Atack, "America: Capitalism's Promised Land," Jeremy Atack in *The Cambridge History of Capitalism*, vol. 1, ed. Larry Neal [Cambridge: Cambridge University Press, 2014], 560)

income for Vermont farmers, wood and lumber was the third most valuable (8 percent), well behind milk (61.5 percent) and slightly behind cattle and calves (9.2 percent).[46]

With a lack of access to common forests to sustain themselves and build capital, the smallest farmers and squatters no longer had a chance. Instead, producers with capital or access to credit, those who could make industry-specific investments in logging and could bear the risk of trespass, got more chances. On the Coe lands, the median cut per job for sole proprietors rose from 549 saw logs in the 1863–64 season to 3,549 in 1920–21.[47]

These small- and moderate-sized sole proprietors were the essential units of production. They intentionally straddled the line between manufacturers and agrarians, growing commodity and subsistence crops when not logging. After working in the woods, "come spring, everybody raised stuff," one logger remembered.[48] Maintaining connection to the farms ensured employment during the summer. But for many, woodskills, the generational knowledge

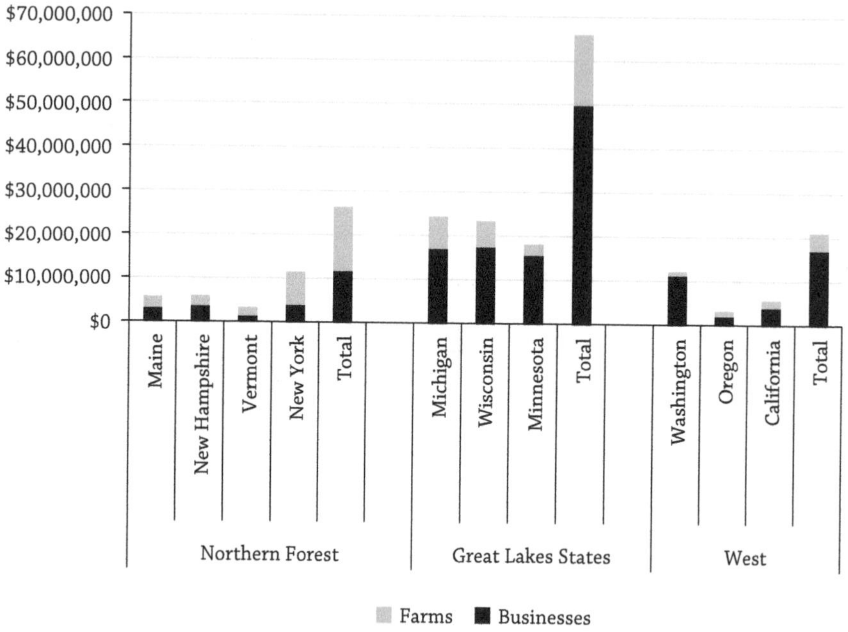

Figure 3.2. Value of wood products cut by farmers vs. businesses in major lumbering regions, 1899 (James H. Blodgett, *Wages of Farm Labor in the United States: Results of Twelve Statistical Investigations, 1866–1902* [Washington, DC: US Department of Agriculture, Bureau of Statistics, 1903], 46)

described in the last chapter, was their most valuable asset, if they could get a chance.[49]

Farmer-loggers filled an important niche in the changing business environment. With intensive agriculture not economically sustainable, speculators and landholders became desperate to transform any resource on their land into cash. New York City land speculator Stephen Mulliany made this clear in a letter to Mainer Nathan Weston, writing, "The object of the proprietor is to make the land yield a large amount of money." The problem was that Mulliany didn't have woodskills and so had no ability to do this. Mulliany and Weston made this venture happen through jobbing, a contract-based system of production that has remained vital to industrial forest product production in the Northern Forest to the present day. Jobbing connected those like Mulliany who lacked woodskills to Northern Foresters who had these skills.

Jobbing did not imply complete specialization, however. On legal documents, Weston and his partners were sometimes referred to as "lumberers," though he was a farmer according to the census. Despite that title, he employed dozens of men in logging and paid hundreds of dollars in wages in what often looked like scrip. Some of his jobs involved at least six oxen teams. In 1870, the farm was making $800 from forest products alone, about a quarter of the value of all the products sold.[50]

Jobbers (this term was synonymous with contractor and subcontractor) like Weston had to be vetted, however, to ensure they had the skill, ability, connections, and capital to make land yield money. Eben Coe took notes about the personality, capital holdings, and abilities of those requesting chances. For example, in 1889, a Mr. Bartell asked for a permit and Coe wrote in his ledger: "40 to 50 years old—has farm & 2 horses rigged." David Eastman was another prospective logger and Coe wrote, "work small farm—operated one winter, always worked in the wood[s]." He was hesitant to give J. J. Wheelock a permit because Wheelock had not paid a trespassing fee. A primary concern for Coe was horses, an animal slowly replacing oxen in the woods. Coe wrote about another permittee "work 6 to 8 horses. Keep 4 on all winter." If he trusted the party, he first would permit a small job. For large operators, Coe also made sure the jobber had a supplier.[51]

Coe "managed risk by managing identity," as historian Scott Sandage found to be the case with many long-distance financial transactions at the time. The contracting system was a way of policing the forest and ensured efficient and legal production. It also mimicked the way that previous generations of loggers had worked together in small groups to harvest resources. Across the Northern Forest, jobbers shared certain characteristics. They had high status in their communities, woodsmen skill or access to those with it, some farm capital, and some specialized logging equipment. They weren't necessarily highly capitalized, though some were. Without a doubt they had a monopoly on human capital. In many cases, however, they remained indistinguishable from farmers.[52]

Jobbing remained important as other aspects of the business environment changed, such as the increased demand for pulpwood for the papermaking industry. This began around the late 1860s and 1870s. Paper mills shredded logs, meaning that small second- or third-growth trees growing on the cutover land of the Northern Forest provided the perfect resource base. Unlike shingle weaving or lumber milling, paper milling was a capital-intensive chemical process that was only profitable on a large scale. Between 1869, the year that pulpwood paper production statistics were first recorded in America, and 1922, production nationwide increased eighteen times over. The amount of timber extracted for pulp increased 800 percent. By 1920, Maine and New York were first and second in terms of pulp production nationally.[53]

Paper production brought new chances to the forest. Companies like Great Northern Paper, International Paper, Santa Clara, and Brown bought extensive tracts of cutover land and timberland deemed inaccessible by previous generations.[54] Pulp mills, like other companies at the time, were concentrating and becoming more powerful. In Maine between 1892 and 1900, the top quartiles of firms, namely Great Northern and International, increased their share of production from roughly 55 percent to roughly 75 percent.[55] These companies were largely owned by Boston and New York City capitalists. In 1880, Boston businessmen owned one third of production in Maine and another third was owned by Portland capitalists. Between 1900 and 1921, more than 80 percent of production in Maine was owned by Boston and New York investors. Between 1880 and 1930, the number of pulp mills in Maine grew from twenty-nine to forty, but the number of firms who owned them stayed the same: twenty-four.[56]

Despite their size and power, paper companies didn't take the chance of moving into procurement. It was risky and seasonal. Logging assets or employees would have been idle most of the year. It could have been profitable for a large company to move into procurement if it could have been done on large continuous tracts of timber that would have sustained them over long timeframes. In most of the cutover Northern Forest these tracts were rare, dispersed, and in difficult topographies. This natural variability meant that metering or tracking worker and capital productivity was difficult and costly.[57] As logging historian Ian Radforth found, the natural environment made it impossible for a central authority to "maintain close, direct supervision."[58] Paper companies tapered integration, cutting some pulp on the land that was least risky but contracting for the rest.[59]

Jobbing meant that forest product production often looked like it was being performed by highly capitalized mills, but it was actually being done by nonspecialist farmer-loggers. For example, in 1895 the Ashland Company had 400 to 600 workers cutting directly under them, but they still got about half of their wood from independent jobbers. In 1916, Great Northern Paper Company contracted out 54,700 cords of pulpwood for their railroad operations. Of that amount, 15,500 cords were contracted to companies, and 41,000 (about 75 percent) were contracted to sole proprietors or other informal business forms.[60] As one forestry student found, "the camps are run by operators who pay stumpage to the Great Northern Paper Company and sell them the spruce and fir."[61] Even by 1955, in the Brown Company of New Hampshire, the people working for jobbers "far outnumber the people employed by Brown" according to a senate subcommittee investigation. That year, the *Brown Bulletin* reported that 60 percent of their 150,000 cords came "from concerns and individuals throughout Maine, New Hampshire and Vermont."[62]

Anecdotal evidence and corporate messaging suggested that working conditions were more relaxed in the large company-owned camps. Yet workers on mill payrolls were likely unaware that they were always competing with contract loggers. If company camps weren't as productive as contractors, or if costs in company camps rose due to better accommodation or food, the mill could always outsource a larger percentage of raw material procurement.

These new paper companies accepted bids from jobbers on "large contracts running from 10,000 to 100,000 cords."[63] Those who got these chances subcontracted shares of production, perhaps raising stumpage costs so that the subcontracts could skim money off the top of the transaction. Legal formality diminished with the scale of operations, and subcontractual agreements were sometimes verbal.[64] John Toothaker, Lincoln's father, engaged in an oral contract in 1884.[65] These agreements could be as simple as being told "to get what I could off the land," as one Adirondacker remembered.[66]

Contracting gave farmer-loggers the independence they were used to when cutting on the commons.[67] Once they got a chance, the jobbers could get the wood to its destination however they wanted and there were several methods depending on the jobber and the land. Forest product production was "not the repetitive work of the machine tender . . . men work somewhat under the conditions of the handicraft," a Canadian sociologist found in the 1920s.[68] A comparative study of jobbing versus consolidated company camps in the 1930s found that jobbing incentivized pulp production and typically distributed profits evenly between contractors and subcontractors. Jobbing also reduced labor overhead because some supervisory roles were eliminated.[69]

The system deferred a small amount of risk and the startup costs to financing parties. A subcontractor who was hired to cut and haul logs to a riverside, for example, avoided the risks of actually getting the logs downriver to the mill. Some contracts also stipulated that the financier pay stumpage. A jobber could further dissipate the risk of a variable forest landscape by implementing piecework for their cutters and haulers.

Jobbing made it difficult for state and private parties to prosecute trespass, subverting the policing that privatization was supposed to bring to the woods. "The scheme of 'letting jobs,'" the *New York Times* reported in 1889, "is partly responsible for the difficulty of fastening the fault of the illegal cutting [in the Adirondacks]."[70] In 1895, an Adirondack land agent found that "a contract . . . usually passed through many hands before it comes to the man who actually does the work" and there was "an effort to shift the responsibility for cutting."

Small producers had some solidarity and were resistant to reveal trespasses. "They are all neighbors," one New York State agent found, "and they all want to trespass some if they can get a chance, and, as a rule, they won't squeal."[71]

Though mills, landowners, and farmer-loggers all had a desire to continue the tradition of locally controlled small production, this arrangement put workers in a unique position in the emerging industrial economy. Jobbers were independent firms, not servants, hirelings, workmen, or even employees, the last a new ill-defined category in the industrializing United States. That meant they were legally equal to the mills and landowners they contracted with and were not entitled to the paternalistic benefits that defined the common-law master-servant relationship.[72]

Jobbers contracted to deliver products, meaning they were subject to the "entire contract doctrine." If they failed to deliver, "the employer was under no legal obligation . . . to make good on his promise to make the one entire payment," as historian Robert Steinfeld found. In those cases, all labor and capital costs were sunk. After 1830, contract law in the United States changed to protect people engaged to work under a contract, allowing them to leave any time without fear of monetary or judicial punishment. These protections did not apply to those contracted to deliver goods. This is important because after building and supplying the camp, it was typical that a contractor would have accrued substantial debt.[73] Cash advances varied in relation to the size and complexity of the job and could be as much as $16,000 or as little as $300. To ensure payment, smart contractors stipulated payment on predetermined dates, or after certain stages of the logging were completed. However, others left with debt and no payment.[74]

More than benefiting jobbers, these contracts shifted much of the risk of the chance of success onto jobbers. They were the parties operating in highly variable environments. Contracts could stipulate that the jobber was responsible for trespass or for damages caused by forest fires. Financiers and landowners could use confusing log rules, which determined how logs were measured and thus what they were worth.[75] One worker remembered: "scalers sort of gypped the men who was lumbering [sic]. . . . it happened with me right down here. . . . I was cutting pine down by the thousand, and we scaled our own logs . . . and we had to cut 1200' to get a thousand."[76] Original contract holders might force subcontractors to pay higher than market stumpage prices, a practice that was common in other sweated industries.[77]

In this business environment, scrimping became the jobber's obsession. As opposed to increasing the capital available to workers for production, a common characteristic of industrialization, they reduced it. They cut outlays on tools, food, and housing. They attempted to get more work from fewer men and animals. The prevalence of oral or informal contracts meant that partners and employees could jump camp, leaving the jobber alone or with only his family to take on the responsibility of the contract. Small contractors and their workers endured the poorest conditions in the Northern Forest. Those who profited made a "serious sacrifice of their health," Canadian sociologist Edmund Bradwin found.[78]

Jobbing worked well for land and mill capital, but when companies wanted more control over cutting, they coopted jobbers, absorbing the woodskills of woodsmen.[79] The Great Northern Paper Company convinced several important jobbers in Maine to work directly for them. Fred Gilbert was a "veteran west branch logger" who began working for the company directly in 1900. He moved up the ranks to become the head of the Spruce Woods Department.[80]

More often than coopting workers, jobbing incorporated families into industrial commodity production informally through the vagaries of contracts. Depending on the size of the job and the distance from the farm, camp cooks, foremen, and jobbers might bring wives and children to camp with the expectation that women and children worked for little or no money.[81] Harry Dyer remembers that when jobbing for the Ray Fraser Lumber Company in Maine it was "just a [. . .] little home crew" composed of his stepfather, his brother, himself and "one man besides, or two besides . . . our family." Male children, some as young as eleven, helped with small tasks and gained woodskills.[82]

These children were exposed to the rigors of commodity production in an industrializing country. Harold Dyer remembers that "our old step-father was pretty rough. And he used to get right after us and we used to have to run. We didn't have time to walk and monkey around. We didn't have no time to play and fool like kids now a days do. We had to keep our end up and when . . . we counted the logs at night, we-we [sic] had to have as many as anybody."[83] Mainer Jim Gardner remembered working in the woods with two men who couldn't read. He told them, "Jesus . . . the school's right just a little way from [where] you lived. 'Yes . . .' [they replied] [']When we get 7 or 8 years old, we think about making money.[']"[84] Working for a relative on a small family job eased the transition into large camps run by high capital jobbers or paper mills.[85]

By 1880, states were setting minimum legal ages for manufacturing work. These protections were broad, holding mills accountable for children working with parents under contract. In Alabama in 1926, Clinton Robinson, a boy under fourteen years old, was caught in lumber mill machinery and died while he was helping his father, who was a formal employee. Because this was a manufacturing facility, the mill was found liable even though it did not directly employ the child. These laws covered contractors working for manufacturers, but farmers were exempt. On the farm, it was expected that children would contribute to production. Contracting with producers who were often farmers, in spaces far from state authorities and that were not clearly manufacturing spaces or farming spaces, created many legal ambiguities.[86]

Wives and daughters also worked for jobbers, typically cooking and cleaning, but sometimes working alongside men. In 1899, *The Ogdensburg Advance and St. Lawrence Weekly Democrat* reported that "Mrs. Rosalie Charrow wife of Contractor Louis Charrow" died of being "overworked." French-Canadian immigrant Tina Daigle remembers working on a multifamily operation with her children.[87]

Hiring systems for nonfamily workers were informal.[88] A potential worker might "see . . . [an operator] around town and hire out with them." Some loggers remembered never working with anyone from out of state. "Most of the time they were just family people from the area or towns close by," a worker recalled. Drawing on neighbors, relatives, and in-laws, operators could employ dozens of workers.[89]

Because of contract work performed by mixed agriculturalists, employment numbers are difficult to determine.[90] The isolation of camps made counting difficult, as the New York State legislature found in 1912, reporting, "it has not been possible to obtain a list of lumber camps or to make any investigations of conditions."[91] Census data from 1905, around the time of peak lumber production, shows that in all the Northern Forest states, there were 1,346 camps employing between 11,304 and 14,570 people.[92] The transition to pulp production increased the number of people working in the woods for companies and jobbers both. Figures from 1952 indicated there were 24,000 workers in the woods exclusively that year.[93]

Though women sometimes worked in camp, that was not always the case. When partners were separated for logging, they could not provide emotional support to each other as they adjusted to new work regimes. The diary of an anonymous woman living around Weld, ME, in the 1870s expressed the loneliness and anxiety that industrial work in the woods could cause. Secluded in a house by herself, time seemed to move slowly: "Have been here to this hated place a week . . . it seems like [a] month." She "dreaded" the cold of winter and diminished daylight. She became melancholy and morbid. The woman kept a necrology and on her birthday she wrote, "today would any hearts be made sad if I should be taken away? A few more weary year [*sic*] will roll around and I shall be done with earth."[94] Investigator Harriet M. Rice wrote in 1896 that while rural men were away at work, they still had the chance for social engagement but "with women it is different." Women "wished they might live where neighbors weren't so far away."[95] To soothe their woes, one commenter in *The Atlantic* wrote in 1897, women "take refuge . . . in floods of unwholesome patent medicine, and in the nostrums of quacks who appear at regular intervals in the village."[96] Lust too was exacerbated by separation. Lincoln Toothaker's wife Ida made her desires clear in a letter, "I shall be glad to see you when you do get home. I am getting kind of buggy haint [*sic*] you. I want you to get one of those nightcaps so we won't have a baby the first thing. Be sure and get one and let it be a good stout one."[97]

Relying on local jobbers remained efficient because desperate farmer-loggers were cheap and, on cutover land, it did not pay for mills, landowners, or producers to experiment with or invest in infrastructure or high-capital machinery. The cutover environment created "hold-up problems." When a farmer-logger specialized in logging and made industry-specific investments, a mill or landowner might determine they were "locked-in" to logging. They could then bargain the jobber down to the level of their investment. For example, if Coe permitted with a farmer who had "6 to 8 horses" but whose farm only required two or four horses, Coe might observe that the surplus horses were kept for logging exclusively. This farmer was spatially locked in to contracting with Coe because of the location of his farm. Coe could, hypothetically, subtract the cost of surplus horses and their upkeep from the final contract price. As farmer-loggers specialized, their dependence on the industry increased.

Therefore, farmer-loggers preferred to use mostly farm equipment and tested agrarian production methods. They avoided all but the most necessary industry-specific investments.[98] If they lost or didn't get a chance, they could go back to farming with few financial losses. Axes, for instance, were farming and logging tools. Northern Forest producers knew of new logging technologies like steam- and gas-powered skidders, and cable systems, but these were expensive niche technologies and not as flexible as muscle power.[99] Even those who wanted to borrow money to specialize might not have been able to. The telegraph allowed eastern credit, which could have gone to loggers in the Northern Forest, to flow to the more lucrative forests of the Lake States, the South, and the West.[100]

For these reasons, a government study of logging in Maine in 1904 reported that "methods of lumbering . . . and the management of camps have changed less than in some other regions."[101] Emporium Lumber Company of New York thought that the system could be improved and wrote that jobbing "cost this industry much money in direct excess cost, and much more in stagnation of development."[102] Even in a 1955 Senate committee meeting on French Canadian guest-working loggers, a lumber company representative testified about new technology but wrote, "new equipment . . . has made possible a new life and new approach for those who seek work in the woods. Some employers, especially jobbers . . . ignore this new situation."[103]

The primacy of jobbing continued into the second half of the twentieth century. In the 1955 Senate subcommittee meeting, the jobbing system was described to officials, but it was such an anachronism it confused many.[104] In 1970, 57 percent of all pulp cut in Maine was cut by contractors, and some large paper companies used only contract-cut wood.[105]

A Walk in the Woods with Alfred Chandler

Labor historians see contracting in market economies as a transitional stage between artisanal-craft production and later-stage capitalism, but contracting has not been seen as a vital part of corporate capitalism. In the colonial period and the early Republic, capital-intensive industries like iron mining, forging, shipbuilding, canal projects, coal mining, and most skilled trades were organized through contracts. Cottage industry, a system of production that involved layers of contracts organized by merchants and middlemen, was an essential step toward the factory system.[106]

The period between roughly 1840 and 1910 has been depicted as a period of business concentration. Business historians like Alfred Chandler Jr. and economists like Ronald Coase and Oliver E. Williamson argued that large, hierarchical corporations became more efficient than contracting in the market economy. As businesses became larger, more complex, and technologically advanced, firms became specialized and interconnected in divisions of labor that extended outside firms. Transaction costs emerged between these firms when contracting, typically in the form of negotiations over prices, delivery time, or other conditions of work, making contracting less efficient. It was cheaper to integrate units of production into a larger hierarchical organization. This was what Chandler meant by the "visible hand." The merger and monopoly wave of the late nineteenth century began. Concentrated corporations led to the creation of monopoly or oligopoly markets, and this phenomenon captivated the attention of Progressive reformers but also sociologists and historians.[107]

At the same time, a nascent management class emerged. Frederick Winslow Taylor, his acolytes and antecedents sought direct control of work to deskill labor processes. These conditions created a low-skilled industrial workforce that was easily replaced and hard to organize. The paternalist master-servant common-law tradition, in which masters directly supervised workers who had no control over production but, in return, got a commitment to a modicum of care and security, was eclipsed by the modern "at will" employee-employer relationship. These conditions also established the legal framework for labor relations. Courts and legislators were reluctant to police work that fell outside the new corporate, manufacturing-based, at-will employee framework. New Deal labor regulations infamously passed over agricultural work and related industries like logging for the exact reason that these workers, and perhaps more importantly their environment of work, did not fit neatly into how this new type of industrial work was imagined.[108]

With the historical gaze set at the level of rural small producers, a different type of business history emerges in which history does not proceed linearly toward concentration or the standard employer-employee relationship. Chandlerian historians and economists believed that contracting created transaction costs because contracting parties were equals—politically, economically, and in terms of their access to information. Historically, bargaining was not equal. Many contracts for labor and products involved large power gradients that made frictions disappear from the perspective of the powerful party. This is clear from reading neat form contracts presented to logging workers who signed them with an "X," denoting illiteracy. Power imbalances did not incentivize concentration. Farmer-loggers served at the whims of the landowner, their debtholders, and mills, all of whom they depended on for a chance. These power imbalances began around 1850 and grew greater over time. The goal of powerful parties was to use loggers to obtain products cheaply while shifting the risk of production onto them. These free-market relations controlled jobbers better than any wood procurement manager could.

There are several important industries where power imbalances created decentralized yet industrialized market economies. As late as 1904, inside the factories of Winchester Repeating Arms Company, skilled contractors received 32 percent of the payroll.[109] In early twentieth-century New York City, the needle trades, or finishing clothing, grew to depend on contracts with desperate immigrant families in slums. In 1919 in New York City, 16 percent of dresses were made in contract shops; in 1936, 75 percent.[110] On the streets of the city, newsboys bought newspapers from publishers as contractors attempting to sell them for profit. In the South, a violent racist economic structure pushed tenant farmers into debt and threatened them with racial terrorism, making these independent producers more obedient than any wage worker in the North.[111]

Market economies prevented workers from cooperating through cutthroat competition that suppressed class consciousness and solidarity. Competition is why loggers only ever had a chance for work. In the first half of the nineteenth century, unions, cooperatives, or other worker associations attempted to subvert cutthroat competition by fixing prices for labor time or products, ending the downward spiral of wages and piece rates.[112] Common-law conspiracy statutes were used to ban coordination, though trade unions of skilled workers emerged as a form of cooperation that was generally accepted in American law.[113] By the late nineteenth century, court-issued injunctions against coordinated boycotts of goods or employers replaced conspiracy laws as the method used to prohibit coordination. Courts were particularly punitive when it came to secondary actions—actions taken against firms that producers were not employed by. For example, it might have been illegal for jobbers to collectively refuse to cut for one mill or one landowner, or for workers across the Northern Forest to refuse to work for one jobber, or for teamsters to refuse to move the logs of one jobber, one mill, or one landowner, though it would have been legal for the employees of a large company camp like Emporium or Great Northern to strike. Union busting was built into this business environment, which is why it was preferred by landowners and mills.[114]

When producers could organize they employed tactics like price fixing, blacklisting, violence, intimidation, and boycotting to fight the deleterious effect of contracting. In NYC's sweated needle industry, the International Ladies Garment Workers Union and the American Clothing Manufacturers Association blacklisted contractors who did not meet certain production size minimums. Small firms harbored the worst conditions and undercut ethical production.[115]

Cooperation of the type that these textile unions participated in was supposed to be federally banned by the 1890 Sherman Act. The 1914 Clayton Act asserted that labor was "not a commodity or article of commerce" and thus not restricted by antitrust laws. The Clayton Act opened up the possibility for contractors, farmers, or those selling labor time to coordinate, although there were loopholes that permitted injunctions in the case of "injury to property" or to "a property right."[116] This was of little avail to contract laborers and wage workers because close to 80 percent of antitrust cases against labor between 1890 and 1929 were brought after the Clayton Act, typically for secondary strikes and boycotts. Courts used injunctions, at least 4,300 of them nationally between 1880 and 1930, to prevent cooperation.[117] Thus, throughout industrial American history the default legal position in regard to contracting work and industrial labor was, according to legal historian Sanjukta Paul, to "support the right [of management] to control while denying the right [of workers] to cooperate."[118]

The Limits of Cooperation

The situation was different for rural producers. Starting in the 1850s, farmers in New England, New York, and elsewhere began to set up cooperatives to maintain prices at a livable level.[119] This type of cooperation might have rubbed against a growing antimonopoly sentiment, but farmers held a special place in the country's imagination. The Grange began organizing dairy cooperatives in the 1870s and by 1887, ten out of the thirteen butter factories in New Hampshire were cooperatives.[120] In 1910, the Boston Cooperative Milk Producers' Company kept 33,000 cans of milk out of the hands of dealers, "striking" for maintenance of high winter prices year-round. In 1916, the Aroostook Shipper Association controlled 75 percent of the potatoes grown in the county and in 1920, New England milk cooperatives controlled over 80 percent of production.[121] The powers of farmer cooperatives were limited and both those organizations eventually faced legal impediments but the ability of farmers to organize was recognized by federal law in 1922. Forest product producers were left out of all types of cooperation.[122] Though farmers could cooperate, and many jobbers were farmers, due to an odd development in American law, nonedible forest products were excluded from protection.[123] As Maine worker Ralph Thornton put bluntly "there never was a labor union here in the woods" and in retrospect there are clear reasons why. Not quite farmers, not always wage-workers, loggers were alienated from both industrial and agricultural labor relations.[124]

This chapter demonstrated that as forests modernized, enclosure made it costly for producers to access forest resources. Between roughly 1860 and 1890 a mixed class of jobbers and wage workers emerged. Lincoln Toothaker took the path of the wage worker. Jobbing was another path, and it was a type of compromise between traditional farmer-logger and modern industrial practices. Through jobbing, many small producers remained in control of production even though this was not always beneficial for them.

The idea of independence was important culturally, however. Descriptions of loggers highlighted their autonomy. In 1896, *Godey's Magazine* described loggers as "a bold independent and manly set of fellows."[125] A forester wrote that "the lumber-jack of Northern New York is a man of hardihood and of self-reliance."[126] Speaking of the Northern Forest specifically, environmental humanist Stephanie Kaza wrote that "private small-scale loggers may speak for a middle ground . . . seeking community-based decision making while still using the forest for [global] commodity trading."[127]

While jobbing made workers independent, and made forest products cheap, it was the bodies of jobbers and their families that ultimately created the value.

The situation in these smaller camps was similar to post–World War II broiler chicken production where Michael Watts and William Boyd found that "the self-exploitative qualities of [these] household enterprises . . . could be captured by capital via forms of vertical integration . . . a form of capitalist development in which there was [financial] centralization without . . . [geographic] concentration." Jan De Vries called the family's move into commodity production "a final frontier of capitalism" but family production could actually be made more efficient as chapter 4 will show.[128]

The Northern Forest business and natural environment acted as firmer control on contractors' freedom in production than even the most demanding manager. This business environment made the Northern Forest into a "black box" where cheaply produced and abundant forest products flowed downriver but the details of production were hidden under the canopy. A zoomed-out view of the Northern Forest reveals a type of coordination emerging out of disaggregation, however. As the following interlude explains, water organized and centralized production.[129]

INTERLUDE

Organic Networks

A majority of production in the Northern Forest was done by small logging firms who were legally independent and in control of production. Yet industrialization requires concentrating and coordinating the disparate activities of markets to increase economies of scale. This was often done through mergers that increased the size of firms and put them under the control of fewer people. By the end of the nineteenth century, these large firms were using the latest technology to coordinate their sourcing, production, and distribution—things like trains, telegraphs, the postal service, and new print technology.[1] Again, the Northern Forest took a different route to coordination that is seemingly primitive but vastly complex and effective.

It was very often the case that small logging contracts dictated that products were delivered to a river or lake, and there the responsibility of the jobber ended. The water and the company drivers mentioned in chapter 2 did the work of delivering logs to mills, but to do this the rivers needed to modernize and industrialize. This happened through materially manipulating the rivers but also through immaterial changes in the law.

Streams and rivers were nodes of collection and arteries of transportation that connected all parties with a stake in production. The ultimate control that waterways played in the Northern Forest meant that entire watersheds became like giant firms. They were "envirotechnical landscapes" in the words of historian of technology Sara Pritchard, systems with internal logics, order, and power imbalances.[2] Watersheds and creatures that worked in and on them were a specific kind of technology; however, they were networks, machines for processing the economic information that traveled down rivers with logs. These organic networks coordinated producers and thus helped to industrialize the forest. The process of creating these networks is described in this interlude.[3]

As explained in chapter 2, in the early nineteenth century, legal precedent on Northern Forest rivers changed to allow the driving of loose single logs downriver. Monopoly companies were created to improve rivers and drive logs in large company or union drives. By the 1830s, the idea of rivers as aquatic commons that everyone could use equally, was dissipating. Legal historian Morton J. Horowitz found that nationwide, courts tried to find a balance between "first in time, first in right" and "reasonable use." In these compromises, Horowitz contended, "the doctrine of reasonable use could assimilate its historic antagonist—the rule of priority—and thereby make monopoly [of rivers] reasonable once again."[4] Courts in the United States regularly ignored "little inconveniences" to downstream parties, judging fair use by the "relative efficiencies of conflicting property uses." Prioritized river use was contingent on "the needs and wants of the community," Horowitz showed, and this often meant that economic efficiency was valued above equal use by courts. In areas with abundant lumber resources, forest product production was given explicit preference in terms of the use of the rivers' natural flow. Preferred river users were even allowed to access land adjacent to the water.[5]

In this changing legal environment, the natural flow of the river needed to be preserved, and the flow had to remain open to all users, but what was judged as a natural flow was whatever was regionally economically important. In southern New England, water privileges were granted to mills, sometimes at the expense of other users. In rural regions, special usage concessions were given to users moving bulk commodities like logs.[6] In 1854, forty-six years after the original designation requiring all lumber to be rafted, New York's Salmon River was declared "a public highway for the purpose of floating saw-logs and timber," as were other rivers in the state.[7] In Maine, the courts argued that if they did not give lumberers special access to rivers, "much of the wealth of the State would be locked up in inaccessible forests." In *Knox v. Chaloner* (1856), the Maine courts ordered that a dam that had stood for seventy-two years prior to lumberers reaching the watershed could not obstruct the flow of logs. From the 1840s to the 1860s, the courts deemed all rivers in Maine, regardless of size, depth, the property they passed through, or their past usage, to be public highways, the assumption being that even small streams could eventually be "improved" to float logs. In these forest hinterlands, waterways became industrial modes of transportation that could be improved by people over time, while still considered legally natural.[8]

On the Mississippi and rivers east of it, two logistical changes occurred during the first half of the nineteenth century that allowed for more efficient transportation of forest products. First, logs cut by different jobbers or farmer-loggers became both distinguishable and fungible with the use of log marks. Second, rivers were redesigned to better facilitate the movement of logs and the information contained on them.[9]

Log marks were symbols cut or stamped into logs. Every large firm had their own mark, often registered with the state. Evidence from New York suggests that logs were marked as early as 1804, before cattle branding was systematized.[10] Given the complex structure of contractual hierarchy, some workers couldn't remember their bosses, only the mark. The mark signified all the value of the cut. Marked logs were abstractions that represented a combination of nature and labor time.

As described in chapter 2, all logs were put to float into the river, so all the marked logs were mixed together on the drive. But because marked logs were scaled in the woods before the drive, the total monetary value of a producer's cut became associated with that mark, and this information traveled downriver autonomously but fragmented. Information—the mark—now became the most important thing moving on these currents. This informational environment, the interplay between different information technologies, the natural, and the designed environment, was essential for coordinating production and determining the autonomy of producers in the Northern Forest.[11]

The Penobscot River in Maine provides a good example of how these rivers became infrastructure for the movement of commodities and information. Including the south and west branches, the length of the river is about 264 miles, and its watershed opened 2.5 million acres of timber to utilization. It is the largest river basin completely in the state of Maine, containing 1,604 streams and 185 lakes. Most of the logs floated on the river were destined for Milford, Old Town, Orono, Veazie, Bangor, and Brewer, where 154 single saws, 15 gang saws, and many lath, shingle, and clapboard machines were operating. The boom to hold logs north of Orono was run by a private corporation until 1847, when the legislature created the Penobscot Log Driving Company (PLD). In 1854, the Penobscot Lumbering Association (PLA) was incorporated to improve rivers and to drive and sort logs.[12] These organizations were producer cooperatives and because of that they charged about one third less than the private booming company that preceded them. Similar cooperatives were established elsewhere in Maine, and also on the Connecticut and Hudson Rivers. When pulp cutting boomed, lumber operations built on this same riparian transportation infrastructure. By the 1890s, railroads allowed new companies to move processing facilities further upriver, shortening the distance of the drive. By 1892, there were significant pulp mills operating as far north as Enfield, ME, and between 1900 and 1909 the largest operations in the state were in Rumford Falls and Millinocket, well up the watercourse. Water transportation remained essential, however.[13]

In the tradition of agricultural cooperatives, the PLA was mandated to put producers in charge of transportation. It had a board, president, clerk, treasurer, and six board members, all of whom were voted into office and held the office for one year. The laws of incorporation show that there were power dynamics operating within the cooperative that might have undermined its mandate. As opposed to the Rochdale model where each member was given only one vote, the charter for the PLA gave votes by capital holding. Under the original charter of the PLA, every timber landowner was given one vote in elections. One vote was also given to members for every 100,000 board feet floated on the Penobscot, and one vote for every six-oxen or four-horse team working in the woods. These requirements meant that many of the smallest producers in Maine had no vote. Similar provisions applied to the PDL.

Theoretically, all people could put their logs in the Penobscot to have them driven to the mill, but the way that the system was organized incentivized concentration. Logs cut by small nonspecialists or farmers on smaller tributaries were often bought by a few dozen concerns because the more lumber one floated on the river, the more votes one had in the boom and drive corporations. This member would scale and mark the logs with their own marks, cutting down on the number of marks on the drive. The PLA's board and president set their own salaries and gave out lucrative contracts to drive logs on the company drive, paying between $500 and $1,000. When the charter of the PLD was rewritten in 1864, it included the provision that the president could not give the contract to drive to themselves.[14]

To facilitate driving and to open upstream timberlands to lumbering, the state of Maine granted monopolies to operate dams on remote areas of the Penobscot and its various tributaries. These monopolies were given franchise to alter the river level and thus change the river flow. Dam owners charged fees to all lumberers who landed logs on the dammed waterway.[15]

With enough river improvement, some accounts say 75 to 90 percent of the logs might make it to the mill with little human labor needed. Workers kept jams from forming and broke them when they did with peavies, axes, pick poles, or dynamite. They also patrolled the shores, keeping logs moving, sometimes using horses. Crews "picked the rear," following the drive, moving stragglers into the current. In some parts of the country, forest product producers were given the legal ability to trespass on river adjacent lands.[16]

Rivers thus improved gave Northern Forest loggers a crucial advantage in forest product production. Few areas of the country had the same prolific network of waterways with a reliable spring freshet. This water resource and its legal definition kept exploitative railroad rates in check. Log marks, cooperatives, driving, and dam companies made entire watersheds into networks designed for the efficient movement of logs and the information stamped on them. They were organic networks.[17]

As the logs made their way downriver they would sometimes travel through fluvial lakes. Here logs were corralled into a pocket boom that was moved by a simple machine called the headworks, a technology borrowed from the maritime trades. The headworks could also be used at the start of the drive to get the logs moving down river. A wooden raft of about forty to fifty square feet was constructed with a capstan with three hundred or four hundred feet of hawser. The raft would be anchored with a large ship anchor several hundred feet away from the boom and men would wind the capstan, pulling the boom toward the headworks. A capstan can increase the amount of weight that a worker can lift sixfold or more. The headworks and anchor would be moved by a bateau further down the lake and the winding repeated until the logs could be released into an outlet. The wind helped or hindered depending on its direction. Workers worked in shifts, winding the capstan twenty-four hours a day until the logs made their way to the outlet. A small bunkhouse was sometimes built on the raft for resting. Before camps became dry around 1850, men on the headworks were given rum to numb the physical pain and monotony of the work. Often these workers were paid twice as much as a normal river driver because the work was so grueling. A headworks device was patented in 1824 but the process was in use more than a decade before then. The patent meant little, as most crews made their own headworks on site. In this way, a boom full of as much as three million board feet of logs—or three thousand tons—was moved up to twenty miles with muscle power (figure I.1).[18] One observer wrote about the process in 1864: "the labor is incessant; night and day the capstan bars go round; fresh men take the place of the weary; every man walks as long as he can endure it. Some will hold out three days and four nights without stopping, except to eat, and without sleep, except the doze into which they fall as they tread around the capstan. . . . Here is where men make horses of themselves for nine shillings a day."[19]

In 1907, there was an effort in the Maine legislature to limit the hours that river drivers could work, but it failed to pass.[20] By World War I,

Figure I.1. Headworks raft in operation, Maine woods, ca. 1900 (Collections of the Patten Lumbermen's Museum, courtesy of MaineMemory.net, item 8493)

gasoline-powered motors sometimes did this work, but headworks were still part of the driving system on some tributaries in 1932.[21] The Penobscot drive ended between June and October. Approximately 2,500 people worked for the first six weeks driving the tributaries and about 200 men stayed on for the main drive. If logs did not make it to the mills before the freeze, the value of the entire season was lost.[22]

Though the drive reduced labor costs and moved logs with the free power of the water's natural flow, logs with different marks and different owners were mixed together in the process of driving. The series of booms called the Argyle boom, located north of Orono, ME, was a mainframe for the processing of logs and information that moved downriver. During the busiest seasons, the logs held back by the boom extended twelve miles upriver. Legally, a channel needed to be left in the river to allow other users to pass. The prospect of boatmen unassociated with the drive using the river during booming season seems dubious, however. It was also obstructing to fishers.[23]

Logs were slowly released via a capstan that could be cranked to open a "sorting gap." Below the sorting gap, a series of four or five workers called "checkers" stood in a row behind one another, many yards apart on individual logs or small rafts. A rope was extended across the river above the head of the workers for them to grab onto. As the logs were released, the first checker jumped onto the first passing log. They spun the log with their feet searching for one of the two or three marks that this checker was assigned to check. If the mark was his, he would kick the log toward the shore where another worker double-checked the mark and collected similarly marked logs together into rafts called "joints." If the log was not one of the first checker's marks, he would jump to the next log, allowing the log to flow to the second checker. The checker repeated the process for all the logs released from the boom. The checker behind the first checker mimicked his upriver counterpart but he was assigned different and more marks than the first checker. The third checker was assigned more marks than the second, and so on. Sorting involved a tremendous amount of brain and muscle work for checkers and the rafters who made the joints. One worker stated he lost nine pounds his first week at the boom. The checking and rafting crew extended a mile downriver and at the busiest times 200 people worked there. Similar sorting methods were used on rivers across the United States, although they had regional idiosyncrasies.[24]

The job of the checker was to process information, but checkers understood more than marks. The first checker was the most skilled worker at the boom and was often an experienced logger. Though only assigned a few marks, this worker had a knowledge of all the season's marks, perhaps 150. They could often connect the mark with a specific geographic location and to the faces of operators who cut them. They could tell tree species by sight and feel. There were first-growth pines cut on a mountain a hundred miles away and small second growth spruce. There were crooked, rotted logs, or damaged logs. The first checker saw work and forests flow under his feet.[25]

Each checker only worked for an hour at a time, after which they were replaced to take a "soak." This was supposedly free time, but during this time they had to correct any mistakes they made while checking. The boom system had a redundancy in the form of another boom below the main boom. During their break, checkers would have to manually drag missed logs upriver to their corresponding rafts, an arduous task. In 1901, both booms broke and about 7,000,000 board feet, or $100,000, floated to sea.

After sorting, the logs were scaled a second time in their joints before the joints were connected into a "swing" containing all the logs of one mark. This final scale would account for lost or damaged logs on the drive and it was also the basis on which the PLA and PLD charged operators for driving and sorting. The charge was ten cents per thousand board feet in 1854, nine in 1869, seven and a half in 1884, and four in 1931. The network became cheaper and more efficient over time, allowing it to compete with trains and trucks. Deduction of boomage charges of up to 6 percent were given to members who paid promptly and in cash.[26]

If the logs weren't under contract, members had mills bid on the season's harvest, and then rafts were floated to the mills. Rafts were sometimes broken again and driven further downriver to the mill boom. After 1903, control of the boom and drive was relinquished to the Great Northern Paper company. The boom and drive likely operated as it did before the takeover, with contractors taking the place of members. On the jobber's chance and in these sylvan waterways, nature and labor was abstracted, deconstructed, and entangled to the point of illegibility. The sorting booms made nature and labor legible and thus salable. Marking, driving, and sorting made entire watersheds into organic information networks—envirotechnical landscapes whose primary purpose was moving and sorting information.[27]

Marking, driving, and sorting benefited all parties involved in forest product production but there were problems with the process, which cost small producers money. Some logs sunk or were destroyed on the drive. Operators were charged by the PLA and PLD on the "Full Bigness Scale" accounting for the size and thickness of the logs regardless of their salable quality. Mills bought them on the "Straight and Sound Scale," which discounted or rejected less valuable rotten, crooked, or heavily damaged logs. Operators were charged for unsalable logs. Scaling, whether in the joints or in the woods, always caused conflict because scalers translated the marks—these representations of nature and labor—into a monetary value. Scalers were supposed to be independent from any operation, mill, the PLA, and PLD, but they could be biased. Due to mistakes or the nature of the drive, some logs arrived at the boom with no mark. This happened because someone forgot to mark a log or the marks wore away on the drive. The latter event was called "dehorning."[28]

Any dehorned logs that arrived at the boom were declared "prize logs" by the charter of the PLA and they were collected and auctioned at the end of the season. The logs of operators who did not pay their boomage fees could also be auctioned off. Each log lost or left unmarked could cost an operator from $10 to $25.[29] The profits from the auction were meant to help fund the operation of the PLA but the PLA administration set their own salaries, incentivizing them to make money above operating costs. Drivers worked for the PLD, so they should have been neutral, but bribery or parochial loyalty could have caused a driver to mark dehorned logs. To ensure the PLA got all the prize logs, the PLA and PLD established harsh rules for anyone caught marking dehorned logs. These workers were fired and fined $20, two thirds of one month's pay. In many states, intentionally dehorning or re-marking logs was a felony. By the 1890s, there could be as much as ten or fifteen thousand board feet of prize logs in a season in the PLA booms.[30]

Prize logs show how, in the process of industrialization, labor and commodities were often transformed into information. Without a mark, the log was still a commodity, but ownership was ambiguous. The actual party who created the object could not claim it. The only thing that mattered was the mark. Jobbers were not paid for the commodities they produced but by the board foot calculation made based on log marks. Marking, river driving, and sorting alienated workers and even firms from the product of their labor.[31]

In preindustrial agrarian economies, many workers produced tangible goods and remained with these goods until the point of sale. Proximity was how a producer claimed ownership. This was slow and inefficient. To speed up transactions, labor is often made into abstractions: numbers or symbols like log marks. More common examples are the mathematical product of wage rate and hours worked, or dollar amount and piece produced. This abstraction allows for quick transactions, adding value to products. This is essential for centralization of business over large physical distances. Most industries used the post, the telegraph, the telephone, and later, computers to do this information work. These abstractions, whatever form they take, are stand-ins, symbols that represent something. When abstract labor, nature, or time is moved around quickly, symbols can be lost or misinterpreted and in that process, value is taken from producers. This is what happened on the drive.[32]

One example of how the organic information network could harm producers is the case of Royal Jordan of Colebrook, NH. In the 1890s, Jordan was hired to cut logs for the Turner Falls Lumber Company, 110 miles away in Turner Falls, Massachusetts. In about six weeks, Jordan's logs were driven on the Connecticut River by the Connecticut River Lumber Company, the monopoly driving organization on that waterway. Like all loggers, Jordan's labor was converted into information, mixed around with other logs on the river, and processed at the boom. This was a complex series of abstractions that was even difficult for Jordan, an experienced logger, to understand. He was concerned that the scaler was taking advantage of him, that his labor was being misrepresented. He wanted something to show for his work besides information, something tangible.[33]

On March 5, 1892, the Turner Falls Lumber Company received an urgent message from an agent around Colebrook via telegram, a series of electrical pulses traveling nearly instantaneously from point to point. In Morse code the message read .——.-. -.. .—. / .. . . . /—.—.- .. -. —. / -.-. . -.. .- .-. / . . . .—— . / .—. -.. / . . . . .-.. .-.. .. -. —. / ..—. When these abstractions were decoded by the telegraphist in Turner Falls, it read "Jordan is taking cedar home and selling it." This was against the contract and illegal. A code traveled back to New Hampshire to the company agent: . . .—— .—. / . . . . ..—; "stop him."[34]

It would be tempting to think that the river provided these industrial logistical services for free but actually, flora and fauna paid a price. Death by flooding was common. The Setting Pole Dam built in 1871 for logging on the Raquette River in New York caused flooding that killed trees along a thirty-mile stretch of the river. Also, objects that floated came to monopolize water rights on driving rivers. The law gave less recognition to things that lived in or under water. Small mouth bass and lake trout spawn in the late spring during the drive. They lay eggs in water as shallow as an inch. Dams fluctuated water levels and over time logs beating against the shorelines widened the river, lowering water levels. These changes killed fish eggs. Booms, dams, and logs disrupted the movement of anadromous fish like alewives, upon which many marine ecosystems and Northeastern fishermen depended.[35]

Logs were also pollutants. Mills depended on the river to soften and sometimes remove bark during the drive. Wood debris sank to the river bottoms. Large pulpwood drives lost between 4 and 10 percent of their logs to sinkage, as many as 12,000 cords a season. While wood debris is important for stream ecosystems, they had not developed to support massive seasonal influxes like this. Maine's Wyman Lake storage area had as much as five inches of accumulated organic debris altering the composition of the riverbed. Sludge worms and algae accumulated in these places, draining oxygen from the water and killing fish. Driving altered the chemical composition of the water so much that some paper mills had to treat it before they could use it for paper making.

It was only because operators, lumber, and paper companies did not have to pay for all the damages caused by driving that this remained a cheap alternative to land transport. By 1953, only 24 percent of the wood cut along the Penobscot River was transported by truck. River drives were banned in Maine in 1976 because of their harmful environmental impact. Great Northern Paper Company continued to drive until that year.[36]

The market economy meant that no single firm had a full grasp on production, yet production happened "efficiently" and regularly. This production followed a simple trajectory of more diffuse concentration of ownership upriver, deep in the woods, with ownership becoming increasingly concentrated and coordinated as logs made their way down to the mill. The grand overseer in this industry was seasonal change and forest watersheds.

Decentralized production meant that experiences of loggers were as diverse and numerous as the camps in which they worked. Key methods of production on the chance, namely how producers utilized the cold weather and the bodies of workers and animals, created bright lines between small-scale, agrarian farmer-loggers and new industrial loggers operating in large camps. The next two chapters examine these differences in the scales of production to show how a lumberjack class emerged.

Part 2

THE RISE OF INDUSTRIAL CAPITALISM

CHAPTER 4

THE WINTER WORKSCAPE

Industrializing with Ice

The 1908 Emerson lumber operation was run by thirty-five-year-old Herbert E. Robinson, the son of a Maine potato farmer with a seventh-grade education. Robinson was a tall man with a medium build, blue eyes, and hair which was starting to gray. As a youth, he transitioned between work on the farm and in the woods but began to specialize in woods work as he grew older. In 1908–1909, Robinson was planning an operation in an unincorporated territory in Penobscot County, ME, where thousands of dollars and the well-being of seventy men was at stake.[1]

The stumpage on this tract was $4 per thousand board feet for spruce and $5 for pine. These could be sold for $18 and $25 respectively, manufactured as lumber. Robinson needed to deliver the wood to the mill for between $14 and $20 per thousand feet just to break even, though he hoped to get it there for $12. Regardless of the stakes, the company sent no "professionally" trained man to assist "simply because . . . [they] have such confidence in their boss, [and] know he is getting as many logs as possible and as cheaply as any man can get them."[2] Using woodskills gained from a life of work in the Northern Forest, Robinson employed the latest, most efficient method of production. To quicken the pace, workers tapped into new sources of cheap nature. To do this they made the landscape, the winter weather, and the bodies of workers and animals work more efficiently.

Zooming the scope of analysis into Robinson's operation shows that capitalism, industrialization, and class all happen when the correct historical conditions align. The most important cause for the manifestation of class was changes in the way workers corporally interacted with the material world. Class in this industry and others was inscribed on and inside the body through work. In the case of the Northern Forest, the cutover landscape was an essential causal factor for class formation. As valuable resources became rarer, value creation became more dependent on the metabolic work of bodies. Class formation should not just be thought of as developing over time, but also across space, as operations existing at the same time employed different production processes that ultimately dictated class. The three chapters in this section focus on how a class of wage-working loggers—or lumberjacks—emerged from a class of farmer-loggers. The formation of a working class is an essential part of industrialization. In the lumbering woods, changes in the labor process didn't center on making more forest products more quickly, though that did happen incrementally. Instead, it was about moving products more efficiently. Between 40 and 75 percent of the cost of bringing wood to market was transport.[3]

The pages below explain the changes in the labor process that distinguished preindustrial from industrial production. The chapter begins with a discussion of the cutover landscape ca. 1910 and the small-scale logging labor process of a farmer-logger named Arthur Westcott. It then goes on to explain how the lives of producers changed as they moved into larger labor camps where their work was managed more closely. Finally, the chapter moves to a discussion of the ways that cold weather and ice increase the scale and speed of production more than any other factor.

Fossil fuels were the most common type of cheap nature used to speed the movement of goods in the industrial United States. It is important to remember that the United States only became more than half fossil-fueled by roughly 1900. There were other paths to industrialization.[4] As chapter 3 explained, the hold-up problem made contractors hesitant to invest in industry specific high-capital technologies. Moreover, in the cutover Northern Forest, valuable trees were far removed from settlement, on high altitude or otherwise rough terrain.[5] Coal and even gasoline powered machines were not up to the task, as one Maine worker remembered: "They had one [tractor]. Didn't stay too long."[6] Even in the 1960s, a Canadian film on French-Canadian pulp contractors proclaimed, "Man and horse tackle paths where the tractor admits defeat." Tellingly, this was followed by, "The horse ages two years in a year."[7] Alongside the unreliability of new technology, a dwindling resource base and the conservation mentality limited the possibility of large capital investment. A steam hauler in 1916 cost about $7,000 and a gasoline hauler $2,200, about forty and twelve times the price of the average working horse, respectively. The roads required to run a steam hauler in Maine in 1916 cost $1,000 a mile, or a little less than ten times the cost for horse logging roads.[8]

In the Northern Forest, industrialization involved the creation of *winter workscapes*. *Workscape* is how historian Thomas Andrews defines "a place shaped by the interplay of human labor and natural processes. . . . [The term] treats people as laboring beings who have changed and been changed in turn by a natural world that remains always under construction." To Andrews, workscape explains the strong class affiliations that led up to the 1914 Ludlow Massacre in Colorado.[9] Adding winter to the term draws attention to the effect of the seasons on workscapes. The earth's tilted axis, and its motion around the sun, shaped and reshaped material realities on the surface of the planet annually, affecting all aspects of human and nonhuman nature. The creation of winter workscapes helps identify when, where, and how both class and industrialization happened.[10] In the Northern Forest, dependence on the winter workscape increased as operations grew in scale and speed. The slickness of snow and ice was an economic lubricant, and frozen water, not timeclocks, set the pace of production. As the interlude showed, rivers linked these winter workscapes into envirotechnical landscapes that operated like giant firms.

In *Fossil Capital*, Andreas Malm shows that understanding the phase change of water is essential for understanding industrialization. Steam, Malm claims, was a tamer version of H_2O compared with the flowing liquid. It was also more conducive to the exploitation of workers. In the case of Northern Forest logging, ice was tame as well. Chemically, it is the least dynamic form of water. This chapter explains how logging operators "rationalized" ice by replacing hard packed fallen snow with thick sheets of frozen water. In the process they made production more predictable, faster, and ultimately more profitable. All the new methods of production that defined the new class of industrial loggers made the work more dangerous.[11]

Scaling Up

To create the winter workscape, an operator like Robinson first "cruised," or surveyed his tract. On the cruise, Robinson surveyed the "boundaries . . . reposting these where it was necessary, [he] located the camp and in a general way decided how much area could be profitably logged from the camp, decided on the location of the main roads including the tote road, and estimated the stand." The most important tool for this job was woodsmen's knowledge. Some loggers considered the winter to be the best time to cruise. Snow leveled the ground and snowshoes aided travel. With the leaves gone from hardwood trees, the cruiser could see more of the forest.

There were hundreds of factors that needed to be considered when cruising but before the 1910s, cruises were almost always conducted by people with no formal credentials. "Usually the jobber'd do his own cruising," worker Benjamin Cole remembered: "It wasn't until the paper companies began to get the upper hands that . . . you heard much about professional cruisers." Through "eye estimates," a woodsman like Robinson could "look out a block 'a timber and see if it would pay to put a road [through it.]"[12]

Robinson was cutting on burnt and cutover land but nevertheless, it was considered "typical of the spruce forest of northern Maine." For example, when Hollingsworth & Whitney Co. went into Squaw Mountain township, Maine, for their 1911–12 season, they were cutting on a tract that was logged in 1867–68 and 1870–77, and after 1883, the tract was lumbered "nearly all the time."[13] On Robinson's tract, the burnt section had about "4000 [board] feet of dead timber per acre." The cutover section was divided into a spruce tract and a mixed growth stand that included hardwoods, white pine, and spruce. On these types of second-growth tracts, each tree was worth less than first-growth trees in terms of board feet, though they "require[d] about as much effort to fell" and transport.[14] Up until the 1860s and 1870s, only trees twenty inches in diameter had been considered merchantable. After that period, merchantable diameters decreased from twelve to fourteen inches.[15] The larger tracts with more merchantable trees per acre, like those in northern Aroostook, were often the tracts that lumber or paper companies like Great Northern Paper bought and operated on, leaving cutover land for contractors. Giving contractors access to the less lucrative ground is also typical in mining.[16]

While some operators like Robinson were logging second growth, others were pushing the limits of their technology by cutting into higher altitudes and ridge tops where first growth remained.[17] For example, during the 1906–1907 season, B. W. Howe & Co. attempted to log the northern side of Traveler Mountain in Maine, a tract that had been attempted twice before without success.[18] New and dangerous methods of hauling allowed cutting long lumber at about 2,000 feet altitude while pulp operations were pushing into high altitude fir-spruce regions of 3,000 to 4,000 feet.[19] On these high altitude operations, gravity-powered chutes were typically used. These simple earthen slides were slickened by snow, ice, water, and the passage of logs. Specially constructed reusable chutes were also employed by the larger operations such as those of Emporium Lumber Company in the Adirondacks. These could cost as little as three cents per foot length with an average cost of perhaps 33–36 cents per foot.[20]

Robinson was not logging a mountainside, but the topography was still difficult: "Just north of . . . [the] water line the country rises in a low chain of hills. The tract has a general northerly slope from the mountains in the south to this waterline in the north. On this slope are rock ridges and low marsh land and all gradations between the two." It was also remote. The township contained only forty-three people, so all supplies had to be hauled in. Robinson, like nearly all other operators in the Northern Forest, had to take "great care" to "keep the expense . . . as small as possible." It was these poor logging conditions that pushed many producers to give up on the Northern Forest and move to factories further south or westward to the loggers' frontier after 1850.[21] The conditions described above are also what made capital search for new sources of value in the labor process. If there were no large trees available that guaranteed large returns, the prerogative of investors was to cut expenses to a minimum and rely on the minds and bodies of locals as the primary source of pecuniary value.

Even as the process of cutover capitalism was industrializing the Northern Forest, there were still Yankee farmers who continued to log as an adjunct to farming in a way that would have been familiar to colonists. Arthur Westcott is a good example. He worked and lived in the Green Mountains of Vermont in the first decade of the twentieth century. Though he made most of his money in the woods, Westcott identified as a farmer. Westcott had no grown children, so typically he logged with one other man, but sometimes he worked alone in the woods.[22]

When cutting by himself, Westcott used many of the same methods that loggers would have in large camps. He cleared debris from the cutting area so he could move quickly away from a falling tree and so branches or bushes would not catch his axe on the backstroke. Accurate felling was accomplished through "notching."[23] Loggers cut a notch in the tree on the opposite side they planned to cut, to direct its descent. He likely tested the accuracy of his notch by placing "the blade of an ax on the horizontal bottom of the notch, with the tip of the ax against the inside of the cut. If the ax handle then pointed in the direction in which the tree was intended to fall . . . he would begin to cut."[24] Conditions varied by the tree; no two cuts were the same.

On the small jobs that Westcott took there were only a few ways to make the process more efficient. He could cut logs so that they fell parallel to the hauling road. Logging in the winter meant deep snow provided a cushion that ensured the product was not damaged. He could also fell a tree across another log so it was not resting completely on the ground and limbs were easy to remove. This could damage a log, though. To avoid having to move the cumbersome log too far, a farmer would "practically . . . [fell] the timber right into the slough."[25]

After cutting the tree and bucking or removing the branches and cutting the tree to length, the result was a saw log, a handcrafted item that was nearly worthless until it was transported out of the wilderness. Typically, Westcott would cut all day for months, arranging his logs in piles, then return with animals so he could load the logs onto a dray or sled. Some farmer-loggers would cut logs then skid or drag them by animal to a more open space, load them with animals, and repeat the process until the sled was full. The idea was to do this quickly and cheaply.

Besides cushioning the logs, the snow aided their movement. Westcott relied on snowfall to improve his route by covering ruts and obstacles. If there was too much or too little snow, he typically just stayed home. As oxen or horses pulled logs, they packed the snow, increasing its density so it resisted melting longer and became slicker. Though Westcott had experience building public roads on crews, alone in the woods he might build a mile of poor road in three days. The roads ideally led to some predetermined location for another contractor to pick up, or perhaps to a riverside or lake.

The type of farming-logging Westcott was engaged in was not lucrative. In 1904, he was married, renting a house, with a child on the way, making about $220 a year in cash or credit, not including bartering or the money his wife brought in from washing laundry and "selling trunk goods." He also hunted and cut his own firewood. Of his total income, $148.37 came directly from logging, sawing, or drawing wood by the piece, making on average $20.57 a month from these tasks.

His monthly income when logging was unpredictable and some months he could make as little as $15 (he averaged $0.98 a workday when in the woods and at most made $1.80 a day at these tasks). He also had good months doing things like sugaring when he made $24.55; peeling hemlock bark, $21.98; and working in a local mill, $28.07. Working at what must have been an exhausting pace, he had his best month that year cutting and drawing saw logs, making $29. In some nonlogging months, he made as little as $3.62. Westcott was poor compared to national and regional averages. Average unskilled workers in the United States made $40.84 a month, and in New England, farm work paid on average $32 with board. He also made less than even the least skilled worker would have in an industrial logging camp in the Northern Forest where wages were between $26 and $30, with the average around $28.[26]

Westcott was not desperately poor in his community, however. These were good years for Vermont farm laborers in terms of purchasing power at average wages.[27] He was never compelled to work on days when the weather was "rotten as hell," in his words, or when "snow blowed like damnation all day," as he wrote. He took some Saturdays and most Sundays off work, sometimes to go "to church with the old women." In 1902, in a 111-day period (January 1 to April 21), he had twenty-five days in which he did not work at all, sixteen of which were Sundays. One day in 1902, he cut "his damn finger half off in the morning" and allowed himself three weekdays of "loafing" while it healed. He had time for recreation too. One workday he wrote, "I went up and cut 4 logs on Wills 650 ft. of Maple and played ball all the afternoon." He went to friends' homes for dinner, and nearly every day he slept at home. On occasion, when he did not feel like working, he did not, and instead, as he wrote in his journal, he "stayed home and rested with my wife." Westcott lived and worked in a way that Yankee farmer-loggers had since settlement, a type of life that was, as E. P. Thompson suggested, "one of alternate bouts of intense labor and of idleness [the same pattern that is found] wherever men were in control of their own working lives."[28]

Had Westcott left home and moved into a logging camp like the one Robinson was setting up, every aspect of his life would be controlled to ensure he worked consistently and efficiently. Days when the weather was cold and snowy were not times of relaxation in these camps but times when logs moved easiest and workers worked longer and harder. In these camps, men and animals were pushed to the limits of their physical ability for months at a time and more logs were produced cheaper and quicker than if each man worked alone from home. Westcott would have benefited from this efficiency, receiving more pay and a more predictable income, but he would have sacrificed time, freedom, and the comfort of resting with his wife.

To imagine how logging transitioned from the agricultural/preindustrial form that Abner Toothaker or Henry Conklin participated in, to an industrial pace like that of Robinson's operation, it is only necessary to build upon Westcott's basic work form. For example, the oxen that had powered the movement of logs since the colonial period were, starting in the 1850s, being replaced by horses. Horses were expensive but essential power sources.[29] These were large, well-bred horses that weighed as much as 2,700 or 3,400 pounds per team and cost about $175 each but could be double or triple that price depending on the team. Horse prices rapidly declined after World War I as government surplus inundated the market.[30] A farmer or a jobber might own teams or rent them from local farmers or suppliers. Rented horses show up on timesheets, and a team earned wages like human workers. Big contracts were given to operators with six or eight teams. Each team had two to eight men working with it so an eight-team operation might employ sixty-eight workers.[31] Horses were smart power sources that gained experience over time. They memorized simple orders, operations, and directions. Lee Roberts remembers that his horses Fan and Blossom were "experts." Roberts proudly recalled that "All the other hosses made three trips [a day] an' I made four with them."[32]

Bringing expensive horses away from farms and stables required hauling in new equipment and supplies and even the building of new and different buildings. With horsepower, workers could lift logs to great heights and the small shacks and lean-tos that typified agrarian resource gathering could be replaced with substantial cabins. Operations with multiple teams erected three structures: one for house workers, one to cook in, and one for animals. This specialization in construction of buildings signified a move away from agro-forestry and towards industrial production.[33]

The location of the camp was an important factor in facilitating timely production. It was "not considered profitable to walk men for more than 1½ miles from camp to work" because a walk of a mile or more could consume between 10 and 20 percent of the day. On cutover land, larger operations logged up to nine square miles around the camp. Robinson located his camp "near the center of the area [to be logged]," close to a fresh water supply in a well-drained spot near a good supply of nonmerchantable wood for fire.[34]

Before 1930, most camps were built using only "axes, broadaxes, saws, shovels, logging chains, hammers, [and] canthooks." One company owner remembered, "no hardware was used; the hinges of doors and the like, being made of wood on the ground." It took about twelve to fifteen men, two horses, and a week to build a medium-size camp. Though camps made with boards with tarpaper roofs provided the most warmth and protection from the elements, they were not regularly seen in the woods until 1930 and were not often constructed by small jobbers and farmers.[35]

Many camps were made from whole logs, so they were large, between twenty-five by twenty-five and thirty by thirty. Based on oral histories and university studies from the turn of the century, there were about twenty-seven square feet per worker, though small camps allowed half of that. Labor demands fluctuated during the season, so overcrowding was possible. New arrivals might have to sleep on benches, the floor, or in the barn during busy times in camp.[36]

Unlike the typical Northern Forest farm that was a space for recreation and work, camps were only spaces of work. They had few comforts. Formal tables and chairs were rare. Some had "deacon seats," long benches made by splitting a log and using small poles for legs. Other camps might have had "a block of wood or two here and there . . . or something like that" for seating or for table space. It was common for workers to share beds in camp but that was even common on frontier farms.[37] As the next chapter will show, a well-equipped cookhouse was essential for the pace of production to increase. It was sometimes built before the bunkhouse so that workers could eat while they constructed buildings and roads. Eating facilities were "rude, homemade tables, all [men] being seated on a long, hewn bench."[38] In Maine and New Hampshire, it was common to "build a cook room right near . . . [the bunkhouse] within ten to twelve feet [with] a little roof over [the space between the buildings to] . . . keep the snow out, and you kept your provisions out there." This was called the dingle or the dog trot and it also helped keep the smell and unsanitary conditions of the bunkhouse away from the cookhouse.[39]

As operations sped and scaled up, improvisation and tool maintenance were required, and a blacksmith served that purpose. Small operations with no blacksmiths used wood and haywire to repair nearly everything. This gave rise to the term haywire, a term that was perhaps conceived in northern New York, referring to a camp that was unorganized and less formal than the larger, industrial-scale facilities. A blacksmith from a larger company camp might be sent out to jobbers' camps as well.[40]

In larger camps, foremen, clerks, foresters, and scalers sometimes had their own camp, which was of superior quality. This spatial barrier separated higher-paid, educated, or experienced workers from lower-paid, menial workers. This spatial barrier signified industrial order and thus class. It was a break with agrarian tradition, traditions still alive among small contractors, where the boss and all other workers slept in the same building, the sign of looser camp hierarchy. These "camp offices" had comfortable accommodations. On Squaw Mountain, Maine, there were "several unique chairs" including "a cut down barrel with rocker attachment[s]." Others had handmade desks and "chairs of a more artistic design, resembling . . . chairs found on . . . [middle-class urban] porches and lawns." These workers often had metal framed beds with mattresses.

This was in stark contrast to the sleeping arrangements of the other workers who had one continuous "spread" or "puff" blanket, some up to thirty feet long that went across all of the bunks. Sometimes one puff went under workers and one over. These blankets were not cleaned often and took on a "heavy and musty" smell, and some workers caught "abominable skin disease[s]" from them.[41] Workers were still using these puffs and sleeping on gathered spruce boughs into the 1930s.[42]

In the process of buying horses and scaling up camp, an operator would have accrued substantial debt. Cash advances from a mill or landowner varied in relation to the size and complexity of the job. They could be as much as $16,000 or as little as $300. Some contracts dictated a contractor was paid as they met targets—$1.25 per thousand board feet after cutting and peeling, $1.25 per thousand when logs were yarded, $0.65 when landed, and $0.85 when "put to float" in the river. An operator could then pay wages or reinvest in the operation over the course of the season. Others got one or more advances until the full contract was complete. Even while a foreman like Herbert Robinson was constructing camp in late fall, the weather was getting colder, and cutting was beginning.[43]

Ice and Industrialization

By the end of November, only about six inches of snow had fallen on Robinson's tract. For his operation to be successful he would need colder temperatures and precipitation.[44] The middle of December had been a fine time for cutting and yarding. Temperatures were below freezing, it was not too cold for comfortable work, and there was regular snowfall. Around Christmas, temperatures rose above freezing for two days, the consistent snow stopped, and the thirteen inches on the ground was melting (figure 4.1). If the warm weather continued, the operation would be ruined. Robinson and thousands of other Northern Forest producers were praying for snow.

Snow was important for production for many reasons. One was its effect on the labor market. Winter increased the amount of labor available and thus lowered the price for labor, creating the conditions for what economist Kaoru Sugihara called "labor-intensive industrialization."[45] Economists Stanley Engerman and Claudia Goldin suggest the largest discount for winter labor in the North Atlantic, about 50 percent lower than at harvest time, was in the 1880s and declined thereafter but never reached below 20 percent by 1910, the end of their dataset.[46] In Vermont, the lowest seasonal farm labor rates were consistently in the winter for both wages paid by day and by month. The average differences between logging season wage rates (November to March) and nonlogging season wages (April to October) decreased from 19 to 14 percent from 1790–99 and 1900–09. But the largest variation in rates was in the period from 1870–79 when there was a 38 percent difference between July to November wage rates.[47] This continued into the twentieth century. In 1938, January wages were about $3.00 per month below October levels. Premiums for day labor also reflect the fact that days were longer in the summer than the winter, but as will be explained later, that did not necessarily mean loggers worked fewer hours.[48]

The slack labor market allowed logging operators to hire many workers cheaply and increase the division of labor in camps. This made work more efficient but also very different from the type of work that farmer-loggers like

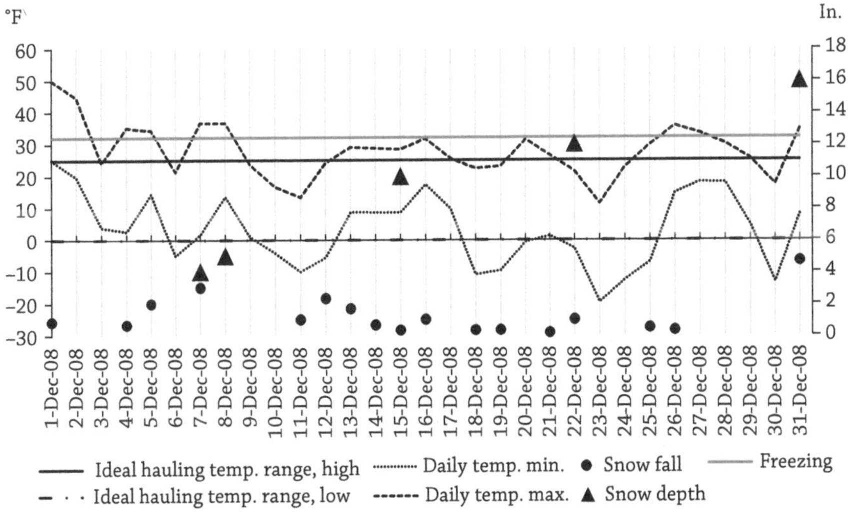

Figure 4.1. December 1908, Emerson Operation. This figure and figures 4.3 and 4.5 reconstruct weather at two operations in Maine at different times and places. They show that when daily temperatures and snow depth were ideal, operations could run smoothly. Operations could be improved if they were not completely dependent on daily temperatures and snowfall. (M. J. Menne, I. Durre, B. Korzeniewski, S. McNeal, K. Thomas, X. Yin, S. Anthony et al., 2012: *Global Historical Climatology Network, Daily* [GHCN-Daily], version 3, NOAA National Climatic Data Center, http://doi.org/10.7289/V5D21VHZ [4/1/2015] Stations: Houlton ME US [GHCND:USC00173897]; Millinocket ME US [GHCND:USC00175304])

Westcott experienced. As explained in chapter 2, the division of labor was not completely new to Northern Forest farmer-loggers. It was common for children to do menial tasks, while adults did complex and taxing jobs. Just like farmers, large operators employed children, sometimes paying as little as $0.35 a day.[49]

Grown men were more vital to increasing the scale and speed of logging. Winter meant there was extra adult labor and so cutters could work in teams, typically three to five men to a team of horses. Each cutting team was assigned a strip of land. Unskilled and young workers, called "swampers," cleared the cutting areas and made skid roads. Another worker directed the horse team, while the best axmen cut. On larger operations, a "head chopper" was a subforeman, directing one cutting crew. This division, the separation of a crew from the logging process as a whole, allowed some operators to pay each cutting crew by the piece or sometimes give production rewards. Bark was sometimes peeled to reduce friction as the log was skidded, or dragged, on the snowy ground to a collection point. Peeling also increased buoyancy for the river drive. If bark was peeled, cutting was done before fall because sap congealed in the cold.[50]

Small changes in tools accompanied the increased division of labor. The double-bitted axe was invented around the middle of the nineteenth century but did not come into wide use in the Northern Forest until around 1860 or 1870. One side of the head had a bit that was finely sharpened for cutting while the other was kept duller and used for bucking, delimbing, or swamping. Having two tools in one saved time but the two blades clearly made logging more dangerous. Traditionally, Northern Forest farmers made their own axe handles and hung the bit to fit their grip and stroke. As operations got bigger, machine-made axe handles were purchased in bulk. These axes tended to be more cumbersome. Between 25 and 50 percent of accidents in the woods were "axe-caused." Minor axe wounds were deadly because dirty camp conditions meant workers were prone to blood poisoning.[51]

Working alone, a worker like Westcott used an axe for all tasks. With a cutting crew, a crosscut saw could be employed. Introduced into the woods sometime between 1876 and 1880, selling at four to five times the price of an axe, these tools were more difficult to upkeep than an axe but were less energy intensive and quicker to use when cutting. With the introduction of the crosscut saw, workers could cut about 10 percent more trees a day. With a crosscut saw, the tree was cut further down the stump, saving ten to twenty board feet per tree. With the crosscut saw, the labor process was often divided further. The tree was notched by axe by a special worker ahead of the sawyers.[52] With this method, workers cut about forty or sixty trees a day, and some "stunt performers" cut 100 to 110. As the speed of the work increased, choppers, sawyers, and draft animals worked harder and faster, sometimes to the point of exhaustion, but brisk winter air kept workers from overheating.[53]

The snow did more than cool the worker, it gave Northern Forest production a crucial advantage. W. C. Sykes, owner of Emporium Lumber Company, relied on snow to keep his jobs in the Adirondacks moving, but not for his Pennsylvania and southwestern New York operations.[54] A knowledge of the area's weather was an essential aspect of the job that an operator needed to be aware of. "To reduce the . . . risk of 'getting caught' by unfavorable weather, full use of past year's experience and authoritative meteorological prediction is important," one 1941 study on hauling found.[55] In the winter of 1908 to 1909, Robinson decreased the value of his logs by about 20 percent in his preseason estimates to account for possible weather problems.[56]

This dependence on weather meant that the lack of snow could freeze production. Logger John Sharpe remembered a season in northern Maine when there were only eight inches of snow for the haul: "they had to haul in mud all winter." During a "freak winter" of light snow in January 1915, the *Bangor*

Daily News reported that loggers were rejoicing because of a fifteen-inch snowfall. "The great lumber interest of northern Maine as well as the various industries which depend on the snow" could now continue work as normal, the newspaper reported.[57] Small producers suffered most due to inconsistencies in the weather: "those who depend upon snow for hauling cord wood, country produce[,] and other heavy loads have waited many weeks for favorable conditions" the *Bangor Daily News* reported in 1915. The lack of snow meant there were "large numbers" of idle workers, both loggers and people who were typically hired for snow removal. The weather was "overburdening the city with unemployed." Under these conditions, horse teams "came out of the woods . . . rather than remain idle there and incur board bills."[58]

Cold weather was not solely a blessing. American businesses preferred predictability, but winter conditions varied.[59] By 1941, when scientific studies of logging methods were finally being made, they found that "the presence of deep snow is . . . a serious handicap" for cutting, though it was a boon for hauling. Two feet of snow increased the time it took to cut wood by 25 percent and three feet of snow, 50 percent. Frozen wood increased the time taken to buck the wood after cutting by 31.8 percent.[60] In extreme cold, frostbite was a risk for workers. Workers lost dexterity in their hands. Axes slipped, cutting workers, and horses were harnessed incorrectly and dangerously. If it got cold too early in the season, the sap in trees thickened and peeling bark was impossible. For these reasons, operators attempted to end cutting by the end of December, before the serious snowfall began. The blizzard of 1886 in Aroostook, ME, blocked men and animals from leaving camps and farms, putting people in danger of starvation. Deep snow packed into horses' shoes, reducing their traction. If the snow was not the correct type for sledding, too dry and powdery for example, it hindered transport. If the snow did not melt fast enough, there was not enough of it by the end of the season, or if the spring rains were insufficient, driving the logs downriver to mills was slow or impossible. Dams helped with the latter problem, as the previous chapter made clear. If the inconsistencies of weather were not made more constant, operations in the woods could not grow in scale or speed; they could not industrialize.[61]

On Robinson's job, after cutting he started the process of secondary transportation in which logs were "brought from the stump to . . . [a] central location" called a "skidway" or "yard."[62] This meant ensuring proper road systems in the woods. New York Superintendent of Forests William F. Fox wrote that the roads leading to the skidways "would resemble a tree with subdividing branches." In this analogy, on a small job, the tree branches represented skid roads. Where the branches met the trunk of the "tree" represented the place

Figure 4.2. Yarding-sled trails leading down to a skidway on a two-sled road, Maine (Ralph Clement Bryant, *Logging; The Principles and General Methods of Operation in the United States* [New York: J. Wiley & Sons, 1923], 162)

where the logs were collected on skidways. On the skidways, logs were stacked parallel to and above haul roads on a slight slope so they would roll onto sleds one after another. The main haul road was the trunk of the tree where the horse teams would collect logs from each skidway in January when the snowpack was deep. The base of the tree represented the final landing, sometimes called a breaking ground or rollway (figure 4.2).[63] Haul roads were major projects. A twelve- or fifteen-foot road cost between $50 and $15 per mile to build and $12.50 a mile to maintain. This was almost all labor costs, as nearly all the materials for construction were procured from the woods. Robinson and some of his workers were woodsmen and had the ability to build primitive roads with little capital. If there was not a good snowpack for hauling as the cutting and yarding was taking place, logs were stored in the woods on the skidways awaiting snow for the haul. The forest became a warehouse for forest products.[64]

Piling wood, whether pulp or long logs on the skidway, was labor intensive, requiring four to five workers. In a twentieth-century ergonomic study, 50 percent of loggers found piling logs and pulp to be the most strenuous job. If it was snowing during cutting, piling was often rushed because the longer it took to pile the logs, the shorter time allowed for hauling. When jobber John Toothaker, Lincoln's father, was out of camp in 1891, he told his son Lincoln to "tell Gary to look after the choppers [so] that the timber is chopped [and piled] so it can be hauled without killing the [hauling] horses."[65]

Skidways allowed for easy hauling but had limitations. Logs were only piled high enough to be found after a snowfall because high piles of heavy logs or pulp were dangerous. But millions of board feet needed to be piled for large jobs, and short piles meant skidways took up a lot of land, land that needed to be swamped, shoveled, and graded. If skidways were stacked short, and snow fell, the level of the roads rose to the height of the snowpack, so more logs needed to be lifted onto sleds instead of rolled down onto them. Short piles also meant there were more piles spread over a larger area and more movement from pile to pile for the hauling, meaning more roads were necessary.[66]

On large jobs, fewer, more dangerous skidways were preferred over larger numbers of skidways. Higher piling was done by "parbuckling" or "cross hauling" logs. This required more rope chain, tackle, extra horses, and extra workers, but skidways could be stacked fifteen or twenty feet high. Parbuckling reduced the physical storage space, a typical strategy in modern supply chain management, reducing costs significantly. The winter workscape became a more efficient warehouse. From the skidways, logs were loaded onto sleds, low-capital tools made in the woods by skilled woodsmen using mostly forest materials.[67]

Despite Robinson's best effort, by Christmas 1908 the operation was in jeopardy. Little snow had fallen. New Year's Day was a time for celebration for more than one reason, however: more than ten inches of snow fell and temperatures plunged. The conditions were perfect for the haul, the final step before the logs left the woods (figure 4.3).

The main haul was a hectic time. If roads were not planned correctly or if there was little snow, there would be delays and the logs may not make it to the river before the spring freshet started. If logs were left in the woods during the summer, they were susceptible to rot, infestation, and fire. Since mills bought logs based on board foot, or volume, as water evaporated out of logs as they dried in the piles, value likewise evaporated. It was considered "very discreditable for a foreman to leave logs in the woods."[68]

Successful operators learned to mitigate the negative effects of unpredictable weather while also quickening the speed of logistics. Woodsmen knew snow made hauling easier and cheaper. Specific snow conditions were better than others, however. Snow is ice, but as snow falls the ice crystals are interspersed with gaps filled with air. As snow sat on the ground and was exposed to sun and wind, it underwent a destructive metamorphosis: the jagged edges of the flakes collapsed into a packed mass. Given the right conditions, in a few

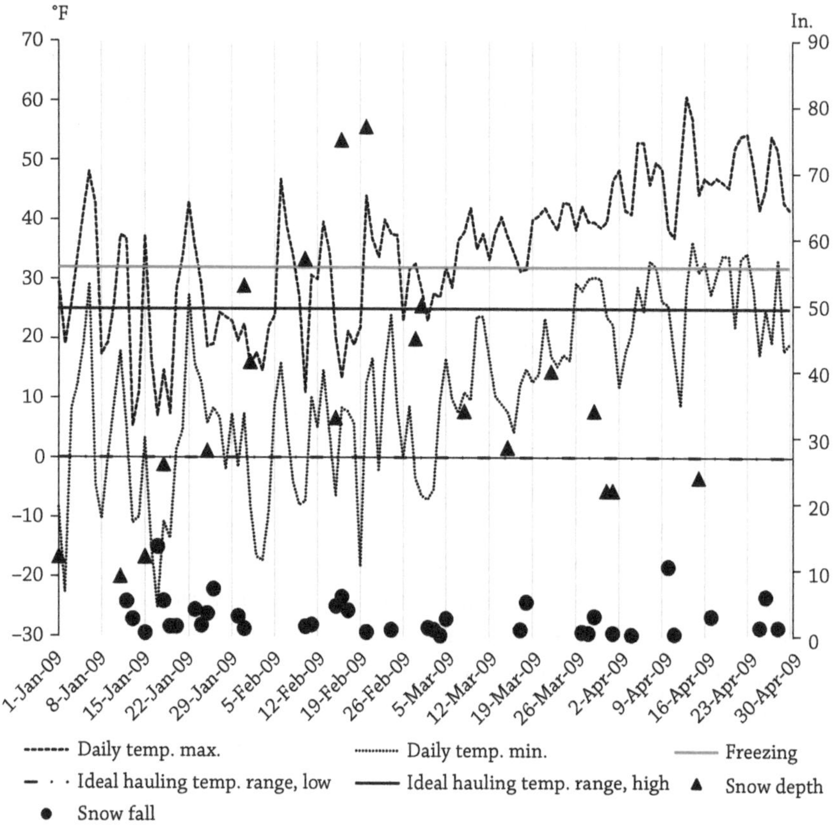

Figure 4.3. January–May 1909, Emerson Operation. In March the snowpack melts and daytimes temperatures move outside the hauling range. Nighttime temperatures—daily lows—remain below freezing, making sprinkling possible (M. J. Menne, I. Durre, B. Korzeniewski, S. McNeal, K. Thomas, X. Yin, S. Anthony et al., 2012: *Global Historical Climatology Network, Daily* [GHCN-Daily], version 3, NOAA National Climatic Data Center, http://doi.org/10.7289/V5D21VHZ [4/1/2015] Stations: HOULTON ME U.S. [GHCND:U.S.C00173897]; MILLINOCKET ME U.S. [GHCND:U.S.C00175304])

hours after falling, snow density can double or, in a few days, quadruple. This compact snow provided a slicker and sturdier surface than freshly fallen snow. Over time, the bottom layer of snow will weaken due to temperature gradients across depth. Thus the process of constructive metamorphosis begins. The integrity of the snowpack can only be maintained through manually packing the snow with more traffic.[69]

No matter how deep and dense the snowpack, there was always a risk of melting. As mentioned in chapter 2, canopy cover slows melting. So too does the albedo factor of white snow, but over time snow collected debris, lowering the reflectance. While snow reflects sunlight, it readily absorbed long-wave radiation emitted by other things in the environment. Snow around tree trunks and other objects melts quicker than the surrounding area. The snowpack was dynamic, becoming more or less conducive to production over time. It needed to be stabilized and rationalized.[70]

Woodsmen knew ice was better for hauling than snow. Generations had been using frozen lakes and rivers for that purpose. Ice is nearly two times as dense as packed snow, so it melts slower. Ice was more stable, leveler, and slicker than snow. These properties meant that operators were desperate to harness and control the substance. When they did so, it produced something remarkable to the eye, but something that was essential to industrialization.[71]

When visiting a camp in the Adirondacks with her forester husband in the 1930s, Barbara Bird found an amazing sight: "in order to make hauling easier the roads [were] covered in ice up to two feet thick." Bird's assessment of two feet may have been an exaggeration, but these ice roads must have been impressive. This process, called "watering" or "sprinkling," gained popularity between 1872 and 1890 and it was an essential aspect of industrializing the Northern Forest. Lubrication was a vital aspect of industrialization, just as vital as coal, steam, or steel. Without lubricants, forces of friction made new workplace efficiencies nearly impossible. This is especially true as competitive industrial markets forced man and machine to move at faster speeds. Snow and ice were the lubricant of this workplace.[72]

This type of lubrication, icing, was made possible with the "sprinkler box," a large watertight box typically eight by eight by four, built on runners that held up to sixty barrels of water (figure 4.4). These niche devices were made locally or even in the woods with materials at hand. Improvised spigots spread water two feet in either direction as the sled moved forward in the dark of night, when teams were off the roads and temperatures were coldest. As each gram of water froze it released 335 joules of heat, initially melting and compacting the snow, giving the dense ice a firm foundation.[73] Two workers operated the device, one driving the horses, the other watching the spigot and chipping away ice buildup. One cartload could ice four to six miles. To fill the box, the men parked by a stream, unharnessed the horses, and drew barrels of water up with guide poles, block, tackle, and horsepower. The earthen gravity chutes built for logging on high altitude could be iced by sliding a barrel full of water with holes in it down the chute.[74]

Temperatures between zero and twenty-five degrees were ideal for hauling ice, and on Robinson's tract the frequency of these cold days increased

Figure 4.4. A sprinkler being filled with water from a brook, Adirondacks (Ralph Clement Bryant, *Logging: The Principles and General Methods of Operation in the United States* [New York: J. Wiley & Sons, 1923], 175)

in January. Some of the best and most consistent hauling weather occurred toward the end of February that year, as it did most years (see figure 4.3).[75] It was best to get the haul done as soon as possible when a period of good weather appeared. Cutting ruts into the ice to form tracks kept sleds from tipping and sped up transport. Ice roads had to be plowed, shoveled, or re-iced when there was snow, and sometimes fences made from brush and windfall were constructed to keep blowing snow off roads. Ice has a lower albedo factor than snow, meaning it will melt easily, so re-icing was always necessary.[76]

Thick ice roads allowed hauling to continue through the warm weather. Without an ice road, the length of the hauling season was dependent completely on consistent cold weather. With an ice road, an operator could count on a ten-week hauling period even if the weather became unseasonably warm. Ice roads rationalized the erratic winter workscape and made it dependable for business. Most American businesses in this period were freeing themselves from dependence on natural cycles by building electrified structures with artificial lighting and heating. In contrast, as forest product production scaled up, it became more dependent on the cold.[77]

With so much invested in roads, crews of workers called “road monkeys” or “chickadees” were assigned for maintenance. On a fourteen-horse operation, there were about six to eight employees doing this work. They fought a constant battle with the weather to make sure conditions were ideal for the teams. In the midday sun, "roads get soft and . . . [loads would] get stuck. They called that calving, when they had . . . [to] throw off half their logs off [to keep moving] . . . that happened a lot" one worker remembered.[78]

Depending on the length of the haul, on unimproved snow roads alone a team could haul 700 to 1,000 board feet of lumber. In typical camps with improved ice roads, "a four-horse team could haul 5,000 to 8,000 board feet per load, while two horses can haul from 2,500 to 4,000 feet." If the ground was rough, as on Robinson's tract, 2,000 to 3,000 board feet for four horses and 1,250 to 1,500 feet for two was common.[79]

A good iced road was an essential attribute that differentiated large industrial operations from the smaller jobs of farmer-loggers. Simply grading roads for ice cost 100 percent more than snow roads, not counting additional equipment and labor. Some estimated ice roads cost between $200 to $1,000 a mile to build and maintain. If it fell in the cheaper range, it was a better method than building roads for tractors.[80]

Snow and ice helped make transport more efficient, but there was a tradeoff. On a downhill slope, a sled could catch up with horses and kill them. Operators limited grades to about 5 percent. On steeper grades, the road monkeys "guarded" the descent by throwing sand, gravel or a special stringy "road hay" onto the snow. If the weather warmed, guarded tracts needed to be covered with snow again. With guarding and icing, operators could increase grades to "10 [percent] on descents and 1–20 [percent] or less for ascent." Logging experts attested that "haulers in the Adirondack mountains . . . carried fifteen cords of spruce pulpwood over roads having 10 and 11 percent grades."[81] As time progressed and valuable tracts receded to the most rugged terrain, limiting grades to 20 percent was not always an option. Tree branches, logs, or chains were attached to the back of the sled to increase friction and slow the sled. Chains or U-shaped "roller braces" could be attached to runners to "tear right into the ice and snow."[82]

Another option was to use a "snub warp," a simple pulley that lowered a load down a steep grade gradually. A rope was wrapped around a tree stump and a lever was constructed to push against the rope to control speed. Patented "Barienger Brakes" could be used, which were adjacent metal drums around which an iron cable was wrapped with levers to control speed. Snub warps and Barienger Brakes allowed teams to transit forty-degree grades. Tremendous tension was put on the line, and getting an arm caught between the rope and a tree or drum resulted in serious injury.[83]

Ice roads and snub warps allowed immense loads to seemingly defy physics, moving quickly on flat surfaces and descending impossible grades. Still there was a systematic flaw in the secondary transportation process: time and resources were wasted building, loading, and unloading skidways. Parbuckling made this more efficient, but time and energy were still lost in the redundant movement of logs or pulp.

During good winters, some bright operators realized they could haul right after cutting, thus avoiding excessive loading and unloading of skidways. At strategic locations, operators built one or two skidways where logs were drawn right after they were cut. The logs were loaded onto the skids quickly in short piles called the "hot yard," and when a haul sled was available, they were loaded onto them for the haul. This was called "hot landing," "hot yarding," or "hauling from the stump."[84]

Hot landing saved time and energy by saving space. Fewer yards had to be constructed or shoveled off, no parbuckling was required, and operators did not have to worry about logs getting frozen together, burned, or otherwise damaged as they sat in the woods awaiting the final haul. This method depended on a good winter snow, but it saved "quite an additional expense," according to one operator. Though totally unconnected practically, hot yarding was conceptually a rudimentary form of "just-in-time" supply chain management that would be perfected by automobile manufacturers in the late twentieth century.[85]

When hot yarding, any delay in the cutting, skidding, yarding, or hauling meant that there was a surplus of logs at the hot yard. As with the assembly line, hot yarding sped up the entire operation and forced all the workers to perform as an interconnected unit. Work in these camps drifted away from the relaxed agricultural labor regimes Westcott experienced toward more controlled and fast industrial regimes. The changes in tools and methods described above were a type of revolution in the logging industry but almost completely unrelated to fossil fuels.[86]

Debora Cowen argues in her book on logistics that it was often biological bodies that bore the physical stresses of "accelerating" logistics. In the winter workscape, animals were affected most. In the past, oxen and horses were large investments. Farmers had to be careful not to work animals too hard or put them in danger.[87] As logging sped up, horses became a source of power and were worked as hard as they could be for as often as they were physically able. Workers would inevitably "get mad and abuse their horses." Axe handles and pulp hooks were used to drive the horses forward.[88] In 1891, Lincoln Toothaker got a letter from his sister, who heard about the abuse of two teams he brought into the woods from the farm, warning Lincoln that he was "going to kill his horses" by working them too hard.[89]

To ensure the logs were at the breaking ground before the spring melt, "in some camps, big, bigger lumber camps for big companies" an operator might "put up a watch or a suit of clothes to the one that hauled the most lumber through the winter."[90] Even when not directly incentivized, teamsters would compete for fun. In a big pulpwood operation with 5,000 to 6,000 cords of wood to cut, it was expected that eleven to fourteen cords would be hauled per team, per day. That was about 500 cords a season, or between 500 and 1,000 tons, moved by each team in a roughly ten-week period.

For operations that weren't hot yarding to be more productive, they needed to move more logs per load. Here there were incentives to overload sleds. Properly iced and maintained roads allowed for heavy loads of eighty logs weighing twelve tons with a half-ton of binding chain stacked ten feet high. Some "champion loads" were said to have weighed thirty tons, which needed extra help to get moving.[91]

On cutover land where profitable tracts were further from rivers and lakes, horses had to make longer trips. Operators estimated how much work horses could take before dying, though it was assumed some would die. Feeding recommendations in the beginning of the twentieth century were eleven pounds of oats and hay a day, though the hardest working city horses pulling omnibuses could eat as much as thirty-five pounds of oats and hay. This would mean as much as 51,000 calories a day.[92] In logging camps it cost about $0.75 to $1.50 to feed each animal per day, about 50 to 100 percent more than it cost to feed the workers. Even with this much food, horses still lost weight.[93] Because they were paying to house and feed the animals, operators did not want horses "standing idle" so they might only rest the animals four hours a day.[94]

The two teams that Lincoln Toothaker brought from his father's farm had to haul twenty-two to twenty-four miles a day, the maximum recommended distance for draft animals. His team, horses named Phil and Dick, were "looking quite well" with four weeks left, while another team, Pepper and Ginger, were "awful poor." "They have been sick," Lincoln wrote his wife, "they done a lot of work since the 15th of December . . . [and] they got to go 24 [miles] every day now till they come home."[95]

Besides working faster and longer, horses took on increasingly risky routes as operators pushed into rougher terrain. Logger Lee Roberts had two mares who were supposedly "experts," though once on the haul they went "over th' side a th' mountain . . . a'course th' snow was deep 'n' kinda saved 'em. But it cut Blossom, my off Mare, right through the brisket—right between th' for'ard legs."[96]

When hot landing, teamsters had to rush to get to and from the hot yard so the logs did not stack too high on the skids as they were coming out of the woods. Some teamsters perfected a method of unloading whereby they used the speed and momentum of the loaded sled to intentionally "sluice" or tip their load to avoid unloading by hand. This saved time and labor in unloading but put the lives of the horses and workers at risk.

On steep terrain, operators became more reliant on failure-prone braking and snubbing systems. When ropes broke on snub warps, full sleds overtook horses, killing or maiming them. After an eight-ton load caught up with a team on a Santa Clara job in northern New York, a witness reported "there wasn't a semblance left of either horse." Smart horses were not only valuable but could ensure their own survival.[97]

A student at the University of Maine in Orono in the 1911–12 season, found that well-treated horses "depreciated" 15 percent during a season, though some estimates were higher. Workers remember buying horses for $375, working them until they were "all used up" and selling them for $25 in April or May. Horses were cheap nature, expendable flesh that allowed the overtaxed resource base of the Northern Forest to industrialize.[98]

Abuses of horses and people were connected. Ralph Thornton was working on the steep slopes of Maine's Farrow Mountain. Each "turn" required two different snub warps. He almost got killed on one turn and his horses were injured. When driving a different team, he wasn't able to get back to camp until 10:00 p.m. and didn't get dinner until 1:00 a.m. The next day the boss, Linscott, asked for three turns and the workers refused. Linscott told them to take their pay and leave, saying, according to Thornton, "I'm going to run this outfit, you fellers ain't." When Thornton and the other teamsters started to leave, Linscott shouted to Thornton he would give him a raise of $0.50 a day to stay and drive a horse that had kicked another worker. The details are unclear, but it seems that this wildcat strike lasted one day and that Ralph either broke ranks and accepted the pay raise, or that all the workers returned.[99]

Thornton didn't strike for his horses' sake. People also worked harder, faster, and longer as the production process sped up.[100] It is hard to find productivity data per worker in logging, but farming labor was getting more efficient and thus more expensive over time, increasing in price by about 1.8 percent per year between 1869 to 1940 in Vermont. Factory labor was likewise getting more efficient and more expensive. Though the winter labor glut attracted workers to the forest, logging labor would have to increase in productivity over time to remain viable. While the increased productivity of farm labor and factory labor was the result, in large part, of new machines and new artificial power sources, this was not necessarily the case in the forest. By the 1920s and 1930s, a three-man crew was expected to cut and yard about five cords per day, or between 3,500 and 7,500 board feet, depending on the tract. In a ten-camp study, with an average of fifty-three men per camp, each camp produced about 469 cords a week, or about 5,160 cords (720,342 board feet) in a typical eleven-week season.[101]

The demand for the eight-hour workday was not heard on the farm nor the more distant camp. A good jobber planned the camp so it was close to the timber, but this was not always possible. Some workers recall a three-mile walk to the job. Zealous foremen made sure the men were at the jobsite by daylight and did not leave until dark. This sometimes meant waking up at 4:00 a.m. More typically, wake-up time was between 5:00 and 6:00 a.m. One worker remembered, "you had breakfast when the stars were shining and you ate supper when he [*sic*] stars were shining at night." Icing had to be done at night, so the two-man icing crew often used lanterns. Twelve- to fourteen-hour workdays were normal in the summer and fall and up to eighteen hours was common in the winter, more if the haul was behind schedule.[102]

Lincoln Toothaker was struggling to stay on schedule during the 1891 haul at the Black Cat camp. Temperatures had been erratic that hauling season, consistently above freezing during the day but dipping to nearly negative thirty degrees in the middle of February. Starting around March 6, however, daytime temperatures rose considerably and remained above freezing for multiple days. On March 7, the hauling crew of six teams had hauled 1,106,010 board feet or about 6,628 logs, and still had about two million board feet to go. With mid-March temperatures reaching sixty degrees, the operation would have been in a panicked rush (figure 4.5).

On these warming days, the early morning was the best time to haul because ice roads were in the best condition and calving was not a problem. Haulers like Toothaker woke up between 3:00 and 4:30 a.m. to prepare their horses and could never get to bed before 9:30 p.m. When behind schedule, two workers might run one team for twenty-four hours.[103]

During this rushed haul, Toothaker reported that he was "awful sleepy," but told his wife in a letter that he would have to "make up for what sleep I have lost" in the spring. Chronic lack of sleep was a problem during busy hauling seasons. Just as with other industries, as logging work sped up and workers lost sleep, tiredness became a symbol of a proper manly attitude toward work. However, overworked and overtired people are more likely to have accidents. The American Engineering Council did a study between 1922 and 1925 and found that production in logging increased 27 percent nationwide but "accidents had increased in severity 464 percent," a "natural concomitant of the

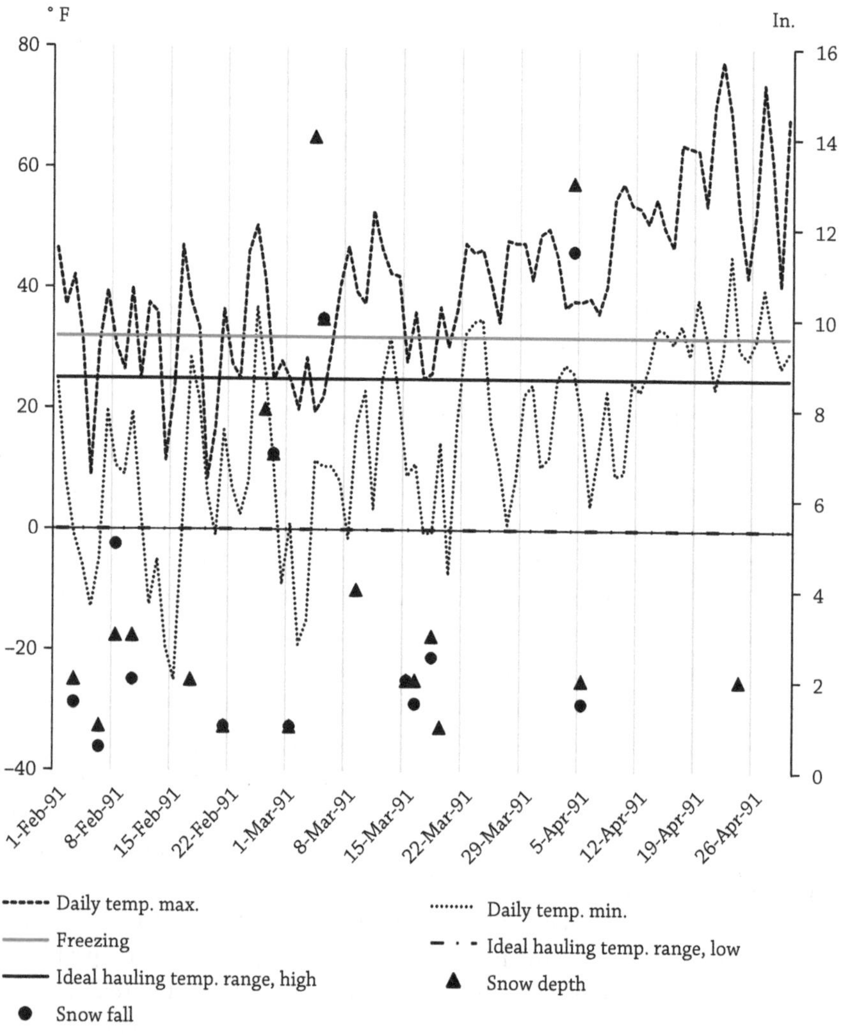

Figure 4.5. February–May 1891, Toothaker Operation (M. J. Menne, I. Durre, B. Korzeniewski, S. McNeal, K. Thomas, X. Yin, S. Anthony et al., 2012: *Global Historical Climatology Network, Daily* [GHCN-Daily], version 3, NOAA National Climatic Data Center, http://doi.org/10.7289/V5D21VHZ [4/1/2015] Stations: BERLIN NH U.S. [GHCND:U.S.C00270690]; WEST MILAN 1 NH U.S. [GHCND:U.S.C00279307])

increased intensity of the industrial process." On one occasion, a log "rolled and struck" an exhausted Toothaker during work, leaving him "quite lame." Toward the end of the 1892 hauling season, he suffered an accident that resulted in the amputation of his leg. It is impossible to say if this was a result of the increased pace of work, but this accident correlated with the busy time in the season and a period in the history of the Northern Forest when the labor process was speeding up.[104]

The type of injury that Toothaker suffered could be very difficult on workers' families. Levi and Esther Austin were poor farmers on a small, unproductive plot in the Adirondacks. As they aged, the Austins came to depend on the wages of their only son, George. In the winter of 1891, thirty-one-year-old George was injured on the job. According to Esther, his "collar bone and breast bones [were] broken and out of place." Attempting to overcome the limitations of his body, George "went back to work before his bones could heal," but his injuries worsened, and he felt "them great with every draw of the saw." With few options left in the middle of an unforgiving winter, Esther decided to write to George's boss, lumberman Luke Usher: "It seems hard for us old people to have to suffer for food and clothing," she wrote, "but hush, I am not a beggar, I am only a little hungry and a little cold."[105]

Along with increased hours and danger on the job, there was more discipline in camps that sped up. Unlike Westcott, who took time off work for "extremely nasty" winter weather, workers in large operations, with new, fast, and interconnected production methods had to endure the worst weather. Workers remember cutting and hauling when it was forty degrees below zero. Government documentation calculated the loggers' work month at twenty-six days, the same as a farm worker. On the farm, holidays and Sundays meant time off, but in the camp that was not always the case. One student studying a camp in Maine reported that three workers refused to work on Christmas, but the threat of expulsion eventually impelled them.[106]

In large operations, the boss needed more direct control over the crew. The bosses were no longer fellow workers but demanding overseers who "urged workers forward with relentless energy."[107] A boss like Herbert Robinson rarely settled into a task but instead walked the job site, inspecting and disciplining workers, giving him the common title of "walking boss." To keep the haul on schedule, he needed to know "exactly what each man is doing, and whether or not the work is well done."[108]

Higher ranking workers asserted authority even during rest times. "The Cook . . . has to run his cook room . . . and have some discipline" one worker recalled, "the boss set at the head of the table . . . and you set down and mind your business and eat all you want." Yet discipline varied by the scale of the job. The same worker remembered, "in little crews like I worked in most time, it would be a family affair. Some fellow you know . . . some neighbor up the river there would have a little operation—have three or four men or five or six and stay at the house, and the woman would do the cooking, and that's a different story, see[?]" Workers' financial gain was tied to the success of the operation. They knew if the logs did not get out of the woods, they would not get paid and so were self-disciplined. There was less differentiation between bosses/owners and workers.[109]

Specialized logging bosses like Robinson were adept at manipulating the winter workscape. Using his own "practicability in devising methods, and . . . his familiarity with men and horses" an operator like Robinson could build bridges, corduroy roads and, with some dynamite, even blast boulders, remove stumps, and excavate hills. One of Santa Clara Lumber Company's jobbers in northern New York was named Fred LeBoeuf and although he was "unable to read or write," he was a "practical engineer of great ability."[110] Successful operators "owe their success largely to a knowledge of executive and mechanical detail, from the efficiency of labor to the varieties of saw practices, that has taken years to acquire, and which has crystallized into a larger and complicated organization." Foremen had to be mildly efficient at all jobs and they maintained the diversity of skills of the preindustrial woodsmen. This type of informal knowledge extended down the hierarchy to head choppers, teamsters, and yardmen. Through observation, this knowledge grew in the minds of young workers swamping or doing menial tasks.[111] From their survival-based woodskills, they built a specialized industrial knowledge.

Some thought this "hard-won insight" could only be approximated by the college-educated foresters who were required to do the same type of work in the growing acreage of national forests in the United States. One forestry professor wrote "the expert knowledge of the forest was generally not possessed by the man at the central office and by the owners; the forest expert of the lumber industry was the foreman of the logging camp and the cruiser, and what little these men had of forestry knowledge they keep to themselves." Nevertheless, foresters and engineers would seek to emulate the work of Robinson and even integrate their knowledge into college curricula.[112]

The US Census of Occupation classified lumber work as a "semiskilled" occupation, but evidence shows that at all levels of the job there remained a "touch of a master handicrafts-man."[113] One early forester commented that "The woods superintendent and foremen are left largely to their own devices, so long as logs are delivered in sufficient quantities and at cost they are deemed proper. It is difficult for the manager under such circumstances to appreciate how a more intelligent care and greater skill in the woods will result in a financial gain, and the woods problem, with all the complications of topography, character of soil, occurrence of trees, varying character of log grades, etc., are such that it is easy for the foreman to convince the manager that no modifications of prevailing methods are possible."[114] In other words, outsiders saw the Northern Forest methods as primitive but they were profitable. For Robinson, the forest landscape was a workbench; workers, horses, snow, ice, and landscapes were his only conceivable tools. His finished product was the workscape. Just like any craftsmen, who can never be completely sure they will make a saleable item out of a given set of raw materials, loggers had no assurance they would get logs out of any tract of woods on time or at cost.[115]

At the height of the industry around 1905, logging had become dependent on the construction of winter workscapes. Operators who harnessed the power of weather to increase the scale and efficiency of production distinguished themselves from agrarian forest product extractors. There were distinct differences between Robinson's operation and Westcott's, though they were in the same business working around the same time. In Westcott's work, preindustrial agricultural norms continued, and the winter weather was the ultimate boss. Operations that skewed toward the industrial needed more order, and they wrought regularity from unpredictable nature. Large operators with ice roads were still at the mercy of the winter but the relationship was more even-keeled. Forming relationships with these cheap natures allowed operators to squeeze profit from the cutover land. Variations in the workscape of camps of different sizes affected how workers within them experienced the transition to industrialization. Industrialization depended on the scale of operations rather than the time in which they existed—geography rather than chronology.[116]

The winter increased the division of labor, sped up production, increased its scale. Workscapes were connected by rivers, creating vast envirotechnical landscapes, ecological networks of human and nonhuman actors. These specific landscape alterations allowed organic power sources to remain viable into the second half of the twentieth century. With the free gifts of ice and snow and the free power of the spring freshet, why spend money on experimental technology? Industrialization here did not free people from dependence on nature but further imbedded them into natural cycles.[117] Thinking otherwise, that industrialization is essentially a move away from organic power and natural cycles, limits our understanding of the phenomenon. After all, climate change proves that, despite the hubris of the twentieth century Anthropocentric milieu, over the last two hundred years parts of humanity have only further embedded themselves in the natural cycle of carbon exchange that helps regulate global temperatures.

Changing relationships with nature define industrialization but these are interdependent relationships. Industrial production in the Northern Forest remained profitable not just because of the weather but because of organic bodies working with nonhuman nature. Industrialization therefore depended on the people and animals who, for better or worse, were not replaced by fossil fuel-powered machines.[118] For bodies to become profitable sources of cheap nature they needed fuel, and a lot of it.

CHAPTER 5

THE BODY AS CHEAP NATURE

As the last chapter hinted at, the industrialization of the Northern Forest meant increased use of fuel, but in this case the most important fuel was food and fodder. One source makes it clear how vital food was to this industry. In the winter of 1902–03, two chemists working for the Maine Agricultural Experiment Station, Edward Raymond Mansfield and Charles Dayton Woods, trekked deep into the forests around Lake Onawa, ME, to do a study on loggers' diets. In order to find out how these workers could work so hard, the scientists recorded everything that they ate. They also collected their feces in glass jars, keeping them preserved in the snowpack for later dissection. In their report, titled "Studies of the Food of Maine Lumbermen," the scientists wrote they were pleased at the outcome "because of the uniformity of the diet, the regularity of the men in stooling, and the long duration of the experiment." Using these meticulous methods, Mansfield and Woods concluded that the diet of these loggers was "as regards to protein and energy, the highest yet recorded for any class of American laboring men." Workers ate on average 6,995 calories a day, though one group averaged 8,198![1]

Using this study among many other sources, this chapter argues that as the speed of production quickened in the period between roughly 1870 and 1900, workers had difficulty adjusting their metabolisms to keep pace.[2] Facing diminishing returns on investment in the overexploited forest of the Northeast, operators relied on the cheapest and most readily available power sources to aid production: human and animal muscle, a type of power that had sustained the world's economy before roughly 1800. Because of the hold-up problem discussed in chapter 3, it was uncommon for contractors to invest in high-capital machinery. Into the first half of the twentieth century, the general rule in the woods was to hire "two French Canadians in preference to any machine."[3] These immigrants and others exerted tremendous effort in the woods, and it was sometimes said that "nothing can swing an axe, or move a saw, or roll logs, like baked beans." Yet no amount of food was actually adequate. Workers bodies suffered from this deficit.[4] This remained the case into the 1950s, when fossil fuel-powered machines finally gained advantage over older methods.

Overcoming the insecurities inherent to local food production—escaping the "Malthusian trap"—was both a cause and effect of the transition to industrial capitalism.[5] Nutritional deficiencies and seasonal diets hampered the amount of work that previous generations of Americans were capable of. Starting in the 1870s, industrial food production gave workers who could afford it access to large quantities of nutritious, high-calorie food, year-round. Businesses, scientists like Woods and Mansfield, and government officials worked in concert to gather and disseminate the latest information about proper nutrition so that they could increase the productive potential of humans. Each of the publications of America's agricultural experiment stations were supposedly read by half a million people. Nutrition became a "popular science" and these efforts improved workers' diets across the country.[6] Historian Nick Cullather found that the "invention of the calorie" was essential for determining how to get as much energy into as many people as possible. This was true, but there was another motive behind the proliferation of the nutritional sciences: figuring out how to get as much work out of workers as possible. Nutrition became another tool of scientific managers, a way to control workers from the inside of their bodies.[7]

When confronted with new types of industrial work like those developing in the industrializing Northern Forest, workers found that they had to fight the limitations of their bodies. The body became a natural barrier that these workers individually and collectively struggled against to create value. When people stopped working to eat, external nature and human muscular work met materially.[8] This aspect of work—the process of metabolism—has not been a major topic of environmental or labor history.[9] The metabolic work of animals has been considered to a greater extent. "Industrial animal husbandry," Les Beldo argued, "depends upon nonhuman vitalities to predictably exceed human inputs to production." Though Beldo makes the case that this is unique to the "metabolic labor" of animals, in some cases, this held true for human vitalities.[10]

Industrialization was dependent on this increased intensity of work but, as shown in the previous chapter, industrial wage work in the Northern Forest was also dependent on weather. Upon first observation these two productive forces seem different. Weather was not part of the cash nexus because nobody paid for its benefits, though some used these gifts effectively. The physical labor of humans and animals was part of the cash nexus. In fact, the supposedly voluntary exchange of money for caloric expenditure was the foundational premise of the "free labor" concept. Free labor differentiated industrial capitalism from its precursory economic systems.

In the Northern Forest, the muscle power of free laborers was so important that workers were guaranteed all the high-quality food they could eat for free in addition to wages. Contracting systems of production were often referred to as "sweated labor" because profit was achieved only through the sweat of workers.[11] Logging work was so demanding, however, that even with virtually unlimited food, workers still suffered from fatigue, injury, and weight loss. The metabolic processes of free laboring bodies became cheap nature like the work of horses, or the weather, forces of nature that owners of productive property could take from unsustainably and without proper compensation.[12] When eating to work, industrial capitalism seeped into the veins of these workers' bodies and fed the fibers of their muscles, transforming them into creatures of capitalism: a class of industrial wage workers.

Wilderness Rations

As chapter 2 showed, the lack of local food in the winter was one of the many obstacles that forest product operations faced. By the 1870s, profitable tracts were far removed from productive farms. The freight costs into the lumber depot of Chamberlain Farm were around $20–$60 for a sled that might be able to carry 2,000 pounds.[13] For these reasons, before 1900, there were few luxuries in camp diets. Operators toted only enough to give workers calories for production, not frivolities for taste, and they did not even achieve the former goal.[14] Like isolated farmers, early industrial loggers complained of the monotony of winter fare.[15] Dedicated lumberers started their own farms, vertically integrating supply chains. The Great Northern Paper Company owned farms that could keep 800 horses, produce 5,000 bushels of potatoes, and 300 hogs.[16]

Hog production was important because until the 1930s, it was the primary protein in camps. Even when fresh beef was available it was not always desired by the loggers, who found it difficult to eat quickly and low in energy when compared to fatty pork. Woods and Mansfield heard a story about a camp where "the men were satisfied with their wages . . . but didn't like . . . 'fresh meat.'" The boss gave them "salt pork three times a day, and peace at once resumed."[17] Beans also remained a vital and celebrated dish. In 1891, Lincoln Toothaker's younger brother wrote to him in the logging camp excited that, "school closes next Friday. We are going to have a 'bake bean supper.'" Loggers in the Woods and Mansfield study derived 20 to 33 percent of their protein and 10 to 14 percent of their total energy from baked beans.[18] Game meat continued to be important. After returning to camp from a hunting trip, Lincoln Toothaker wrote home saying they "lived like kings in here the week past. We have coffee for breakfast and great big mince pies." When game meat was served, the forest ecology entered workers' bodies, fueling production.[19]

The industrialization that was changing work in the Northern Forest was also changing food production. By the time of the pulp boom around 1900, increased railroad mileage made supplying camps easier. A national infrastructure of beef production and distribution was developing. This allowed for more "fresh meats, vegetables, fruits, and even eggs, butter, and milk." Salt pork and beans remained staples, but cuts of beef were now available if workers desired it. Even with increased railroad mileage, supplies were still toted directly into most camps by sled, but the distance was often reduced, and operators were less reliant on frozen rivers for transport.[20]

Industrial food manufacturers were also producing cheaper and safer canned food. High temperature canning technology and food regulation increased consumer confidence and demand.[21] The number of canneries in the United States almost doubled between 1899 and 1914.[22] Camps now had access to tasty, high-calorie canned foods like pie fillings, cooking lard, jellies, jams, and condensed milk. Some camps had access to more complex dishes like macaroni, puddings, custards, and chocolate. Large jobbers and mills invested in specialized, high-quality cooking implements and new ingredients. Doughnuts, pies, cookies, and cakes appeared on camp menus. Like pork and beans, these new foods were easy to eat and digest, yielding calories to workers quickly. As shown in chapter 2, the type of paternalism that characterized the common-law master-servant relationship remained a part of the wage system in the Northern Forest into the twentieth century. Cash wages were infrequent and unpredictable but free food was provided daily.[23]

Who Would Work for Food?

In the harsh winter climate of the Northern Forest, the promise of high-quality food in unlimited quantity pushed farmers and their sons into camps. Into the 1920s, the poorest still grew about half of all their food.[24] For these farmers, the season was the most important determinant of rural diets. Historian Robert Dirks found that "the difference between being relatively affluent and frankly poor from a nutritional standpoint was more palpable from the onset of winter through early spring." Even when there were abundant calories for home consumption, in many parts of the Northern Forest the diet was monotonous.[25] Separated from the growing network of American icehouses and refrigerated railcars, the diet of isolated farmers would not be completely untied from the "great trinity" of bread, bacon, and beans until the 1920s. Day after day of "bean porridge," boiled cornmeal purchased from a store, or potatoes and salt, would have been common.[26] Maine logger John Sharp remembered that a blizzard kept his father from returning home from an outing for four days, so the rest of the family melted snow for water and "lived . . . on just potatoes and salt."[27] Diets were universally lacking in fruits and vegetables, and gathered berries were an important source of nutrition. As downeast Mainer Laura Beam reported, "winter food depended greatly on the woman's skill in canning, drying, preserving, pickling and jelly making."[28]

Observers witnessed the effects of poor nutrition. An *Atlantic Monthly* study published in 1897 on the town of Dickman, a pseudonym for a real farming township "in the interior of one of the New England States" found that the diet was mainly pork "supplemented . . . with hot cream-of-tartar and saleratus biscuits, doughnuts, and pies." Other "meats, vegetables, mushrooms, and fruits" were "either . . . not known or . . . ignored." The author observed, "The men are listless, sullen, stolid. Chronic dyspepsia and other internal disorders are common."[29]

National economic trends also negatively affected the diets of Northern Forest farmers. Though below national averages, rates of tenancy in Northern Forest states increased between 1880 and 1930.[30] Facing new western competition, small mixed farmers were incentivized to abandon subsistence farming to plant cash crops that could then be sold to lumbering operations or on the national market. These farmers mostly grew potatoes, oats, and hay.[31] Fluctuating market prices, increasing debt, and railroad monopolies meant cash profits were rare. To maximize yields, farmers planted over home gardens with cash crops. They spent less time fishing, hunting, and foraging and more time working on their cash crops or for wages.[32] By 1930, only 12 percent of farms in New Hampshire, 10 percent in Maine, and 6 percent in Vermont were considered "self-sustaining."[33] Those isolated farmers who avoided (or were avoided by) the push to commercial agriculture could have procured more of certain micronutrients from gardens and foraging but were not much better off than struggling commercial farmers.[34] While there is evidence that the height of farmers—a general indicator of health—was decreasing between 1830 and 1890, generally farmers and rural workers were healthier than their urban counterparts. This was both a result of and essential for the rigorous manual labor jobs rural people were engaged in. These occupations excluded the unhealthy and demanded extreme levels of work from the healthy.[35]

Forest product operators had an advantage in their attempt to feed rural workers. The logging camp concentrated people in one spot, avoiding the need to distribute food to a geographically disparate rural population. Knowing this, workers' neighbors, relatives, and even strangers made the long hike into camps for the lavish meals. Woods and Mansfield's study recorded sixty-one meals given to "Visitors" during two seasons in Maine. Despite this charity, the bulk of camp food went to workers. Workers took these jobs and stayed at camp for the food. Doing this also took strain off their families' winter food supplies.[36]

Like isolated Northern Forest farmers, the transient and migrant workers who made up a larger part of camp populations after 1890 were drawn to camp by food.[37] From 1800 to 1900, there was a gap between the cost of living and wages for Northeastern farm workers.[38] Nationally, it was not uncommon for wage workers to spend half of their income on food, not counting cooking tools and fuel.[39] Accounts from transient workers consistently highlight the hunger of "the road." For mobile workers traveling between jobs, dinner could be as meager as "a dish of bread and milk." Often, they ate nothing for days. Some traveling wage workers only expected to earn enough to eat, drink, and stay mobile.[40] One recalled he would "gladly do anything that offered . . . bread and board."[41]

Like the hobos who were pulled to sources of food, immigrant workers were drawn to the United States by promises of "reefs of roast beef and apple pie."[42] By 1901, half a million French Canadians had settled in New England. They were the largest foreign labor group employed in the American pulp and paper industry. The period from 1873 to 1896 was one of great economic contraction in Québec.[43] Facing an agricultural crisis, poor banking systems, the rise of commercial agriculture, and interest rates that were generally higher than the United States (as high as 20 percent for some), French-Canadian farmers often found it necessary to work in the American woods as a supplemental or often a primary source of cash.[44]

Canadians who came to the United States ate double the amount they had in Canada. One study calculated they ate 28 percent more calories, 32 percent more protein, and double the amount of fat.[45] The situation was similar for other immigrants. After overviewing statistics on the American diet, Dr. Wilber Olin Atwater, the USDA's chief nutrition scientist, confidently concluded that "the American working man is vouchsafed the priceless gift which is denied to most people of the world, namely . . . the liberal nourishment, which . . . [is] essential to large production, high wages, and the highest physical existence."[46]

Modern Food, Industrial Bodies

There are many contradictions of industrialization. It was labor-saving, but also demanded more work per capita. It also produced an abundance of nutritious food and made no guarantees that workers could access it. Unknowingly, the Woods and Mansfield series of studies on loggers revealed these contradictions, but their studies were actually part of a larger effort by the USDA to solve these problems.[47] The agenda of this and other USDA diet studies was distinctly part of the Progressive movement, designed to reform the diets of rural, immigrant, and working-class Americans to instruct them how to be healthy, frugal, and maximally productive.[48] Giving little heed to cultural preferences, the designer of the agricultural experiment station studies, Wilber Olin Atwater and his colleagues, "gave the highest praise to those who just met the standard [nutritional] requirements at the lowest cost" and commonly blamed the poor for their own malnutrition.[49]

The goal of the "Studies of the Food of Maine Lumbermen" was slightly different than some other studies on immigrant and working-class communities. The reputation of loggers as hard workers and tremendous eaters preceded the study. The first goal was to quantify what many assumed to be the most robust diet in the United States. The second goal was to show that a high level of nutritional efficiency was possible in austere environments when free market processes dictated food distribution and preparation. The third goal was to make some suggestions on how to improve these workers' diets for increased efficiency.[50]

In these USDA studies, the accounts of the amount of calories, carbohydrates, fat, protein, water, "minerals," and nitrogen found in food met current scientific standards but these scientists had little or no understanding of vitamins and essential amino acids.[51] They warned against spending too much money on green vegetables, argued that tomatoes were nutritionally useless, and promoted the use of refined white flour over what we now know to be healthier options. One historian suggested that "if America turned *en masse* to follow [their] advice, rickets, beriberi, scurvy, and other vitamin-deficiency diseases may have reached epidemic proportions [emphasis in the original]."[52]

This lack of attention to the quality of diets makes sense given these scientists' perceptions of human metabolism. As scientists in the nineteenth century began to discover that food contained quantifiable amounts of potential energy, they very quickly began to compare food to wood and coal.

Food was a production input, capital that created more capital. As Cara New Daggett has argued, technocrats like these food scientists "embraced capitalism." It was central to the structure of their professions and their training. Scientists "treated work as energy conversion, and labor governance as the striving for discipline efficiency over those energy flows."[53] The calorie was an easily understandable and objective unit of measurement that could be used to achieve these ends. Calories became a unit in industrial management similar to the second, minute, hour, piece, or dollar.[54] Ideally, workers would benefit from metabolic efficiency too. Echoing Fredrick Winslow Taylor's ideas on the utility of management, Atwater found that the "general principle" when it comes to proper diet is "that liberal food, large production, and higher wages go together."[55] A writer for *The Review of Reviews* interpreted the experiment station studies this way: "The power of a man to work depends upon his nutrition. A well-fed horse can draw a heavy load. With less food he does less work. A well-fed man has strength of muscle and brain, while a poorly nourished man has not."[56]

But humans were actually better than animals, scientists found. In 1887, when Atwater was beginning his work on food, he found that healthy human bodies were better at converting the potential energy of food into work than were horses, oxen, or even "the most efficient steam engines." With a sense of pride, Atwater proclaimed how rigorously the American body could work and consistently reported the highest calorie expenditure that the USDA had found, a number that continued to increase up until the results of "Studies of the Food of Maine Lumbermen."[57] Nutritional sciences and the Progressive assumption of human perfectibility meant that it wasn't certain that machines would replace the work of humans in some manual labor professions. Science conceived of the digestive processes as something apart from human agency, a part of nature that could be improved and adjusted for production.[58]

The "Studies of the Food of Maine Lumbermen" was conducted like many of the other USDA studies. The researchers measured the weight and cost of food before consumption, considering leftovers. The amount of protein, carbohydrates, fat, and calories in all the different foodstuffs consumed were measured with bomb calorimeters and recorded. Weighing the participants before and after gave the scientist information on total caloric excess or deficiencies. With this information, the scientists deduced the composition of what was consumed. Isolated camp workers were ideal for this study because they had no access to outside provisions. The camp was an insulated chamber, ideal for experimentation. From a modern perspective, the studies are flawed in several ways, but not so much so that the historian cannot draw any conclusions from them. They relied on accurate calorie bomb measurements and their understanding of the protein and carbohydrate compositions of food is trustworthy.

Woods and Mansfield conducted five dietary studies, lasting from six to sixteen days, involving forty-seven workers total. "The men were for the most part from 25–30 years old, of good working weight . . . and were an active, rugged set of men," the study declared. They also conducted six digestion experiments that recorded the consumption and excretion of six workers who were "typical of the camp in vigor . . . the amount . . . they ate, and in their capacity for work."[59]

As mentioned above, workers ate on average 6,995 calories a day, more calories than any other workers studied internationally. No other dietary study up to 1954 found numbers as high.[60] Northern American diets were on average between 3,100 and 5,000 calories a day.[61] In "Study 390," the loggers ate a high of 8,198 calories a day. This was around six pounds of food total. The efficiency of free market food distribution and preparation was assumed as fact, once the amount of food that loggers ate was recorded.[62]

The food was as varied as the food of people who lived closer to markets, the study found. According to other sources, variation in food was demanded by the workers, who saw "eating . . . [as] the chief amusement in the lumber camp."[63] Typical dishes were baked beans, biscuits, cold meats, sugar cookies, doughnuts, stewed prunes, mashed potatoes, mashed turnips, boiled fish, regular bread and gingerbread, roast beef, beef smother, cake, and vegetable soup. Between 10.5 and 16.1 percent of the food consumed was vegetable products, foods that were often absent in the winter diets of Northern Foresters. Workers ate on average 337 grams of fat and 812 grams of carbohydrates a day, both of which were easy to digest and energy dense.[64]

The amount of food consumed was reported to be in proportion to the "amount and kind of work performed" and the work was difficult.[65] As late as 1951, one study showed "that the pulpwood cutter used his axe almost half of his working time; the saw log cutter used his about one-third."[66] Axes ranged from 2.5 to 4 pounds.[67] With a typical two-pound axe working at a moderate rate of thirty-five swings a minute, a worker burned about ten calories per minute, at fifty strokes the number rose to 19.3. Bucking logs took 8.6 calories a minute, trimming 8.4, barking 8, and carrying or dragging logs 12.1. Simply walking on hard packed snow is two times as energy intensive as walking on dirt and walking in loose snow with a forty-four-pound load requires 20.2 calories per minute. For comparison, mining coal took 6.1 calories per minute, laying bricks 4, and typing about 1.4.[68] During the winter, energy expenditures increased by as much as 5 percent because of the cold and because of wet and heavy clothes. Workdays were typically from sunup to sundown, six days a week. River drivers and teamsters worked longer.[69] These grueling schedules continued past 1936, when the Fair Labor Standards Act mandated a forty-hour week (this loophole will be discussed in chapter 7). Use of cross-cut saws may have decreased calories-per-minute expenditures, but they increased expected production quotas, forcing workers to do more work in a shorter period.[70]

Work was hardest in pulpwood camps where cutters and haulers were paid by the piece, the commonest form of payment in the United States in the 1910s and 1920s.[71] One of the most important effects of the transition to pulpwood cutting was that long logs, which were cut twelve-foot or longer, began to be cut into four-foot lengths. This change allowed for fewer jams on the river drives. But long logs had necessitated horses, or two workers with peavies, to move all wood. Peavies used the power of leverage to make the job bearable. When cutting pulpwood, one worker with pulp-hooks could move piles of four-foot wood short distances: for example, from a yard into a river or up onto a sled. Piecework on pulp operations drove cutters to skip breaks and work longer hours, sometimes until they were hot, sick, and delirious.[72] One Canadian worker reported, "I nearly killed myself making eight-foot piles [of pulpwood] . . . I found myself crying, it was such strenuous work. Once I was off work for two weeks, I strained myself so badly." Peer pressure was physically oppressive, as a logger named Gerry Fortin remembered: "I went at it just like a maniac, anxious to show I could hold my own with the old-timers. But I soon started to slow up, until I couldn't even move my arms. Each morning it took me longer before I could really get going. Then I became swollen all over." Fortin had to quit.[73] One worker remembered that, when working in negative forty-degree weather, "[I had to] work so hard to keep from freezing to death that [I] pretty near worked myself to death." Turnover was high in piecework camps.[74]

As described in chapter 3, the jobbing system of production along with piecework removes what economists call "the principal agent problem." This is the idea that salaried workers and some wage workers are incentivized to do only just enough work to not get fired. When jobbing, many of the workers, like the boss, had a stake in the profitability of the operation. If they didn't meet the contract terms, nobody was paid. This forced all workers to push their bodies to the maximum physiological limits. To save money, contractors scrimped on modern tools, food, and housing. They got more work from fewer men and animals. Small contractors and their workers endured the poorest conditions. Those that profited often made a "serious sacrifice of their health."[75] Piecework in camps of larger scales similarly made each worker their own businessperson, providing the allusion of flexibility but in reality provoking maximum bodily effort.

River drivers had simpler food because of the constant mobility during the season. During the drive, operators spent 25 percent less money on food. Typical meals included baked beans, biscuits, and some type of cookie or pie. USDA scientists considered driving to be more difficult than winter logging. These workers typically ate four meals a day and an impressive number of calories, but not as many as haulers in the woods.[76] One aspect of the drive required more power and endurance than any other: the incessant winding of the headworks described in the interlude. Despite how torturous the work seemed, the government study insisted "the general health of the men in the studies recorded remained good" and their work environment was "favorable to health."[77]

Observers agreed that rigorous work, long hours, and food wages transformed bodies, for good and for ill. Most loggers were not large. Woods and Mansfield's crew was "of good, working weight, generally about 160 pounds" each, and only the camp blacksmith was over 200 pounds.[78] Some loggers reported gaining weight in camp. A logger named Julius Joel recalled gaining twenty pounds in his first season. Similarly, Maine logger Lincoln Toothaker wrote his wife, "I am just as big as any of [the other workers] or will be soon. Well we have just finished supper and I am unable to write much more for I am full as a tick. . . . I have gained 10 pounds in the last two days."[79]

Most loggers did not gain weight, however. Instead, they would have likely gained lean muscle mass and lost fat in near equal proportion. In Woods and Mansfield's study, workers ate between 152 and 247 grams of protein per day, more than any other worker examined by the USDA, and at minimum 2.5 times the modern recommended daily allowance. One-third to half of this was animal protein with all the amino acids required for muscle growth and increased strength.[80] A meat-heavy diet like this would "increase both the amount of work (through iron, which will prevent anemia) and the ability to do more work (by staving off infection through greater zinc absorption)."[81] The dissection of workers' feces determined they had high nutrient absorption rates—85.3 percent for protein, 97.4 percent for fat, 98 percent for carbohydrates, and 92.6 percent for calories in general. This is a sign of their general health.[82] A lean muscular body would have been a requirement of the job because, as one worker put it, the men "didn't work with brute strength, they worked with skill." Despite the Paul Bunyan myth, observers didn't describe bodily bulk but sinewy or cord-like musculature.[83]

Hard work and long hours could hamper the digestive processes, subverting the system of food wages that was meant to increase output. During intense physical labor, blood flow in the digestive system decreases, causing improper absorption of nutrients and sometimes diarrhea. Overwork can also cause rhabdomyolysis, whereby circulating broken muscle tissue damages the kidneys. Neither of these problems was reported in logging camps, but they also weren't well understood at the time.[84] Sometimes workers were simply too tired to eat. Logger Frederick Burke remembered times "when I come in, I was so tired I couldn't eat supper. I had to go right to bed. And a lot of other men, bigger men and rugged men than me couldn't eat no supper, they'd go to bed."[85] Consecutive seasons of logging degraded bodies. Workers suffered chronic pain and used medication and alcohol to self-medicate, as described in the next chapter. Many young loggers even "in the full pride of strength bore an awkwardness and an angularity of motion." Among loggers, fifty-five was old age and these older workers were noticeably disfigured.[86]

Workers didn't necessarily understand what was happening in their bodies, but they understood the importance of food wages, as the ubiquitous mealtime "silence rule" exemplified. Workers were, as an unwritten rule, mute at meals. Mealtimes could be as short as ten minutes and they had to eat about 2,000 to 3,000 calories.[87] When asked why workers were quiet at the table one former logger simply said, "so they could eat."[88]

Pushing their bodies to maximum physical potential day after day created a deep hunger. It was not "a hunger which comes from a day's shooting, and which whets your appetite to the point of nice discriminations in an epicure's dinner," sociologist and hobo Walter Wyckoff wrote, but one of desperation, "a ravenous hunger which fits you to fight like a beast for your food, and to eat it raw and in brutal haste for gratification." Another worker found that "hunger takes on a different aspect in the woods it becomes the real absolute starvation of the world, a veritable savageness for food, such as no city park or street can give."[89]

Woods and Mansfield understood that food wages were an important part of the implicit negotiations between workers and management. They wrote, "the demand for labor . . . [has] caused competition not only in wages but also in the food and care of the men while in the woods."[90] Without proper meals three or four times a day, worker's contracts, whether formal or informal, were void, and loggers walked. If the appropriate quality and quantity wasn't presented to workers at the frequency they expected, work stopped. Loggers even collectively bargained over the type of tableware.[91]

On a cold January night in 1908, in a camp near Wildwood, ME, dinner was late. In protest, sixty workers walked, some making their way sixty miles to

Rumford Falls. It was a Saturday and workers had just walked two miles from the worksite to camp. They expected dinner promptly at 5:15 p.m. One worker, Henry Conlon, said that the "hungry crowd" was in a "general protest" when food was not presented that minute. The camp boss offered the door to complainers. "The result was that all but a few teamsters and one or two camp men asked for their time right on the spot," the *Rumford Citizen* reported. These types of protests were likely common, but most were resolved in favor of the workers and went unreported.[92]

For workers, getting timely meals in unlimited quantity meant they were getting the most out of their employment relationship. The USDA scientists calculated that it cost the operator an average of $0.256 a day for food per man, but this ignored the cost of freight, tote, preparation, service, and cleaning.[93] If the average cost of transportation and food service is reconstructed, the figure comes to about $0.307 a day per man.[94] Each worker was costing the operator about $0.563 a day in food. A forestry student estimated the real cost for food per worker per day at a similar camp to be $0.55.[95] The workers in the USDA study had wages between $26 and $30 a month, with the average around $28, typical in the industry.[96] Considering actual food costs, loggers in this study made an average of $42.64 a month. This new figure means loggers made $14 less per month than the average factory worker. But the average unskilled workers made $40.84 and average farm workers only $22.11, both spending on average 40–50 percent of their income on food.[97] In 1902, farm work with board paid an average of $16.40 a month nationwide, $19.08 in the entire Northeast, $21.50 in Vermont, and $20.84 in Maine. When food costs are added to loggers' wages, they were making about double what they might have in similar occupations. Taking advantage of the food in logging camps made rural wage workers slightly more secure, and this kept them returning to work season after season.[98]

More important than real wages was what was happening inside workers' bodies. The rigor of the work meant that the nine loggers in the study who worked the entire season, from the start of cutting in December to the end of the drive in May or June, lost from one to nine pounds with an average loss of six pounds. One worker gained a pound. Much of this loss was blamed on the harsh conditions of the drive. Weight loss was an externality, literal pounds of flesh, not kept track of on the books of operators, though operations depended on it.[99]

The Body as Cheap Nature

Trees, snow, and the landscape were all natural obstacles that workers had to overcome to make a wage, but their bodies were also natural obstacles. In the transition into industrial modernity, many workers had to work harder and longer. Human bodies resisted these speedups. Those who could withstand season after season of rigorous work in camps with an adequate supply of food made their bodies into industrial power sources. They came closer to becoming a class of industrial wage workers. Those rural people who logged in small operations or from the farm, with meager or unpredictable rations, remained preindustrial workers with preindustrial bodies, and could not compete, though they might persist in trying. The food wage system, like ice roads, exemplifies how the Northern Forest could industrialize without the widespread implementation of fossil fuels. Food sciences made metabolism into nature and this nature was worked more than it was compensated, a clandestine but essential feature of industrial capitalism.[100]

Partaking in large camp meals was one step that many farmers and sons of farmers made into the industrial world. These workers could and often did move back into agriculture, seasonally or sometimes permanently, the latter finding the work in camp too rigorous. The next chapter shows the steps that some workers took, willingly and unwillingly, to cement themselves into a class of industrial, wage-working lumberjacks.

CHAPTER 6

THE LUMBERJACK PROBLEM

In 1927, twelve-year-old Frederick Burke started working in his family's logging camp in Maine. He had the option of attending school but Burke, like many other young men, was eager to become a lumberjack. He remembered, "[my family] was trying to keep me in school and I was trying to get out . . . [to] work in the woods with my father." As he got older, he worked for jobbers with ten other workers, and in the Great Northern Paper Company camps alongside hundreds. Admittedly he was "quite a boozer." "I was just a young feller" he recalled "but that was the only way I could make a living, going in the woods, as I say I was an alcoholic. I used to go up in the wood with them [older workers] an[d] come down and drink booze with . . . [them]." During these drinking "sprees" in Bangor he bought Right Hand Brand "pure alcohol" 190 proof at $0.50 a pint, half a days' wage.[1] The move back to camp after a spree of many months prompted workers like Burke to get sober, at least until the drive was over and they could have another spree. Workers sometimes attempted to bring alcohol into camps but it was against the rules. To get their fix, some sneaked into the kitchen and drank the alcoholic cooking extracts (figure 6.1).[2]

Years of repeated cycles of work and drinking sprees solidified Burke's position as a lumberjack but harmed his health. Old men who were never able to "keep their stake" could be found in camps doing light chores or mending roads, enfeebled by alcoholism and grueling labor. To sociologist and one-time logger Walter Wyckoff, these workers looked independent on the outside "but confronted with temptations, the difficulties of their inner life, there they had no strength; and lust and passion mastered them. . . . Here, in respect of mastery, they were slaves."[3]

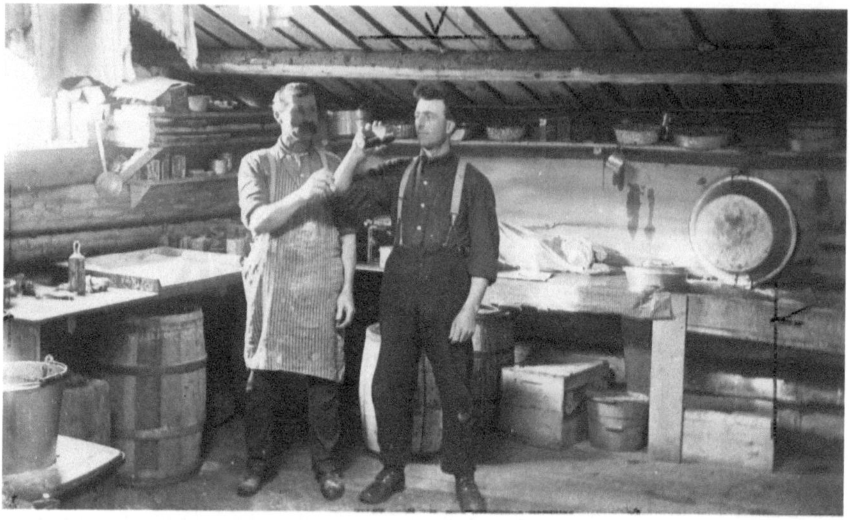

Figure 6.1. "Don't Drink the Vanilla!" (The Isaac Simpson Collection, Collections of Maine Historical Society, item 135680)

In the period from the 1890s to the 1950s, many rural Americans experienced the transition to industrial capitalism working in rural labor camps for logging, construction, mining, and many other industries. In the North, these workers were depicted as prototypical free laborers who worked of their own volition and perhaps even enjoyed their jobs.[4] This chapter shows that despite this depiction, cycles formed in this industry that followed the Northern Forest seasons and these cycles determined the extent to which these workers were free. These cycles also created class, however.[5]

Seasonal cycles were made possible by credit, the lifeblood of camps. Credit flowed from distant financiers, mills, and landowners to contractors and then workers, who used their share to turn "future income into present consumption" in camp stores. Workers' consumption aided production but it was often used to gratify needs and wants.[6] But credit could be dangerous, as contemporaneous labor economist John R. Commons observed: "It is an easy matter to get a working man in debt."[7]

When workers left camp, many participated in spending or drinking sprees. These spectacles of consumption, witnessed by government officials, business owners, and local mill town populations exemplified a blending of two ethoses. The first was an agricultural/artisanal "producerist" ethos typical of the first half of the nineteenth century, when labor was defined by production. The second was a new "consumerist" ethos, where labor's power manifested in spending.[8]

Wage-working loggers who recently emerged from agriculture held both ethoses simultaneously. The result was that workers who lived austerely and worked intensively, then spent lavishly in order to signify their class identity, were left destitute and in poor health, forcing them back to camp. Workers became path dependent, locked into inefficient pathways that were dependent on their previous actions. The concept of path dependency can be applied to national development, businesses, historical trajectories, the evolution of species, the evolution of ecosystems and, as I argue here, to class formation.[9] Social, economic, and ultimately natural forces—both human and nonhuman—led these workers to repeat prior actions. These were path-dependent, seasonal cycles of work, debt, and spending that involved movement from austere spaces of production to spaces of leisure with abundant consumer choice.[10]

Seasonal cycles of work were common in the United States into the 1930s at least. Cowboys, miners, fur traders, ice cutters, railroad workers, seamen, construction and demolition workers, prisoners, soldiers, canners, some factory workers, and farm workers participated in similar cycles.[11] These types of cycles also define the lives of hobos who traveled across the country, but this chapter focuses on regionally mobile workers who specialized in one specific industry.[12] These cycles demonstrate a type of coercion that was detached from working agreements or labor laws but was sometimes aided by them. At its most extreme this path dependency caused physical and psychological dependence on alcohol, or ensnared workers or entire families in debt peonage. Something that Commons or even Wyckoff could not understand, but that Burke did, was the chronic mental and physical pain that industrial work caused, pain which required soothing.[13]

The type of path-dependent cycles described below existed across the country, but it became less important to class formation when the work and environment changed in at least two ways: (1) when and wherever work sites were easily accessible from permanent family living spaces, (2) when and wherever work became detached from seasons. For example, these cycles were less important in the South where logging did not depend on the snow and also at times workers had access to trucks, trailers, and cars and could travel to and from work regularly.[14]

The actions that path-dependent workers took were at odds with their long-term interests but it became a crucial part of class identity. It was one of the most important signs that a rural producer had cut ties with agriculture and moved into industry. When workers fell deep into physical and psychological dependence on the routines of their class, capital could rely on their bodies. They were propelled by forces outside their control, their own nature ensnared them.

Vice and Solidarity

Between the 1850s and 1950s, the Northern Forest experienced a constant drain of young workers. The sons of farmers who had provided the labor for the forest product industry since the Colonial Era were moving to factories or out West. While Yankee farmers maintained high paying positions in camps, operators increasingly drew on immigrants and American migrant workers to do the lowest paying jobs. By 1890, French Canadians had taken American farmers' places in the logging camps, a subject we will turn to in the next chapter.[15] They were joined by people from across the world. In 1913, the *Bangor Daily News* reported that, "Congress of all Nations in Maine's Lumber Camps, Russians, Poles, Finns, Swedes and Lithuanians Have Succeeded the Canadians Who Displaced Native Loggers."[16] Along with immigrants, some of the roughly three million migrant or "hobo" workers, both foreign and domestic, could be found in Northern Forest camps.[17] These workers were "in their prime—men twenty, twenty-five, thirty years old. [Many of whom] had just two thoughts in mind . . . rum and women," one worker recalled.[18]

These new workers challenged community norms. "You can't expect me to be much of a fellow hereafter," native Maine logger Lincoln Toothaker wrote to his wife from the Black Cat camp of western Maine, "being in such a crew of workers as I have since the 15th of Dec. last . . . for they lie, steal, swear and everything bad that I can think of." For Lincoln, the son of a local farmer-logger, the Black Cat camp was an initiation into the culture of industrial wage work. Lincoln observed himself changing, writing, "they are liable to spoil the Person after he had been virtuous all his life."[19]

This new working population created a camp environment that was seen as inappropriate for women. The exception was those very small contractors who were forced by the pressures of the market to employ all family members. Whereas Henry Conklin worked alongside his mother and sisters in the 1850s and 1860s, by the 1890s, "women were unknown."[20] Camp visitor Barbara Bird reported that living in the woods with strange workers was taboo, "a lady . . . did not do such things!"[21] Prospective female workers or visitors might have had reasons to be worried, as one worker made clear:

> H: "I worked one place where they had a woman cook. [the interviewer's thoughts next] (Here, he pauses awhile, deciding what's appropriate to say, so I prodded him by asking, bluntly:)
> B: Did the workers ever pester her while she was there?
> H: No her husband was right there . . . He was the boss.

> H: Yeah, but I got my leg hurt, and I stayed in one day. (B. Uh-huh.) (pause) Jesus Christ, y'know uh, I think I could have screwed her, but I didn't dare to try . . . her husband was in the woods. . . . If I'd said anything to her, and she wasn't . . . willing, why, she could have told him, see?"[22]

Workers admitted that "they wouldn't dare to bring a nice woman in there where there was thirty good men. . . . She'd be so nervous she couldn't sleep nights."[23] Another worker said that a jobber's wife who stayed in camp "didn't want to stay alone and I can't tell the rest on tape."[24]

The lack of women and the isolation allowed for more sexual freedom than in settled farm communities. Migrant work cultures drew workers with aversions to family life and those who were ostracized because of transgressive sexuality. Unattached workers learned homosexual culture from the "schools of crime" fostered in prisons, places many frequented for reasons discussed below.[25]

Camp sleeping arrangements would have invited sexual activity. Two workers often shared a bed. In small operations, relatives or friends slept together, but as operations scaled up this was not always possible.[26] In 1880, seventeen-year-old Edwin H. Eddy visited one of his father's camps and wrote the following about sleeping arrangements:

> On either side [of the bunkhouse] were the beds for the men—One long bed on each side—the workers slept head to the wall feet to aisle—the mattress was made of small spruce or fir boughs covered with one long blanket . . . over the workers who slept like so many clothes pins over the outside blankets sewn together as one . . . The first night when . . . all were required to "turn in" . . . the foreman said, ["]Mr. Eddy I have only one extra bunk in my little place, what about the boy? [meaning Eddy himself]." Then a man spoke and said ["]give him to me Mr. Eddy[,] Joe and I can make room for him between us["]—so off with coat[,] vest[,] trousers and shoes and in I went, workers to the right of me, workers to the left . . . and across the aisle another bed full the same way.[27]

The "spread" or "puff" blanket described in chapter 4 also increased intimacy.

Gerald Averill remembers a situation like Eddy's, yet more nefarious. Right after he finished high school in the 1920s, he and a friend went into a camp and, Averill recalled, "when I saw the greasy, bearded foreigner that I was supposed to turn in with and sensed a peculiar gleam in his eye, we both slipped outside and spent an uneasy night in a . . . sawdust pile."[28] Another worker reported, when he bunked with an older man, "I hated sleeping with him the first night—I weren't only 15. I thought he was old—he was only 52, but he looked awful old to me then."[29]

Historians have found evidence of same-sex relations in Western camps but the evidence is rare in the Northeast. Newspapers report arrests for "sodomy," but as historian George Chauncey found, "most sodomy laws applied equally to male-male, male-female, and human-animal sexual activity."[30] Many loggers simply had no same-sex desires, abstained from sex and later visited prostitutes, dated, or courted when in towns or on the farm. Marriage among native workers often meant a change in occupation, typically into some ownership position on a farm or in the woods or a move into less dangerous and isolating wage work.[31] A minority of workers were resigned to bachelor life and some regularly engaged in same-sex activity.[32] There is some direct evidence of this same-sex activity in camps of the East, such as the following anecdote from a worker in Ontario: "I slept with a quiet, decent fellow who was going to get married in the spring. Unfortunately, I guess in anticipation of the event, he lost control of himself during one night. Imagine! I woke up with this fellow busy giving me the works. Not my ring (my ring is intact to this day in spite of my many misadventures) but he was massaging both of us."[33]

Camp Consumption

The bachelor culture that emerged with industrialization was distinct from mainstream Northern Forest culture in many ways. Unlike the farmer-loggers, these bachelor workers did not always have a desire to save and invest, nor were these always options. Some gave up on the prospect of ownership and their financial time horizon shortened. Items of immediate pleasure became more important than they might have been for farmer-loggers. Loggers were sometimes depicted as individualists who could produce with few modern amenities and there was some truth to this. Skilled woodsmen could craft many tools and structures from forest material alone. When consumer goods became accessible in the decades around the turn of the century, however, these workers did not hesitate to spend.

As explained in chapters 2 and 3, systems of remuneration and consumption were different in camps than in urban spaces. Wage relations were rooted in older agrarian practices where accounts were informal and there was little separation between the finances of business and personal life.[34] Farmers, loggers, and their families depended on credit that flowed and seized-up with the seasons. Records of the Turner Falls Lumber Company, a mill in Massachusetts that funded operations all along the northern part of the Connecticut River, show that liberal amounts of credit were extended in the late summer and in the fall when camps were constructed, during the hauling season (January and February), and in preparation for the log drive in the spring.[35] Unfortunately, this was also when interest rates in the Northeast tended to be highest. Based on numbers from New York City between 1890 and 1908, which were representative of New England, interest rates on short-term loans were lowest in the middle of July and August, just over 2 percent. They increased to between 4 and 7 percent between the middle of October and early January.[36] Debts, including wages owed to workers, were paid off in March when the log haul ended, as well as in July and August when the log drive ended. This latter period was the traditional season of debt-settling in the rural United States. For farmer-loggers, November and December was also a time to pay debts after selling crops.[37]

Historian Louis Hyman and other scholars of American finance have argued that preindustrial systems of credit quickly gave way to industrial wage relations circa 1900. In the urban industrial United States, it was presumed that cash flowed readily, and credit via open account systems, which had been common in the preindustrial era, became unnecessary. Payment in the urban corporate economy no longer depended on the seasons but instead "workers got paid every two weeks like clockwork."[38] In the hinterland, industrialism developed differently. Old agrarian and new industrial financial regimes existed side by side into the 1950s. Credit gave rural owner/operators and wage workers what they needed for production and what they wanted for themselves or their families. Laborers could buy tobacco with value they attained from cutting logs that were still dozens of miles from a mill, and currency might never exchange hands.

In the isolation of the forest, it often made little sense for workers to hold cash. Numbers next to names in a book kept by a trustworthy boss was a safer system. Open accounts prevented workers from betting away wages in camps where gambling was one of the few entertainments. Good operators kept careful track of the invisible flow of credit from financier to operator to worker, and back to operator through camp store purchases, in systems that were remarkably like the open accounts of early nineteenth-century shopkeepers.[39]

Most camps kept a store, van, or "wangan" where yet-to-be-realized wages could be spent. Shortened from the Montagnais Indian word *atawangan*, *wangan* was a regional term originally used to describe certain riverboats, or containers on riverboats, that were used to store goods. Like many aspects of logging camp culture, the word was probably borrowed from the language of French-Canadian fur traders. Depending on the size of the operation, the wangan could be a locked box with $100 worth of goods or a full room with $6,000 worth of items.[40] In some camps, workers could order special items at the camp office to be brought in on the tote road with the next team. Any goods ordered or bought by workers during the winter were, according to one worker, "charged up to you . . . and . . . settled in the spring." Few workers came into camp with money but almost all had access to credit at the wangan.[41]

Merchants, traders, and farmers walked from camp to camp with trinkets on their backs or on sleighs, attempting to tap into the value created in camp. Workers could "ask for their time" and get cash, if any was on hand, to pay traders. Some provided services like barbering, photography, and tailoring. Toothaker wrote to his wife from camp, reporting that a farmer named H. A. Furbish "got $175.00 of trade" in his camp one season. One logging family described them as "jewelry sales workers that'd come in [with] . . . watches and rings and stuff." Some reported that the goods were always cheap and broke readily, which is what happened to a pendant that Lincoln Toothaker bought from a "cutthroat peddler." Sometimes the workers got the better of the peddlers, as Toothaker reported: "German Peddlers lost $28 worth of clothing here and sold $179.41 so I guess their profit was small for their board bill was $10. And when old Murphy was here he lost about $25 worth of Goods and the man I bought the watch off lost two or three dozen Pipes some worth $1.00 or more."[42]

Buying wangan or a merchant's cheap goods was an important way workers transitioned from the agricultural world, where many goods were produced at home or nearby, into industrial capitalism, where goods were bought and often mass-produced by strangers far from home.[43] The items that workers bought fell into two categories: wearables and consumables. Some items, like clothes, boots, and painkillers, were investments in production. Other goods, like tobacco and candy, were for immediate gratification.

Many groups of workers came into the camp looking very different from one another. Heterogeneous dress was alluded to in the logging song "The Hoboes of Maine": "[workers will] come by the hundreds, those hardy young bloods, / All neatly attired in their own native goods."[44] Homemade clothes were common in the Northern Forest into the 1900s.[45] In Aroostook and Madawaska, ME, domestic cloth production rose in the second half of the nineteenth century.[46] By the twentieth century, native workers were buying more factory-made clothes produced specifically for outdoor work and it was typically only immigrant workers who had homespun clothes. Workers from Prince Edward Island "were noted for the fact that they were always clad in pure-white wool—underwear, mittens, caps—spun and knitted by their mothers."[47] The same was true of many French Canadians. Immigrants were teased and ostracized for their homespun clothing, incentivizing them to buy from the wangan.[48]

Workers needed the right kind of factory-made clothes to fit in. For example, when jobbers and companies looked to urban areas for unskilled labor after the pulp boom, they often hired people who had "never seen a log" and "never been in water." In New England these workers were called "Boston men" and they would come to camp "with . . . dress clothes on." They had "little thin coats and dress shoes" one worker recalled, "they'd freeze their damn feet." Boston men brought suitcases rather than bindles (bundles of items tied to the end of a stick) and, as one worker recalled, a "suitcase didn't make a good pillow."[49]

Besides being a fashion faux pas, homespun and urban clothes wore out. Even high-quality wangan goods might not last the season. Workers often had to buy new clothes on credit after a few weeks and typically a whole new set at the end of the season. In 1895, in northern New York, the J. B. Mertens & Co. clothing establishment had to bring a sleigh full of clothes because "the whole woods was all ragged out."[50] Maine logger Lee Roberts remembers that when driving a team wearing good leather gloves "th' friction o' the' reins—one leather against the other- will wear leather mittens out terrible fast—in about ten days." One winter after his gloves wore out, Roberts took a fresh pair off the corpse of a Boston man killed on the job. Some workers wore three or four pairs of gloves at a time and layered wool mittens inside leather ones, allowing them to work in temperatures as low as forty degrees below zero.[51] Great Northern Paper Company's South Branch pulp camps employed approximately 160 workers in three separate camps and these workers bought on average ten pairs of gloves in one season in the 1930s.[52]

Most camps had plenty of heavy Mackinaw jackets for sale, a garment that would come to define the lumberjack class. These were made from "a heavy, napped and felted woolen cloth," typically in a plaid pattern, and "double-breasted . . . short and often belted." One worker remembered that in a Mackinaw "you could work all day in the rain. You wouldn't wet through." It was one of the most expensive items in the wangan.[53] The pants available at the wangan were quality but expensive. One worker remembered, "it take [sic] you a week's work there, working for twenty-eight dollars a month . . . to earn a pair . . . of heavy pants." For workers on the sprinkler wagon or the river, slicker coats or greased leather overcoats were available, later replaced by rubber rain jackets that "crack[ed] . . . [and] leak[ed] under the arms" and were replaced often.[54]

Workers bought three types of footwear. The first was moccasins or shoepacks.[55] One worker said the first thing he remembered about the "lumberjacks [was that] a lot of them wore high moccasins." These were rawhide leathers with layers of wool socks underneath. Larrigans were a higher oiled moccasin that were waterproof, allowing workers to "stand right out on the ice in the spring . . . [and the leather remained] just as dry as though it had been besides the stove."[56] Second were rubber work boots for working in mud or in the river. Third were caulk (sometimes spelled cork) boots named for the metal caulks embedded in the sole, giving purchase on wet logs. Like many other clothing items, footwear wore out quickly. New workers who left leather boots, gloves, and shoepacks too close to the fire at night found their shoes and clothes cracked and ruined by the morning.[57]

Workers who purchased items from the wangan would have started to look alike over the course of a season. During his travels among wage workers, Princeton sociologist Walter Wyckoff learned to identify the experienced laborers by "their superiority in intelligence, accompanied by a certain indefinable superiority in dress" while the new workers were "noticeably heterogeneous." Those with full suits of wangan clothes had invested in their trade. They were clearly lumberjacks, distinct from farmers, new immigrants, or Boston men.[58]

Proper clothes were necessary, but for many the most desirable wangan items were consumables that helped workers cope with pain and monotony. In the eighteenth and early nineteenth century, alcohol was a cure-all that alleviated both pain and boredom. By the 1850s, most camps were dry, a rule that reflected cultural and political attitudes toward alcohol and the increased speed of production, which disallowed drunkenness.[59] Small camps and family operations sometimes deviated from the norm and allowed, or at least ignored, alcohol use in camp. In dry camps, traditional spirits were replaced by patent medicines and snake oils, many of which contained alcohol. In the South Branch camps, about 3 percent of sold goods were medicines.[60]

Tobacco was the "ultimate article of consumption" in the Northern Forest.[61] The South Branch sold $2,850.90 in tobacco and smoking paraphernalia in a season. Each worker bought on average $17.79 or nineteen pounds of tobacco, over a half a month's wages for many (figure 6.2). This seems like a lot but some of this was wet chewing tobacco. Also, 160.2 was the average number of workers in camp, though sometimes there were as many as 223 workers.[62] Although workers had a voracious tobacco appetite, it had to be a certain type. Many French-Canadian workers grew tobacco on their farms and brought it to camp. Yankee workers assumed that the homegrown leaf lacked quality and called it "Canadian shag." Even hand-rolled cigarettes were scorned. The preferable tobacco was packaged and name branded.[63] Like name brand tobacco, candy made with refined sugar and chocolate was a special treat for those coming

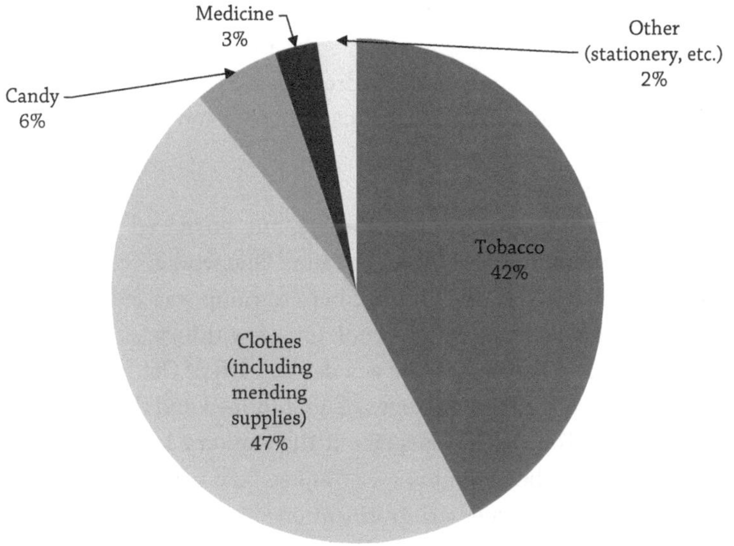

Figure 6.2. Wangan goods per worker (average), South Branch Camps, Maine, 1938 (Cecil Max Hilton, *Rough Pulpwood Operating in Northwestern Maine, 1935–1940* [Orono: University of Maine Press, 1942], 121–22)

from abroad or forest farms. In those places, molasses, brown sugar, maple sugar, or honey were staple sweeteners. At the South Branch pulp camps, workers consumed 1,652 pounds of candy a season, or about 10.3 pounds per worker.[64]

Tobacco and candy provided pleasure and offered temporary release from the boredom, repetition, and pain associated with industrial work. Remote towns in New England already suffered from problems of boredom and social isolation.[65] Loggers were moved even further away from social life, and isolation caused psychic distress. As with clothes, the purchase of brand name tobacco and mass-produced candy signified a movement away from subsistence consumption distinguishing the class of wage-working lumberjacks from farmer-loggers.[66]

The South Branch operators sold $6,746.28 worth of wangan goods in a season, or about $42.11 per man. That is considerably more than a month's wages for almost every worker, and almost two months' wages for the low-paid workers and children. Most operators "did not try to make a lot [of profit] from their wangan but they did not intend to lose anything" either, according to one worker. Goods were more expensive in camp than in settled areas because they were toted long distances over rough terrain. Prices were about

10 to 15 percent above normal market value. Some operators hoped to make enough money to pay the wangan clerk. Some camps charged as much as one third above market price and some railroad camps charged double or triple market price, much more than the cost of transport and clearly exploitative.[67]

Trapped in the Woods

Buying on credit benefited most workers but ensnared others. Lincoln Toothaker kept accounts for his father's camp. One worker "called for a bill of his time" on January 31st and "his bill here to camp was $54.10[,] his work came to $66.89 and after paying the cook for a few things [*sic*] he had of liver he had $8.75 left and he come in the woods the 14th of Oct.[.] He went out to the Hotel and called for ham and eggs. Going to feed and dress well if he did not lay up a cent." Toothaker's surprise at the workers' lack of thrift demonstrates the difference between his own Yankee farming background and the wage laborer's value of immediate gratification.[68]

Labor agents, who connected workers with jobs, added to workers' debt. Some agents lied to nonlocal workers telling them "all kinds of things" to entice them. They lied about camp conditions, distance from town, wages, or job types. According to state officials who investigated these agents some workers were contractually obligated to do work for which "they were entirely unfit" or which was "physically impossible" for them to do.[69] When a worker took the job, the agent fee could be $15, alongside debt for transport, food, and winter clothes. Workers who used an agent could start work with $30–$35 of debt. When they realized the truth about work conditions, they were forced to work a month or more to break even. Wages were withheld during nonproductive days even though time in camp was hardly time off. Workers took $40 or $50 worth of goods, planning to work all season, but might be waylaid by injury, illness, or bad weather. Rarely, a jobber or company might also charge a ten-cent fee per day for tools, or for lost or broken tools, adding further to debt.[70]

Workers were not exclusively victims of credit. When labor was scarce, jobbers were willing to advance considerable money to uncreditworthy workers. Some workers "jumped" camp without paying, though this debt did not typically exceed $10 or $20. The same worker might repeat the act at other camps.

Jumping camp was likely rarer than operators defaulting, underpaying, or overcharging workers for wangan goods, but operators exercised political leverage. In 1907, the Maine legislature enacted a statute that allowed authorities to arrest forest product workers and river drivers with unpaid debt. Guilty workers faced thirty days of jail or a $10 fine. Rural justices did not keep good records and some constables had their pay tied to the number of arrests they made. In Maine, judges either did not understand or willingly ignored the "intent to defraud" provision of the law and punished all debtors, even if workers had reasons for leaving camp, for example, if the labor agent lied. The threat of punishment pressured indebted workers to continue work and few cases made it to the courts. When workers were arrested under this provision, "in nine cases out of ten the workers are made to go back to work," according to one labor agent. Labor advocate John Clifton Elder found that some government officials in Maine were bribed by large forest products interests to persuade these officials to send guilty workers back to camp to work off their debt and fine. Elder testified that this type of labor abuse was common in most of the rural US and thought that "the Labor Laws of Maine . . . make virtual slaves of the laboring classes." The law was decried by some government officials and reform groups like the Maine Federation of Women's Clubs as "class legislation" and they appealed for its removal. The law was repealed in 1917 but only after hundreds of workers had been convicted.[71]

Even when workers were not indebted, the seasonality of forest product production and the varying scale of operations meant cash payments were irregular and infrequent. The smallest camps had very informal remuneration systems, as one worker recalled: "They didn't have any regular pay days you know. You, you happened to want a little money, why . . . you'd go to the timekeeper and get it and . . . when they got done in the spring or when they got done on the drive why they'd just pay them off the whole works."[72] There was a chance that workers might not get paid at all. Working in the woods was "just the same as working on the farm," one worker remembered, "you work there all summer when they dug their potatoes an[d] sold 'em if there was enough left besides the fertilizer bill they paid ya"; if not, the worker was owed money.[73] One operation in Somerset County, ME, in 1908 had an explicit rule posted on the door of the bosses' camp: "No wages paid until time of quitting, credit being given at the wanigan box."[74] Some camps had a system where workers had to collect compensation when they earned a certain dollar amount or else possibly lose wages. Others practiced "switching," which meant they paid by the piece on a bad chance, with less wood, and by the hour on a good chance with more wood.[75] Logging workers in Maine were exempted from an 1887 law that guaranteed payment biweekly. Industry spokesmen argued it was impossible to get the cash into the woods that frequently. There was an attempt to amend the law in 1907 so that it would cover "unincorporated firms or single proprietorships" but the attempt failed.[76]

If workers were not compensated correctly, few had the ability or time to seek legal recourse, particularly if the amount was small. Felix Albert was a

French-Canadian immigrant hired to cut wood near Nashua, NH, at the end of the nineteenth century. After working hard, he "got overheated and became sick" and the woodlot owner came to measure his stack and discounted him one cord for no discernible reason. When the situation was reversed years later, and Albert had another man working for him, Albert was sued for back wages and argued that his worker was a crook. Because profits and payment were never assured, buying many items on credit from the wangan early in the season was sometimes the only way to be sure a worker would get something for their work. Wage relations did not necessarily improve over time but became more reliable in larger operations that could not escape regulation. Here, workers were paid regularly, typically by the month.[77] As late as 1917, however, there were reports in Maine of workers getting paid only once a season. In 1949, there were again debates in the Maine senate over whether loggers should legally be paid biweekly, but loggers again got no legal reprieve.[78]

Experienced workers might think they could get the full value of their labor if they went out on their own and became contractors, but Canadian sociologist Edmund Bradwin found this was rarely the case. Small contractors formed close relationships with local merchants, mills, or landowners to ensure they had a buyer for their forest products, could be resupplied, and could obtain credit with little warning. In the late nineteenth century, a popular way to pay off debt was through wood products. These merchants operated like banks, the reserve capital being forest products.[79] Asa Flagg remembered cutting pulp wood for a jobber where all pay was done through the local supply depot. "If [the boss] got done with a man" Flagg said "[he'd] give them an order . . . [at] R. D. Gardner and Sons . . . for the pay, and they'd go out there and Gardner would pay just, well it seems as though it was a bank really."[80] One worker remembers that when his family was cutting for the Ray Fraser Lumber Company, "in the spring . . . [they'd]—take us down to the—lumber store where they furnished everything. And get summer supply, and buy us some clothes, and maybe a box of .22 cartridges or something for . . . winter's work."[81]

Most often these indebted contractors were obliged to live close to their creditor. Felix Albert moved between the ownership and wage-working classes, a common situation in the Northern Forest. He would take on debt with a local merchant, forcing him to remain in the area until he paid off the debt. Albert's mobility and his ability to see his family were limited while in debt but this was business as usual.[82] Small owner-operators and farmer-loggers sometimes got caught up in a system of peonage similar to systems that entrapped Southern sharecroppers. In fact, a 1911 federal report found "there has probably existed in Maine the most complete system of peonage in the entire country."[83]

Northern Forest contracting, like sharecropping and urban tenement sweating, were all common, decentralized modes of industrial production that had a façade of independent production but could become hierarchical, exploitative, and ensnaring. These production regimes were particularly pernicious when they trapped entire families. French-Canadian families, new to the United States and unfamiliar with American customs and language, were particularly vulnerable to debt peonage.

Besides the contracting system, debt, and labor laws, there were other more direct types of coercion. Pressuring workers by physical force was supposed to be a thing of the past in the postbellum North, but this was not so in the isolation of the Northern Forest, where labor norms straddled the line between familial/agricultural and legal/industrial. As legal historian William E. Forbath found, corporal punishments remained legal into the twentieth century. If a camp boss was not literally the father of workers in camp, he assumed a paternal position. Contractors had considerable personal investments in their operation and could be the most draconian bosses.[84]

It was the boss's job to bring "order out of chaos, by the sheer force of indomitable energy." Bedtime, mealtime, and worktime were strictly enforced. Workers recalled that a boss would "put you to bed" if you chose not to go. A worker remembers the boss having a "fight with one man and knocked this fellow out and beat him up and he quit."[85] They were "hard[est] on the foreign-born" and inexperienced, weeding out the unfit. Wyckoff was admittedly "green" when he started logging, and he was threatened by his boss Fitz-Adams with an axe. Wyckoff was perplexed when he overheard that the boss wanted to kill him rather than fire him.[86] The mental and physical abuses from bosses added to the pain of the logging season.

Apart from bullying bosses, most coercion was not initiated by a bad actor. "It is the system not the man that is at fault," Bradwin found, "the individual contractors, carefree and well-met . . . have not personally the desire to coerce" nor be coerced. Instead it was interest rates, debt, the weather, and the seasons that propelled them to skimp, overcharge, become abusive, or miss payroll. Changes in the contracting system were slow, and coercive debt continued to be a problem. New logging technology that came about in the 1950s was a great boon for some independent contractors. Real income rose for them from 1950 to 1970, but debt became a problem again thereafter.[87]

The Spectacle of the Spree

After spending a portion of wages at the camp wangan, many workers continued to work on the log drive, the most dangerous and demanding part of the logging labor process. The drive brought workers from the hinterland to towns and cities, closer to the final act of consumption of the season, the spending spree. As the interlude explained, the river drive had developed to the point where most wood was moved by "union" or "company" drivers like the Penobscot Log Driving Company or the Connecticut Valley Lumber Company. Unlike loggers, most drivers worked for companies rather than contractors. Drivers were less likely bound to owners by family ties. Because of the danger and strenuousness of the job, workers were typically younger than loggers in the woods, who were themselves typically in their twenties and thirties. The lifestyle was only possible for young workers who could "take more punishment than most men," as sociologist Norman Hayner found.[88] Piece rate pay was not possible on the drive; all workers were paid by the day. Though they could also be loggers in the winter, drivers who worked the entire drive worked during summer, the time when their labor was needed most, and worth the most, on farms. They consciously chose this industrial work over farm work and became a class of industrial wage workers.

Drivers had strong solidarity, a unique identity and reputation. Popular historian Stewart H. Holbrook reported that, growing up in Vermont and New Hampshire, "few of us boys wanted to be soldiers or cowboys or policemen. To be rivermen and go down with the drive was the stated or secret ambition of most of us . . . What we wanted . . . was a cant dog, a pair of new calked boots, and a fast-moving stream of logs." Northern Forest communities saw drives as spectacles of work and nature. In 1947, on the Moose River in northern New York, a dam broke and scores of drivers were called in to control the chaos. Cars crowded a bridge over the river to watch the action. Some spectators drove over two hours to see the event. "The Moose River was a gala performance," an observer reported.[89]

Part of the performance of the drive was the costume. Stewart Edward White, fiction writer and former lumberjack, described the dress well in his short story *The Riverman*: "Nearly all were smoking pipes. Every age was represented in this group, but young workers predominated. All wore woolen trousers stuffed into leather boots reaching just to the knee. These boots were armed on the soles with rows of formidable sharp spikes or caulks, a half and sometimes even three quarters of an inch in length. The tight driver's shoe and 'stagged' trousers had not then come into use. From the waist down these workers were all alike, as though in a uniform, the outward symbol of their calling."[90] Feathered felt hats were also typical.[91]

Drivers worked sixteen or eighteen hours a day at a job that was as difficult on their clothes as it was on their bodies. Maine writer Fannie Eckstorm made special note of the clothes of drivers she witnessed in the 1880s and 1890s. They were, she wrote, "originally a vivid scarlet" but had been "reduced by rains and perspiration to whitish red, once whole perhaps, but now pinned together with huge horse safety-pins and variously adorned with patches of old mittens." Another driver had "neither heels nor toes to the socks he had on." Eckstorm recalled one man, whose wardrobe was still intact, saying "I don't look quite so all fallin' to pieces; but the wangan bills on this drive's goin' to be somethin' hijjus [hideous]."[92]

Caulk boots were the most important part of the river driver's apparel. They were also one of the most expensive, costing around $37 a pair, more than a month's pay for many.[93] They were one of the few logging tools with no use on the farm or in other industries. They signaled a commitment to wage work. These boots were also renowned because of the practice of poxing, whereby drivers stomped and raked foes with the metal caulks, leaving marks resembling scars left by smallpox. Local histories and newspapers from all over the Northern Forest recorded instances of poxing. In one example, a group of eighteen Polish workers fought two French Canadians in Big Moose station in the Adirondacks: "[The] sheer weight of numbers [of the Poles], got the big Canadians down and out. Then, lumberjack style, they put the boots to him. Raking his head and body with sweeping kicks so that the caulks on the boots would slash and rip. . . . The little Frenchman was taken to the doctors and lost his eye as a result of the fight. The big Frenchman, although badly beaten, had nothing seriously wrong with him. . . . His hair and part of his scalp had been removed by the calked boots of the Poles."[94]

Historian Eliot Gorn called poxing a part of the "rough-and-tumbler's art" that "grew out of a pattern of living" characterized by "drinking, treating friends, impulsive pleasure seeking, heroic labor, and vicious fighting." Poxing was likely rare but there are trustworthy reports. Poxing and caulked boots defined lumberjacks and river drivers in the minds of thousands who heard these romantic stories.[95]

Poxing often took place in mill towns between March and August, when river drives ended, logs were sawn into lumber or made into paper, and the entire season's wages were often distributed. The geographic path workers took in a year and the way they spent their wages would either further entrench them in the professional class of lumberjacks, or allow them to be absorbed back into the realm of mixed husbandry.

A contractor or foreman's core crew might go into camp again as early as July or August. One worker remembers that if you were committed, you "didn't come out unless you had some real urgent reason to" and another added that "single workers never hardly ever come out of the woods."[96] Workers who spent nearly a full year in the camp were clearly industrial wage workers, the rare few who might identify as loggers, lumbermen, or lumberjacks on censuses.[97]

Others faced a choice. They could continue to work for wages in town or in the hinterland, or return to their family farm. Northeastern farmers had low rates of seasonal unemployment compared to other workers.[98] They avoided idleness to add value to their property. As figure 6.3 shows, mills likely absorbed some workers leaving the camps and drives, but not all of them. In 1905, around the height of lumber production, logging camps in the Northern Forest states employed a maximum of 20,871 workers and the number sank to an annual low of 3,485 in July. That was a total of 17,386 idle workers coming from the camps. Employment in the mills never dropped below 12,455 workers and only gained an additional 10,145 workers in the busy season of May. Assuming that the mills hired only idle loggers for the busy season, and this was likely not the case, there was a surplus of workers from the camps, at least 7,000, who were not in the mills. Seasonal demand for work in the farm and forest developed countercyclically, as the seasons bent human economic predispositions to its whims. Farming labor demands rose sharply starting in mid-April, reaching an apex in June, when farmers needed help preparing "seed beds, sowing spring small grains," and planting corn where that was possible. Farm labor demands dropped to annual lows from November to April as cold sapped life from fields. Logger Frank Carey remembered in an interview that for him, "that's the way it used to be. . . . In the woods in the winter and, and home it was, work in the sawmill, [or] around the farm." In Eastern Canada, sociologist Edmund Bradwin found that there were "whole villages the families of which, French and English speaking, have grown up in a like circle of activities—in winter camps, the spring drives, and, then, the sawmills for the summer."[99]

As the population in the Northeast increased, patrimony was not always available for sons, and taking up wage work allowed aspiring farmers to buy a plot of land.[100] It was Lincoln Toothaker's plan to make enough in the woods to "get a cozy little home" and farm for his wife and daughter. Maine logger Asa Flagg remembers that after his first winter in the woods in 1914 he was able to buy part of "a junk of land. . . . My father owned half of it, I bought the other half, and we cut the hay on it for years." Toothaker, Flagg, and thousands of others remained farmer-loggers, petit-bourgeois. They "had little to do with the hell-raising gentry" of real lumberjacks, Gerald Averill wrote.[101]

After the camp broke up or the river drive ended, workers had anywhere from $50 to $2,000, while jobbers and foremen might have even more. Much of this money would be spent in "regular blowout[s]" that lasted a month or

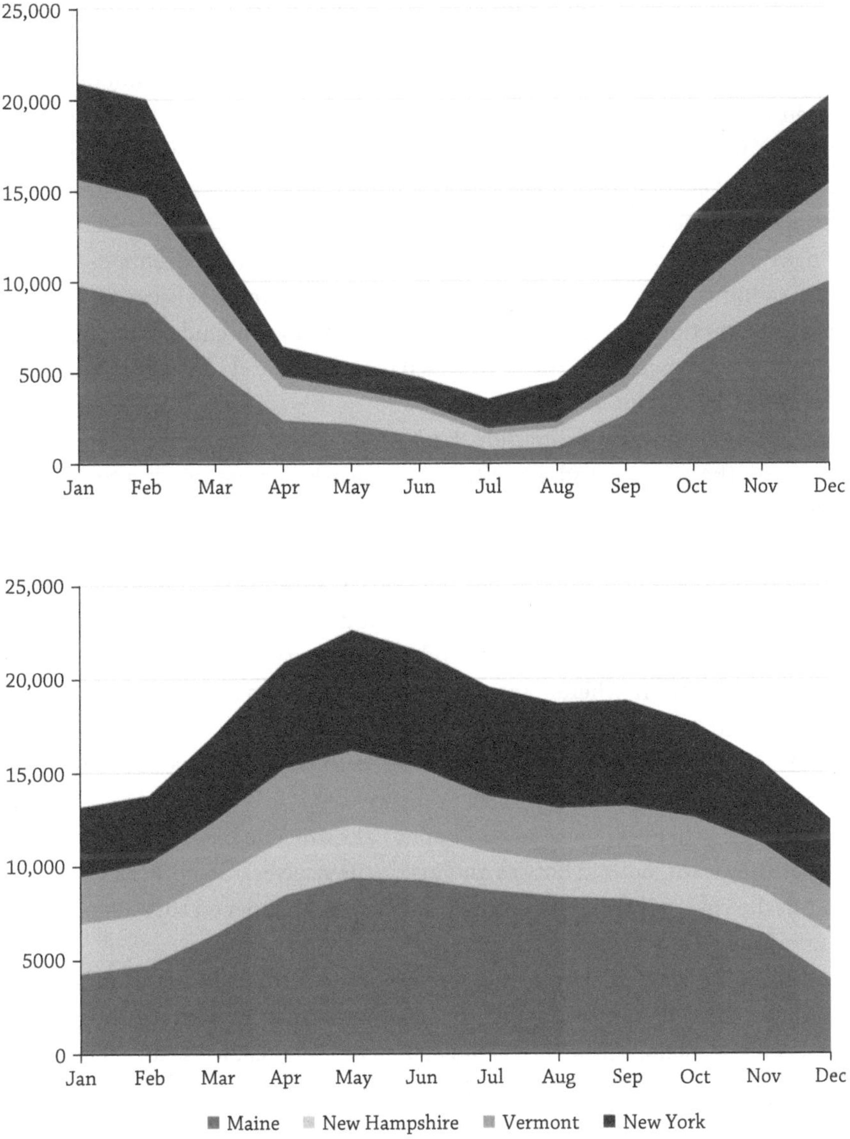

Figure 6.3. Logging camp workers by month (*top*) and lumber mill workers by month (*bottom*), statewide, 1905 (William M. Steuart, Jasper E. Whelchel, and Henry Gannett, *Census of Manufactures: 1905, Lumber and Timber Products* [Washington, DC: Government Printing Office, 1907], 51–53)

more.[102] Sprees were iterations of the celebrations that accompanied bringing goods to market in the rural United States. Before 1840, it was common for workers to drink through the working day. Alcohol consumption increased when the work was done and when people came together for harvests, barn raisings, fishing, political events, musters, different types of working "bees," and other social events. Similar celebrations accompanied the end of a fur-trading voyage in French-Canadian and American frontier cultures. These "communal binges" helped to create rural producer identities. All these events involved a move from isolation, austerity, and intense production to leisure, recreation, and consumption. The spree was a ritual that combined preindustrial traditions of communal binges with the heightened pace, rigor, and consumerist ethos of the industrial revolution.[103]

By 1900, many American industries were freeing themselves from dependence on the seasons and, simultaneously, workers were moving to cities to live. For urban corporate workers, pay came weekly or biweekly as opposed to once or twice a year when commodities were sold. Regular paydays were still times of celebration but they were not as intense as communal binges. In order to end the spree, reformers, the state, and workers' aid groups encouraged workers to start families and buy property. The geography of forest product production, wherein trees receded further from settled areas annually, thwarted attempts at reform.[104]

As these isolated camps were dry, workers thirsted for alcohol to ease their aching bodies. Emporium Lumber Company in New York reported "that our woodsmen, whenever they go to Tupper Lake are able to return with all the liquor they want, both in bottles and inside themselves." Some workers passed out in the cold, got frostbite, or died. This is what happened to "a man named Butler" near Tupper Lake after a spree.[105]

The spree was, of course, not mandatory. Averill used the example of a worker named Jamie McGaskill, a pseudonym, to demonstrate the choices that some workers, perhaps even himself, made. McGaskill was an experienced logger and was prone to drink his wages away. After the 1915 season, he promised himself "there would be no drinking, foregathering with filthy worn out drabs . . . no fighting." Instead, he would invest in new logging gear, have a good dinner, and finally "do the thing he had . . . yearned [to do] for years. He would go home . . . to the rock mountain farm . . . and give the old man four hundred dollars to make up for his lost services." Yet McGaskill was tempted to drink and compelled to spend the $1,000 he saved.[106]

Similar stories were repeated in fiction and nonfiction accounts of logging. Bradwin wrote "all workers in camp have ideas, and dream dreams," and he recounted the story of a worker named Scotty who dreamt of "a snug farm for himself" though was never able to "keep what he had made" in camp.[107] Some workers devised self-docked payment systems to prevent this. Lumberjack Dan Murray was only given his wages "a few dollars at a time so that he wouldn't spend it all drinking or through generosity." To prohibit the reckless spending so common among casual workers, the Civilian Conservation Corps (1933–1942) program required workers send $22 of their $30 monthly wage to a dependent.[108]

Sprees could happen at different times. Sociologist Norman Hayner found that there were "short-stakers" who would take sprees often. Others took sprees on holidays or during seasonal breaks in the work.[109] In 1916, during the Christmas break between cutting and hauling, workers in the Dead River region of Maine celebrated with a large dinner and a dance. A forestry student sent to study the camp witnessed workers "busily engaged at the bar, drinking toast to their freedom" and also saw a "free-for-all fight" among the men, "such as you often read about in novels."[110] The *Turner Falls Reporter*, a newspaper from the Massachusetts town where the Connecticut River drive ended, wrote about several fights and one battle between rivermen and the local baseball club. A driver named Dennis Haggerty, after attempting to bowl in a bowling alley with a lit kerosene lamp, took off his shirt and walked down the street offering to "fight the whole town individually or collectively." Besides drinking and fighting, workers on the spree purchased clothes, watches, and other consumer goods. Stories circulated about workers who would buy automobiles, wreck, and abandon them.[111]

Mill towns and cities perpetuated the spree. Small farm villages in the Northern Forest offered few of the financial and consumer options of mill towns. One young worker remembered getting out of camp with $20 but not being able to find a place to break the bill. Mill towns and cities presented workers with modern institutions, consumer choice, and even a degree of decadence in contrast to the austerity of the forest camp and family farm.[112]

Bars, hotels, and brothels established methods to extract the value that flowed down river with the seasonal swell. Sex workers provided services that allowed the bachelor subculture to continue. It was generally accepted in the Northern Forest that when "men . . . are deprived during months at a stretch of the companionship of women, of home ties, and all that elevates life in a man," they will pay for sex, as Bradwin observed.[113] Madam Fan Jones allegedly had the chimney of her brothel, "the Blue House," in Bangor painted bright blue so workers could easily find it. Outside of sex work, merchants tried different types of gimmicks to get workers to their stores. One observer remembered that in Old Town, ME, the first thing the workers would do was make "for Water Street . . . but they had to get by some people, like 'Humpy' Mishou, first . . . [who was] trying to drag them in to sell them suits of clothes."[114]

Drunken workers were robbed in bars, a practice called "rolling." In March, 1908, the *Bangor Daily Commercial* reported on one worker who was headed from Waterville, ME, to Boston, but woke up at the railroad station and "couldn't remember any of the events of the night and didn't know where he had been, who he had been with or where he had his money [a roll of about $75] last." In another instance, lumberjack Charles H. Reagan met with a man named William Masters in Bangor after coming back from the river drive in June, 1910. They met with two women and went to establishments where "liquor had been purchased and drunk." Reagan began with a roll of $200 and "spent and made gifts to his friends in a most liberal manner" but had $42 directly stolen from him, allegedly by Masters.[115]

At the turn of the century, consumption of spirits dropped to near all-time lows in the United States, so the spree stood out and was reported on widely. The constituent parts of the spree: corked boots, poxing, fighting, drinking, sex, robbery, and, most importantly, reckless spending were, like the drive, spectacles of class. The spree represented a disregard for bourgeois savings and investment habits and thus separated lumberjacks from farmer-loggers.[116]

Becoming a lumberjack meant years or decades of repeated participation in these cycles that broke bodies and minds, sometimes leading to alcohol dependence. The meaning of problem drinking changed over time and by place. Lumberjacks and their communities accepted seasonal excessive consumption. Most workers had a "taken-for-granted attitude toward riotous living." Figure 6.1, a staged shot of a worker sneaking drinks of cooking extracts, shows that the desperation of an alcoholic was dealt with lightheartedly.[117]

When lumberjacks reflected on work later in life, the problems of alcohol dependency became more evident: "You'll find that every woodsman that ever worked in the woods, is a rummy [, an] alcoholic," Maine lumberjack Fredrick Burke remembered. He continued, "they don't classify themselves an alcoholic . . . in them days. . . . He was just a drunk, a woodsman, a lousy woodsman." Other workers emphasized that drinking defined them as a class: "The lumberjack is a fellow that likes to drink. About 90 percent of them were heavier drinkers." Another worker said, "I won't say every man, but pretty near every man that works in the woods is a boozer." Types of dress, debt, and a separation from agricultural work characterized the lumberjack, but for some, heavy drinking was an important characteristic.[118]

The Path Back to Camp

"Sore after a big drunk," with no money left, many workers were lured back to camp where they could find free food, shelter, and credit. The places where lumberjacks bought alcohol and sex were the places that they could find work. French-Canadian immigrant lumberjack Romeo Arsenault often stayed at the American House in Tupper Lake, NY, during seasonal breaks. It cost $9 a week, with as much food as he could eat, and the proprietor would keep the workers informed on jobs.[119] Workers could be drawn back to camps in other ways. In northern Maine, a rural justice admitted that he arrested workers on the spree, checked if they had debt, and, if so, sent them to a camp.[120]

Returning to camp was a return to a familiar, secure setting. Wyckoff commented that those workers returning after a spree seemed to be revived "as by miracle under the touch of their native life." Lumberjack Frank Carey commented that in camp, "you knew every day where you were . . . what you was going to do, you knew what you was going to eat . . . you had everything right up there in the woods, I liked it very much."[121]

The camp was a type of shelter that provided a supportive atmosphere to get sober.[122] "The biggest reason why, I went [back] to the woods," Frederick Burke recalled, was "to get away from the booze. And course you go up there and you make a stake, and then you come down and it's going to be spent for booze. . . . That's why I say, you can always go right back to the same place [the camp] after you got over your drunk."[123] Around the turn of the century, one forestry student reported, "after they get over their spree they calm down and go back to work in the woods where they will work hard for three or four months without any trouble."[124] American labor leaders and reformers argued that reckless spending on alcohol led to workers who were "distressed by . . . [their] vices into slavish necessity of accepting the only terms possible from the most selfish employers."[125] Burke remembers that he and other workers "didn't care," when labor agents charged them $15 "as long as we get out of the city, get back to work again . . . have something to do and get away from the booze."[126] In 1955, a jobber testified to the US Senate that he would recruit "refugees from Alcoholics Anonymous" to work for 80 cents an hour when standard rates were $1.30 to $1.72.[127]

"Shanghaiing," or forcibly moving a worker to camp while intoxicated, was reported in the Northern Forest. According to some, this was not always coercive. Friends, coworkers, and families of workers on a spree brought "lumberjacks into [camp] to sober them up a little bit." There were precedents for this. In England and the United States, rural work camps were established by the state specifically for the rehabilitation of alcoholics. Workers who became embedded in these cycles year after year became dependent on more than just alcohol, they became dependent on the routines of the industry, on how they used their own time and bodies and how their time and bodies were used by others.[128]

These cycles were an important part of nineteenth- and early twentieth-century logging songs. It is debatable to what extent the songs of loggers represent their lived experience. Camps were places to rest and refuel and the songs and dances that were supposedly part of class culture were dismissed by many as romantic fabrications. Specific narratives depicted in songs aren't always trusted accounts of events.

Some songs were authored and sung by workers and some do represent real experiences. Maine folklorist Fannie Eckstorm commented that songs represent "the mental horizon of the pioneer." Most importantly, popular songs demonstrate how outsiders understood the Northern Forest and how they imagined this class of workers. Eckstorm, who collected songs, assumed that some dated back to the early 1800s. They were transcribed from the 1890s to the 1920s and should be assumed to represent attitudes of that time, a time when an industrial lumberjack class was forming.[129]

Songs have comedic tones, treating these cycles as innocent. In "The Falling of the Pine," the narrator sings:

> "Our whistles for to wet
> With whiskey or good wine.
> With some pretty girl we'll boast
> Till our money is all used up
> We're the boys that don't refuse
> To return and fall the pine."

In "The Boys of the Island," a song about Canadian immigrant loggers, the "little P.I. [Prince Edward Island] boys can get drunk / And then sober up under the shades of the trees." The song relates economic cycles to natural cycles and depicts both as burdensome:

> "'Tis true, my brave boys, I have made lots of money,
> But the curse of all bushmen being on me,
> Also my money it flew like the snow in June
> and back to the woods every fall I must go."[130]

By the pulp boom, songsters associated these seasonal patterns with exploitation, most pointedly in "Henry's Concern" and "The Hoboes of Maine."

"Henry's Concern" explains the many pitfalls of logging, such as paying for transport to camps, for broken tools, for board, and for fines after quitting with debt. The narrator says subcontractors in New Hampshire were "apt to lose [their] pay; / There's no lien-law in the state, the logs you can't retain." This meant if contractors were late on delivery they might not get paid and would lose the logs.[131]

"The Hoboes of Maine," recorded by Eckstorm in 1924, provides the most complete example of the annual cycles of workers in verse. In the first stanza, the narrator establishes he is "poor and neglected . . . mean and dejected." Nevertheless, this worker was "in search of employment and earthly enjoyment." Employment and enjoyment were linked, but separated by space and time. The narrator refers to camps as "man traps" that handicapped workers. After spending his winter wages in "some dive" the narrator takes work on the river drive. In the mill town

> "The City Police they plot and connive
> To snare those poor dupes coming off of the drive,
> They'll hang around the station, in deep consultation
> In watch of those victims before they arrive.
> They'll joyfully hail them, all ready to jail them . . .
> Each man, as he'll walk up, is booked for the lock-up."

After the police beat the drivers, the narrator sings, "They'll capture his money, his watch and his chain; / Likewise their design to collect a big fine." The next morning the narrator, "silly from blows of the billy," is brought to "Judge Vose" who says to the worker, "'They tell me young man, you've been drinking again; / a fine I must levy, exceedingly heavy." The narrator serves thirty days in jail, the amount of time that the 1907 Maine statute on loggers' debt prescribed.[132] Lumbering songs demonstrate that workers could be victims of systems with disparate and disembodied nodes of coercive power that were embedded in the land, the seasons, and within workers' bodies and minds. Some songs depict the loggers' early death as part of seasonal cycles. Sometimes this is a heroic death at work. Others songs are less clear on the cause of demise.[133]

For some, suicide offered an escape from the repetition of seasonal cycles. Sobering up after a spree, workers were stricken by the pain of their supposed failure. Twenty-one cases of attempted or actual suicide of lumberjacks can be found in newspapers published in the Adirondacks between 1850 and 1950, though fourteen took place between 1906 and 1929. It is likely there are many more cases, but they are impossible to find because workers only rarely identified as loggers, lumberjacks, or lumbermen specifically. Victims were between twenty-five and sixty years old, and three were identified as immigrants. In nine cases, workers were described as on a spree, binge, or had just spent their roll. Workers killed themselves in various settings: at camp, during the spree, and right after a spree in town.

In 1914, the *Ogdensburg Journal* wrote that a lumberjack killed himself "as a climax to a spree." James Shattuck returned to camp from a "drunken debauch" and was "out of his head." "He produced a razor," the reporter wrote, "and cut his throat from ear to ear, dying almost instantly." A young worker named William Oryell was working in his brother's lumber camp, a small operation that allowed alcohol. Oryell awoke after a night of drinking and shot himself in the chest with a shotgun, leaving "a gaping wound." He reportedly "staggered to his feet, shook hands with his brother, bade him goodbye," and died. This aspect of camp life rarely makes it into the romantic narratives or songs.[134]

Why did workers drink to excess, spend recklessly, and sometimes kill themselves instead of saving, investing, and finding a more secure economic position? High rates of alcohol consumption are correlated with high rates of suicide, but why did loggers drink so much?[135] Historian Mark Lawrence Schrad has argued that distilled liquor has often been used as a tool of colonial oppression but pays less attention to alcohol as a tool of management. Historian Peter Way, on the other hand, argued that antebellum canal companies used alcohol to cause dependence and curb absenteeism. The same was true of employees of seamen, soldiers, and many other workers before 1850. This was not the situation in the turn-of-the-century Northern Forest because production was too scattered and irregular for any entity to control the workforce.[136]

Several factors compounded to create these cycles. For workers drawn from small European or North American farming communities—where capital was tied up in land, livestock and equipment—abundant cash was a novelty. Formal saving institutions were also rare. For young workers, the spree was the first time with a peer group away from family, neighbors, and the church.[137] In these settings and groups, other social norms and etiquettes were cast aside. Wyckoff was shocked by the swearing and irreligiousness of lumberjacks. When Wyckoff asked a worker "if he felt no sense of wrong in using lightly the name of the Almighty" the worker responded that he just got back from town where he "ain't swore for a month," but now that he was back in the camp "that's the way that us fellows talk." Less experienced workers followed older workers. Lincoln Toothaker, who declared himself a "virtuous" person, wrote to his wife near the end of a season, "I shall be glad when I get out of here and have a good drunk and I shall feel better[,] that is what most of the fellows are talking about." Toothaker was displaying solidarity in his desire for drink.[138]

According to anthropologist Samuel Martinez, "any interpretation of consumption that . . . [excludes] sensation-seeking is flawed." Camps were austere.[139] One jobber remembered, "it wasn't often that they had any amusement of any kind in the camp between practically the 15th of December as a rule, until [the] 15th of March . . . because from that time on . . . when the workers got in[,] then they slept." Bradwin wrote that camp life was "often solitary and humdrum, with little change in scene." He continued, "monotony predominates and . . . [a] mental sluggishness can accompany life continued under such environments. . . . A restlessness pervades their days which ultimately infects not only their thinking, but their habits of life." Wyckoff witnessed the "acute suffering . . . of enforced idleness." During nonwork hours in the camp, "the movement of time was slow torture" a torment that was not as obvious as the physical taxation of the work. Emerging from the forest created a desire for novel stimulations to sooth mental ills.[140]

Adding to this was the long period of isolation. A forestry student wrote in 1916 that "the men, when confined to the woods for several weeks, become very wild, and whenever an opportunity offers itself, may go to the village to celebrate, which to most workers of this caliber means to get drunk and have a good fight." Bradwin wrote, "there is a tendency, even under the best of conditions, for the heavy monotonous labor of the campman to become merely routine drudgery endured for a time in the hope of subsequent release, marked by a period of license."[141] The spree was interpreted as a natural reaction. Wyckoff described the spree as a release of the "cumulative storage of energy, financial and psychical." Writing in 1916, Dr. George Thomas White Patrick gave the entire American working class the following clinical diagnosis:

> The use of alcohol has commonly followed the law of rhythm. Among primitive tribes drinking was periodic, wild orgies of intoxication following considerable periods of plodding life. This periodicity . . . is a familiar fact in every community at present. . . . The power of self-restraint, strengthened by public sentiment and private prudence, deters from the use of alcohol up to a certain point, when the cumulative forces of desire, which is the cumulative need of release from painful tension, overthrows all barriers, and excess and complete relaxation follows for a season. . . . the effect of alcohol is a kind of *catharsis* . . . a kind of escape. The spirit of the age proclaims

> that we must be efficient. Efficiency, and ever more efficiency, is demanding, and the desire for alcohol is the desire for rest, for release from tension, for freedom and abandon [emphasis in the original].[142]

Perhaps people with an impulse for intense sensation-seeking were drawn to this type of work and drawn to other people with the same disposition. Some people "crave exotic and intense experiences, despite physical or social risk," according to psychologist Kenneth Carter. In a world where workers had limited choices economically, sensation-seeking gave them a sense of control over their environment and themselves, a sense that was temporary and perhaps illusory.[143] Lumberjacks preferred hard liquor in a period when American tastes were shifting to low-alcohol, mild-tasting lager beer. The intense sensation was what workers sought. Wyckoff remembers the thirst that quarry work caused: "water had long since ceased to satisfy . . . I have never tasted gin, but I remembered in one of Froude's essays a reference to it as much in use among working-men, and as being seasoned to their taste by a dash of vitriol, and eagerly I longed for that." Lumberjacks sought intense sensation in other consumables like the previously discussed tobacco and candy, but also vinegar, molasses, pork fat, syrup, and tea that was so strong, dark, and bitter it could "tan sole leather."[144]

This was a job of extreme sensory and emotional fluctuation. There were micro fluctuations, the movement from the fasting of the day's work to the gluttony of the camp meals, or from the bitter arid cold of winter work to the smelly, moist heat of camp. There were also longer-term fluctuations like the move from the nuclear family to the homosocial camp; from sexual abstinence to sexual promiscuity; from the danger of work to the safety of the town; taxing labor and responsibility to rakish relaxation; the austerity of camp to the luxury of the mill town; the manic spree to the depression afterwards. Intense sensations numbed broken bodies. It numbed too the psychic pain of market pressures and the prospect of a future of grueling wage labor and poverty.[145] Lumberjacks lived dangerous, risky lives. Psychologists today link financial, physical, emotional, legal, and social risk-taking with alcoholism, gambling, violence, and suicide.[146]

The feeling that industrial wage work was inescapable might have led workers to drink and to take the drastic action of suicide.[147] As the economy was industrializing, the rhetoric of free labor promised that frugal workers could become owners or operators, but in the declining agricultural economy of the Northern Forest and in the jobbing systems, advancing to an ownership position was not always possible or rational. The feeling that a person could not live up to the standards of industrial capitalism sometimes resulted in self-harm or suicide.[148] The lack of unions meant workers could find little economic support among their fellow laborers.

Attempting to represent the above disposition, novelist and former lumberjack Stewart Edward White created the character of a jobber named John Radway who failed to meet a contract, leaving him bankrupt. When asked what he was going to "do," Radway responded, "'Do! I'm going into the woods, by God! I'm going to work with my hands, and be happy! I'm going to do other men's work for them and take other men's pay. Let them do the figuring and worrying. I'll boss their gangs and make their roads and see to their logging for 'em, but it's got to be THEIRS. No! I'm going to be a free man.'" Free meant the relative freedom of a working-class bachelor life but, as this chapter has shown, bachelor life came with its own snares.[149] Historian of alcohol use W. J. Rorabaugh argued that the oscillation "between abstinence and binges . . . blurred the reality, lessening simultaneously . . . [the] frustration and . . . hope of ever ameliorating [the wage workers'] condition." He argues that anxiety and high aspirations mixed with low motivation caused alcoholism. Lumberjacks were motivated and capable, but moving out of wage work was not logical or viable.[150] Workers unable to escape the seasonal cycles had their very nature turned against their interests, compelling them to work until their bodies and minds were broken. They became "slaves to the bottle," a phrase often used to refer to alcoholics.[151]

When alcohol dependence occurred, it was at least partially the result of a geographic and seasonal pattern of production and consumption that brought unattached workers from extreme isolation, austerity, and boredom to settled areas with abundant cash, consumer choice, and a work culture that encouraged uncontrolled spending and drinking. Just as the leaves fell from trees in the fall and regrew in the spring, lumberjacks went to camp, worked to an extent that was mentally and physically unhealthy, and had a cathartic, class-defining spree. Workers who took part in these cycles for many years in a row were resigned to their positions and their natural inclinations. The reason for the spree and alcoholic dependence was resignation. Workers understood that ownership, a condition that defined manhood for their fathers and grandfathers, was no longer possible or rational. The industrial work they were stuck performing was some of the most physically demanding in the country. Career lumberjacks likely thought their lives had not turned out as they hoped.[152] All of this created immense physical pain and psychic pain. Angus Deaton and Anne Case argued that social upheaval, like burgeoning industrialization, can cause chronic pain that can cause self-harm and suicide.[153] Loggers' propensity for violence could be directed inwards. The spree exemplified the violence of industrial capitalist commodity production, a spectacle marking a time when trees and workers were delivered to industrial hubs to be dismantled and destroyed for profit.[154]

Most loggers maintained a connection to the farm and weren't entrenched in the class cycle of logging. Others chose to remain in the woods but did not get caught in the cycle, or escaped after a few years. Some saved their wages and took the risk of becoming an owner/operator. "If they kept at the work of the woods," one forestry student found, workers could often "rise up to be scalers, camp bosses and jobbers."[155] A few of these upwardly mobile workers even succeeded and attained wealth and stability.

Workers' consumption "was simultaneously a marker of group identity and a way to assert one's individuality," as historian of rural consumption Béatrice Craig found. Consumption helped create a lumberjack class in an industry in which the line between owners and the proletariat was blurred. As one worker put it later in his life, only those workers who "came [back to camp year after year] developed into real lumberjacks."[156]

The word lumberjack was important. In the nineteenth century, terms like "logger," "lumberer," "woodman," "woodsman," and especially "lumberman" were used to describe those who engaged in forest product production, but none distinguished between owner/operators and wage worker. This ambiguity represents the role of farmer-loggers or casual laborers who were sometimes owners, jobbers, bosses, manual laborers, or all of the above.

By the turn of the century, terms emerged for woods wage workers specifically. These were "lumber worker," "woods-worker," "woods labor," and "lumberjack," though early on, the last word often appeared hyphenated. The *Oxford English Dictionary* cites the use of the term "lumberjack" as early as 1831, but the term really became popular in the late 1890s, as seasonal cycles were ensnaring more and more workers.[157] By the 1920s and 1930s, "lumberman" was beginning to denote an owner of a lumber business who did little or no manual labor. Starting in the 1910s, some experts in forestry and sociology began to refer to the cycles described above as "the problem of the lumberjack" or the "lumberjack problem."[158]

As this chapter has shown, the elements of class creation were also aspects of the industry that assured mills and landowners had annual access to the metabolic processes of workers' bodies. There was another element of production that also linked class with bodies. That was race, to which we turn next.

CHAPTER 7

HALF-WILD FOLK

In 1852, the Brown Company was a small, water-powered sawmill on the banks of the Androscoggin River in Berlin, NH. By 1897, it was one of the largest and most successful lumber, pulp, and paper companies in the Northeast, producing 55 million board feet of lumber per year. Its success depended on the French-Canadian immigrant laborers it employed to cut and drive its wood. Brown established a labor agency in Coaticook, Canada, to ensure a steady supply of these workers.[1] These immigrants worked long hours, withstood difficult living conditions, and accepted low wages. As early as 1878, Northern Forest people were commenting on the advantages of the "cheap labor" of French Canadians. The going wage then was $0.75 a day, paid in buckwheat.[2] Perhaps most importantly, however, these immigrants were seen as innately suited for logging. Officials wrote they were a "hardy type, accustomed to the work in the bush, such as portaging, running rapids, etc., . . . [and were] as a rule, pretty high-grade men."[3]

The French-Canadian affinity for logging was recognized across the Northern Forest. Adirondack scholar Alfred Donaldson wrote that they "seemed naturally endowed with the agility, recklessness, and immunity to exposure that must combine to make them expert. They have always predominated as a race in the lumbering operations." One Canadian sociologist wrote that they "have the lure . . . of the woods tingling in their blood."[4] Another Canadian operator wrote, "lumbering seems to be born in his blood, and with it goes a profound, instinctive knowledge of the forest and all its ways. To him the forest is not merely a place wherein he earns his livelihood . . . It is a personality he knows." Officials for the Chicago newspaper company Tribune wrote, "99 [percent] of the labor used [in pulp procurement] . . . was [the] migratory French Canadian lumberjack."[5] It was these workers,

French-Canadian immigrants, who would supply the Northern Forest with cheap nature in human form into the 1950s and beyond.

By 1901, almost a quarter of the population of Québec was in the United States. Ninety-two percent settled in the "border states or in states immediately south of them."[6] Most settled in cities, but in the Northern Forest there were logging camps composed entirely of French Canadians. Conditions in jobbers' camps had degraded to the point where Americans refused the work. An 1890 Congressional report found that "American farmers' sons no longer follow wood chopping for a business, and their places have been filled by the French Canadians."[7] In 1900, 33.6 percent of New England "woodchoppers, lumbermen [or] raftsmen" were French Canadian.[8]

The Foran Act of 1885 should have banned from entry those immigrant laborers who had already signed contracts to work before arriving in country. The law seemed to be broken regularly in Maine, disappointing labor unions who disliked seasonal surges in the labor market.[9] The Immigration Act of 1917 allowed "skilled workers" to be imported to the United States if there was no native-born labor available. The Santa Clara Lumber Company of New York was one company that lobbied the Department of Labor, arguing that French Canadian loggers were skilled.[10] Under this act, immigrant workers were subject to an $8 to $10 head tax, a charge that was often factored into a labor agents' fees.[11] The 1924 Johnson-Reed Act imposed a quota on immigration but there were exceptions for countries in the Western Hemisphere.[12] The northern border was lightly policed until 1924 and even then the newly militarized border patrol targeted Europeans who were crossing into the United States illegally, not native-born Canadians. When the border patrol disrupted the movement of much needed cheap Canadian labor, local American communities resisted these new policing efforts.[13]

Once at work in the American woods, these foreigners were isolated, separated from their communities and from vital church support. Unfamiliar with the English language and American labor laws, they were especially vulnerable to mistreatment, contract violations, and debt peonage. In the Adirondacks, the Emporium, Santa Clara, and A. Sherman lumber companies conspired to set low wages for immigrants.[14]

Temporary migration of French-Canadian workers eventually became a government-sponsored contract labor program. During the labor shortages of World War II, the Canadian and American governments created a guest labor program that "bonded" a specific number of "Canadian woodsmen to their American employers for fixed terms," usually six months. Employers could simply fill out requests via a "Woodsman Order Form" with state or federal employment agencies. This continued after the war. Between 1951 and 1955, an average of 5,920 French Canadian workers were "bonded" to logging companies throughout Northern Forest states per year, though some years there were more than 7,000. During these years, the pulpwood cutting force in Maine was on average 78.4 percent French Canadian. In some years in New Hampshire, French Canadians were 100 percent of the workers. Industry representatives found 80 percent of these were "cutters" and that "no Canadian labor is imported to work in . . . other parts of the industry." One US senator investigating the bonded labor system in the 1950s called it "temporary peonage."[15]

Other immigrants worked in the woods too but were systematically routed to different types of jobs depending on their country of origin. Lumberjack Arnold Hall said that he only ever saw "one or . . . two Italians in the woods in my life. They don't work in the woods much. Pick and shovels all right, but they don't seem to go for the woods." The Maine Department of Labor found that "Italians who work on our dams, railroads, and other construction operations in the summer are not to be found in [logging] camps. It is too cold for them." An Adirondack newspaper from 1883 reported that, "excepting the French Canadians, the Latins have an insurmountable aversion to the ax."[16]

The supposed French-Canadian affinity for forest products work and the odd exclusion of Italians exemplifies how North Americans in the late nineteenth and early twentieth centuries connected their ideas about race, nonhuman nature, and work. Businesses, academics, unions, and government officials used pseudoscientific methods to construct racial taxonomies that situated French-Canadian workers as closer to nature than native-born American workers. This designation gave jobbers, mills, landowners, and government officials a rationale to exploit French-Canadian workers as if they were another part of the wilderness. This also created schisms in the working class, which, alongside the jobbing system, served to disrupt workers' organization, as a 1955 unionization attempt among Brown Company woods workers, which is described below, shows clearly.

By the early twentieth-century, eugenic and racial thinking had become "so pervasive . . . that it attained the state of common sense."[17] This was particularly true among the well-educated. Between 1914 and 1928, the number of universities offering courses that taught eugenics increased from 44 to 376.[18] Experts like sociologist Edward A. Ross asserted that even "economic virtues . . . [were] a function of race." Ross's comments on these issues carried weight. A renowned but controversial academic, Ross's popular audience widened in 1900 when he was fired from Stanford University for supporting Chinese exclusion which, he argued, would prevent "race suicide," a phrase he coined.[19] Influential labor historian and economist John R. Commons agreed, observing that each race had "varying industrial gifts and capacities."[20] In writing and in practice, businesses, unions, academics, and governments sorted immigrant and African American workers into specific industrial niches based on their perceived racialized bodily characteristics.[21] This is what David Roediger and Elizabeth Esch have called "race management." This chapter expands on Roediger and Esch's thesis, showing how these racial-industrial categories were constructed, implemented in business, and finally institutionalized through legislation.[22]

This chapter uses three terms to describe thinking about race. (1) Scientific racism: the encompassing academic pursuit of investigating racial differences through many disciplines in the social and natural sciences. It was used in (2) race management, a term described above. Those who believed in scientific racism or race management were typically (3) eugenicists, a term describing people who believed in racial differences, race degeneration, and also the supremacy of the "White" races, though they could not always agree on which groups were White.

Race management created patterns in the type of work that different immigrant groups engaged in, as the reports of the US Congressional Joint Immigration Commission (hereafter referred to as the Dillingham Commission, after its Chairman William P. Dillingham of Vermont) found in 1911:

> The Austrians have gone principally into construction work and to the iron ore fields. The Finns have been furnished with about the same class of labor. The Greeks and Italians almost without exception have gone into section work for some railroad system. The Scandinavians and Americans have gone into almost every kind of work, but the largest percentage of them have gone into the logging camps. . . . The Poles and Bulgarians, almost without exception, have gone into construction work. . . . The Cuban and Spanish races are employed exclusively in the manufacture of cigars and tobacco . . . North and South Italians are most extensively employed in silk dyeing, railroad and other construction work, bituminous coal mining, and clothing manufacturing . . . the Slovaks seem to be industrial laborers rather than farmers.

Canadian sociologist Edmund Bradwin expressed similar sentiments in his investigations of labor camps.[23] Immigrant labor agents, "coolie" labor streaming, and tenement sweating in New York City were also propelled, in part, by scientific racism, which streamed immigrants into the type of work and work environments that they were seen as racially suited to.[24]

At their most extreme, immigration policies that followed racial dictates led to draconian exclusionary laws such as the Chinese Exclusion Act (1882) and the Johnson-Reed Act (1924), among others. Before Johnson-Reed, however, less than 2 percent of the roughly twenty-six million immigrants who came to the country since 1870 were excluded.[25] Therefore, up until 1924, the more important "immigration question" was what was to be done with the immigrants already in the country. Historians disagree on whether racist arguments or arguments for economic efficiency guided American immigration policy. Race management shows racism was often perceived as economically efficient. Bigoted ideas crept into supposedly objective racial sciences. Confirmation bias plagued these fields of study. Therefore, it was not coincidental that those races who were considered "undesirable" were also considered to be suited to low-paying jobs, monotonous factory work, and grueling manual labor. Robert DeCourcy Ward, climatologist, eugenicist, and cofounder of the Immigration Restriction League, wrote, "It is a general rule . . . that weaklings resort to the less desirable occupations." Race management was therefore appealing to racists, unions, restrictionists, and businesspeople.[26]

In his book *Barbarian Virtues*, Matthew Frye Jacobson focuses on how Americans created and reacted to what he calls the "image" of the immigrant, "[seemingly] unshakable demonstrations of this or that ethnological truth about this nation and the nature of the world's diverse populations." This chapter uses Jacobson's concept of the immigrant image to demonstrate how race management schemes were constructed.

These immigrant images were shaped by environmental factors as well as observations of work. One way to justify routing immigrants into bad jobs was by interpreting culturally valuable types of labor—clearing and cultivating wild land—as work that only real "White" people could do with success.[27] White Northern Europeans pushed west to civilize supposedly free, wild land. Immigrants of questionable whiteness who were capable of improving wilderness land might be more than just expendable industrial workers, they might have the ability to become independent agriculturalists, the bedrock of American democracy. This logic was circular: any person descended from a group with a long history of citizenship in the United States was presumed to have descended from pioneering, wilderness-conquering people and was therefore de facto White, or a superior racial type. In other words, White people were White because they were pioneering people and White people were pioneering people because they were White people. Those who were not pioneering were therefore fit for the factory, or some other menial wage work. Eugenicists argued that there were groups of people who were "in between" White and non-White, groups whose whiteness remained in question even after being tested by wilderness work. This was where the French Canadians fit into this logic, and these racial discourses are the primary reason they were exploited in the woods for more than a century.[28]

According to Jacobson, it was an imperial prerogative to see foreign people as "wilderness in human form."[29] Racial management incorporated the nature/society dualism into industrial management explicitly. The nature/society dualism is an idea central to Jason W. Moore's conception of cheap nature. This is the idea that anything defined as natural can be used by civilized "humans" to make more capital. Workers who were uncivilized or wild could be exploited endlessly for profit just like the rest of the natural world. Unlocking the cheap nature of racialized bodies was the same as unlocking the cheap nature of the weather or human metabolism. These processes allowed operators to wrest profit from the dwindling resource base of the cutover forest. In this era of logging, when the industry remained dependent on muscle power, ice, and water, the French Canadians acted as complements to native-born workers rather than substitutes. They made native born farmer-logger bosses more "efficient."[30] Inhuman treatment of immigrants was a production technology, an idea best exemplified in the quote that was used earlier in this book, which came from a British-Canadian lumberman who declared in 1918, "give me two French Canadians in preference to any machine you can introduce."[31] Racialized bodies and race management were cost-saving innovations that, in the words of historian Julie Greene, "do the work of capital."[32]

As the previous chapter showed, the state, through legislation and the courts, collaborated with industry to limit workers' choices, keeping labor flexible and seasonally available. Emboldened by the urgency of World War II, the federal government became complicit in systematizing seasonal labor flexibility, and they did so along race lines. The Bracero program of Mexican agricultural guest workers on the southwest border is the best example. This system was propelled by images of immigrants, the belief that Mexicans were innately suited for difficult, uncomfortable "stoop labor" in American fields.[33]

The bonded labor program of French Canadian workers challenges historian Mae Ngai's assertion that guest worker programs, and their racist intellectual foundations, separated workers along the lines of "European and non-European immigrant groups."[34] In 1955, Arizona Senator Barry Goldwater called the bonded labor program and the Bracero program a "very comparable situation."[35] As this chapter shows, French Canadians' whiteness, and their suitability for citizenship, was suspect in a way that was similar to that of Mexicans.[36]

The comparison between the situation of Mexicans and French Canadians is not perfect but it is necessary for this narrative because scientific racism depended on racial comparisons. After first exploring how the French-Canadian image emerged in literature, this chapter continues with comparisons of the images of different immigrants. The images of French Canadians are compared with the images of Jewish, Italian, and Polish immigrants to show how race management ideas were created and implemented in the United States through the period of the bonded labor program.

Literature and the French-Canadian Image

As historian Reginald Horsman found, in the mid-nineteenth century there was no "sharp separation between a precise scientific racialism and literary racial nationalism."[37] The influence of literature in forming immigrant images continued into the late nineteenth and early twentieth centuries, complementing emerging scientific and social scientific explanations of racial differences.

The French-Canadian image was deeply influenced by perceived racial mixing with Native Americans during colonization. This connection explained the reported Québécois "swarthy" or "copper" complexion and their affinity with the forest.[38] James Fenimore Cooper's *Leatherstocking Tales* shaped beliefs in this racial connection, as did nonfiction works by Zadok Cramer, Francis Parkman, Henry David Thoreau, and historian George Bancroft.[39] According to Parkman, "the French became savages," as he wrote in *The Conspiracy of Pontiac* (1851). Parkman continued, "hundreds [of French settlers] betook themselves to the forest, never more to return."[40]

There is evidence to support the history of French and Native American connections but little to support widespread sexual intermingling.[41] Even though most French Canadians were not of mixed heritage, by 1911 this belief was so widespread that the US Immigration Commission felt the need to address it in its *Dictionary of Races*, stating "the French Canadian race is not widely intermingled with Indian blood, as some misinformed persons think." By the middle of the nineteenth century, American attention was fixated on the expansion of Anglo-Saxon peoples westward and on the domination and disappearance of Native Americans. Early writers on racial differences assumed the French weakened their European blood by intermingling with Native Americans just like Mexicans had. People with Native American blood were on the wrong side of history, destined to be destroyed.[42]

The French-Canadian connection to nature and Native Americans was reinforced by the popular image of the French voyageurs and *coureurs de bois*, frontier workers who defined the early Canadian experience in the wilderness.

Nineteenth-century texts on the voyageurs depicted them as blending into rather than civilizing the frontier. The French entered the woods not to "clear and colonize" but to range. The only enduring marks they left on the land were "names upon the map." Thoreau wrote that they had "overrun the great extent of the country . . . without improving it."[43] One American author, reflecting on the settlement of the United States, wrote, "if these countries had continued to belong to the French, the population would certainly have been more gay than the present American race . . . but it would have had less comforts and wealth, and ages would have passed away, before man had become master of those regions." French Canadians, like Native people, were a "vanishing" part of the landscape.[44]

The French-Canadian image not only reflected American writing about these people, but it also reflected political and racial tensions in Canada. *La survivance* was a cultural and political repatriation movement that formed as a reaction to the mass exodus of French Canadians to the United States in the late nineteenth and early twentieth centuries. La survivance inspired a plethora of popular books, many of which depicted the bucolic and wild Canadian landscape as preferable to industrial modernity.[45] Most popular among these books was Louis Hémon's 1916 *Maria Chapdelaine*, which narrates a young woman's struggle to decide whether to leave Québec for the United States or to stay in her forested homeland. One of Maria's suitors was Eutrope Gagnon, a forest farmer who, like the Chapdelaine family, was endlessly engaged in a "battle" to clear the forest. This was the passion of these people: "'Make land!' Rude phrase of the country, summing up in two words all the heart-breaking labor that transforms the incult woods, barren of sustenance, to smiling fields, ploughed and sown. Samuel Chapdelaine's [Maria's father] eyes flamed with enthusiasm and determination as he spoke. For this was the passion of his life; the passion of a man whose soul was in the clearing, not the tilling of the earth."[46] These people didn't labor to civilize the land but did it merely for pleasure. Maria's choice to stay in Québec and continue the life of clearing forest land "symbolizes Québec's determined struggle to secure a foothold for rural, Catholic, French society away from the onslaught of modern, urban, English-dominated life," according to literary scholar Paul Socken. *Maria Chapdelaine* was translated into English multiple times and made into three different motion pictures.[47]

Americans and British Canadians confused fictions with facts when it came to French-Canadian culture. Adding to this confusion was folklorist Honore Beaugrand, who presented his collections of French-Canadian folklore as nonfiction.[48] The voluminous and popular poetry of William Henry Drummond, a

British Canadian, was a type of French-Canadian minstrelism that furthered the idea of French Canadians as simple, comical, backwoods people most at home working in the woods. His characters were nearly all lumbermen, simple habitants (peasant farmers), or voyageurs.[49] A particularly poignant example of the French-Canadian image is Felix-Antoine Savard's *Menaud Maître-draveur* (1937), a book twice translated into English. It depicts the French nearly exclusively as loggers and river drivers working under a despotic Anglo-Canadian lumberman. The main character, Menaud, is driven mad when his son dies trying to break a log jam. There are several other authors who employed similar themes in their works on French Canadians.[50]

Jack London's immensely popular *The Call of the Wild* (1903) solidified the French-Canadian image in the American imagination. The French-Canadian characters Francois and Perrault are vital to the protagonist Buck's reconnection with nature. The two were couriers and expert woodsmen who led dog teams across thin ice, slept on the snow, and employed natural resources to help them on their journey.[51] Characters similar to Francois and Perrault appear in the plethora of popular lumbermen novels published around the turn of the century. In his most famous work, *The Blazed Trail* (1902), Stewart Edward White, writer, outdoorsmen, and friend of Theodore Roosevelt, employed the French-Canadian image in the character of expert woodsman Fabian Laveque, who "typified the indomitable spirit of these conquerors of a wilderness." Similar characters appear in White's *Conjuror's House, A Romance of the Free Forest* (1903), *The Forest* (1903), and *The Westerners* (1901) and in Maine forest fiction writer Holman Day's *Joan of Arc of the North Woods* (1922) and *The Landloper, the Romance of a Man on Foot* (1915). Both Day and White had their books made into films.[52] These French-Canadian ancillary characters are too numerous to mention. In these books, French Canadians are rarely leads themselves but are instead tools that helped Americans civilize the wilderness. Alternatively, they were villains who disrupted American attempts to do so.[53]

Industrializing Racism

In fictional works, French-Canadian idiosyncrasies were vaguely explained. Around the turn of the century, the emerging field of race science increasingly attempted to fit all immigrants into what Jacobson calls a scientific "hierarchy of evolutionary economic stages." The construction of this hierarchy would serve to explain causes of racial differences and also the industrial virtues of these differences. French-Canadian affinity for Native Americans and their connection to the forest became not the cause of racial difference, but the consequence. The disciplines of sociology, history, climatology, geography, biology, and anthropology were the methods used to create and arrange immigrant images.[54]

As scientific racism developed, experts like anthropologist Franz Boas posited that people were shaped by their environment and shaped their environment in turn as part of the progression of human evolution. Scientific racists erroneously mixed Lamarckian and Darwinian ideas, assuming that the use and disuse of physical actions, actions determined by environmental necessity, could be passed down to progeny as "acquired characteristics." Races that were out of place were physically and economically disadvantaged.[55] Race determined which temperatures different groups of people could optimally perform manual labor within, for instance, and their ability to do this labor made their children more able to do the same. Therefore, certain people were less capable of making American wilderness land valuable. Popular travel writer Richard Harding wrote in 1903 that "there is no more interesting question of the present day, than that of what is to be done with the world's land which is laying unimproved, whether it shall go to the great power that is willing to turn it to account, or remain with its original owner, who fails to understand its value."[56] The ability to cultivate and properly utilize wilderness land was a sign of social progress. Groups who conquered and profited from wilderness land were "civilized," and those who couldn't, or who merely subsisted from it, were "savage."[57]

The United States had a long tradition of adjudicating property rights and citizenship based on an individual's ability to mix their labor with the land to create value. Common-law squatters' rights, the original Homestead Act (1862), and the many additional homesteading acts are the best examples. Independent landholding had been a key requirement for citizenship since colonial times, and aspects of this idea remained relevant in the industrial era.[58]

In making wilderness land profitable, "the inherent superiority of the Anglo-Saxon or the Germanic or the Teutonic or the Aryan race was a common intellectual assumption of the day," historian Gilman M. Ostrander found.[59] "Savages" like Native Americans were bodily inefficient in this pursuit. The Germans, on the other hand, were better able to "apply their industry and energy" to valuable work than were Southern Europeans, according to the Dillingham commission. Theodore Roosevelt, Frederick Jackson Turner, Herbert Baxter Adams, Edward Perkins Channing, George Bancroft, and other eugenic thinkers agreed: the "free land" of North America was a place that only White people had the ability to utilize to its full economic potential.[60]

This way of thinking implied that racial characteristics determined the type of work that racial groups were predisposed to perform. In his popular

Passing of the Great Race, Madison Grant wrote, "The Alpine race is always and everywhere a race of peasants, an agricultural and never a maritime race. . . . The Nordics are, all over the world, a race of soldiers, sailors, adventurers and explorers, but above all, of rulers, organizers and aristocrats." Ward wrote that "the Syrians and Armenians take naturally to non-agricultural occupations."[61] Sociologists and businesspeople witnessing African Americans migrating to northern cities during World War I argued they were "particularly fitted for some occupations," typically agricultural work. The focus was on the worker's biological body. For example, businesspeople argued that Black people naturally walked slower than Whites, making them less efficient at certain jobs.[62]

Eugenicists roughly agreed that to civilize wilderness land, a racial group needed three characteristics: (1) to be bodily able, (2) to have familiarity (personally or hereditarily) with wilderness land of the type found in North America, and (3) to have independent inclinations. These characteristics come up repeatedly in texts on race and wilderness. For example, famous turn-of-the-century historian Fredrick Jackson Turner described these pioneering traits as "coarseness and strength combined with acuteness and inquisitiveness; that practical, inventive turn of mind, quick to find expedience; that masterful grasp of material things, lacking in the artistic but powerful to effect great ends; that restless, nervous energy; that dominant individualism." The last attribute, individualism, was particularly important in qualifying races as civilized. Independence meant a people could use a small amount of capital to create more capital, using little besides their own labor. Capitalism was therefore embedded in the race sciences.[63] John R. Commons argued that French and Spanish colonists were "accustomed to a paternal government and they had not . . . the self-reliance and capacity for [the] sustained exertion required to push forward as individuals . . . to cut themselves off from the support of a government across the ocean." To Commons, it was only the English and Scotch-Irish that had the "preliminary training" to establish homes and agriculture in the wilderness of North America. "The Spaniards and the French were pioneers and adventurers, but they established only trading stations."[64] Farm owners in the West found that Mexicans "require constant supervision and driving[,] . . . do not possess initiative . . . [and] like authority."[65] White people tamed the wilderness individually, civilized it, and eventually lorded over others. Americans on Canadian frontier rail grades were often bosses who "take hold of a group of workers and get something done," Bradwin wrote.[66]

The forest environment was a crucial part of creating civilization because it gave White people vast resources while also imposing a barrier to weed out weaker peoples. According to Turner, "American democracy came from the forest." In Roosevelt's words, "there was scant room for cowards and weaklings in the ranks of the adventurous frontiersmen . . . who first hewed their way into the primeval forest."[67] George Bancroft wrote that "the century-training in backwoods life" gave White Americans advantages over the immigrant germ.[68]

The swinging of an axe was a metaphor for the advancement of civilization, but there was a literal element to this metaphor. Only those people who were good axemen, good at clearing land, could make good civilization from wilderness. Northern Europeans, eugenicists argued, had a propensity for "unbroken forest land" and naturally avoided urban, industrial work.[69] According to Ross, the Scandinavian "insisted on getting his living in connection with soil, water and wood" and looked for "good land rather than for land easy to subdue." The German "chopped his homestead out of the densest woods" because, according to Ross, he knew "heavy forest growth proclaims rich soil."[70]

The study of ancient and medieval history supported scientific racism. Still influential at the end of the nineteenth century, the works of the Roman historian Edward Gibbon reinforced the idea that the Gallic, Nordic, or Teutonic surpassed Mediterranean people in vigor and independence.[71] Although he became famous for his ideas on the environment, George Perkins Marsh was also inspired by race. According to his book *Man and Nature or, Physical Geography as Modified by Human Action*, Roman decadence and weakness had caused this culture to become out of sync with the environment, leading to the fall of the empire. To Marsh and Ross, the ability to make land profitable in the long term was an inheritable racial trait.[72]

Racial scientists were nuanced in their analysis of Whiteness. For example, there were vast differences between northern Italians and southern Italians. Northern Italians were "cool, deliberate, patient, practical . . . [and] capable of great progress" while the southerners were "excitable, impulsive . . . imaginative, impracticable . . . having little adaptability to highly organized society." Southern Italians could not and, according to Turner, did not contribute much to the advancement of the frontier.[73] Similarly, Russian and Romanian Jews, sometimes assumed to be of Mongolian blood, sometimes Mediterranean, were always depicted as bad pioneers.[74] Referring to native-born Americans, Ross asked, "to this roaming, hunting, exploring, adventurous breed what greater contrast is there than the denizens of the Ghetto?"[75]

Though most immigrant groups were subject to categorization by eugenicists and government officials, not all fit neatly into the emerging racial taxonomy. For example, the Polish and French Canadian had an uncertain racial heritage. The Polish were not clearly a Nordic, Gallic, Celtic, or Mediterranean people.[76] Prominent racial theorist Carl Campbell Bringham used intelligence tests to calculate that the Polish were precisely 90 percent Alpine/Celtic and 10 percent Nordic.[77]

American government reports and racial scientists agreed that perceived French Canadian racial deficiencies were caused by the evolution of French society in ancient and medieval Europe, though there was mixed opinion on their exact genealogy. It was assumed by some that the French were Celtic or Gallic people who shared the bellicose nature of other ancient frontier peoples like the Germans or the Scandinavians. The *Dictionary of Race*, along with a few other sources, defined the French as Teutonic, or purely White. The Gauls and Celts, however, had succumbed to the ancient Roman conquest of their land easier than German, Teutonic, Nordic, or Anglo-Saxon people, demonstrating their weakness. Still other racial thinkers saw the French as a bifurcated people, the peasant class comprised largely of Roman slave blood, while the aristocracy maintained Teutonic traits. European origin mattered little given the presumption of widespread intermixing with Native Americans, however. This unstable genealogical position meant that French Canadians, like the Polish, could not immediately be considered White, civilizing people.[78]

Immigrants in the Wilderness

The Dillingham Commission investigations into the active settling of wilderness land reinforced the idea that immigrants of questionable whiteness were unfit to create value from wilderness. These investigations demonstrated how government, science, and industry worked in unison to create a schema of racial management. Two volumes on "Recent Immigrants in Agriculture" explored how new immigrants took to "pioneer farming" or the clearing and civilizing of wild land. The authors exposed confirmation bias in the abstract, writing that they selected only those "races . . . which we are accustomed to consider inclined to industrial rather than to agricultural pursuits," those that "come from southern or eastern Europe, and the Japanese." The term *pioneer farming* is never fully defined in the report, but it is used throughout to refer to those farmers who lived in isolated areas, in inhospitable climates, and who cultivated wild or cut and grown over lands. According to the study, wild land was any land that was valueless until hard work made it valuable.[79]

The site of investigation was the wilderness of northern Wisconsin. Cold, long winters, a short growing season, rugged isolated terrain, and tree- and rock-strewn soil all combined to make it a difficult landscape for any farmer, regardless of race. The commission gave a brief description of what type of work was required to cultivate this landscape: "The first industry to be carried on in this whole region was lumbering . . . The farm was at first a mere adjunct to the lumber camp. Many of the early farmers were first woodsmen or 'lumberjacks.'" "It is just such land as this . . . that hundreds of Germans, Scandinavians, Poles and Swiss have been buying, clearing and making good living on since the early [eighteen] nineties," the report found.[80]

The Dillingham Commission reported that southern Italian immigrants were naturally ill-equipped. They also found "a sharp cleavage" between northern and southern Italians. Northern Italians showed a disposition for wild land, while southern Italians disproportionately settled in cities. Northern Italians, though not accustomed to lumber work, were able to make a profit from the forest: "the best of the Italian farmers are fully up to the average of their German and American neighbors," one case study found, but "are a little behind the Scandinavians."[81]

"Progress in citizenship is less rapid among the South Italians," the study declared. According to Ross, the southern Italian was physically weak, partially because they were vegetarian. When southern Italians did excel at heavy labor it was not because of their "physical strength, but because of their endurance of heat, cold, wet and muck."[82] On the frontier, southern Italians "perhaps" worked in the woods as a supplement for farming, but most did railroad work.[83]

It was believed that southern Italians lacked independence. They did not possess the "self-reliance, initiative, resourcefulness nor self-sufficing individualism that necessarily marks the pioneer farmer. . . . The Southern Italians, especially, run in groups and follow a leader," according to the Dillingham Commission. They could not "endure the chill loneliness of the American Homestead," Ross argued, and they "haven't the head" for extensive farming. The lack of independence in southern Italians was tied to their devout Catholicism.[84]

Southern Italians were comparable to Jewish immigrants. In 1904, the "Milwaukee Jewish Agricultural Society under the management of its president, a wealthy and philanthropic Hebrew, secured 720 acres of 'wild lands' for the settlement of refugee Russian and Romanian Jews." To help the colony, the society employed a "young man who had had considerable practical experience as a farmer and woodsman," but he could not better the Jews' position. The Dillingham Commission found these immigrants completely inept. The local woodsman reported that the Jews knew little "about clearing new lands and crops" and "were ignorant of even [the] simplest operations. . . . No one could handle or sharpen an ax or a saw, or milk a cow, care for stock or conduct any sort of farming operations." The Jews lacked in physical ability, the commission found, and "the pioneer work . . . proved too severe a strain on the patience and endurance of many a prospective Hebrew farmer." There were a few exceptions, and these exceptional settlers cleared a "large quantity of timber."

Jewish agricultural colonies in the West generally failed because of the supposed "nonagricultural character of the colonist."[85]

Crucially, the study depicted the Jews as unable to comprehend independent proprietorship. They mistook cash advances for wages and when they received the advances they assumed "sustenance [was] assured . . . [so] few of the settlers were willing to do any very hard work, relying solely on the advances." Several Dillingham Commission case studies found that the Jewish settlers were inclined to "pay more and acquire fields ready for the plow." Even then, "crops, tillage, quality and quantity of produce, show up rather more poorly than in most of the colonies . . . investigated." "The Hebrews are the polar opposite of our pioneer breed," Ross argued.[86]

The Polish were a new immigrant success story and "made excellent pioneers." They could cultivate land with $1,000 less credit than other immigrant groups. Instead of being oppressed by the forest, they utilized it, logging for themselves or for companies during the winter. They had the ability for frontier ingenuity because "they work by rule of thumb," a woodsmen skill. Tracts "that twenty years ago was heavy forest or unproductive swamp" were, under the Polish reign, "80 to 90 percent in tillage, producing profitably." The Dillingham Commission agreed with a growing consensus that some immigrants were not fit for independent production in the wilderness.[87]

Placing the Canadians

French Canadians were not included in the Dillingham Commission because their history in the Americas proved that they excelled at aspects of wilderness work, yet this did not mean their whiteness was unquestioned. French Canadians had White people's aptitude and ability in the woods, but they lacked the third element required for civilization: an independent inclination. The collection of essays edited by James George Aylwin Creighton, *French Canadian Life and Character: With Historical and Descriptive Sketches* (1899), demonstrates the common conception of French-Canadian workers at the time: "[the] Canadian experiences developed in the old French stock new qualities, good and bad, the good predominating . . . *such men needed only a leader* who understood them to go anywhere into the untrodden depths of the New World, and to do anything that man could do [emphasis added]."[88]

French Canadians had a natural affinity for hierarchy expressed in their religion. Gerald Morgan argued in the pages of *The North American Review* in 1917 that the will of the French-Canadian people was the same as the will of their priests, who desired to keep the laity ignorant, isolated, and bound to tradition. The result was the "stoppage of national progress." In many texts, French-Canadian Catholicism is depicted as almost pagan or a type of nature worship. To Creighton, the French Canadian was "a genuine survival of the Old Regime . . . smoke-dried into perpetual preservation."[89]

The French-Canadian allegiance to hierarchy created beliefs in the business and labor communities that French Canadians were less likely to stand up to bosses or to unionize. The Knights of Labor found this to be the case also.[90] "The French Canadian is a capital laborer," Grant argued "he is docile and willing and his light-heartedness gets over all difficulties." "No other class among the navvies [general construction laborer] seems possessed with the lightheartedness and cheerfulness of these men," Bradwin found "the spirit of youth seems not to desert them."[91] Despite this reputation, French Canadians did participate in direct action in the mills of the Northern Forest and elsewhere when the correct conditions arose.[92]

As described in chapter 2, Americans had long depicted French-Canadian agriculture as regressive, and this became associated with their race.[93] In 1887, travel writer Frederic Gregory Mather found that the exhausted soil left them destitute. Thousands, Mather argued, travel to "help the Vermont farmers, or to work in the brick-yards of New England . . . they return with almost the only money they ever see." They reproduced their ignorance, according to the author, who supposedly witnessed streets full of "neglected children . . . [proof that] one generation of illiterate, unkept idlers succeed another." Turner wrote that "the simple and ignorant Acadian farmers, continu[ed] the primitive customs of the basin of Grand Pre, along the tranquil water of the Tesche, remote from the corroding touch of busy modern life."[94] French Canadians could clear wilderness land under direction, but like African Americans, southern Italians, Jews, and other "savage" races, they could never bring civilization to it. In 1881, a year before Chinese exclusion was passed, the Massachusetts Bureau of Statistics of Labor infamously wrote that French Canadians were "the Chinese of the Eastern states." Commons declared the French Canadians had a "a standard of living lower than that of the Irish or Italians." Conveying both the French-Canadian lack of independence and their racial inferiority, Madison Grant wrote they were "a poor and ignorant community of little more importance to the world at large than are the Negroes in the South."[95] One northern New York newspaper published an article in 1904 proclaiming, "these French Canadian inhabitants of the woods are half-wild folk." They were a people in between White and savage.[96]

There was a growing disdain for these immigrants outside work camps. In 1919, the Maine legislature considered banning French in public schools, an action meant to exclude or assimilate French Canadians.[97] By the 1920s, eugenicists were arguing that French-Canadian "defectives" retreated to mountain valleys in New England to interbreed to produce more defectives. Eugenicists found that French Canadians were disproportionately represented among the states' degenerates and delinquents. The Ku Klux Klan, an organization that might have had as many as 150,000 members in Maine alone at its peak, targeted the French. The organization was instrumental in breaking up the effort of the IWW to organize French-Canadian lumber workers in Greenville, ME, in 1924.[98]

The reasons why French Canadians faced discrimination—their unique racial traits—were the same reasons mills and landowners coveted them. Once in camp, there is evidence that French Canadians were subject to very harsh treatment. Bullying bosses pushed foreigners hard and disciplined them severely. A boss in St. Lawrence County, NY, shot and killed a French-Canadian worker in 1908 after a disagreement about food.[99] This type of rough treatment may have caused the famous French-Canadian "jumping" disease, a type of posttraumatic stress disorder reported in a few Northeastern camps.[100]

Beginning in the 1930s, the explicit racial thinking of the first two decades of the twentieth century was becoming dated.[101] Anthropologists and sociologists from the University of Chicago and some other schools adopted new narratives and methods. They used ethnographic observation and other data to explain differences between groups. These narratives reinforced all the characteristics of the French-Canadian image created by eugenicists, however. Examples can be found in Elin L. Anderson's *We Americans: A Study of Change in an American City* (1937), Horace Miner's *St. Denis: A French Canadian Parish* (1939), Everett C. Hughes's *French Canada in Transition* (1944), and Robert Redfield's *Peasant Society and Culture: An Anthropological Approach to Civilization* (1956).[102]

Not a New Deal for Everyone

Into the 1950s, French Canadians were considered a primitive or wild people, a people whose bodies were considered another part of cheap nature. Progressive and New Deal labor reforms were meant to end the exploitation of vulnerable working bodies but only the bodies of citizens. For example, the influx of immigration created labor competition that was degrading for the American working class, so the Johnson-Reed Act limited immigration to limit competition, but Canadian workers were excluded. They could continue to work at wages below the American standard of living. Northern Forest logging was an industry of small, outdoor contractors who were historically connected to farming. New Deal labor protections were designed for male, head-of-household, manufacturing workers whose work environments were vertically integrated, urban, and indoors. Logging was at the intersection of three loopholes in these Progressive and New Deal protections: the immigration restriction loophole described above, the small business loophole, and the farming loophole, the latter two of which were described in chapter 3. For instance, the 1938 Fair Labor Standards Act banned child labor but exceptions were carved out for farmers and certain small firms. In all cases, children were not legally allowed to participate in "felling, bucking, skidding, loading, or unloading timber with butt diameter of more than 6 inches."[103] Despite the regulations, a 1945 film produced in part by the Brown Company and the War Production Board unabashedly shows young children helping to buck logs. Jobs like swamping, tending roads, cooking, and many others were all legal for children, immigrant and native born alike.[104] New Deal regulators were aware of the detrimental effects that contracting had on labor conditions but enforcing these labor regulations for small businesses in the hinterland was difficult or unconstitutional, and so they were explicitly ignored by legislation. Single men who traveled between many occupations were likewise unregulatable and also not protected.[105]

By the 1950s, a "shacking system" of forest product production evolved in the Northern Forest that epitomized the loopholes in the New Deal as well as the general search for cheap nature that has been described in this book. An employee of Maine's Great Northern Paper Company described it thus:

> A shacker is a [French Canadian] man, usually with a family, and one or two relatives who will move onto company land, build himself a shack to live in, cut pulp through the cutting season and haul it to the designated hauling point. . . . Usually the whole family, regardless of age, works with the father in the woods. The children rarely attend school. . . . The shacker invariably is semi-literate. . . . If a contract can be drawn that will make these shackers independent contractors we will be able to relieve ourselves of a great deal of responsibility and will be able to produce wood much cheaper.[106]

The shacking system, a labor arrangement typically used by jobbers and large mills, mimicked the way that French-Canadian habitant families were thought to have lived in Québec. Maine American Federation of Labor president Benjamin Dorsky testified to the Senate that Canadian children as young as four or five were working in the woods. In one instance in the 1950s, eight Canadians reportedly lived together in the winter, in a dirt floor shack alongside their horses. In another instance, French-Canadian workers were housed in "an old abandoned bus." These conditions made production cheap. In 1955, Brown made 145 petitions for bonded workers, each petition requesting a dozen workers or more. Ninety of these petitions came from Brown's jobbers.[107]

Racializing workers created an idea that these people did not deserve good conditions or wages. According to one Mainer in the 1950s, "[French Canadians] are accustomed to a somewhat lower living standard." Maine jobber Joseph Pooler was candid: "I would save money by using 'bonds.' If I scaled his wood, I see a bad log . . . [I] don't pay for that. Then I will load the wood, I will take it. I will get my pay. The Canadian will be gone . . . he won't know anything . . . I am in business to make money, and Canadians are available, those are the boys I am going to have . . . I can scale them down. You can make them work harder. They will live under worse conditions."[108] Another Maine jobber, Roland Lang, testified "I think we agree . . . [the Canadian] has been exploited. . . . He knows he is not loved." But exploitation of labor was necessary in the cutover forest. When defending the bonded labor program, a pulp mill representative declared: "[we] must compete with . . . the industry in the Northwest, where 1 tree produced more wood than 10 trees in the Northeast." This treatment of labor made the cutover forest more valuable over time. Between 1947 and 1953, the pulp industry increased gross annual production value by $450 million to reach a valuation of $1.18 billion.[109]

The perpetuation of the French-Canadian image filtered down to American-born workers, making it possible for the Brown Company to use one of the most common forms of racial management—divide and conquer. In 1952, American-born loggers for the Brown Company approached officials from the International Brotherhood of Pulp, Sulphite, and Paper Mill Workers (IBPSPMW) to try to form a union. The workers believed that the going rate of price per cord of pulp was being undercut by French Canadian guest workers, dropping from $7.50 to $5.50–$6.00 between 1952 and 1955. The result of this meeting was, according to one company official, that Brown became "the first company in the Northeast in which the attempt at organization of woodcutters was . . . made."[110]

There was confusion about whether guest workers could vote in National Labor Relations Board (NLRB) elections, and the IBPSPMW wanted to define the bargaining unit as American workers exclusively. IBPSPMW lawyer Samuel E. Angoff argued bonded workers disrupted the union drive because "you can't get in to see these Canadians in the woods. If you do get them to sign cards, by the time the National Labor Relations Board comes down with a decision, they have gone, so you have to start all over again."

In November 1954, Brown refused to meet with union representatives and a strike was called. According to Angoff, the Immigration and Naturalization Services, the New Hampshire state organization in charge of bonded workers, and the Attorney General's office threatened to "permit as many Canadian laborers to come in and take the jobs of Americans who were on strike." The police were there guarding the "entrance to the woods" and protecting "imported scabs," the union argued. Brown Company vice president of Woods Operations Clarence S. Herr disagreed, saying only sixty out of 700 workers struck and "no effort was made . . . to fill in back of those men." He continued, "we did . . . in the . . . unaffected portion of our operation, bring in Canadians." The strike lasted a week and collapsed.[111]

By September 1955, IBPSPMW was again organizing woodcutters. This time, according to NLRB instructions, they were including bonded workers. They wanted a $2 increase per cord cut, a demand that would have cost the company "approximately $200,000 a year." For comparison, that year Brown was making investments in their physical plants that amounted to somewhere between "$10 and $16 million" and had profits of $3,411,175. The company waged, in their own words, an "intensive campaign" in the camps and in their labor agency in Canada to convince workers, Canadians specifically, to vote against the union. To exacerbate the ethnic schism between American and Canadian workers, Brown sent flyers indicating the IBPSPMW's initial purpose was to exclude Canadians from the union, and ultimately from the Northern Forest in general. In November the union was certified, with only 25 percent of the workers voting against. The United Northeast Woods Workers Local 809 was the first recognized union of woodcutters in the history of the Northern Forest.[112]

United Northeast Woods Workers was short-lived and relatively ineffective in the face of larger changes transpiring in the Northern Forest after the 1950s, changes discussed in the Epilogue. The union proves that French-Canadian and American workers understood their common conditions and that Americans could see past the French-Canadian image that had been drilled into the heads of generations of Americans. After all, by the 1950s many of these native-born New Hampshire loggers could trace their family history back to Québec.[113] The image of the French Canadian was a result of these peoples' connection with the forest, a connection that many Northern Forest residents shared.[114] Illinois Senator Paul Douglass, who was raised in Maine and worked as a logger, reported in the investigation on bonded laborers that, in the Northern Forest, "small farmers [are] very similar to the small farmers on the Canadian side of the border."[115]

The use of racialized French-Canadian bodies was another type of cheap nature that allowed the cutover forest to remain profitable. This racialization was one example of a larger historical phenomenon that Jason W. Moore described, whereby "Some people became Human, who were members of something called Civilization . . . most humans were either excluded from Humanity . . . or were designated as *only part* Human [emphasis added]." Those who were conceived of as not human, or only part human, were nature and could be justifiably exploited like other natural resources. This process is as old as colonialism, but the more recent race science gave this specific type of search for cheap nature renewed vigor.[116] Though some workers were conceived as less than human, nearly every group had a unique and maximally efficient place in the industrial economy. Racist industrial policies were synonymous with economically robust industrial policies. By the 1950s, systematic racism had been a part of American political and economic thought for more than a century and its effects were hard to dislodge.[117] Despite the victory of the United Northeast Woods Workers, the exploitation of French-Canadian immigrant workers and hostilities between American and Canadian loggers on the border remain problems in the Northern Forest in 2023.[118]

EPILOGUE

Land, Labor, and Local History

The events leading to the formation of the United Northeast Woods Workers Local 809 demonstrate many of the defining features of cutover capitalism. In this case, the rhetoric on race and French-Canadian difference obscured the fact that cutover capitalism depended on treating all workers like disposable nature, regardless of their ethnicity. After the 1950s, as fossil fuels were implemented to profitable effect in the Northern Forest, local communities began to understand and respect the history of an older type of work, where people worked in unison with their environment. To explain this veneration of the past, this epilogue returns to contemporary Tupper Lake, the place where this book began.

When I visited Tupper Lake as a child, I was disappointed that I didn't encounter the lumberjacks of my imagination. The only things left were symbols of these workers in the form of school mascots, statues, and lumberjack competitions. Other important parts of the Northern Forest workforce—the trees, the snow, and the rivers—were still thriving. Across the street from my camp was a dense forest of mixed second growth. This was private property but also conservation land, part of the wider system of private-public conservation that makes the Adirondacks unique. Forest products production on most public lands in the Adirondacks is forbidden, and cutting on private land is regulated in many instances across the Northern Forest. In 1989, Maine, perhaps the least regulated of the Northern Forest states, passed a law that limited the size of clear cuts for the sake of maintaining biodiversity.[1] Even when legal, development and industry is unpopular among many locals.[2] Above all other concerns, preservation in the Adirondacks means mitigating or eliminating extraction of forest products from protected land. Local communities in league with their state governments now choose to preserve the forest instead of extracting value from it. This celebration of the lumberjack and the regional popularity of conservation seems like a contradiction, but a deeper understanding of history as locals understand it lends clarity to this inconsistency.[3]

Of course, the shift away from industrial production cannot be blamed solely on the desire to preserve the forest. As economist Michael Hillard has shown, the paper industry in the Northern Forest was dismantled by a neoliberal management style beginning in the 1970s. Management and owners' priorities shifted to shareholder profitability, and mills across the Northern Forest, mills that had supported entire communities for generations, were shuttered because they were not profitable enough.[4]

As neoliberalism was closing mills, a new type of cheap nature altered production in the woods, which drew attention to the historical significance of the older type of logging labor described in the second section of this book. Understanding the place of this new cheap nature in local narratives helps unravel the apparent contradiction between forest conservation and the celebration of the lumberjack. Fossil capital, the term Andreas Malm uses to describe production regimes dependent on coal or petroleum, took an inordinate amount of time to reach the Northern Forest, but when it did it reorganized the position of people in relation to the seasons and the nonhuman things that they worked with. After World War II, the gas-powered chainsaw slowly began to de-skill and reduce the cutting workforce, while the bulldozer, logging truck, and the feller-buncher replaced horses and also made isolated camps, river drives, and winter-dependent cutting inefficient. Bodies ceased to become the most important throughput in this industry. This new type of production did not end the search for cheap nature, however; it just shifted where the externalities were. Fossil fuel-powered production meant increased emissions that added to the greenhouse effect and climate change, the textbook examples of negative externalities.[5] While forest product production hasn't disappeared, both conservation and new management styles meant that the industry no longer held the predominant economic place it once had.[6]

The rise of fossil capital in the Northern Forest led to a reinterpretation of the past. For example, International Brotherhood of Pulp, Sulphite, and Paper Mill Workers representative Samuel Angoff told the US Senate in 1955, "The old-fashioned logger or lumber worker . . . is gone. A bulldozer makes a good road into the woods . . . men working in the woods . . . take . . . their little Fords . . . and go home every night. [The worker is usually] a married man with several children, perfectly sober, owns a home . . . and participates in every aspect of community life." Angoff stressed the bodily effort required for logging work before fossil capital: "A third piece of equipment that has changed everything in the woods is the crane. Instead of lifting these logs by hand, these huge logs are now lifted, sometimes in packs of 10, 12, or more." Ending his eulogy of this older labor process, Angoff testified, "I have watched what we call the spring drive, but they are nothing like the old-fashioned spring drives." Harold K. Hochschild, local Adirondack historian and founder of The Adirondack Museum (now the Adirondack Experience), agreed. In 1962 Hochschild wrote "The lumberjack has gained in health, in safety of life and limb and in steady employment. He has become respectable and commonplace."[7]

The nostalgic stories of logging history and the accounts of lumberjack bodies at work were shaped, in part, by a long history of actual observations of Northern Forest workers. In the 1850s, during his trips to Maine, Henry David Thoreau wrote: "our woods are sylvan, and their inhabitants woodsmen and rustics . . . men nearer of kin to the rocks and the wild animals than we." He called the backwoodsmen camp "a slight departure from the hollow tree which the bear still inhabits." To Thoreau these people were like "the deer and moose, the bear and wolf."[8] By the turn of the century, loggers were depicted as "a pure strain apart from the ordinary run of men."[9] They were said to be able to lift horses and wrestle with moose.[10] One industrial observer reported that loggers' "woodcraft blends with, rather than destroys, what is picturesque in nature."[11] They were called "timber beasts," "tigers," and later "riverpigs."[12] To those who spent time with these workers, there was something special about them and their work. For close readers there is plenty of evidence to suggest that contemporaries understood that the real value in the Northern Forest came from the inhabitants and workers, not the land.

People who were very close to the workers and the land began to see the work of "old time" lumberjacks—this synchronicity between people, snow, water, trees, and horses—as something special. This nostalgia for a defunct labor process fills the pages of the dozens of local history books written on the industry after the 1950s.[13] These stories are powerful in shaping perceptions. For example, on September 2, 2010, in Tupper Lake, the local library held a "reading marathon" of the popular local history book *Mostly Spruce and Hemlock* (1976) by Louis Simmons, a book currently in its second edition. According to the *Adirondack Daily Enterprise*, the "reading event . . . [featured] 76 people reading 461 pages for 19 hours" to "promote reading and local literature."[14]

To locals who trust these histories, who read them out loud together for hours, the Northern Forest as a historical landscape was a place where men worked hard alongside other living and nonliving things. Reflecting on the height of the forest products industry, one Northern Forest denizen wrote around 2001 that "the [area] is defined by hard work . . . Here, and north of us, the whole lifestyle, ecosystem—they're hardworking folks."[15] Speaking about economic development in Maine in 2015, then-Governor Paul LePage said that "Maine has had a work ethic for hundreds of years. And while I would be the first to admit it's not as good as it was 150 years ago, it's still the best in America."[16] This book has made explicit an implied assumption that helps define modern Northern Forest culture, that it was workers' bodies who were the primary contributors to value creation and economic development. In doing so, the book has cautiously considered local history, folklore, and oral history, both for the insights they provide into the history of capitalism and for what they reveal about how locals understood loggers and the land.[17]

To understand this veneration of past workers, it helps to understand the interconnected relationship between the stories that people told about the Northern Forest, the work, and the land. Adirondack historian Philip G. Terrie explains: "People tell stories about the land that reflect their needs. They project their needs onto the land in the stories they tell about it. They define—in a sense, create—the land in their stories. These stories either achieve currency in the popular imagination or they fail to do so. . . . By 'story' I do not mean fiction; I mean widely shared understanding about the land's meaning deriving from accounts of actual encounters with the land."[18]

Terrie's analysis is correct, but can be extended further. The relationship between land and people is symbiotic and dialectical. Landscapes are defined by people, but people become defined by or even absorbed into their landscapes in the process of working on them. As they work, they change the land, and the process repeats in a new form.

The celebration of logging workers in the Northern Forest, whether it is in local history books, statues, or mascots, is not a celebration of labor exclusively. These narratives are celebrations of a labor process, an envirotechnical landscape that emerged after the enclosure of forest land and as the forest industrialized using snow, ice, seasonal change, horses, and racialized bodies. Celebrations of the lumberjack are also celebrations of the forest ecosystem. People who were deeply connected to cutover capitalism witnessed their bodies, or the bodies of their narrative subjects, friends, or relatives, entangled with the forest and used in the same callous way as the trees. This is reflected in the long lineage of local history and memory, and is evidence of a type of solidarity that bridged the gap between workers and the forest. Northern Forest people could not preserve the old lumberjack class and their venerated labor process, and that is probably a good thing. They could and did preserve the landscape that once created the lumberjack class and the landscape that still held within it the memory of this class. When I look at the wood-carved and hand-painted lumberjack statue in Tupper Lake today, the statue that opened this book, I don't see it as a commemoration of labor power as it is typically conceived. This statue represents nature, an all-encompassing nature that includes workers.[19]

MANUSCRIPT COLLECTIONS

Albany, NY. Cultural Education Center. New York State Library. Manuscripts and Special Collections.

Albany, NY. Cultural Education Center. New York State Library. New York State Archives.

Barre, VT. Vermont Historical Society. Leahy Library.

Berlin, NH. Berlin and Coös County Historical Society.

Blue Mountain Lake, NY. Adirondack Experience (Formally the Adirondack Museum).

Cambridge, MA. Harvard Business School. Baker Library Historical Collections.

Cambridge, MA. Harvard University. Radcliffe College. Schlesinger Library.

Concord, NH. New Hampshire Historical Society.

Durham, NC. Forest History Society. Oral History Interview Collection. (FHS) (OHIC)

Orono, ME. Maine Folklife Center. University of Maine at Orono. "Lumberman's Life Collection." (MFC) (LLC)

Orono, ME. University of Maine. Raymond H. Fogler Library. Special Collections.

Portland, ME. Maine Historical Society. Brown Library.

Rangeley, ME. Rangeley Lakes Region Logging Museum.

Syracuse, NY. State University of New York College of Environmental Science and Forestry. Moon Library. Special Collections & College Archives.

NOTES

Introduction

1 Louis J. Simmons, *Mostly Spruce and Hemlock* (Saranac Lake, NY: Hungry Bear Publishing, 1979), 159.
2 Jerry Jenkins and Andy Keal, *The Adirondack Atlas: A Geographic Portrait of the Adirondack Park* (Syracuse, NY: Syracuse University Press, 2004), 112, 130, 124; Stephen C. Harper, Laura L. Falk, and Edward W. Rankin, *The Northern Forest Lands Study of New England and New York: A Report to the Congress of the United States on the Recent Changes in Landownership and Land Use in the Northern Forest of Maine, New Hampshire, New York and Vermont* (Rutland, VT: Forest Service, US Department of Agriculture, 1990), 35.
3 J. M. Long and Peter Bauer, *The Adirondack Park and Rural America: Economic and Population Trends 1970–2010* (North Creek, NY: Protect the Adirondacks!, 2019).
4 Gary M. Walton and Hugh Rockoff, *History of the American Economy* (Boston: Cengage Learning, 2013), 300.
5 John G. Franzen, *The Archaeology of the Logging Industry* (Gainesville: University Press of Florida, 2020), 22.
6 Christopher McGrory Klyza and Stephen C. Trombulak, *The Future of the Northern Forest* (Middlebury, VT: Middlebury College Press, 1994), 1; Harper, Falk, and Rankin, *The Northern Forest Lands Study of New England and New York* 1, 33; Pavel Cenkl, "Reading Place in the Northern Forest," in *Nature and Culture in the Northern Forest: Region, Heritage, and Environment in the Rural Northeast*, ed. Pavel Cenkl (Iowa City: University of Iowa Press, 2010), 12.
7 Mark Paul Richard, "'This Is Not a Catholic Nation': The Ku Klux Klan Confronts Franco-Americans in Maine," *New England Quarterly* 82, no. 2 (2009): 296–297.
8 Charles Andrew Scontras, *Organized Labor in Maine: War, Reaction, Depression, and the Rise of the CIO 1914–1943* (Orono: Bureau of Labor Education, University of Maine, 2002), 180–181.
9 Brown Company Records, Brown Company Management v. Mv14, "Program for Special Meeting of Board of Directors to Be Held in New York, September 12, 1955," p. 7, New Hampshire Historical Society; John B. Allen, *Reflections of Berlin* (Berlin, NH: Berlin City Bank, 1985); Charles A. Scontras, *Collective Efforts among Maine Workers: Beginnings and Foundations, 1820–1880* (Orono: Bureau of Labor Education, University of Maine, 1994), 112.
10 Michael G. Hillard, *Shredding Paper: The Rise and Fall of Maine's Mighty Paper Industry* (Ithaca, NY: Cornell University Press, 2020), 140.
11 Franzen, *The Archaeology of the Logging Industry*, 36; Melvyn Dubofsky, *We Shall Be All: A History of the Industrial Workers of the World* (Chicago: Quadrangle Books, 1969).

12 Karl Marx, *Capital: A Critique of Political Economy* (Harmondsworth: Penguin, 1990); Louis Hyman, "Why Study the History of Capitalism?" in *American Capitalism: A Reader*, ed. Louis Hyman and Edward E. Baptist (New York: Simon and Schuster, 2014); Jonathan Levy, *Ages of American Capitalism: A History of the United States* (New York: Random House, 2021); Charles Sellers, *The Market Revolution: Jacksonian America, 1815–1846* (New York: Oxford University Press, 1991), 6, 128, 227; Max Weber, *The Protestant Ethic and the Spirit of Capitalism* (New York: Scribner, 1930), 52–54; Fernand Braudel, *Civilization and Capitalism, 15th–18th Century*, vol 2: *The Wheels of Commerce* (New York: Harper & Row, 1982), 232–243; Karl Polanyi, *The Great Transformation: The Political and Economic Origins of Our Time* (Boston: Beacon Press, 2001), 145–147.

13 Joseph A. Schumpeter, *Capitalism, Socialism and Democracy* (Florence: Taylor & Francis Group, 2010), 73.

14 There is a growing body of literature that connects environment, work, body, nature, and/or food. Christopher Sellers, "Thoreau's Body: Towards an Embodied Environmental History," *Environmental History* 4, no. 4 (1999), https://doi.org/10.2307/3985398; Bathsheba Demuth, *Floating Coast: An Environmental History of the Bering Strait* (New York: W. W. Norton, 2019); Joseph E. Taylor, *Persistent Callings: Seasons of Work and Identity on the Oregon Coast* (Corvallis: Oregon State University Press, 2019); Neil M. Maher, "The Body Counts: Tracking the Human Body through Environmental History" in *A Companion to American Environmental History*, ed. Douglas Cazaux Sackman (Chichester, UK: Wiley-Blackwell, 2010); Neil M. Maher, *Nature's New Deal: The Civilian Conservation Corps and the Roots of the American Environmental Movement* (Oxford: Oxford University Press, 2008), 13, 54, 84, 34; Ava Baron and Eileen Boris, "'The Body' as a Useful Category for Working-Class History," *Labor* 4, no. 2 (2007): 23–43; Stefania Barca, "Laboring the Earth: Transnational Reflections on the Environmental History of Work," *Environmental History* 19, no. 1 (2014): 3–27; Richard White, "Are You an Environmentalist or Do You Work for a Living?" in *Uncommon Ground: Rethinking the Human Place in Nature*, ed. William Cronon (New York: W. W. Norton, 1996); Gunther Peck, "The Nature of Labor: Fault Lines and Common Ground in Environmental and Labor History," *Environmental History* 11, no. 2 (2006): 213; Thomas G. Andrews, *Killing for Coal: America's Deadliest Labor War* (Cambridge, MA: Harvard University Press, 2008); John Field, *Working Men's Bodies: Work Camps in Britain, 1880–1940* (Manchester, UK: Manchester University Press, 2013), 5; Rachel Louise Moran, *Governing Bodies: American Politics and the Shaping of the Modern Physique* (Philadelphia: University of Pennsylvania Press, 2018); Cara New Daggett, *The Birth of Energy: Fossil Fuels, Thermodynamics and the Politics of Work* (Durham, NC: Duke University Press, 2019); Anson Rabinbach, *The Human Motor: Energy, Fatigue, and the Origins of Modernity* (Berkeley: University of California Press, 1992); Carolyn Merchant, *The Death of Nature: Women, Ecology, and the Scientific Revolution* (New York: Harper & Row, 1989).

15 E. A. Wrigley, *Energy and the English Industrial Revolution* (Cambridge: Cambridge University Press, 2010); Vaclav Smil, *Energy and Civilization: A History* (Cambridge, MA: MIT Press, 2017); John Robert McNeill, *Something New Under the Sun: An Environmental History of the Twentieth-Century World* (New York: W. W. Norton, 2000).

16 Murray Bookchin, *Post-Scarcity Anarchism* (Montreal: Black Rose Books, 1986), 85.

17 John F. Sitton, "Critique of the Gotha Programme," in *Marx Today: Selected Works and Recent Debates*, ed. John F. Sitton (New York: Palgrave MacMillan, 2010), 146.

18 Charles F. Carroll, *The Timber Economy of Puritan New England* (Providence, RI: Brown University Press, 1974), 9.

19 Carroll, *The Timber Economy*, 8.
20 Carroll, *The Timber Economy*, xi.
21 Ted Steinberg, *Down to Earth: Nature's Role in American History* (Oxford: Oxford University Press, 2002), 68.
22 Romeyn Berry, "A Natural History of Trees of Eastern and Central North America" (Book Review), *New York History* 32, no. 1 (1951): 81.
23 Franzen, *The Archaeology of the Logging Industry*, 5.
24 Keith Pluymers, *No Wood, No Kingdom: Political Ecology in the English Atlantic (The Early Modern Americas)* (Philadelphia: University of Pennsylvania Press, 2021), 3.
25 Carroll, *The Timber Economy*, 14.
26 Carroll, *The Timber Economy*, 11, 28; Yasuhide Kawashima and Ruth Tone, "Environmental Policy in Early America: A Survey of Colonial Statutes," *Journal of Forest History* 27, no. 4 (1983): 170.
27 Carroll, *The Timber Economy*, 19–21, 86.
28 Franzen, *The Archaeology of the Logging Industry*, 22.
29 Manuel González de Molina and Víctor M. Toledo, *The Social Metabolism: A Socio-Ecological Theory of Historical Change, vol. 3* (New York: Springer, 2014), 202.
30 Carroll, *The Timber Economy*, 14; Marc D. Abrams, "Eastern White Pine Versatility in the Presettlement Forest," *BioScience* 51, no. 11 (2001): 967–979.
31 Raj Patel and Jason W. Moore, *A History of the World in Seven Cheap Things: A Guide to Capitalism, Nature, and the Future of the Planet* (Berkeley: University of California Press, 2017); Joshua Specht, *Red Meat Republic: A Hoof-to-Table History of How Beef Changed America* (Princeton, NJ: Princeton University Press, 2019); Bryant Simon, *The Hamlet Fire: A Tragic Story of Cheap Food, Cheap Government, and Cheap Lives* (New York: The New Press, 2017); John R. McNeill, "Cheap Energy and Ecological Teleconnections of the Industrial Revolution, 1780–1920," *Environmental History* 24, no. 3 (2019): 463–533; Joshua R Eichen, "Cheapness and (Labor-)Power: The Role of Early Modern Brazilian Sugar Plantations in the Racializing Capitalocene," *Environment and Planning D: Society and Space* 38, no. 1 (2018): 35–52; John F. Richards, *The Unending Frontier: An Environmental History of the Early Modern World* (Berkeley: University of California Press, 2003), 347, 355, 377.
32 Carroll, *The Timber Economy*, 71, 9, 58, 83, 95, 110, 118–119; Strother E. Roberts, *Colonial Ecology, Atlantic Economy: Transforming Nature in Early New England* (Philadelphia: University of Pennsylvania Press, 2019), 141–142.
33 Nancy Langston, "Global Forests," in *A Companion to Global Environmental History*, ed. John Robert McNeill and Erin Stewart Mauldin (Hoboken, NJ: Wiley, 2012), 272–273.
34 Gunther Peck, "The Nature of Labor," 212–238; Liza Piper and John Sandlos, "A Broken Frontier: Ecological Imperialism in the Canadian North," *Environmental History* 12 no. 4 (2007): 759–795; William Buckhout Greeley, Earle Hart Clapp, Joseph Kittredge, Herbert Augustine Smith, Ward Shepard, William Norwood Sparhawk, and Raphael Zon, "Timber: Mine or Crop?," vol. 886 (Washington, DC: US Government Printing Office, 1923), 118–119.
35 William Cronon, "Turner's First Stand: The Significance of American History," in *Writing Western History: Essays on Major Western Historians*, ed. Richard Etulain (Reno: University of Nevada Press, 2002), 82.
36 Greeley et al., "Timber: Mine or Crop?," 83; James Willard Hurst, *Law and Economic Growth: The Legal History of the Lumber Industry in Wisconsin, 1836–1915* (Cambridge, MA: Harvard University Press, 1964), 83; Franzen, *The Archaeology of the Logging Industry*, 101.
37 Hurst, *Law and Economic Growth*, 112–113.

38 David C. Smith, "The Logging Frontier," *Journal of Forest History* 18, no. 4 (1974): 96–106; Thomas R. Cox, *The Lumberman's Frontier: Three Centuries of Land Use, Society, and Change in America's Forests* (Corvallis: Oregon State University Press, 2010). This also adheres to Johann Heinrich von Thünen's argument on wages, rents, and distance from markets in his 1826 *Isolated State*. Johann Heinrich von Thünen, *Isolated State: An English Edition of Der Isolierte Staat*, ed. Peter Geoffrey Hall (Oxford: Pergamon Press, 1966).

39 Marian Brown, "Technology and The North American Forest," *Scientia Canadensis* 16, no. 2 (1992): 195; Louis T. Steyaert and Robert G. Knox, "Reconstructed Historical Land Cover and Biophysical Parameters for Studies of Land-Atmosphere Interactions within the Eastern United States," *Journal of Geophysical Research: Atmospheres* 113, no. D2 (2008); Norman S. Hayner, "Taming the Lumberjack," *American Sociological Review* 10, no. 2 (1945): 217; Ted Steinberg, *Down to Earth: Nature's Role in American History* (New York: Oxford University Press, 2002), 64–67; Cox, *The Lumberman's Frontier*; Smith, "The Logging Frontier"; Michael Williams, *Americans and Their Forests: A Historical Geography* (Cambridge: Cambridge University Press, 1992); Hurst, *Law and Economic Growth*, 183.

40 Tom Hull, "'More Deadly Than War': High-Lead Steam Logging Unit," *Technology and Culture* 44, no. 2 (2003): 355–358; Brown, "Technology and The North American Forest," 196; Franzen, *The Archaeology of the Logging Industry*, 82.

41 Michael R. Redclift, *Frontiers: Histories of Civil Society and Nature* (Cambridge, MA: MIT Press, 2006), 21–22; Franzen, *The Archaeology of the Logging Industry*, 19; Cox, *The Lumberman's Frontier*.

42 Edelman and Wolford, "Introduction: Critical Agrarian Studies in Theory and Practice Symposium: Agrarianism in Theory and Practice," *Antipode* 49, no. 4 (2017): 967.

43 Naomi Klein, *The Shock Doctrine: The Rise of Disaster Capitalism* (New York: Macmillan, 2007); Anna Lowenhaupt Tsing, *The Mushroom at the End of the World: On the Possibility of Life in Capitalist Ruins* (Princeton, NJ: Princeton University Press, 2015), 18, 30, 62–63.

44 Gerard George and Simon J. D. Schillebeeckx, *Managing Natural Resources* (Cheltenham, UK: Edward Elgar Publishing, 2018), 14.

45 David Edgerton, *The Shock of the Old: Technology and Global History Since 1900* (London: Profile Books, 2011), 187.

46 Daniel Immerwahr, *How to Hide an Empire: A History of the Greater United States* (New York: Random House, 2019), 18, 271.

47 David E. Nye, *America as Second Creation: Technology and Narratives of New Beginnings* (Cambridge, MA: MIT Press, 2004); Harry Braverman, *Labor and Monopoly Capital: The Degradation of Work in The Twentieth Century* (New York: NYU Press, 1998).

48 Margaret Elley Felt, *Gyppo Logger* (Seattle: University of Washington Press, 2017), 52–53.

49 Felt, *Gyppo Logger*, 9–10; Steven C. Beda, "'Tie a Yellow Ribbon for the Working Man': Environmental Conflict and Working-Class Politics in Oregon Timber Country, 1970–Present," *Labor* 20, no. 1 (2023): 85–111.

50 E. B. Mittelman, "The Gyppo System," *The Journal of Political Economy* 31, no. 6 (1923): 840; Robert E. Walls and Dora Zimpel, "Lady Loggers and Gyppo Wives: Women and Northwest Logging," *Oregon Historical Quarterly* 103, no. 3 (2002): 362–382.

51 Felt, *Gyppo Logger*, 4.

52 Quoted in Mittelman, "The Gyppo System," 850.

53 Frank Barkley Copley, *Frederick W. Taylor: Father of Scientific Management*, vol. 2 (New York: Harper and Brothers, 1923), 395–396.
54 Frederick Winslow Taylor, *The Principles of Scientific Management* (New York: Harper, [1911] 1913), 5.
55 Edmund Russell, "Introduction: The Garden in the Machine: 1 Toward an Evolutionary History of Technology" in *Industrializing Organisms: Introducing Evolutionary History*, ed. Susan Schrepfer and Philip Scranton (New York: Routledge, 2004), 2.
56 Levy, *Ages of American Capitalism*, 236–237.
57 Edward E. Baptist, *The Half Has Never Been Told: Slavery and the Making of American Capitalism* (Boulder, CO: Basic Books, 2012), 136; Mark Fiege, "King Cotton: The Cotton Plant and Southern Slavery," in *The Republic of Nature: An Environmental History of the United States* (Seattle: University of Washington Press, 2012), 119; Caitlin Rosenthal, *Accounting for Slavery: Masters and Management* (Boston: Harvard University Press, 2019).
58 Patel and Moore, *A History of the World in Seven Cheap Things*, 19.
59 Moore, *Capitalism in the Web of Life*, 53.
60 Jason W. Moore, "The Rise of Cheap Nature" in *Anthropocene or Capitalocene?: Nature, History, and The Crisis of Capitalism*, ed. Christian Parenti and Jason W. Moore (Oakland, CA: PM Press, 2016), 92.
61 Craig G. Lorimer, "Eastern White Pine Abundance in 19th-Century Forests: A Reexamination of Evidence from Land Surveys and Lumber Statistics," *Journal of Forestry* 106, no. 5 (2008): 258.
62 Harold F. Wilson, *The Hill Country of Northern New England: Its Social and Economic History, 1790–1930* (New York: Columbia University Press, 1936); Hal S. Barron, *Those Who Stayed Behind: Rural Society in Nineteenth-Century New England* (Cambridge: Cambridge University Press, 1984).
63 Steyaert and Knox, "Reconstructed Historical Land Cover," 48; Charles E. Oak, *Annual Report of the Forest Commissioner of the State of Maine* (Augusta, ME: Burleigh & Flynt, 1896), 137; Bernard Albert Chandler, "Lumbering in Northern Maine: As Illustrated by an Operation of the Emerson Lumber Company" (Thesis, University of Maine Orono, 1909), 9–10; David Nathan Rogers, *Lumbering in Northern Maine* (Thesis, University of Maine Orono, 1906), 9.
64 Hillard, *Shredding Paper*, 5; William Parenteau, "The Rise of the Small Contractor: A Study of Technological and Structural Change in the Maine Pulpwood Industry" (PhD diss., University of Maine, Orono, ME, 1986), 4.
65 Quote in Charlotte Todes, *Labor and Lumber* (New York: International Publishers, 1931), 120; Glenn C. Prescott and Raymond E. Rendall, "Lumbering in the Dead River Region, Somerset County, Maine" (Ph.D. diss. University of Maine–Orono, 1916), 42–47; William James Henry Miller, James Plummer Poole, and Harlan Hayes Sweetser, "A Lumbering Report of Work on Squaw Mountain Township, Winter of 1911–1912" (Thesis, University of Maine–Orono, 1912), 2–3; Rogers, "Lumbering in Northern Maine," 7; Chandler, "Lumbering in Northern Maine . . . Emerson Company," 10; David C. Smith, *A History of Lumbering in Maine, 1861–1960* (Orono: University of Maine Press, 1972), 22–23.
66 Franzen, *The Archaeology of the Logging Industry*, 102–103.
67 Smil, *Energy and Civilization*, 388.
68 Parenteau, "The Rise of the Small Contractor," x; Evelyn M. Dinsdale (Evelyn Stokes), "Spatial Patterns of Technological Change: The Lumber Industry of Northern New York," *Economic Geography* 41, no. 3 (1965): 255; Ian Walter Radforth, *Bushworkers and Bosses: Logging in Northern Ontario, 1900–1980* (Toronto:

University of Toronto Press, 1987), 4, 26, 78–79, 192; Edmund W. Bradwin, *The Bunkhouse Man: A Study of Work and Pay in the Camps of Canada, 1903–1914* (Toronto: University of Toronto Press, 1972), 161; Richard William Judd and Patricia A. Judd, *Aroostook: A Century of Logging in Northern Maine* (Orono: University of Maine Press, 1988), 130, 188; Alexander Koroleff, *Pulpwood Cutting: Efficiency of Technique*, no. 630 (Montreal: Woodlands Section, Canadian Pulp and Paper Association, 1941), 43–44; Alexander Koroleff, *Pulpwood Skidding with Horses: Efficiency of Technique*, no. 694 (Montreal: Woodlands Section, Canadian Pulp and Paper Association, 1943); Brown, "Technology and The North American Forest," 196.

69 Daniel Auerbach and Brett Clark, "Metabolic Rifts, Temporal Imperatives, and Geographical Shifts: Logging in the Adirondack Forest in the 1800s," *International Critical Thought* 8, no. 3 (2018): 468–486; John Bellamy Foster, *Marx's Ecology: Materialism and Nature* (New York: Monthly Review Press, 2000).

I. The Work of Trees

1 Jamie Organski, "A Fallen Giant," *Adirondack Explorer*, January 10, 2022; Susan Orlean, "The Tallest Known Tree in New York Falls in the Forest," *The New Yorker*, January 18, 2022.

2 Henry David Thoreau and Jeffrey S. Cramer, *The Maine Woods: A Fully Annotated Edition* (New Haven, CT: Yale University Press, 2009), 74.

3 Harold F. Wilson, *The Hill Country of Northern New England: Its Social and Economic History, 1790–1930* (New York: Columbia University Press, 1936), 5.

4 Jerry Jenkins and Andy Keal, *The Adirondack Atlas: A Geographic Portrait of the Adirondack Park* (Syracuse, NY: Syracuse University Press, 2004), 9; Christopher McGrory Klyza and Stephen C. Trombulak, *The Future of the Northern Forest* (Middlebury, VT: Middlebury College Press, 1994), 1; US Department of the Interior and US Geological Survey, *Elevations and Distances in the United States* (Reston, VA: US Department of the Interior, US Geological Survey, 1991), 5–7.

5 Richard W. Judd, *Second Nature: An Environmental History of New England* (Amherst: University of Massachusetts Press, 2014), 101.

6 Barbara McMartin, *The Great Forest of the Adirondacks* (Utica, NY: North Country Books, 1994), 8; Jenkins and Keal, *The Adirondack Atlas*, 18; Stephen C. Harper, Laura L. Falk, and Edward W. Rankin, *The Northern Forest Lands Study of New England and New York: A Report to the Congress of the United States on the Recent Changes in Landownership and Land Use in the Northern Forest of Maine, New Hampshire, New York and Vermont* (Rutland, VT: Forest Service, US Department of Agriculture, 1990), 22–23; Richard William Judd, *Common Lands, Common People: The Origins of Conservation in Northern New England* (Boston, MA: Harvard University Press, 1997), 16; Christopher McGrory Klyza and Stephen C. Trombulak, *The Future of the Northern Forest* (Middlebury, VT: Middlebury College Press, 1994), 15.

7 Andrew Barton, "Introduction: Ecological and Historical Context" in *Ecology and Recovery of Eastern Old-Growth Forests*, ed. Andrew Barton and William Keeton (Washington, DC: Island Press/Center for Resource Economics, 2018); Peter J. Marchand, *North Woods: An Inside Look at the Nature of Forests in the Northeast* (Boston: Appalachian Mountain Club, 1987), 3–5.

8 Marchand, *North Woods*, 6–7.

9 Marchand, *North Woods*, 6–7; Anthony W. D'Amato, Patricia Raymond, and Shawn Fraver, "Old-Growth Disturbance Dynamics and Associated Ecological Silviculture for Forests in Northeastern North America," in Andrew Barton and William Keeton, *Ecology and Recovery of Eastern Old-Growth Forests* (Washington, DC: Island Press/Center for Resource Economics, 2018).

10 Mark S. Monmonier, *Lake Effect: Tales of Large Lakes, Arctic Winds, and Recurrent Snows* (Syracuse, NY: Syracuse University Press, 2012), 16.
11 Monmonier, *Lake Effect*, 5–13, 92–93.
12 Marchand, *North Woods*, 88.
13 Thoreau and Cramer, *The Maine Woods*, 17.
14 Béatrice Craig, "Agriculture and the Lumberman's Frontier in the Upper St. John Valley, 1800–70," *Journal of Forest History* 32, no. 3 (1988): 128; State of Maine, Department of Agriculture, *Sixth Annual Report of the Secretary of the Maine Board of Agriculture, 1861* (Augusta, ME: Stevens & Sayward, 1861), 30–31, 349–350, 352, 435; David R. Foster and John D. Aber, *Forests in Time: The Environmental Consequences of 1,000 Years of Change in New England* (New Haven, CT: Yale University Press, 2004), 23; Harper, Falk, and Rankin, *The Northern Forest Lands Study*, 23; Jenkins and Keal, *The Adirondack Atlas*, 4–5, 8–11, 22.
15 Marchand, *North Woods*, 11, 87.
16 Peter J. Marchand, *Life in The Cold: An Introduction to Winter Ecology* (Chicago: University Press of New England, 2014), 55-62.
17 Marchand, *Life in the Cold*, 81; Marchand, *North Woods*, 87, 125–131.
18 Marchand, *North Woods*, 41; Marchand, *Life in the Cold*, 53.
19 Changhong Liu, Tingting Liu, Fengfeng Yuan, and Yucheng Gu, "Isolating Endophytic Fungi from Evergreen Plants and Determining Their Antifungal Activities," *African Journal of Microbiology Research* 4, no. 21 (2010): 2243–2248.
20 Peter Wohlleben, *The Hidden Life of Trees: What They Feel How They Communicate : Discoveries from a Secret World* (Vancouver, BC: Greystone Books, 2016), 10–11.
21 M. F. Bekker and G. P. Malanson, "Linear Forest Patterns in Subalpine Environments," *Progress in Physical Geography* 32, no. 6 (2008): 645–648.
22 Jeffrey R. Foster and William A. Reiners, "Vegetation Patterns in a Virgin Subalpine Forest at Crawford Notch, White Mountains, New Hampshire," *Bulletin of the Torrey Botanical Club* (1983): 144.
23 Raymond D'Amato and Fraver, "Old-Growth Disturbance Dynamics."
24 Satoshi N. Suzuki, "Non-Equilibrium Dynamics of a Wave-Regenerated Forest Subject to Hierarchical Disturbance," *Journal of Vegetation Science* 27, no. 5 (2016): 969–979.
25 Marchand, *North Woods*, 96–99.
26 Barton, "Introduction: Ecological and Historical Context."
27 Harper, Falk, and Rankin, *The Northern Forest Lands Study*, 22, 24.
28 Marchand, *North Woods*, 2.
29 Trombulak, "A Natural History of the Northern Forest," 15–16.
30 Marchand, *North Woods*, 20.
31 William Freeman Fox, *A History of the Lumber Industry in the State of New York* (US Department of Agriculture, Bureau of Forestry, 1902), 77; McMartin, *Great Forest of the Adirondacks*, 118–122.
32 Jeremy S. Wilson, "Nineteenth-Century Lumber Surveys for Bangor, Maine: Implications for Pre-European Settlement Forest Characteristics in Northern and Eastern Maine," *Journal of Forestry* 103, no. 5 (2005): 222.
33 Barton and Keeton, *Ecology and Recovery of Eastern Old-Growth Forests*, 6, 111.
34 Richard William Judd and Patricia Judd, *Aroostook: A Century of Logging in Northern Maine* (Orono: University of Maine Press, 1988), 12; Thoreau and Cramer, *The Maine Woods*, 133; Harper, Falk, and Rankin, *The Northern Forest Lands Study*, 101; John Dickerson, "Plant Fact Sheet: Eastern White Pine, USDA, accessed January 15, 2015, http://plants.usda.gov/factsheet/pdf/fs_pist.pdf; Robert E. Pike, *Tall Trees, Tough Men* (New York: W. W. Norton, 1967), 23; William Cronon, *Changes in the Land: Indians, Colonists, and the Ecology of New England* (New York: Hill and Wang, 1983), 50, 145.

35 William M. Steuart, Jasper E. Whelchel, and Henry Gannett, *Census of Manufactures: 1905, Lumber and Timber Products* (Washington, DC: Government Printing Office, 1907), 58; Barbara McMartin, *Hides, Hemlocks and Adirondack History: How the Tanning Industry Influenced the Region's Growth* (Utica, NY: North Country Books, 1992), 43–44.
36 McMartin, *The Great Forest of the Adirondacks*, 38.
37 Wohlleben, *The Hidden Life of Trees*, 44.
38 Marchand, *North Woods*, 49; David R. Foster, Glenn Motzkin, and Benjamin Slater, "Land-Use History as Long-Term Broad-Scale Disturbance: Regional Forest Dynamics in Central New England," *Ecosystems* 1, no. 1 (1998): 114.
39 Barton and Keeton, *Ecology and Recovery*, 9.
40 Christine L. Goodale and John D. Aber, "The Long-Term Effects of Land-Use History on Nitrogen Cycling in Northern Hardwood Forests," *Ecological Applications* 11, no. 1 (2001): 254.
41 Judd and Judd, *Aroostook*, 103, 13; Judd, *Common Lands, Common People*, 92; Lloyd C. Irland, "New England Forests: Two Centuries of a Changing Landscape" in *A Landscape History of New England*, ed. Blake A. Harrison and Richard William Judd (Cambridge, MA: MIT Press, 2011), 65; Foster and Aber, *Forests in Time*, 24, 42.
42 Judd and Judd, *Aroostook*, 12, 108; Pike, *Tall Trees, Tough Men*, 30–31; Elbert L. Little; Sonja Bullaty, Angelo Lomeo, and National Audubon Society, *National Audubon Society Field Guide to North American Trees: Eastern Region* (New York: Alfred A. Knopf: 1980), 281–282.
43 Marchand, *North Woods*, 68.
44 Carroll, *The Timber Economy*, 123; Little et. al., *National Audubon Society Field Guide*, 406.
45 Carroll, *The Timber Economy*, 35–36.

2. Common Labor, Common Lands

1 Henry Conklin, *Through "Poverty's Vale": A Hardscrabble Boyhood in Upstate New York, 1832–1862* (Syracuse, NY: Syracuse University Press, 1974); Lloyd Blankman, "Henry Conklin—Pioneer," *York State Tradition* 19, no. 4 (Fall 1965): 47.
2 Conklin, *Through "Poverty's Vale,"* 38–39, 132.
3 Peter C. Welsh, *Jacks, Jobbers, and Kings: Logging the Adirondacks, 1850–1950* (Utica, NY: North Country Books, 1995), 28.
4 Richard White, "Are You an Environmentalist or Do You Work for a Living?" in *Uncommon Ground: Rethinking the Human Place in Nature*, ed. William Cronon (New York: W. W. Norton & Company, 1996).
5 Andrew M. Barton, "Introduction: Ecological and Historical Context" in *Ecology and Recovery of Eastern Old-Growth Forests*, ed. Andrew M. Barton and William S. Keeton (Washington, DC: Island Press, 2018).
6 Allan Greer, "Commons and Enclosure in the Colonization of North America," *The American Historical Review* 117, no. 2 (2012): 365–386; George R. Milner and George Chaplin, "Eastern North American Population at ca. AD 1500," *American Antiquity* 75, no. 4 (2010): 707–711; Marc D. Abrams and Gregory J. Nowacki, "Native Americans as Active and Passive Promoters of Mast and Fruit Trees in the Eastern USA," *The Holocene* 18, no. 7 (2008): 1127; Charles F. Carroll, *The Timber Economy of Puritan New England* (Providence, RI: Brown University Press, 1974), 28–30; Melissa Otis, "'Location of Exchange': Algonquian and Iroquoian Occupation in the Adirondacks before and after Contact," *Environment, Space, Place* 5, no. 2 (2013): 11–12.

7 Abrams and Nowacki, "Native Americans," 1130–1133; Tim Parshall and David R. Foster, "Fire on the New England Landscape: Regional and Temporal Variation, Cultural and Environmental Controls," *Journal of Biogeography* 29, no. 10-11 (2002): 1312; F. Herbert Bormann and Gene E. Likens, "Catastrophic Disturbance and The Steady State in Northern Hardwood Forests: A New Look at The Role of Disturbance in the Development of Forest Ecosystems Suggests Important Implications for Land-Use Policies," *American Scientist* 67, no. 6 (1979): 662.

8 Though the debate over indigenous land use is active, the consensus seems to be that "aboriginal populations were small and their impacts light in northern New England," Andrew M. Barton and William S. Keeton "Conclusion: Past, Present, and Future of Old-Growth Forests in the East" in *Ecology and Recovery of Eastern Old-Growth Forests*, ed. Andrew M. Barton and William S. Keeton (Washington, DC: Island Press/Center for Resource Economics, 2018); Wyatt Oswald, David R. Foster, Bryan N. Shuman, Elizabeth S. Chilton, Dianna L. Doucette, and Deena L. Duranleau, "Conservation Implications of Limited Native American Impacts in Pre-Contact New England," *Nature Sustainability* 3, no. 3 (2020): 241–246; Christopher McGrory Klyza, and Stephen C. Trombulak, eds., *The Future of the Northern Forest* (Middlebury, VT: Middlebury College Press, 1994), 14; Jerry Jenkins and Andy Keal, *The Adirondack Atlas: A Geographic Portrait of the Adirondack Park* (Syracuse, NY: Syracuse University Press, 2004), 9; Philip G. Terrie, *Contested Terrain: A New History of Nature and People in the Adirondacks* (Blue Mountain Lake, NY: Adirondack Museum, 1997), 3, 24; Harper, Falk, and Rankin, *The Northern Forest Lands Study*, 100; Foster and Aber, *Forests in Time*, 8, 63–64, 69; William Cronon, *Changes in the Land: Indians, Colonists, and the Ecology of New England* (New York: Hill and Wang, 1983), 50; Susy Svatek Ziegler, "Postfire Succession in an Adirondack Forest," *The Geographical Review* 97, no. 4 (2007): 468; Andrew Lipman, *The Saltwater Frontier: Indians and the Contest for the American Coast* (New Haven, CT: Yale University Press, 2015) 54, 66–69.

9 State of Maine, Department of Agriculture, *Sixth Annual Report of the Secretary of the Maine Board of Agriculture, 1861* (Augusta, ME: Stevens & Sayward, 1861), 6, 349, 356–357.

10 Lloyd C. Irland, The Northeast's Changing Forests (Petersham, MA: Harvard Forest, 1999), 150; Harper, Falk, and Rankin, *The Northern Forest Lands*, 22–23.

11 Cronon, *Changes in the Land*, 50.

12 Alexander Koch, Chris Brierley, Mark M. Maslin, and Simon L. Lewis, "Earth System Impacts of the European Arrival and Great Dying in the Americas after 1492," *Quaternary Science Reviews* 207 (2019): 13–36.

13 Jeremy S. Wilson, "Nineteenth Century Lumber Surveys for Bangor, Maine: Implications for Pre-European Settlement Forest Characteristics in Northern and Eastern Maine," *Journal of Forestry* 103, no. 5 (2005): 219.

14 Ann Norton Greene, *Horses at Work Harnessing Power in Industrial America* (Cambridge, MA: Harvard University Press, 2008), 28–29.

15 John G. Franzen, *The Archaeology of the Logging Industry* (Gainesville: University Press of Florida, 2020), 117; John S. Springer, *Forest Life and Forest Trees Comprising Winter Camp-Life Among the Loggers and Wild-Wood Adventure, with Descriptions of Lumbering Operations on the Various Rivers of Maine and New Brunswick* (New York: Harper, 1856), 90–91.

16 Ralph Clement Bryant, *Logging; The Principles and General Methods of Operation in the United States* (New York: J. Wiley & Sons, 1923), 129, 130, 131; Springer, *Forest Life and Forest Trees*, 90; Wood, *A History of Lumbering in Maine*, 17; Vaclav Smil, *Energy and Civilization: A History* (Cambridge: MIT Press, 2017), 67–70.

17 Harriett Sewall Harmon and William Wingate Sewall, *Recollections of William Wingate Sewall (1845–1930) of Island Falls, Maine: Dedicated to the People of Island Falls in Observance of Centennial Year 1972* (Island Falls, ME: 1972), 49; Horace Miner, *St. Denis, a French Canadian Parish* (Chicago: University of Chicago Press, 1963), 20, 158; Craig A. Gilborn, *Adirondack Camps: Homes Away from Home, 1850–1950* (Syracuse, NY: Adirondack Museum, 2000), 39–60; Susan McVetty, "Interviews about Dan Murray," 1970, transcript, p. 578018 (LLC) (MFC); Robert E. Pike, *Tall Trees, Tough Men* (New York: W. W. Norton, 1967), 90; Edmund W. Bradwin, *The Bunkhouse Man; A Study of Work and Pay in the Camps of Canada, 1903–1914* (Toronto: University of Toronto Press, 1972), 15, 85, 133, 135.

18 Springer, *Forest Life and Forest Trees*, 148, 169.

19 Conklin, *Through "Poverty's Vale."*

20 Harry Dyer (b. 1896), interviewed by Jeanne Milton, 1970, p. 568023, transcript (LLC) (MFC).

21 Michael Williams, *Americans and Their Forests: A Historical Geography* (Cambridge: Cambridge University Press, 1989), 115–114; Prescott and Rendall, "Lumbering in the Dead River Region," 15; Geraldine Tidd Scott, *Isaac Simpson's World: The Collected Works of an Itinerant Photographer* (Falmouth, ME: Kennebec River Press, 1990), 39–41, 89; Béatrice Craig, *Backwoods Consumers and Homespun Capitalists: The Rise of a Market Culture in Eastern Canada* (Toronto: University of Toronto Press, 2009), 141–146; Bradwin, *The Bunkhouse Man*, 76.

22 Judd Richard William and Patricia Judd, *Aroostook: A Century of Logging in Northern Maine* (Orono: University of Maine Press, 1988), 114; Bryant, *Logging; The Principles and General Methods*, 60; Springer, *Forest Life and Forest Trees*, 68, 72; Pike, *Tall Trees, Tough Men*, 90; John F. Flanagan, "Industrial Conditions in the Maine Woods," *First Biennial Report of the Department of Labor and Industry* (Waterville, ME: Sentinel Publishing Company, 1912), 209; Bradwin, *The Bunkhouse Man*, 78, 132.

23 Ferris Meigs, "The Santa Clara Lumber Company vol. I, " Santa Clara Collection, Adirondack Museum, New York, typeset 1941, 84; Conklin, *Through "Poverty's Vale,"* 102; Springer, *Forest Life and Forest Trees*, 68; Bryant, *Logging*, 63.

24 Springer, *Forest Life and Forest Trees*, 70–82.

25 Thomas M. Wickman, *Snowshoe Country: An Environmental and Cultural History of Winter in the Early American Northeast* (Cambridge: Cambridge University Press, 2018), 6–7, 12; William B. Meyer, "Boston's Weather and Climate Histories," in *Remaking Boston: An Environmental History of the City and Its Surroundings*, ed. Anthony N. Penna and Conrad Edick Wright (Pittsburgh, PA: University of Pittsburgh Press, 2009), 220; Anya. A Zilberstein, *Temperate Empire: Making Climate Change in Early America* (Oxford University Press, 2016), 10.

26 Karen Ordahl Kupperman, "Climate and Mastery of the Wilderness in Seventeenth-Century New England," *Seventeenth-Century New England* 63 (1984), 9.

27 Judith Fingard, "The Winter's Tale: The Seasonal Contours of Pre-Industrial Poverty in British North America, 1815–1860," *Historical Papers/Communications Historiques* 9, no. 1 (1974): 86; William B. Meyer, *Americans and Their Weather* (New York: Oxford University Press, 2014), 34; Bernard Mergen, *Snow in America* (Washington, DC: Smithsonian Institution Press, 1997), 38–39; K. Sokoloff and D. Dollar, "Agricultural Seasonality and the Organization of Manufacturing in Early Industrial Economies: The Contrast Between England and the United States," *The Journal of Economic History* 57, no. 2 (1997): 288–321; Thurston Madison Adams, *Prices Paid by Vermont Farmers for Goods and Services and Received by Them for Farm Products, 1790–1940; Wages of Vermont Farm Labor, 1780–1940* (Burlington, VT: Vermont Agricultural Experiment Station, 1944), 12, 85; Stanley L. Engerman, Claudia Dale

Goldin, and National Bureau of Economic Research, "Seasonality in Nineteenth Century Labor Markets" (Cambridge, MA: National Bureau of Economic Research, 1991), 29, http://proxy.library.cornell.edu/login?url=http://www.nber.org/papers/h0020; 85.

28 Cotton Mather, *Winter Meditations, Directions How to Employ the Leisure of the Winter . . .* (Boston: 1693); Thomas Wickman, "'Winters Embittered with Hardships': Severe Cold, Wabanaki Power, and English Adjustments, 1690–1710," *The William and Mary Quarterly* 72, no. 1 (2015): note 36; Harold F. Wilson, *The Hill Country of Northern New England: Its Social and Economic History, 1790–1930* (New York: Columbia University Press, 1936), 31.

29 George Rogers Taylor, *The Transportation Revolution, 1815–1860* (New York: Rinehart & Company, 1951), 15.

30 Pike, *Tall Trees, Tough Men*, 29; Robert Volney (b. 1890), interviewed by Linda Hubbard, 1970, p. 571070, transcript (LLC) (MFC); Bradwin, *The Bunkhouse Man*, 49; James L. Garvin, "Early White Mountain Taverns," *Historical New Hampshire*, 50, no. ½ (Summer 1995): 22–37.

31 Wilson, *The Hill Country of Northern New England*, 17; Adams, *Prices Paid by Vermont Farmers*, 47.

32 Peter J. Marchand, *Life in The Cold: An Introduction to Winter Ecology* (Chicago: University Press of New England, 2014), 35.

33 Meyer, "Boston's Weather and Climate Histories," 222–224.

34 Henry David Thoreau and Jeffrey S. Cramer, *The Maine Woods: A Fully Annotated Edition* (New Haven, CT: Yale University Press, [1864] 2009), 140; Stephen C. Trombulak, "A Natural History of the Northern Forest," in *The Future of the Northern Forest*, ed. Christopher McGrory Klyza and Stephen C. Trombulak (Middlebury, VT: Middlebury College Press, 1994), 17, 24; The State of New Hampshire, *New Hampshire Water Resources Primer* (Concord, NH: New Hampshire Department of Environmental Services, 2008), 5.1.1; Harper, Falk, and Rankin, *The Northern Forest Lands Study*, 23.

35 J. L. Turner to Shepard Cary, Fort Kent, M. E., April 2, 1857, Shepard Cary papers, box 1, folder 12, Maine Historical Society, Portland, Maine; Springer, *Forest Life and Forest Trees*, 88–89.

36 John Hector St. John, *Letters from an American Farmer and Sketches of Eighteenth-Century America* (New York: Penguin, 1981), 239.

37 Moses Greenleaf, *A Survey of the State of Maine: In Reference to Its Geographical Features, Statistics and Political Economy* (Augusta, ME: Maine State Museum, 1829), 103–105.

38 Greenleaf, *A Survey of the State of Maine*, 103–105.

39 Richard G. Wood, *A History of Lumbering in Maine, 1820–1861* (Orono, ME: University of Maine Press, 1935), 17–18.

40 Alfred Geer Hempstead, "The Penobscot Boom and the Development of the West Branch of the Penobscot River for Log Driving," *Maine Bulletin*, 33 (1931), 43; Erik Reardon, "Managing the River Commons: Fishing and New England's Rural Economy, 1783–1848" (PhD diss., The University of Maine, Orono 2016) Proquest, https://www.proquest.com/dissertations-theses/managing-river-commons-fishing-new-englands-rural/docview/1844966807/se-2?accountid=14605; Ralph Clement Bryant, *Logging: the Principles and General Methods Of Operation in The United States* (New York: J. Wiley & Sons, 1914), 38; William Freeman Fox, *A History of the Lumber Industry in the State of New York* (Washington, DC: US Department of Agriculture, Bureau of Forestry, 1902), 22, 23–40; Hugh G. E. MacMahon, *Progress, Stability, and the Struggle for Equality: A Ramble Through the Early Years Of Maine Law, 1820–1920* (Portland, ME: Drummond Woodsum & MacMahon, 2009), 59; John T. Cumbler,

Reasonable Use: The People, the Environment, and the State, New England, 1790–1930 (Oxford: Oxford University Press, 2001), 6; Samuel C. Wiel, "Natural Communism: Air, Water, Oil, Sea, and Seashore," *Harvard Law Review* 47, no. 3 (1934): 425–457; James Willard Hurst, *Law and Economic Growth: The Legal History of the Lumber Industry in Wisconsin, 1836–1915* (Cambridge, MA: Harvard University Press, 1964), 174.

41 Andreas Malm, *Fossil Capital: The Rise of Steam-Power and The Roots of Global Warming* (Westminster, MD: Random House, 2016), 117; Theodore Steinberg, *Nature Incorporated: Industrialization and the Waters of New England* (Cambridge: Cambridge University Press, 2003); Jamie H. Eves, "Shrunk to a Comparative Rivulet: Deforestation, Stream Flow, and Rural Milling in 19th-Century Maine," *Technology and Culture* 33, no. 1 (1992): 38–65; Graeme Wynn, *Timber Colony: A Historical Geography of Early Nineteenth Century New Brunswick* (Toronto: University of Toronto Press, 1981); Evelyn M. Dinsdale (Evelyn Stokes), "Spatial Patterns of Technological Change: The Lumber Industry of Northern New York," *Economic Geography* no. 3 (1965): 41, 255.

42 Theodore Dwight, *The Northern Traveller: And Northern Tour* (New York: G. &. C. Carvill, 1828), 201, 220, 272.

43 Bryant, *Logging: The Principles and General Methods*, 413.

44 Wilson, *The Hill Country of Northern New England*, 34.

45 Barbara McMartin, *The Great Forest of the Adirondacks* (Utica, NY: North Country Books, 1994), 50.

46 Wilson, *Hill Country*, 127, 34.

47 Thomas R. Cox, *The Lumberman's Frontier: Three Centuries of Land Use, Society, and Change in America's Forests* (Corvallis: Oregon State University Press, 2010), 38, 80–85; Bryant, *Logging*, 407; Alexander Koroleff and John Fortune Walker, *River Drive of Pulpwood: Efficiency of Technique* (Canada: Canadian Pulp and Paper Association, Woodlands Section, 1946), 9; Wilson, *The Hill Country of Northern New England*, 18, 34.

48 Judd and Judd, *Aroostook*, 103, 13; Richard William Judd, *Common Lands, Common People: The Origins of Conservation in Northern New England* (Cambridge, MA: Harvard University Press, 1997), 92; Lloyd C. Irland, "New England Forests: Two Centuries of a Changing Landscape" in *A Landscape History of New England*, ed. Blake A. Harrison and Richard William Judd (Cambridge, MA: MIT Press, 2011), 65; David R. Foster and John D. Aber, *Forests in Time: The Environmental Consequences of 1,000 Years of Change in New England* (New Haven, CT: Yale University Press, 2004), 24, 42.

49 Edward D. Ives, *Argyle Boom* (Orono ME: Northeast Folklore Society, 1977), 128; Dwight, *The Northern Traveller*, 348; Bryant, *Logging*, 389; Cox, *The Lumberman's Frontier*, 13–14.

50 Bryant, *Logging*, 413–415; Joel Tyler Headley, *Letters from the Backwoods and the Adirondac* (New York: J. S. Taylor, 1850), 36.

51 Hempstead, "The Penobscot Boom," 16; Cox, *The Lumberman's Frontier*, 103.

52 Fox, *A History of the Lumber Industry*, 23; Hempstead, "The Penobscot Boom," 35.

53 Hempstead, "The Penobscot Boom," 16; Rand E. Rohe, "The Myth of the Wild Wolf: Logging and River Improvement on a Wisconsin River," *The Great Lakes Review* 10, no. 2 (1984): 24–35; Cox, *The Lumberman's Frontier*, 60; Bryant, *Logging*, 389.

54 Bill Gove, *Log Drives on the Connecticut River* (Littleton, NH: Bondcliff Books, 2003); Thomas R. Cox, "Transition in the Woods: Log Drivers, Raftsmen, and the Emergence of Modern Lumbering in Pennsylvania," *The Pennsylvania Magazine of History and Biography* 104, no. 3 (1980): 345–364; McMartin, *The Great Forest of the Adirondacks*, 50.

55 Morton J. Horwitz, *The Transformation of American Law, 1870–1960: The Crisis of Legal Orthodoxy* (Oxford: Oxford University Press, 1992), 72.

56 Horwitz, *The Transformation of American Law*, 138–139; Susan Pace Hamill, "From Special Privilege to General Utility: A Continuation of Willard Hurst's Study of Corporations," *American University Law Review* 49, no. 1 (1999): 81–180; Pike, *Tall Trees, Tough Men*, 109; Rogers, "Lumbering in Northern Maine," 50; Prescott and Rendall, "Lumbering in the Dead River Region," 52; John Sharpe (b. 1881), interviewed by Lillian Shirley, 1970, p. 37, transcript (LLC) (MFC); Harry Dyer (b. 1896), interviewed by Jeanne Milton, 1970, p. 581031, transcript (LLC) (MFC); Andrew Chase (b. 1888) interviewed by Linda Edgerly, 1971, p. 697031, transcript (LLC) (MFC); Frederick Burke (b. 1915) interviewed by Norma Coates (1971), transcript, p. 7020064 (LLC) (MFC).

57 Quoted in Peter J. Marchand, *North Woods: An Inside Look at the Nature of Forests in the Northeast* (Boston: Appalachian Mountain Club, 1987), 14.

58 Kenneth Lockridge, "Land, Population and the Evolution of New England Society 1630–1790," *Past & Present* 39 (1968): 62.

59 Richard W. Judd, *Second Nature: An Environmental History of New England* (Amherst: University of Massachusetts Press, 2014), 85; Jenkins and Keal, *The Adirondack Atlas*, 79; Gerald E. Morris, Richard D. Kelly, and Ronald F. Banks, *The Maine Bicentennial Atlas: An Historical Survey* (Portland: Maine Historical Society, 1976), plate 22 and p. 14.

60 Joel T. Headley, *Letters from the Backwoods and the Adirondac* (New York: J. S. Taylor, 1976), 42.

61 Judd, *Common Lands, Common People*, 32.

62 Alan Taylor, *American Colonies: The Settling of North America (The Penguin History of the United States)* (New York: Penguin Books, 2002), 309; Judd, *Common Lands*, 45; Alan Taylor, *Liberty Men and Great Proprietors: The Revolutionary Settlement on the Maine Frontier, 1760–1820* (Chapel Hill, NC: University of North Carolina Press, 1990), 28.

63 Craig, *Backwoods Consumers*, 170; Judd, *Common Land, Common People*, 24; Judd, *Second Nature*, 78; Jan Albers, *Hands on the Land: A History of the Vermont Landscape* (Cambridge, MA: MIT Press, 2000), 170.

64 Benjamin Rush and Jacob Rush dedicatee, *Essays, Literary, Moral & Philosophical by Benjamin Rush, M.D. and Professor of The Institutes of Medicine and Clinical Practice in The University of Pennsylvania* (Philadelphia: Thomas & Samuel F. Bradford, 1798), 213–214.

65 Judd, *Common Lands*, 15; Charles Sellers, *The Market Revolution: Jacksonian America, 1815–1846* (New York: Oxford University Press, 1991), 18.

66 Wilson, *The Hill Country of Northern New England*.

67 Judd, *Common Lands, Common People*, 16; Harper, Falk, and Rankin, *The Northern Forest Lands Study*, 101; Judd, *Second Nature*, 94, 111; Klyza and Trombulak, *The Future of the Northern Forest*, 15; David R. Foster, Glenn Motzkin, and Benjamin Slater, "Land-Use History as Long-Term Broad-Scale Disturbance: Regional Forest Dynamics in Central New England," *Ecosystems* 1, no. 1 (1998): 114; Wilson, *The Hill Country of Northern New England*, 128.

68 Laura Beam, *A Maine Hamlet* (New York: W. Funk, 1957), 28.

69 William, *Americans and Their Forest*, 112–117; Craig, *Backwoods Consumers*, 141–142.

70 Beam, *A Maine Hamlet*, 28; Maine Department of Agriculture, *Sixth Annual Report*, 344; Henry David Thoreau and Jeffrey S. Cramer, *The Maine Woods: A Fully Annotated Edition* (New Haven, CT: Yale University Press, 2009), 21; Jenkins and Keal, *The Adirondack Atlas*, 17.

71 Judd, *Common Lands, Common People*, 32.
72 Thoreau and Cramer, *The Maine Woods*, 21.
73 Wilson, *The Hill Country of Northern New England*, 22; Elizabeth Mancke, *The Fault Lines of Empire: Political Differentiation in Massachusetts and Nova Scotia, Ca. 1760–1830* (New York: Routledge, 2005), 39, 61.
74 Conklin, *Through "Poverty's Vale,"* 48, 35, 37, 51, 134, 152.
75 Conklin, *Through "Poverty's Vale,"* 45; Harvey A. Levenstein, *Revolution at the Table: The Transformation of the American Diet* (New York: Oxford University Press, 1988), 25, 175–176, 178; Julian D. Boyd, "The Nature of the American Diet," *The Journal of Pediatrics* 12, no. 2 (1938): 250; Wilson, *The Hill Country of Northern New England*, 30; Elaine N. McIntosh, *American Food Habits in Historical Perspective* (Westport, CT: Praeger, 1995), 110; Béatrice Craig, "Agriculture and the Lumberman's Frontier in the Upper St. John Valley, 1800–70," *Journal of Forest History* 32, no. 3 (1988): 129, 136.
76 Roger Horowitz, *Putting Meat on the American Table: Taste, Technology, Transformation* (Baltimore, MD: Johns Hopkins University Press, 2006), 16; Sarah F. McMahon, "'All Things in Their Proper Season': Seasonal Rhythms of Diet in Nineteenth Century New England," *Agricultural History* 63, no. 2 (1989): 144–145; Sarah F. McMahon, "'A Comfortable Subsistence': A History of Diet in New England, 1630–1850" (PhD diss., Brandeis University, 1982), 157; Beam, *A Maine Hamlet*, 15; Levenstein, *Revolution at the Table*, 29; Catherine Leonard Turner, *How The Other Half Ate: A History of Working-Class Meals at the Turn of the Century* (Berkeley: University of California Press, 2014), 29; Mancke, *The Fault Lines of Empire*, 39, 61.
77 Judd, *Common Lands*, 25; Wilson, *The Hill Country of Northern New England*, 129.
78 Maine Department of Agriculture, *Sixth Annual Report of the Secretary of the Maine Board of Agriculture, 1861* (Augusta, ME: Stevens & Sayward, 1861), 83–84, 30–31, 349–350, 352, 435.
79 Wilson, *The Hill Country of Northern New England*, 44; Jenkins and Keal, *The Adirondack Atlas*, 88–89; Cox, *Lumbermen's Frontier*, 66; Morris, Kelly, and Banks, *The Maine Bicentennial Atlas*, 30–31; Bill Gove, *Logging Railroads of New Hampshire's North Country* (Littleton, NH: Bondcliff Books, 2010), vii; Albers, *Hands on the Land*, 169–170.
80 Judd, *Second Nature*, 85; Jenkins and Keal, *The Adirondack Atlas*, 79; Morris, Kelly, and Banks, *The Maine Bicentennial Atlas*, plate 22 and p. 14; Wilson, *The Hill Country of Northern New England*, 17, 130, 8; Craig, *Backwoods Consumer*, 146, 144, 37, 42; Michael Merrill, "Cash Is Good to Eat: Self-Sufficiency and Exchange in the Rural Economy of the United States," *Radical History Review*, no. 13 (1977): 42; Bettye Hobbs Pruitt, "Self-Sufficiency and the Agricultural Economy of Eighteenth-Century Massachusetts," *The William and Mary Quarterly* (1984): 334; Judd, *Second Nature*, 91; Judd, *Common Lands, Common People*, 60.
81 Thoreau and Cramer, *The Maine Woods*, 19.
82 Ralph Waldo Emerson, *Poems* (Ann Arbor: University of Michigan Humanities Text Initiative, 1996), 185, http://name.umdl.umich.edu/BAD1982.0001.001, accessed 8/1/2023.
83 Eric Sloane, *A Museum of Early American Tools* (New York: Wilfred Funk, 1964), 2; Harry Dyer (b. 1896), interviewed by Jeanne Milton, 1970, p. 581055, transcript (MFC) (LLC).
84 Ian Walter Radforth, *Bushworkers and Bosses: Logging in Northern Ontario, 1900–1980* (Toronto: University of Toronto Press, 1987), 57; Taylor, *Liberty Men*, 1–2; Adams, *Prices Paid by Vermont Farmers*, 79.
85 Judd, *Common Lands*, 25.

86 Conklin, *Through "Poverty's Vale,"* 48, 51, 54, 124, 107–108, 126, 134, 144, 188; Thoreau and Cramer, *The Maine Woods*, 139; Cronon, *Changes in the Land*, 145–146; Karl Jacoby, *Crimes against Nature: Squatters, Poachers, Thieves, and the Hidden History of American Conservation* (Berkeley: University of California Press, 2005), 19–23; 54–55; John Mack Faragher, *Sugar Creek: Life on the Illinois Prairie* (New Haven, CT: Yale University Press, 1986), 1–17; McMartin, *The Great Forest of the Adirondacks*, 59; David N. Borton, "Adirondack Lumbering—The Jessup Operation" (unpublished), 1965, p. 1–2, Adirondack Museum, Blue Mountain Lake, NY, object number, 2389, MS 65–13; Stewart H. Holbrook, *Yankee Loggers: A Recollection of Woodsmen, Cooks, and River Drivers* (New York: International Paper, 1961), 30–31.

87 One cord is a pile of wood or bark stacked four feet high, eight feet long, and four feet deep. There are approximately twenty-four small trees in a cord of wood, or 1,536 board feet., and one cord of green wood is approximately 2,000 to 4,000 pounds. C. Max Hilton, *Woodsmen, Horses, and Dynamite: Rough Pulpwood Operating in Northwestern Maine, 1935–1940*, (Orono: University of Maine Press, 2004), 33; Cronon, *Changes in the Land*, 25; Irland, *The Northeast's Changing Forests*, 234; Adams, *Prices Paid by Vermont Farmers*, 168; Theodore Steinberg, *Down to Earth: Nature's Role in American History* (Oxford: Oxford University Press, 2002), 64; Foster and Aber, *Forests in Time*, 56.

88 Walker Family Diaries, 1828–1893, vol. 8, Daniel Walker Diary 1873, March 15, March 29, April 11, June 7, June 10–12, Maine Historical Society, Portland, Maine.

89 Michael Hillard, *Chapter 2 Introduction—Maine: A Rags to Riches Story* in "The Fall of the Paper Plantation: Ownership Eras, Labor Histories, Memories and Resistance in Maine's Paper and Logging Industries Over the Twentieth Century" (unpublished manuscript, November 2013), 21.

90 Judd and Judd, *Aroostook*, 89.

91 Wilson, *The Hill Country of Northern New England*, 47.

92 Philip L. White, *Beekmantown, New York: Forest Frontier to Farm Community* (Austin: University of Texas Press, 1979), vii; Irland, *The Northeast's Changing Forests*, 138–140; Maine Department of Agriculture, *Sixth Annual Report*, 349–350, 435; Craig, *Backwoods Consumers*, 168; Wilson, *The Hill Country of Northern New England*, 125–126.

93 Daniel Hammond to The Trustees and Proprietors of the Boston & Eastern Mill & Land Co., Boston, January 1848, Boston and Eastern records, box 1, folder 2, Maine Historical Society, Portland, ME; Allan Kulikoff, *The Agrarian Origins of American Capitalism* (Charlottesville: University Press of Virginia, 1992), 58.

94 Wynn, *Timber Colony*, 84.

95 Charles A. Scontras, Collective Efforts among Maine Workers: Beginnings and Foundations, 1820–1880 (Orono: Bureau of Labor Education, University of Maine, 1994), 2.

96 Maria Mackinney-Valentin, "The Lumberjack Shirt: The Fabric and Fabrication of Zeitgeist," *Catwalk: The Journal of Fashion, Beauty, and Style* 1, no. 1 (2012): 7; Craig, *Backwoods Consumers*, 182; Robert Eric Wall, *The Making of the American Logger: Traditional Culture and Public Imagery in The Realm of the Bunyanesque* (PhD diss., Indiana University, 1997).

97 Reardon, "Managing the River Commons," 59.

98 Adams, *Prices Paid by Vermont Farmers*, 90–91; Judd, *Common Lands*, 25.

99 US Census Bureau, Federal Census Non-Population Schedules, 1880, Henry Conklin, Wilmurt, Herkimer, New York, accessed August 11, 2014, ancestry.com; historical geographer Graeme Wynn found that "[t]he seasonal demands of part-time lumbering and subsistence farming were almost diametrical. They were often combined with success." Judd and Judd, *Aroostook*, 88, 89, 90, 95; Conklin, *Through*

"Poverty's Vale," 130, 187, 188; Radforth, *Bushworkers and Bosses*, 28; Wynn, *Timber Colony*, 186.

100 Stephen J. Hornsby, Richard William Judd, and Michael J. Hermann, *Historical Atlas of Maine* (Orono: University of Maine Press, 2015), plate 42; Marcus Lee Hansen, and John Bartlet Brebner, *The Mingling of the Canadian and American Peoples*, vol. 1 (New Haven, CT: Yale University Press, 1940), 180–181; Gerard J. Brault, *The French Canadian Heritage in New England* (Hanover, NH: University Press of New England, 1986), 52–53.

101 Carolyn Podruchny, *Making the Voyageur World: Travelers and Traders in the North American Fur Trade* (Lincoln: University of Nebraska Press, 2007), 304–305; Brigitte Lane, "Three Major Witness of Franco-American Folklore in New England: Honore Beaugrand, Adelard Lambert, and Romeo Berthiaume," in *Steeples and Smokestacks: A Collection of Essays on the Franco-American Experience in New England*, ed. Claire Quintal (Worcester, MA: Institut Francais of Assumption College, 1996), 414; John Irvine Little, *Crofters and Habitants: Settler Society, Economy, and Culture in a Québec Township, 1848–1881* (Montreal: McGill-Queen's University Press, 1991), 47, 72, 149, 154; John Irvine Little, *Nationalism, Capitalism and Colonization in Nineteenth-Century Québec: The Upper St. Francis District* (Kingston, ON: McGill-Queen's University Press, 1989), 7, 16, 31–35, 47, 81, 83, 89; Bruno Ramirez, *On the Move: French Canadian and Italian Migrants in the North Atlantic Economy, 1860–1914* (Toronto: McClelland & Stewart, 1991), 47, 77–79; Bradwin, *The Bunkhouse Man*, 95; Ralph Dominic Vicero, "Immigration of French Canadians to New England, 1840–1900: A Geographic Analysis" (PhD diss., University of Wisconsin–Madison, 1968), 70, 197–198, 214; Franzen, *The Archaeology of the Logging Industry*, 167; Félix Albert, *Immigrant Odyssey: A French Canadian Habitant in New England—A Bilingual Edition of Histoire D'un Enfant Pauvre* (Orono: University of Maine Press, 1991), 34–37, 40, 56; Judd and Judd, *Aroostook*, 194–195; Bruno Ramirez and Yves Otis, *Crossing the 49th Parallel: Migration from Canada to the United States, 1900–1930* (Ithaca, NY: Cornell University Press, 2001), 5, 8, 63, 11–12, 16; Brault, *The French Canadian Heritage*, 34, 158.

102 Anya Zilberstein, *A Temperate Empire: Making Climate Change in Early America* (Oxford: Oxford University Press, 2016), 125, 131–133.

103 Henry David Thoreau and Jeffrey S. Cramer, *Walden: A Fully Annotated Edition* (New Haven, CT: Yale University Press, [1854] 2004), 139, 143, 141, 142, 143, 144–145; also see, Robert W. Bradford, "Thoreau and Therien," *American Literature* 34, no. 4 (1963): 501; Edward Watts, *In This Remote Country: French Colonial Culture in the Anglo-American Imagination, 1780–1860* (Chapel Hill, NC: University of North Carolina Press, 2006), 48; Philip Cafaro, *Thoreau's Living Ethics: Walden and the Pursuit of Virtue* (Athens: University of Georgia Press, 2004), 36, 37, 87, 118, 119, 210, 211.

104 Springer, *Forest Life, Forest Trees*, 247.

105 Edward H. Elwell, *Aroostook: With Some Account of the Excursions Thither of the Editors of Maine, in the Years 1858 and 1878, and of the Colony of Swedes, Settled in the Town of New Sweden* (Portland, ME: Transcript Print, 1878), 26.

106 Springer, *Forest Life and Forest Trees*, 246–247; Quoted in Watts, *In This Remote Country*, 40–41.

107 The first printing of *Evangeline* in 1847 sold out and in the following century the poem went through 270 editions and was translated into 130 languages. Naomi Griffiths, "'Longfellow's *Evangeline*': The Birth and Acceptance of a Legend," *Acadiensis* 11, 2 (1982): 28, 37; Andrew J. B. Johnston, "The Call of the Archetype and the Challenge of Acadian History," *French Colonial History* 5, no. 1 (2004): 78; Eric L. Haralson, "Mars in Petticoats: Longfellow and Sentimental Masculinity,"

Nineteenth-Century Literature 51, no. 3 (1996): 343, 344; Henry Wadsworth Longfellow, *Evangeline, A Tale of Acadie* (Boston, MA: Leach, Shewell, & Sanborn, [1847] 1896), 15–16; Watts, *In This Remote Country*, 88.

108 Yves Roby, "The Economic Evolution of Québec and the Emigrant (1850–1929)" in Claire Quintal, *Steeples and Smokestacks*, 6–7; John McCallum, *Unequal Beginnings Agriculture and Economic Development in Québec and Ontario until 1870* (Toronto: University of Toronto Press, 1980), 4; Vincent Geloso, "Unenlightened Peasants? Farming Techniques among French-Canadians, Circa 1851," *GMU Working Paper in Economics*, no. 22–10 (2021), http://dx.doi.org/10.2139/ssrn.3994002; Frank Lewis and Marvin McInnis, "The Efficiency of the French Canadian Farmer in the Nineteenth Century," *The Journal of Economic History* 40, no. 3 (1980): 497–499; "The Farmers in the Province of Québec," *New York Times*, December 27, 1869; Watts, *In This Remote Country*, 56–57; Albert, *Immigrant Odyssey*, 6.

109 Thoreau and Cramer, *Walden*, 139–144.

110 Richard White, *The Middle Ground: Indians, Empires, and Republics in the Great Lakes Region, 1650–1815* (Cambridge, MA: Cambridge University Press, 1991), 60–75, 316; Podruchny, *Making the Voyageur World*, 1, 2, 71, 98; William Dillingham et al., *Dictionary of Races or Peoples* (Washington, DC: Government Printing Office, 1911), 29; Jean Charlemagne Bracq, *The Evolution of French Canada* (New York, NY: The Macmillan Company, 1924), 206; Madison Grant, *The Conquest of a Continent; or, The Expansion of Races in America* (New York, NY: C. Scribner's Sons, 1933), 310–311; Reginald Horsman, *Race and Manifest Destiny: The Origins of American Racial Anglo-Saxonism* (Cambridge, MA: Harvard University Press, 1981), 183, 216, 240, 241, 272.

111 Wayne Franklin, *James Fenimore Cooper: The Early Years* (New Haven, CT: Yale University Press, 2007), xxix; Allan M. Axelrad, "Historical Contexts of *The Last of the Mohicans*: The French and Indian War, and Mid-1820s America," paper presented at the 17th Cooper Seminar, "James Fenimore Cooper: His Country and His Art at the State University of New York College at Oneonta," July, 2009, accessed 8/20/2014, http://external.oneonta.edu/cooper/articles/suny/2009suny-axelrad.html; James Fenimore Cooper, *The Deerslayer* (New York: Dodd, Mead [1841] 1952), 23, 41; James Fenimore Cooper, *The Pathfinder* (New York: Dodd, Mead, [1840] 1953), 164; Zadok Cramer, *The Navigator* (Pittsburgh, PA: Cramer & Spear, [1801] 1824), 44, 254, 388; Fulmer Mood and Frederick J. Turner, "An Unfamiliar Essay by Frederick J. Turner," *Minnesota History* (1937): 393; Peter Cook, "Onontio Gives Birth: How the French in Canada Became Fathers to Their Indigenous Allies, 1645–1673," *The Canadian Historical Review* 96, no. 2 (2015), 165–193.

112 Quoted in Watts, *In This Remote Country*, 72; Henry David Thoreau, *A Yankee in Canada with Anti-Slavery Reform Papers* (Boston: Ticknor and Fields, [1850] 1866), 60, 61; Charles Hallock, "Aroostook and the Madawaska," *The Harper's Monthly* (New York: Harper & Brothers, 1863), 695.

113 Fingard, "The Winter's Tale," 73.

114 State of Maine, Department of Agriculture, *Ninth Annual Report of the Secretary of the Maine Board of Agriculture, 1864* (Augusta, ME: Stevens & Sayward, 1864), 83–87.

115 State of Maine, Department of Agriculture, *Sixteenth Annual Report of the Secretary of the Maine Board of Agriculture, 1872* (Augusta, ME: Stevens & Sayward, 1872), 148.

116 Judd and Judd, *Aroostook*, 46; Judd, *Common Lands, Common People*, 29, 34.

117 Conklin, *Through "Poverty's Vale,"* 105.

118 Quoted in Judd and Judd, *Aroostook*, 25.

119 Robert McCullough, *The Landscape of Community: A History of Communal Forests in New England* (Hanover, NH: University Press of New England, 1995), 50–60.

120 Judd and Judd, *Aroostook*, 49; Wynn, *Timber Colony*, 85.
121 Craig, *Backwoods Consumer*, 222–226, 135.
122 Louis Hyman, *Borrow: The American Way of Debt* (New York: Vintage Books, 2012), 8.
123 Merrill, "Cash Is Good to Eat," 42–71, 53, 54, 58; Craig, *Backwoods Consumers*, 128; Kulikoff, *The Agrarian Origins of American Capitalism*, 6; Bettye Hobbs Pruitt, "Self-Sufficiency and the Agricultural Economy of Eighteenth-Century Massachusetts," *The William and Mary Quarterly: A Magazine of Early American History and Culture* 41, no. 3 (1984): 334–364, 338, 349; Rusty Bittermann, "Farm Households and Wage Labour in the Northeastern Maritimes in the Early 19th Century," *Labour/Le Travail* (1993): 13–45; Christopher Clark, "Household Economy, Market Exchange and the Rise of Capitalism in the Connecticut Valley, 1800–1860," *Journal of Social History* 13, no. 2 (1979): 173; Winifred B. Rothenberg, "The Self-Sufficiency and the Agricultural Economy Market and Massachusetts Farmers, 1750–1855," *Journal of Economic History* 41, no. 2 (1981): 286, 298.
124 Hurst, *Law and Economic Growth*, 16–18; Greer, "Commons and Enclosure in the Colonization of North America."
125 Jan Albers, *Hands on the Land: A History of the Vermont Landscape* (Cambridge, MA: MIT Press, 2000), 86; Robert A. Gross, *The Minutemen and Their World (Revised and Expanded Edition)* (London: Picador, 2022), 94–95; Brian Donahue, *The Great Meadow: Farmers and the Land in Colonial Concord* (New Haven, CT: Yale University Press, 2007), 6–7; Yasuhide Kawashima and Ruth Tone, "Environmental Policy in Early America: A Survey of Colonial Statutes," *Journal of Forest History* 27, no. 4 (1983): 170–171.
126 McCullough, *The Landscape of Community*, 61–62, 76.
127 Judd, *Common Lands*, 45; McCullough, *The Landscape of Community*, 26, 82.
128 Strother E. Roberts, *Colonial Ecology, Atlantic Economy: Transforming Nature in Early New England* (Philadelphia: University of Pennsylvania Press, 2019), 133.
129 Kawashima and Tone, "Environmental Policy in Early America," 171; McCullough, *The Landscape of Community*, 38–40.
130 Greer, "Commons and Enclosure in the Colonization of North America," 369; McCullough, *The Landscape of Community*, 16.
131 Judd and Judd, *Aroostook*, 72; Judd, *Common Land*, 24; Morris, Kelly, and Banks, *The Maine Bicentennial Atlas*, 5.
132 McCullough, *The Landscape of Community*, 70; Alan Taylor, *Liberty Men and Great Proprietors: The Revolutionary Settlement on the Maine Frontier, 1760–1820* (Chapel Hill, NC: University of North Carolina Press, 1990).
133 Judd, *Common Lands*, 29–30, 63; Jacoby, *Crimes against Nature*, 54.
134 J. B. Koetteritz to The Comptroller of the State of New York, Dolgeville, NY April, January 27, 1884, Letters from agents appointed to serve notice on illegal occupants of state lands, 1881–1893, folder 3 (2 of 2), BO942–85, New York State Archives, Cultural Education Center, Albany, NY.
135 Jacoby, *Crimes against Nature*, 24.
136 McMahon "All Things in Their Proper Season," 130; Robert Dirks, "Diet and Nutrition in Poor and Minority Communities in the United States 100 Years Ago," *Annual Review of Nutrition* 23, no. 1 (2003): 95; Beam, *A Maine Hamlet*, 177–179; Richard Osborn Cummings, *The American and His Food; A History of Food Habits in the United States* (Chicago: University of Chicago Press, 1941), 172; Levenstein, *Revolution at the Table*, 180; Judd, *Common Lands, Common People*, 66–67; Dora L. Costa, "Height, Wealth, and Disease Among the Native-Born in the Rural, Antebellum North," *Social Science History* 17, no. 3 (1993): 375–376.
137 Judd, *Common Lands, Common People*, 61–62; Levenstein, *Revolution at the Table*, 30; Dirks, "Diet and Nutrition," 88; Craig, *Backwoods Consumers*,165–179; Judd,

Second Nature, 114; Alvan F. Sanborn, "The Future of Rural New England," *Atlantic* 80 (1897): 80.

138 Judd, *Common Lands, Common People*, 60–61, 64–65; Levenstein, *Revolution at the Table*, 179–181; Julian D. Boyd, "The Nature of the American Diet," *The Journal of Pediatrics* 12, no. 2 (1938): 252; Megan J. Elias, *Food in the United States, 1890–1945* (Santa Barbara, CA: Greenwood Press, 2009), 6; Jacoby, *Crimes against Nature*, 53.

139 Alice Ross, "Health and Diet in 19th-Century America: A Food Historian's Point of View," *Historical Archaeology* 27, no. 2 (1993): 50; Dora L. Costa, and Richard H. Steckel, *Long-Term Trends in Health, Welfare, and Economic Growth in the United States* (Chicago: University of Chicago Press, 2008), 63; Dora L. Costa, "Height, Wealth, and Disease," 365.

140 Craig, "Agriculture and the Lumberman's Frontier," 129.

141 A. K. Moore to Samuel S. Lewis, Machias, ME, May 28, 1837, B&E records, box 1, folder 2, Maine Historical Society, Portland, Maine.

142 C. Whitaker to Shepard Cary, September 28, 1849, St. John New Brunswick, Canada, Shepard Cary papers, box 1, folder 12, Maine Historical Society, Portland, Maine.

143 Thoreau and Cramer, *The Maine Woods*, 19; Judd and Judd, *Aroostook*, 86; Chamberlain farm,[Oxen record April 15, 1848] and "H. W. Sampson account of Supplies sent to Farm by J. Lake April 11, 1848, Chamberlain Farm collection, Maine Historical Society, Portland, Maine.

144 Judd and Judd, *Aroostook*, 47, 56–57, 59–60; J. L. Turner to Shepard Cary, April 2, 1857, Fort Kent, Shepard Cary papers, box 1, folder 12, Maine Historical Society, Portland, Maine.

145 Craig, *Backwoods Consumers*, 21, 74, 115, 120, 137; Maine Department of Agriculture, *Sixth Annual Report*, 344.

146 Maine Department of Agriculture, *Sixth Annual Report*, 345–346; Dean B. Bennett, *The Wilderness from Chamberlain Farm: A Story of Hope for the American Wild* (Washington, DC: Island Press/Shearwater Books, 2001), 4, 77.

147 Maine Department of Agriculture, *Sixth Annual Report*, 348; Judd and Judd, *Aroostook*, 51.

148 Herbert G. Gutman, "Work, Culture, and Society in Industrializing America, 1815–1919," *The American Historical Review* (1973): 531–588; Craig, *Backwoods Consumers*, 95; David Montgomery, *Workers' Control in America: Studies in the History of Work, Technology, and Labor Struggles* (Cambridge: Cambridge University Press, 1980); Paul E. Johnson, *A Shopkeeper's Millennium: Society and Revivals in Rochester, New York 1815–1837* (New York: Hill and Wang, 1985); Peter Way, *Common Labour: Workers and the Digging of North American Canals, 1780–1860* (Cambridge: Cambridge University Press, 1993).

149 Ian Radforth, "The Shantymen" in *Laboring Lives: Work and Workers in Nineteenth-Century Ontario*, ed. Paul Craven (Toronto: University of Toronto Press, 1995), 249; Gunther Peck, *Reinventing Free Labor: Padrones and Immigrant Workers in the North American West, 1880–1930* (Cambridge: Cambridge University Press, 2000), 35; Craig, "Agriculture and the Lumberman's Frontier," 134–135; Bradwin, *The Bunk-house Man*, 63.

150 Daniel Hammond "Report January 1850/Whitnyville Concern," B&E records, box 1, folder 2, Maine Historical Society, Portland, Maine; Accounts with Daniel Hammond, March 1852 to January 1853, B&E records, box 1, folder 2, Maine Historical Society, Portland, Maine; James Popes, agents accounts (goods accounts), B&E records, box 1, folder 11, Maine Historical Society, Portland, Maine.

151 Béatrice Craig and Maxime Dagenais, *The Land in Between: The Upper St. John Valley, Prehistory to World War I* (Gardiner, ME: Tilbury House, 2009), 205, 206.

152 "Peter G. Morrill to Chamberlain Farm," account, 1849, Chamberlain Farm collection, Maine Historical Society, Portland, Maine.
153 Daniel Hammond, "Report January 1850/Whitnyville Concern," B&E records, box 1, folder 2, Maine Historical Society, Portland, ME.
154 Holman Cary to Silas Plummer, May 20, 1851, Shepard Cary papers, box 1, folder 12, Maine Historical Society, Portland, Maine; Holman Cary to Shepard Cary, October 13, 1851, Dept Camp, box 1, folder 12, Maine Historical Society, Portland, Maine; A. K. Moore to Samuel S. Lewis, Machias, ME, July 10, 1837, B&E records, box 1, folder 2, Maine Historical Society, Portland, Maine; A. K. Moore to Samuel S. Lewis, Machias, ME, September 18, 1837, B&E records, box 1, folder 2, Maine Historical Society, Portland, Maine.
155 Horowitz, *Putting Meat on the American Table*, 45; Joseph Robert Conlin, *Bacon, Beans, and Galantines: Food and Foodways on the Western Mining Frontier* (Reno: University of Nevada Press, 1986), 11; Faragher, *Sugar Creek*, 65; Conlin, "Did You Get Enough Pie," 17; Springer, *Forest Life*, 76.
156 Richard James Hooker, *Food and Drink in America: A History* (Indianapolis, IN: Bobbs-Merrill Company, 1981), 169; Susan Williams, *Food in the United States, 1820s–1890* (Santa Barbara, CA: Greenwood Publishing Group, 2006), 24–25; McMahon, "'A Comfortable Subsistence'" [dissertation], 216, 227; Horowitz, *Putting Meat on the American Table*, 18–19; Thoreau and Cramer, *The Maine Woods*, 17.
157 Springer, *Forest Life*, 46.
158 Horowitz, *Putting Meat on the American Table*, 13, 19; Chamberlain Farm to A. Palmer . . . [account January 29—March 9, 1850], Chamberlain Farm collection, Maine Historical Society, Portland, Maine.
159 Thoreau and Cramer, *The Maine Woods*, 119.
160 McIntosh, *American Food Habits in Historical Perspective*, 86; Conlin, *Bacon, Beans, and Galantines*, 58; Horowitz, *Putting Meat on the American Table*, 45.
161 McIntosh, *American Food Habits in Historical Perspective*, 83, 92.
162 Turner, *How The Other Half Ate*; Hooker, *Food and Drink in America*, 214; Gabriella M. Petrick, "The Arbiters of Taste Producers, Consumers and the Industrialization of Taste in America, 1900–1960," (Thesis, University of Delaware, 2007), 16–17, 22; Beam, *A Maine Hamlet*, 64; Conlin, *Bacon, Beans, and Galantines*, 5; Anna Zeide and Darra Goldstein, *Canned: The Rise and Fall of Consumer Confidence in the American Food Industry* (Berkeley: University of California Press, 2018).
163 Thoreau and Cramer, *The Maine Woods*, 9.
164 C. Whitaker to Shepard Cary, December 14, 1849, St. John New Brunswick, Canada, Shepard Cary papers, box 1, folder 10, Maine Historical Society, Portland, Maine.
165 Craig, *Backwoods Consumers*, 207; Carlisle and Shatney, "Report on a Logging Operation in Northern Maine," 9; Rogers, "Lumbering in Northern Maine," 20; Miller, Poole and Sweetser, "A Lumbering Report of Work on Squaw Mountain Township," 12; Andrew Chase (b. 1888), interviewed by Linda Edgerly, 1971, p. 697069, 697070, transcript (LLC) (MFC).
166 "The French Canadians," *All the Year Round* 39, no. 928 (1886): 127; Lady Jephson, *A Canadian Scrap-Book* (London: M. Russell, 1897), 16; Craig, *Backwoods Consumers*, 144; Little, *Crofters and Habitants*, 140–141, 154; Nathaniel Hawthorn, "Diaries" in *No Ordinary Lives: Four 19th Century Teenage Diaries*, ed. Marilyn Seguin (Boston: Branden Books, 2009), 27–29.
167 Matthew Warner Osborn, *Rum Maniacs: Alcoholic Insanity in the Early American Republic* (Chicago: University of Chicago Press, 2014); W. J. Rorabaugh, *The Alcoholic Republic, an American Tradition* (New York: Oxford University Press, 1979), 11, 141; Springer, *Forest Life and Forest Trees*, 149–151; Graeme Wynn, "Deplorably Dark and

Demoralized Lumberers"? Rhetoric and Reality in Early Nineteenth-Century New Brunswick," *Forest & Conservation History* 24, no. 4 (1980), 168–187; Rorabaugh, *The Alcoholic Republic*, 141–142; Robert E. Walls, "The Making of the American Logger: Traditional Culture and Public Imagery in The Realm of The Bunyanesque" (PhD diss., Indiana University, 1997), 252; Anthony Rotundo, *American Manhood* (New York: Basic Books, 1993), 170.

168 Charles A. Scontras, *Collective Efforts among Maine Workers: Beginnings and Foundations, 1820–1880* (Orono: Bureau of Labor Education, University of Maine, 1994), 64.

169 Springer, *Forest Life and Forest Trees*, 151–152; Rorabaugh, *The Alcoholic Republic*, xi; Johnson, *A Shopkeeper's Millennium*; John Koren, *Alcohol and Society* (New York: H. Holt, 1916), 45–46.

170 Franzen, *The Archaeology of the Logging Industry*, 128.

171 Kulikoff, *The Agrarian Origins of American Capitalism*, 58; Judd and Judd, *Aroostook*, 82; Wynn, "'Deplorably Dark and Demoralized Lumberers'?," 168–169, 170, 187.

172 Benjamin Rush, *Essays, Literary, Moral and Philosophical* (Philadelphia: Text Creation Partnership, [1798] 2011), 221–222, https://quod.lib.umich.edu/e/evans/N25938.0001.001/1:7.10?rgn=div2;view=fulltext.

173 Taylor, *Liberty Men and Great Proprietors*, 50, 63; Adams, *Prices Paid by Vermont Farmers*, 90–91.

174 Quoted in Wynn, "'Deplorably Dark and Demoralized Lumberers'?," 168–169; Judd, *Common Lands*, 63; Cox, *Lumbermen's Frontier*, 80.

175 Philip G. Terrie, "Romantic Travelers in The Adirondack Wilderness," *American Studies* 24, no. 2 (1983): 63, 59; Joel Tyler Headley, *The Adirondack: Or, Life in the Woods* (New York: Charles Scribner, [1850] 1864), I; Joel Tyler Headley, *Letters from the Backwoods and the Adirondac* (New York: J. S. Taylor, 1850).

176 Headley, *Letters from the Backwoods*, 41, 43, 48; Headley, *The Adirondack*, 28–29, 47–48, 350.

177 Nancy Isenberg, *White Trash: The 400-Year Untold History of Class in America* (NY: Penguin, 2016), 108, 109–112; Headley, *The Adirondack*, v; Greer, "Commons and Enclosure in the Colonization of North America," 369; Headley, *Letters from the Backwoods*, 44; Terrie, "Romantic Travelers in The Adirondack Wilderness," 73.

178 Headley, *Letters from the Backwoods*, 60.

179 Liza Piper, and John Sandlos, "A Broken Frontier: Ecological Imperialism in the Canadian North," *Environmental History* 12, no. 4 (October 2007): 761.

180 Trombulak, "A Natural History of the Northern Forest," 17, 19; Judd, *Common Lands, Common People*, 38; Mancke, *The Fault Lines of Empire*, 39, 61.

181 Wilson, *The Hill Country of Northern New England*, 7, 56; Mancke, *The Fault Lines of Empire*, 40; USM and UMO, *Farms of Maine*, 2; Judd, *Second Nature*, 85; Jenkins and Keal, *The Adirondack Atlas*, 79; Kelly Morris and Banks, *The Maine Bicentennial Atlas*, plate 22 and p. 14.

182 Wilson, *The Hill Country of Northern New England*, 132, 31; Adams, *Prices Paid in Vermont Farms*, 92–93.

183 Michael Bell, "Did New England Go Downhill?," *Geographical Review* 79, no. 4 (1989); 460–461, 464; David Soll, "Reforestation in Norfolk County, Massachusetts, 1850–1910" in *Remaking Boston: An Environmental History of the City and Its Surroundings*, ed. Anthony N. Penna and Conrad Edick Wright (Pittsburgh, PA: University of Pittsburgh Press, 2009), 150–155.

184 E. R. Pember, "Our Hill Farms," in Hiram A. Cutting, *Eight Vermont Agricultural Reports by the State Board of Agriculture for the Years 1883–1884* (Montpelier, VT: Watchmand & Journal Press, 1884), 364.

185 Wilson, *The Hill Country of Northern New England*, 101.

186 Judd, *Common Lands, Common People*, 64–65; Irland, *The Northeast's Changing Forests*, 141.
187 Irland, *The Northeast's Changing Forests*, 272–242.
188 Christine L. Goodale and John D. Aber, "The Long-Term Effects Of Land-Use History On Nitrogen Cycling In Northern Hardwood Forests," *Ecological Applications* 11, no. 1 (2001): 260; T. J. Fahey, "Belowground Ecology and Dynamics in Eastern Old-Growth Forests"; Goodall and Aber, "The Long-Term Effects of Land-Use History on Nitrogen Cycling," 260–263; Jamie H. Eves, "Shrunk to a Comparative Rivulet: Deforestation, Stream Flow, and Rural Milling in 19th-Century Maine," *Technology and Culture* 33, no. 1 (Jan. 1992): 38–65.
189 Judd, *Common Lands, Common People*, 35.
190 Marchand, *North Woods*, 21; Barton, "Introduction: Ecological and Historical Context."
191 Wohlleben, *The Hidden Life of Trees*, 10–11.
192 Wilson, *The Hill Country of Northern New England*, 9.
193 Jenkins and Keal, *The Adirondack Atlas*, 88–89; Irland, *The Northeast's Changing Forests*, 135; Bennett, *The Wilderness from Chamberlain Farm*, 92.
194 Barton and Keeton, *Ecology and Recovery*, 107; Christopher R. Webster and Craig G. Lorimer, "Single-Tree versus Group Selection in Hemlock-Hardwood Forests: Are Smaller Openings Less Productive?," *Canadian Journal of Forest Research* 32, no. 4 (2002): 598.
195 Susy Svatek Ziegler, "Postfire Succession in an Adirondack Forest," 469–470; Irland, *The Northeast's Changing Forests*, 93; Trombulak, "A Natural History of the Northern Forest," 19; Judd, *Second Nature*, 17, 116, 117; George P. Buchert, Om P. Rajora, James V. Hood, and Bruce P. Dancik, "Effects of Harvesting on Genetic Diversity in Old-Growth Eastern White Pine in Ontario, Canada," *Conservation Biology* 11, no. 3 (1997): 747–758.
196 William Cronon, *Nature's Metropolis: Chicago and the Great West* (New York: W. W. Norton, 2009), 165; Todes, *Labor and Lumber*, 31; Stephanie Kaza, "Ethical Tension in the Northern Forest," in Klyza and Trombulak, *The Future of the Northern Forest*, 74.
197 Thoreau and Cramer, *The Maine Woods*, 36–139; Judd, *Second Nature*, 114; Henry Conklin, *Through "Poverty's Vale": A Hardscrabble Boyhood in Upstate New York, 1832–1862* (Syracuse, NY: Syracuse University Press, 1974), 48, 51, 54, 124, 107–108, 126, 134, 144, 188; Cronon, *Changes in the Land*, 145–146; Jacoby, *Crimes against Nature*, 19–23; 54–55; McMartin, *The Great Forest of the Adirondacks*, 59; Borton, "Adirondack Lumbering—The Jessup Operation," 1–2; Holbrook, *Yankee Loggers*, 30–31.
198 Richard W. Judd, *Common Lands, Common People: The Origins of Conservation in Northern New England* (Harvard University Press, 1997), 35.

3. A Chance

1 "Coe Family Papers, "Logging operations, volume 1, 1862–63," "Logging operations, volume 3, 1890–91," Special Collections, Raymond H. Fogler Library, University of Maine, Orono, ME; US Census Bureau, Federal Census Non-Population Schedules, 1860, Production of Agriculture, Abner Toothaker, Rangeley, Franklin, Maine, p. 23, accessed August 11, 2014, ancestry.com.
2 "The Lincoln and Idella Toothaker Letters, 1890–1892," January 1, 1891, Lincoln to Ida; March 28, 1891; January 18, 1891, Lincoln to Ida; November 16, 1891, Lincoln to Ida. Exhibit edited by Becky Ellis Martineau, 2003. Property of Becky Ellis Martineau and the Rangeley Lakes Region Logging Museum, Rangeley, Maine, http://rlrlm.org.

3 Francis Cherunilam, *Business Environment* (Mumbai: Himalaya Publishing House, 2010), 1; Forough Zarea Fazlelahi and J. Henri Burgers "Natural Imprinting and Vertical Integration in the Extractive Industries," in *Managing Natural Resources*, ed. Gerard George and Simon J. D. Schillebeeck (Cheltenham, UK: Edward Elgar Publishing, 2018), 140; Gary J. Castrogiovanni, "Environmental Munificence: A Theoretical Assessment," *Academy of Management Review* 16, no. 3 (1991): 542–565; Rachel Bouvier, "The Natural Environment as Field-Level Actor: The Environment and The Pulp And Paper Industry in Maine," *Journal of Economic Issues* 44, no. 3 (2010): 717–735; Christine Meisner Rosen and Christopher C. Sellers, "The Nature of the Firm: Towards an Ecocultural History of Business," *Business History Review* 73, no. 4 (1999): 594.

4 Robert J. Steinfeld, *Coercion, Contract, and Free Labor in the Nineteenth Century* (Cambridge: Cambridge University Press, 2001), 3; Olivier Zunz, *Making America Corporate, 1870–1920* (Chicago: University of Chicago Press, 1992); Ralph Gomory and Richard Sylla, "The American Corporation," *Daedalus* 142, no. 2 (2013): 102–118; William G. Robbins, *Colony and Empire: The Capitalist Transformation of the American West* (Lawrence: University Press of Kansas, 1994); Jeremy Atack, "America: Capitalism's Promised Land," in *The Cambridge History of Capitalism*, vol. 1, ed. Larry Neal (Cambridge: Cambridge University Press, 2014), 560; Alfred D. Chandler, *The Visible Hand: The Managerial Revolution in American Business* (Cambridge, MA: Belknap Press, 1977); Cronon William, *Changes in the Land: Indians, Colonists, and the Ecology of New England* (New York: Hill and Wang, 2011), 13–14; Castrogiovanni, "Environmental Munificence," 543.

5 Michael J. Enright, "Organization and Coordination in Geographically Concentrated Industries"; Naomi R. Lamoreaux and Daniel M. G. Raff, eds., *Coordination and Information: Historical Perspectives on the Organization of Enterprise* (Chicago: University of Chicago Press, 2007), 123–124; Christian G. De Vito, "Labour Flexibility and Labour Precariousness as Conceptual Tools for the Historical Study of the Interactions among Labour Relations" in *On the Road to Global Labour History: A Festschrift for Marcel van der Linden* (Leiden: Brill, 2018); Mark Erlich, "Misclassification in Construction: The Original Gig Economy," *ILR Review* 74, no. 5 (October 2021): 1202–1230.

6 David Harvey, *Seventeen Contradictions and the End of Capitalism* (Oxford: Oxford University Press, 2014), 142.

7 Ralph Clement Bryant, *Logging: the Principles and General Methods of Operation in the United States* (Hoboken, NJ: J. Wiley & Sons, 1914), 476–477; "chance, n., adj., and adv." OED Online, Oxford University Press, 2001, accessed July 20, 2016, http://www.oed.com.

8 Allan Greer, "Commons and Enclosure in the Colonization of North America," *The American Historical Review* 117, no. 2 (2012): 365–386; Robert McCullough, *The Landscape of Community: A History of Communal Forests in New England* (Lebanon, NH: University Press of New England, 1995), 83–84; Carolyn Merchant, *Ecological Revolutions: Nature, Gender, and Science in New England* (Chapel Hill: University of North Carolina Press, 2010), 166.

9 McCullough, *The Landscape of Community*, 76–78, 67.

10 Jan Albers, *Hands on the Land: A History of the Vermont Landscape* (Cambridge, MA: MIT Press, 2000), 138; Patricia J. Tracy, "Re-considering Migration within Colonial New England," *Journal of Social History* 23, no. 1 (1989): 100–102; Roberts, *Colonial Ecology, Atlantic Economy*, 115, 117.

11 James Willard Hurst, *Law and Economic Growth: The Legal History of the Lumber Industry in Wisconsin, 1836–1915* (Cambridge, MA: Harvard University Press, 1964), 98–99, 27, 29, 16, 25.

12 Richard William Judd, *Common Lands, Common People: The Origins of Conservation in Northern New England* (Cambridge, MA: Harvard University Press, 1997), 45–46.
13 David C. Smith, *A History of Lumbering in Maine, 1861–1960* (Orono: University of Maine Press, 1972), 191; Dean B. Bennett, *The Wilderness from Chamberlain Farm: A Story of Hope for the American Wild* (Washington, DC: Island Press/Shearwater Books, 2001), 87, 91.
14 Judd, *Common Lands, Common People*, 102.
15 Richard William Judd and Patricia Judd, *Aroostook: A Century of Logging in Northern Maine* (Orono: University of Maine Press, 1988), 95; Béatrice Craig and Maxime Dagenais, *The Land in Between: The Upper St. John Valley, Prehistory to World War I* (Gardiner, NY: Tilbury House, 2009), 140; Judd, *Common Lands, Common People*, 30.
16 "stumpage, n.," OED Online, Oxford University Press, accessed October 20, 2014, http://www.oed.com.
17 Coe Family Papers," box 8, "E. S. Coe: Applications for permits 1886–1899," Special Collections, Raymond H. Fogler Library, University of Maine.
18 Karl Jacoby, *Crimes against Nature: Squatters, Poachers, Thieves, and the Hidden History of American Conservation* (Berkeley: University of California Press, 2005), 11.
19 George Perkins Marsh, *Man and Nature: Or, Physical Geography as Modified by Human Action* (New York: Charles Scribner, 1864), 36.
20 Barbara McMartin, *The Great Forest of the Adirondacks* (Utica, NY: North Country Books, 1994), 30–38.
21 "Circumnavigating the Adirondacks," *Forest and Stream*, 34 (New York: Forest and Stream Publishing, 1891), 104–105; Michael Rawson, *Eden on the Charles: The Making of Boston* (Cambridge, MA: Harvard University Press, 2011), 37–38; Judd, *Common Lands, Common People*, 92.
22 F. Roth, "The School-Trained Forester," *Journal of Forestry* 16, no. 8 (1918): 855; James B. Berry, "The Creation of an Ideal," *Forestry Quarterly* XII, no. 4 (1914): 514–519.
23 Circular of The New York State College of Forestry at Syracuse University, Announcement of Courses no. 30, xix, no. 6 (1910): 10, SUNY ESF Moon Library Archives, Syracuse New York (not catalogued); J. A. Ferguson, "The Development of Forestry Education in The United States," *Penn State Farmer* 3, no. 4 (1910): 73–77.
24 Henry Solon Graves and Cedric Hay Guise, *Forest Education* (New Haven, CT: Yale University Press, 1932), 685.
25 Alfred L. Donaldson, *A History of the Adirondacks* (New York: Century Co, 1921), 163; Jacoby, *Crimes against Nature*, 200–202; Judd, *Common Lands, Common People*, 91, 104, 113.
26 Stephen C. Harper, Laura L. Falk, and Edward W. Rankin, *The Northern Forest Lands Study of New England and New York: A Report to the Congress of the United States on the Recent Changes in Landownership and Land Use in the Northern Forest of Maine, New Hampshire, New York and Vermont* (Rutland, VT: Forest Service, US Department of Agriculture, 1990), 102.
27 Judd, *Common Lands, Common People*, 98, 111, 116.
28 "Coe Family Papers," Logging operations vol. 1–6, Special Collections, Raymond H. Fogler Library, University of Maine, Orono, ME.
29 New York State, *First Annual Report of the Commissioners of Fisheries, Game and Forests of the State of New York* (Government publication, 1896), 7.
30 D. H. Stauton to A. G. Chaplin, Malone, NY, April 7, 1884, Letters from agents appointed to serve notice on illegal occupants of state lands, 1881–1893, folder 2 (1 of 2), BO942–85, New York State Archives, Cultural Education Center, Albany, NY.

31 J. B. Riley to A. G. Chaplin, Malone, NY, April 9, 1884, Letters from agents appointed to serve notice on illegal occupants of state lands, 1881–1893, folder 1 (2 of 2), BO942–85, New York State Archives, Cultural Education Center, Albany, NY.

32 Hurst, *Law and Economic Growth*, 55.

33 Jacoby, *Crimes against Nature*, 169, 137–138, 164.

34 Judd, *Common Lands*, 60–61, 61–62, 64–65; Béatrice Craig, *Backwoods Consumers and Homespun Capitalists: The Rise of a Market Culture in Eastern Canada* (Toronto: University of Toronto Press, 2009), 165–179; Graeme Wynn, *Timber Colony: A Historical Geography of Early Nineteenth-Century New Brunswick* (Toronto: University of Toronto Press, 1981), 132.

35 William Buckhout Greeley, Earle Hart Clapp, Joseph Kittredge, Herbert Augustine Smith, Ward Shepard, William Norwood Sparhawk, and Raphael Zon, "Timber: Mine or Crop?," vol. 886 (Washington, DC: US Government Printing Office, 1923), 146–149.

36 McMartin, *The Great Forest of the Adirondack*, 113.

37 Harold F. Wilson, *The Hill Country of Northern New England: Its Social and Economic History, 1790–1930* (New York: Columbia University Press, 1936), 70–71.

38 Mose Velsor [Walt Whitman], "Manly Health and Training, with Off-Hand Hints Toward Their Conditions," *Walt Whitman Quarterly Review* 33 (2016): 194, 208, 212, 266–267, 205–206, 289.

39 Quoted in Wilson, *The Hill Country of Northern New England*, 143.

40 H. W. Foster, "Physical Education vs. Degeneracy" in Susan Harris Smith and Melanie Dawson, *The American 1890s: A Cultural Reader* (Durham, NC: Duke University Press, 2000), 302–304, 317.

41 Richard Cabot, *What Men Live By: Work, Play, Love, Worship* (Boston: Houghton Mifflin, 1914), 53; Foster, "Physical Education vs. Degeneracy," 302–304, 317; Jackson Lears, *No Place of Grace: Antimodernism and the Transformation of American Culture, 1880–1920* (New York: Pantheon Books, 1981), 31.

42 Thurston Madison Adams, *Prices Paid by Vermont Farmers for Goods and Services and Received by Them for Farm Products, 1790–1940; Wages of Vermont Farm Labor, 1780–1940* (Burlington, VT: Free Printing Co., 1944), 97–98.

43 Charles Sellers, *The Market Revolution: Jacksonian America, 1815–1846* (New York: Oxford University Press, 1994); Wilson, *The Hill Country of Northern New England*, 8–70; Judd, *Common Lands, Common People*, 32; David Soll, "Reforestation in Norfolk County, Massachusetts, 1850–1910" in *Remaking Boston: An Environmental History of the City and Its Surroundings*, ed. Anthony N. Penna and Conrad Edick Wright (Pittsburgh, PA: University of Pittsburgh Press, 2009), 153.

44 James H. Blodgett, *Wages of Farm Labor in the United States: Results of Twelve Statistical Investigations, 1866–1902* (Washington, DC: US Department of Agriculture, Bureau of Statistics, 1903), 46.

45 United States, Fifteenth Census of the United States, 1930: Agriculture: Type of Farm, Summary for the United States, 1929 and 1930 (Washington, DC: US Government Printing Office, 1932), chapter XIII, "Forest Products Cut on Farms and Nurseries and Greenhouses" and "Maine," "New Hampshire," "Vermont," and "New York."

46 Edmund W. Bradwin, *The Bunkhouse Man: A Study of Work and Pay in the Camps of Canada, 1903–1914* (Toronto: University of Toronto Press, 1972), 65; Adams, *Prices Paid by Vermont Farmers*, 8.

47 "Coe Family Papers," Logging operations, volume 3, 1890–1891, Special Collections, Raymond H. Fogler Library, University of Maine, Orono, ME.

48 John Sharpe (b. 1881), interviewed by Lillian Shirley, 1970, p. 37, transcript (LLC) (MFC).

49 Bennett, *The Wilderness from Chamberlain Farm*, 4, 77; John F. Flanagan, "Industrial Conditions in the Maine Woods," *First Biennial Report of the Department of Labor and Industry* (Waterville, ME: Sentinel Publishing Company, 1912), 211; Charles Andrew Scontras, *Organized Labor in Maine: Twentieth Century Origins* (Orono: Bureau of Labor Education of the Continuing Education Division, University of Maine, 1985), 150; Maine Department of Agriculture, *Sixth Annual Report*, 345–346, 348, 6, 349, 356–357; Judd, *Common Lands, Common People*, 16, 17–19, 23, 25–31; Judd and Judd, *Aroostook*, 145; Michael M. Bell, "Did New England Go Downhill?," *Geographical Review* 79, no. 4 (1989): 450–466; David Soll, "Reforestation in Norfolk County, Massachusetts, 1850–1910" in *Remaking Boston: An Environmental History of the City and Its Surroundings*, ed. Anthony N. Penna and Conrad Edick Wright (Pittsburgh, PA: University of Pittsburgh Press, 2009), 164.

50 Weston Homestead Farm Corporation, 1793–2011, finding aid, "Draft: B and N Weston, Merchants, Lumbermen," box 99, folder 1; "Nathan Weston Debt" box 99, folder 7, Maine Historical Society, Portland, ME; US Census Bureau, Federal Census Non-Population Schedules, 1870, Production of Agriculture, Nathan Weston, Madison, Somerset, Maine, accessed August 11, 2014, ancestry.com.

51 "Coe Family Papers," box 8, "E. S. Coe: Applications for Permits 1886–1899," Special Collections, Raymond H. Fogler Library, University of Maine.

52 Scott A. Sandage, *Born Losers: A History of Failure in America* (Cambridge, MA: Harvard University Press, 2005), 100; Bradwin, *The Bunkhouse Man*, 52; Ian Walter Radforth, *Bushworkers and Bosses: Logging in Northern Ontario, 1900–1980* (Toronto: University of Toronto Press, 1987), 35.

53 Earle Hart Clapp and Charles Ward Boyce, "How the United States Can Meet Its Present and Future Pulpwood Requirements," US Department of Agriculture, bulletin no. 1241 (Washington, DC: US Department of Agriculture, 1924), 11; John G. Franzen, *The Archaeology of the Logging Industry* (Gainesville: University Press of Florida, 2020), 6.

54 Arthur Bernhard Recknage, *The Forests of New York State* (New York: Macmillan, 1923), 35; Clapp and Boyce, "How the United States Can Meet Its Present and Future Pulpwood Requirements," 40; Radforth, *Bushworkers and Bosses*, 70–72.

55 John Howard Clark, "The Emergence of The Paper Plantation: Historical Geographies of the Pulp and Paper Industry in Maine, 1880 to 1930" (Thesis, Pennsylvania State University, 2010), 85–86.

56 Clark, "The Emergence of the Paper Plantation," 60–78.

57 David Besanko, David Dranove, Mark Shanley, and Scott Schaefe, *Economics of Strategy* (Hoboken, NJ: John Wiley & Sons, 2009), 183; Franzen, *The Archaeology of the Logging Industry*, 82, 102–103; Armen A. Alchian and Harold Demsetz, "Production, Information Costs, and Economic Organization," *The American Economic Review* 62, no. 5 (1972): 777–795.

58 Radforth, *Bushworkers and Bosses*, 72.

59 Lamoreaux, Raff, and Temin, "Beyond Markets and Hierarchies," 410; Walter W. Powell, "Neither Market nor Hierarchy: Network Forms of Organization," *Research in Organizational Behavior* 12 (1990): 306; Fazlelahi and Burgers, "Natural Imprinting and Vertical Integration in the Extractive Industries," 143; Besanko et al., *Economics of Strategy*, 156; Bradwin, *The Bunkhouse Man*, 49.

60 Judd and Judd, *Aroostook*, 154, 179.

61 Raymond J. Smith and Samuel B. Locke, "A Study of the Lumber Industry of Northern Maine" (Thesis, University of Maine Orono, 1908), 21.

62 US Congress, Importation of Canadian Bonded Labor, 84th Congress, 1st Session, 1955, Hearings before the Subcommittee on Labor of the Committee on Labor and Public Welfare on S. Res. 98, A Resolution to Authorize a Study of the Policy

and Practice of the United States with Respect to Permitting Bonded Laborers from Canada to Enter and Work in the United States, 20; "Today's Modern Lumberjacks," *The Brown Bulletin* 7 (February 1955): 9 http://berlinnhhistoricalsociety.org/wp-content/uploads/2011/06/The_Brown_Bulletin_V3_No7_Jan_1955.pdf.

63 Cecil Max Hilton, *Rough Pulpwood Operating in Northwestern Maine, 1935–1940* (Orono: University of Maine Press, 1942), 21.

64 Radforth, *Bushworkers and Bosses*, 50–51; Peter C. Welsh, *Jacks, Jobbers, and Kings: Logging the Adirondacks, 1850–1950* (Utica, NY: North Country Books, 1995), 38; W. C. Sykes to R. I. Sisson, October 20, 1919, Emporium Forest Company Records box 12, Adirondack Museum; Judd and Judd, *Aroostook*, 87, 88, 89; Bradwin, *The Bunkhouse Man*, 66; R. Boultbee, A. P. Leslie, and J. B. Matthews, "Report of Logging Operation on Limits of the Canoe Lake Lumber Co., Canoe Lake Ont., 1927–1928 (Thesis, University of Maine Orono, 1928), 7; Bruce R. Lyons, "Contracts and Specific Investment: an Empirical Test of Transaction Cost Theory," *Journal of Economics & Management Strategy* 3, no. 2 (1994): 268.

65 *The Atlantic Reporter, vol. 75* (Rochester, NY: West Publishing Company, 1910), 42–43.

66 State of New York, "Report of the Special Committee Appointed by The Assembly of 1895 to Investigate the Depredation of Timber in the Forest Preserve" (1896), 13.

67 Sandage, *Born Losers*, 67, 192–193.

68 Bradwin, *The Bunkhouse Man*, 178.

69 C. Max Hilton, *Woodsmen, Horses, and Dynamite: Rough Pulpwood Operating in Northwestern Maine, 1935–1940* (Orono: University of Maine Press, 2004), 21–23.

70 Quote in Jacoby, *Crimes against Nature*, 55.

71 State of New York, "Report of the Special Committee," 3.

72 Katherine Stone, *From Widgets to Digits: Employment Regulation for the Changing Workplace* (Cambridge: Cambridge University Press, 2004), 13; Frederick Smith Hall, *Forty Years, 1902–1942, The Work of the New York Child Labor Committee* (Brattleboro, VT: E. L. Hildreth, 1943), 83–84; Matthew T. Bodie, "Participating as a Theory of Employment," *Notre Dame Law Review* 89 (2013): 302.

73 Steinfeld, *Coercion, Contract, and Free Labor*, 292.

74 Lyman Sutton (1867–1956) interviewed by John Larson,1954, transcript, p. 2–3 (FHS) (OHIC); Bradwin, *The Bunkhouse Man*, 51; Rogers, "Lumbering in Northern Maine," 18; W. T. Turner to G. W. Sykes, August 21, 1919, Emporium Forest Company Records box 8, Adirondack Museum; Prescott and Rendall, "Lumbering in the Dead River Region," 36; Bradwin, *The Bunkhouse Man*, 122.

75 Steinfeld, *Coercion, Contract, and Free Labor*, 5, 37, 292, 318; Bradwin, *The Bunkhouse Man*, 178; William Boyd, *The Slain Wood: Papermaking and Its Environmental Consequences in the American South* (Baltimore, MD: Johns Hopkins University Press, 2015), chap. 2, "Logging the Mills."

76 Asa Flagg (b. 1898), interviewed by Rhoda Mitchell, 1970, p. 5750013, transcript (LLC) (MFC).

77 Bradwin, *The Bunkhouse Man*, 18; Amy Dru Stanley, *From Bondage to Contract: Wage Labor, Marriage, and the Market in the Age of Slave Emancipation* (Cambridge: Cambridge University Press, 1998), 83, 90; Bill Parenteau, "Bonded Labor: Canadian Woods Workers in the Maine Pulpwood Industry, 1940–55," *Forest & Conservation History* 37, no. 3 (1993): 114–115.

78 Bradwin, *The Bunkhouse Man*, 120–125, 199; William C. Osborn, *The Paper Plantation: Ralph Nader's Study Group Report on the Pulp and Paper Industry in Maine* (New York: Grossman Publishers, 1974), 138.

79 Robert M. Grant, "Toward a Knowledge-Based Theory of the Firm," *Strategic Management Journal* 17, no. S2 (1996): 109–122.

80 Judd and Judd, *Aroostook*, 179–180.
81 Franzen, *The Archaeology of the Logging Industry*, 142; Aaron Howe, "'Men of Good Timber': An Archaeological Investigation of Labor in Michigan's Upper Peninsula" (Thesis, Department of Anthropology, Western Michigan University, Kalamazoo, 2015).
82 Harry Dyer (b. 1896), interviewed by Jeanne Milton, 1970, p. 581012, transcript (LLC) (MFC).
83 Harry Dyer (b. 1896), interviewed by Jeanne Milton, 1970, p. 568029, transcript (LLC) (MFC).
84 Arnold Hall (b. 1892) interviewed by William Bonsall, 1970, transcript, 580051 (LLC) (MFC).
85 Frederick Burke interviewed by Norma Coates, 1971, transcript, p. 702010 (LLC) (MFC); Franzen, *The Archaeology of the Logging Industry*, 144.
86 Bruce Goldstein, Marc Linder, Laurence E. Norton, and Catherine K. Ruckelshaus, "Enforcing Fair Labor Standards in the Modern American Sweatshop: Rediscovering the Statutory Definition of Employment," *UCLA Law Review* 46 (1998): 1045, 1030–1037, 1042.
87 Henry Conklin, *Through "Poverty's Vale": A Hardscrabble Boyhood in Upstate New York, 1832–1862* (Syracuse, NY: Syracuse University Press, 1974), 52, 134, 141, 156; "Canton," *The Ogdensburg Advance and St. Lawrence Weekly Democrat* (Ogdensburg, NY) January 19, 1899, p. 1; Tina and Ivan Daigle, interviewed by Christina Trefethen, 1987, p. 1971007, 1971010, 1971032, transcript (LLC) (MFC).
88 Ian Radforth, "The Shantymen," in *Laboring Lives: Work and Workers in Nineteenth-Century Ontario*, ed. Paul Craven (Toronto: University of Toronto Press, 1995), 240–243.
89 The Dechene Family (Adirondack lumbering family), in communication with the author, September 2010.
90 Irland, *The Northeast's Changing Forests*, 274; Frank Tobias Higbie, *Indispensable Outcasts: Hobo Workers and Community in the American Midwest, 1880–1930* (Urbana: University of Illinois Press, 2003), 101.
91 State of New York Department of Labor, "Annual Report of the Bureau of Industries and Immigration" (Albany, NY: 1912), 62.
92 William M. Steuart, Jasper E. Whelchel, and Henry Gannett, *Census of Manufactures: 1905, Lumber and Timber Products* (Washington, DC: Government Printing Office, 1907), 16–18, 52.
93 US Congress, Importation of Canadian Bonded Labor, 98, 100.
94 Anonymous Diary, 1872–1874, February 9, 1872, March 29, 1872, November 11, 1872, November 8, 1873, January 10, 11, 12, 13, 1872, December 31, 1873, February 22, 1872, Schlesinger Library, Radcliffe College, Harvard University, Cambridge, MA.
95 Harriet M. Rice, "The Young Women and the Farm," in C. M. Winslow, *Fifteenth Vermont Agriculture Report by The State Board of Agriculture for the Year 1895* (Burlington, VT: Free Press Association, 1896), 193–194.
96 John R. Howard Jr., "Social Problems of Rural New England," in *Proceedings of the National Conference of Charities and Corrections at the Thirty-Eighth Annual Session, Held in Boston, Mass., June 7–14 1911*, ed. Alexander Johnson (Fort Wayne, IN: The Fort Wayne Printing Company, 1911), 419; Alvan F. Sanborn, "The Future of Rural New England," *Atlantic* 80 (1897): 76.
97 John Demos, *Circles and Lines: The Shape of Life in Early America* (Cambridge, MA: Harvard University Press, 2004), 13; Gary S. Foster, Richard L. Hummel, and Donald J. Adamchak, "Patterns of Conception, Natality, and Mortality from Midwestern

Cemeteries," *The Sociological Quarterly* 39, no. 3 (1998): 476; Daniel Scott Smith and Michael S. Hindus, "Premarital Pregnancy in America 1640–1971: An Overview and Interpretation," *The Journal of Interdisciplinary History* 5, no. 4 (1975): 556; "The Lincoln and Idella Toothaker Letters, 1890–1892," May 27, 1892, Ida to Lincoln.

98 Inge Geyskens, Jan-Benedict E. M. Steenkamp, and Nirmalya Kumar, "Make, Buy, or Ally: A Transaction Cost Theory Meta-Analysis," *Academy of Management Journal* 49, no. 3 (2006): 521, 530; Todd R. Zenger, Teppo Felin, and Lyda Bigelow, "Theories of the Firm–Market Boundary," *Academy of Management Annals* 5, no. 1 (2011): 117; Bruce R. Lyons, "Contracts and Specific Investment: An Empirical Test of Transaction Cost Theory," *Journal of Economics & Management Strategy* 3, no. 2 (1994): 257–278; Vladimir Smirnov and Andrew Wait, "Hold-Up and Sequential Specific Investments," *RAND Journal of Economics* 25, no. 2 (2004): 386; Jeffrey R. Church and Roger Ware, *Industrial Organization: A Strategic Approach* (Homewood, IL: Irwin McGraw Hill, 2000), 72–75; Besanko et al., *Economics of Strategy*, 137–149.

99 Evelyn M. Dinsdale (Evelyn Stokes), "Spatial Patterns of Technological Change: The Lumber Industry of Northern New York," *Economic Geography* 41, no. 3 (1965): 255; Radforth, *Bushworkers and Bosses*, 4, 26, 78–79, 192; Wynn, *Timber Colony*, 10; Welsh, *Jacks, Jobbers and Kings*, 13, 28; L. T. Murray, Sr. (b. 1885), interviewed by Elwood R. Maunder, November 4, 1957, p. 21, transcript (FHS) (OHIC); Judd and Judd, *Aroostook*, 130, 188; Bradwin, *The Bunkhouse Man*, 161.

100 Hurst, *Law and Economic Growth*, 120, 137; Wilson, *The Hill Country of Northern New England*, 97–184.

101 Charles Dayton Woods, and E. R. Mansfield, *Studies of the Food of Maine Lumbermen* (Washington, DC: Government Printing Office, 1904), 7; David Nathan Rogers, "Lumbering in Northern Maine: A Report Presented to the Department of Forestry of the University of Maine" (Thesis, University of Maine, Orono, 1906), 1.

102 Quoted in Welsh, *Jacks, Jobbers and Kings*, 45, 85. Also see, Franzen, *The Archaeology of the Logging Industry*, 86.

103 US Congress, Importation of Canadian Bonded Labor, 6–7.

104 Michael Hillard, and Jonathan P. Goldstein, "Cutting off the Canadians: Nativism and the Fate of the Maine Woodman's Association, 1970–1981," *Labor: Studies in the Working-Class History of the Americas* 5, no. 3 (2008): 67–89; US Congress, Importation of Canadian Bonded Labor, 1–10.

105 Osborn, *The Paper Plantation*, 135.

106 Dan Clawson, *Bureaucracy and the Labor Process: The Transformation of US Industry, 1860–1920* (New York: Monthly Review Press, 1980), 119–121, 23, 30, 116; Michael V. Kennedy, "Working Agreements: The Use of Subcontracting in the Pennsylvania Iron Industry 1725–1789," *Pennsylvania History* 65, no. 4 (1998): 492–508; Thomas M. Doerflinger, "Rural Capitalism in Iron Country: Staffing a Forest Factory, 1808–1815," *William and Mary Quarterly* 59, no. 1 (2002): 3–38; David Montgomery, *Workers' Control in America: Studies in the History of Work, Technology, and Labor Struggles* (Cambridge: Cambridge University Press, 1980); Robert V. Robinson, and Carl M. Briggs, "The Rise of Factories in Nineteenth-Century Indianapolis," *American Journal of Sociology* 97, no. 3 (1991): 622–656; John R. Commons, Ulrich Bonnell Phillips, Eugene Allen Gilmore, Helen L. Sumner, and John B. Andrews, *A Documentary History of American Industrial Society: Labor Conspiracy Case vol. 3* (Cleveland, OH: Arthur H. Clark Co.), 48–51; Bruce Laurie, *Artisans into Workers: Labor in Nineteenth-Century America* (Urbana: University of Illinois Press, 1989); Sean Wilentz, *Chants Democratic: New York City and the Rise of the American Working Class, 1788–1850* (Oxford: Oxford University Press, 2004), 113.

107 Besanko et al., *Economics of Strategy*, 41, 47; Ronald Coase, "The Nature of the Firm," *Economica*, 4 no. 16 (1937): 386–405; Jesse T. Carpenter, *Competition and Collective Bargaining in the Needle Trades, 1910–1967* (Ithaca, NY: Cornell University, 1972), 37; William Lazonick, *Business Organization and the Myth of the Market Economy* (Cambridge: Cambridge University Press, 1993), 13, 29; Richard White, *Railroaded: The Transcontinentals and the Making of Modern America* (New York: W. W. Norton, 2011), xxv.

108 United States Wage and Hour and Public Contracts Divisions, Small Logging Operations: Data Pertinent to an Evaluation of the 13(a)(15) Exemption of the Fair Labor Standards Act. (Washington, DC: Government Printing Office, 1964); Bruce Goldstein, Marc Linder, Laurence E. Norton, II, and Catherine K. Ruckelshaus, *Enforcing Fair Labor Standards in the Modern American Sweatshop: Rediscovering the Statutory Definition of Employment*, 46 *UCLA Law Review* (1999): 983, 984, 1017; Hall, "Forty Years," 83–84; Nelson Lichtenstein, *State of the Union: A Century of American Labor—Revised and Expanded Edition* (Princeton, NJ: Princeton University Press, 2013); Lizabeth Cohen, *Making a New Deal: Industrial Workers in Chicago, 1919–1939* (Cambridge: Cambridge University Press, 1990); Brian Callaci, "Control Without Responsibility: The Legal Creation of Franchising, 1960–1980," *Enterprise & Society* 22, no. 1 (2021): 158.

109 Clawson, *Bureaucracy and the Labor Process*, 76.

110 Carpenter, *Competition and Collective Bargaining in the Needle Trades*, 32–33, 37.

111 Tiziana Casciaro and Mikolaj Jan Piskorski, "Power Imbalance, Mutual Dependence, and Constraint Absorption: A Closer Look at Resource Dependence Theory," *Administrative Science Quarterly* 50, no. 2 (2005): 173, 189.

112 Clawson, *Bureaucracy and the Labor Process*, 108, 111; Higbie, *Indispensable Outcasts*, 117; Commons et al., *A Documentary History of American Industrial Society vol. III*, 48–49; Thomas Dublin, *Women at Work: The Transformation of Work and Community in Lowell, Massachusetts, 1826–1860* (New York: Columbia University Press, 1979); Alan Dawley, *Class and Community: The Industrial Revolution in Lynn* (Cambridge, MA: Harvard University Press, 1976).

113 William E. Forbath, *Law and the Shaping of the American Labor Movement* (Cambridge, MA: Harvard University Press, 2009), 59.

114 Forbath, *Law and the Shaping of the American Labor Movement*, 83–86, 155–156.

115 Andrew Wender Cohen, *The Racketeer's Progress: Chicago and the Struggle for the Modern American Economy, 1900–1940* (New York: Cambridge University Press, 2004); Carpenter, *Competition and Collective Bargaining in the Needle Trades*, 122.

116 Sanjukta Paul, "Antitrust as Allocator of Coordination Rights," *UCLA Law Review* 67, no. 2 (2020), 398–399; Victoria Saker Woeste, *Farmer's Benevolent Trust: Law and Agricultural Cooperation in Industrial America, 1865–1945* (Chapel Hill: University of North Carolina Press), 195; Forbath, *Law and the Shaping of the American Labor Movement*, 157–158.

117 Sandeep Vaheesan, "Accommodating Capital and Policing Labor: Antitrust in the Two Gilded Ages," *Maryland Law Review* 78 (2018): 790; Marshall Steinbaum, "Antitrust, the Gig Economy, and Labor Market Power," *Law & Contemporary Problems* 82 (2019): 57–58; Forbath, *Law and the Shaping of the American Labor Movement*, 61.

118 Paul, "Antitrust as Allocator of Coordination Rights," 405.

119 Woeste, *Farmer's Benevolent Trust*, 195, 210–211.

120 Jon Lauck, "American Agriculture and the Problem of Monopoly," *Agricultural History* 70, no. 2 (1996): 202; Woeste, *Farmer's Benevolent Trust*, 24, 138, 233; Wilson, *The Hill Country of Northern New England*, 340–341.

121 Franklin D. Jones, "The Status of Farmers' Co-Operative Associations under Federal Law," *Journal of Political Economy* 29, no. 7 (1921): 596; Woeste, *Farmer's Benevolent Trust*, 203, 233, quote from 213–214; Wilson, *The Hill Country of Northern New England*, 340–341; Woeste, *Farmer's Benevolent Trust*, 144; Woodsmoke Productions and Vermont Historical Society, "The Co-Op Movement, 1919," The Green Mountain Chronicles radio broadcast and background information, original broadcast 1988–1989, https://vermonthistory.org/the-coop-movement-1919.

122 Woeste, *Farmer's Benevolent Trust*, 64–69, 157, 194, 165, 200; Wilson, *The Hill Country of Northern New England*, 185, 197, 314–315, 381, 396; Donald A. Frederick, "Antitrust Status of Farmer Cooperatives: The Story of the Capper-Volstead Act," US Department of Agriculture, Rural Business-Cooperative Service Series: Cooperative Information Report 59 (2002): 181, 191.

123 Jon Lauck, "American Agriculture and the Problem of Monopoly," *Agricultural History* 70, no. 2 (1996): 202; "To Promote Cooperative Marketing: Hearings on S. 1910 and H.R. 7893 Before the Senate Committee on Agriculture and Forestry," 69th Congress, 1st Session (1926): p. 9, 18, 32, 69–70, 112, 156, 162; Wikisource contributors, "Tigner v. Texas/Opinion of the Court," Wikisource, https://en.wikisource.org (accessed April 7, 2021).

124 Ralph Thornton (b. 1885), interviewed by Wayne Bean, 1972, p. 717470, transcript (LLC) (MFC).

125 Lee J. Vance, "Lumbering in the Adirondacks," *Godey's Magazine* 113, no. 789 (March 1896): 232.

126 Recknage, *The Forests of New York State*, 31.

127 Stephanie Kaza, "Ethical Tensions in the Northern Forest" in Christopher Klyza and Stephen C. Trombulak, *The Future of the Northern Forest* (Middlebury, VT: Middlebury College Press, 1994), 79.

128 William Boyd and Michael Watts, "Agro-Industrial Just-In-Time: The Chicken Industry and Postwar American Capitalism," in *Globalizing Food: Agrarian Questions and Global Restructuring*, ed. David Goodman and Michael Watts (London: Routledge, 1997), 204–206; Jan de Vries, "The Industrial Revolution and the Industrious Revolution," *The Journal of Economic History* 54, no. 2 (1994): 265.

129 De Vito, "Labour Flexibility and Labour Precariousness," 223; Michael C. Jensen and William H. Meckling, "Theory of the Firm: Managerial Behavior, Agency Costs and Ownership Structure," *Journal of Financial Economics* 3, no. 4 (1976): 305–360; William Lazonick, *Business Organization and the Myth of the Market Economy* (Cambridge: Cambridge University Press, 1993), 13, 29, 39.

Interlude

1 JoAnne Yates, *Control through Communication: The Rise of System in American Management* (Baltimore: Johns Hopkins University Press, 1989).

2 Sara B. Pritchard, "An Envirotechnical Disaster: Nature, Technology, and Politics at Fukushima," in *The History of Technology: Critical Readings*, ed. Suzanne M. Moon and Peter S. Soppelsa (London: Bloomsbury Publishing, 2020).

3 Naomi R. Lamoreaux, Daniel M. G. Raff, and Peter Temin, "Beyond Markets and Hierarchies: Toward a New Synthesis of American Business History," *American Historical Review* 108, no. 2 (April 2003): 410; Christine Meisner Rosen and Christopher C. Sellers. "The Nature of the Firm: Towards an Ecocultural History of Business," *Business History Review* 73, no. 4 (1999): 582; Gordon M. Winder and Andreas Dix, "Commercial Knowledge and Environmental Transformation on and through Frontiers," in *Trading Environments: Frontiers, Commercial Knowledge and*

Environmental Transformation, 1750–1990, ed. Gordon M. Winder and Andreas Dix (London: Routledge, 2015), 6; Richard White, *The Organic Machine: The Remaking of the Columbia River* (New York: MacMillan, 1996).

4 Morton J. Horwitz, *The Transformation of American Law, 1870–1960: The Crisis of Legal Orthodoxy* (Oxford: Oxford University Press, 1992), 42; Jonathan Leitner, "North American Timber Economy: Log Transport, Regional Capitalist Conflict, and Corporate Formation in Wisconsin's Chippewa Basin, 1860–1900," *Review (Fernand Braudel Center)* (2003): 184–194.

5 James Willard Hurst, *Law and Economic Growth: The Legal History of the Lumber Industry in Wisconsin, 1836–1915* (Cambridge, MA: Harvard University Press, 1964), 166–167, 212; Hugh G. E. MacMahon, *Progress, Stability, and the Struggle for Equality: A Ramble Through the Early Years of Maine Law, 1820–1920* (Portland, ME: Drummond Woodsum & MacMahon, 2009); Robert F. Fries, "The Mississippi River Logging Company and the Struggle for the Free Navigation of Logs, 1865–1900," *The Mississippi Valley Historical Review* 35, no. 3 (1948): 430–431.

6 Theodore Steinberg, *Nature Incorporated: Industrialization and the Waters of New England* (Cambridge University Press, 2003); Horwitz, *The Transformation of American Law*, 31–41.

7 William Freeman Fox, *A History of the Lumber Industry in the State of New York* (US Department of Agriculture, Bureau of Forestry, 1902), 23.

8 MacMahon, *Progress, Stability, and the Struggle for Equality*, 260–262; Hurst, *Law and Economic Growth*, 250.

9 Fries, "The Mississippi River Logging Company," 433.

10 David B. Gracy II, "A Cowman's-Eye View of the Information Ecology of the Texas Cattle Industry from the Civil War to World War I," *Information & Culture* 51, no. 2 (2016): 164–191.

11 Fox, *A History of the Lumber Industry in the State of New York*, 23; Ralph Thornton (b. 1886), interviewed by Wayne Bean, 1972, p. 717334, transcript (LLC) (MFC); Richard R. John "Recasting the Information Infrastructure for the Industrial Age," in *A Nation Transformed by Information: How Information Has Shaped the United States from Colonial Times to the Present*, ed. Alfred D. Chandler Jr., James W. Cortada, and Alfred D. Chandler (Oxford: Oxford University Press, 2000), 56.

12 Alfred Geer Hempstead, "The Penobscot Boom and the Development of the West Branch of the Penobscot River for Log Driving," *Maine Bulletin* XXXIII (1931) "Preface," 16; Richard George Wood, *A History of Lumbering in Maine, 1820–1821* (Orono: University of Maine Press, 1935), 14; Edward D. Ives, *Argyle Boom* (Orono, ME: Northeast Folklore Society, 1977), 15, 20–23.

13 John S. Springer, *Forest Life and Forest Trees . . .* (New York: Harper & Bros., 1851), 175; Bill Gove, *Log Drives on the Connecticut River* (Littleton, NH: Bondcliff Books, 2003), 197; Barbara McMartin, *The Great Forest of the Adirondacks* (Utica, NY: North Country Books, 1994), 60–61; John Howard Clark, "The Emergence of the Paper Plantation: Historical Geographies of the Pulp and Paper Industry in Maine, 1880 to 1930" (Thesis, Pennsylvania State University, 2010), 18, 40, 46.

14 Hempstead, "The Penobscot Boom," 21–22, 46, 165, 170; Ralph Clement Bryant, *Logging: The Principles and General Methods of Operation in the United States* (Hoboken, NJ: J. Wiley & Sons, 1914); Leitner, "North American Timber Economy," 189–194.

15 Hempstead, "The Penobscot Boom," 60–61; William W. Geller, "Log Driving on the West Branch of the Penobscot River: An Addendum to Alfred Hempstead's Book *The Penobscot Boom and the Development of the West Branch of the Penobscot River for Log Driving, Maine History Documents* 117 (2016): 8, 21; Hurst, *Law and Economic Growth*, 178–180; Alexander Koroleff and John Fortune Walker, *River*

Drive of Pulpwood: Efficiency of Technique (Brossard, QB: Canadian Pulp and Paper Association, Woodlands Section, 1946), 41.

16 Koroleff and Walker, *River Drive of Pulpwood*, xiii, 172–176; Bryant, *Logging: The Principles and General Methods*, 415–416, 418.

17 Hurst, *Law and Economic Growth*, 145, 167.

18 Robert Little, *The Washington Quarterly Magazine of Arts, Science and Literature*, vol. 1 (Washington, DC: Pishey Thompson and Davis and Force, 1823), 125–127; G.C. Pickering, "A Tramp in the Shadow of Katahdin," in *The Northern Monthly: A Magazine of Original Literature and Military Affairs* (Portland, ME: Bailey and Noyes, 1864), 147–154, 224–232; Robert E. Pike, *Tall Trees, Tough Men* (New York: W. W. Norton, 1967), 214; Nathaniel Hawthorn, "Diaries" in *No Ordinary Lives: Four 19th Century Teenage Diaries*, ed. Marilyn Seguin (Boston: Branden Books, 2009), 27–29; Geller, "Log Driving on the West Branch of the Penobscot River," 122; Frank Carey (b. 1886), interviewed by Rita Swidrowski, 1970, p. 6980061–62, transcript (LLC) (MFC); Henry David Thoreau and Jeffrey S. Cramer, *The Maine Woods a Fully Annotated Edition* (New Haven, CT: Yale University Press, 2009), 42–44; Vaclav Smil, *Growth: From Microorganisms to Megacities* (Cambridge, MA: MIT Press, 2019), 230–231.

19 Pickering, "A Tramp in the Shadow of Katahdin," 147–154, 224–232.

20 Charles Scontras, "Labor Day 2007: Pausing to Reflect on Images of Maine Labor One Hundred Years Ago" (Orono: Maine Bureau of Labor Education, 2007), 7.

21 Geller, "Log Driving on the West Branch of the Penobscot River," 122.

22 Bryant, *Logging: The Principles and General Methods*, 418–419.

23 MacMahon, *Progress, Stability, and the Struggle for Equality*, 264; Bryant, *Logging: The Principles and General Methods*, 419.

24 Ives, *Argyle Boom*, 32–33, 65, 38; Alfred Geer Hempstead, "The Penobscot Boom and the West Branch of the Penobscot River" (Thesis, University of Maine, 1930); Bryant, *Logging: The Principles and General Methods*, 403; 405, 410, 421–423; Thomas R. Cox, *The Lumberman's Frontier: Three Centuries of Land Use, Society, and Change in America's Forests* (Corvallis: Oregon State University Press, 2010), 97–98.

25 Ives, *Argyle Boom*, 38–51, 56, 58.

26 Ives, *Argyle Boom*, 47, 62–63; Bryant, *Logging: The Principles and General Methods*, 385.

27 Ives, *Argyle Boom*, 114; Hempstead, "The Penobscot Boom," 80–86; Bryant, *Logging: The Principles and General Methods*, 405; Henry David Thoreau, *The Maine Woods* (Boston: Ticknor and Fields, 1864), 42–44.

28 Hempstead, "The Penobscot Boom," 29; 57; Ives, *Argyle Boom*, 68.

29 Bryant, *Logging: The Principles and General Methods*, 410–411; Hempstead, "The Penobscot Boom," 166–167; Ives, *Argyle Boom*, 59, 67–68.

30 Springer, *Forest Life and Forest Trees*, 176; Hempstead, "The Penobscot Boom," 170; Bryant, *Logging: The Principles and General Methods*, 411; Ives, *Argyle Boom*, 59.

31 Werner Bonefeld, "Abstract Labour: Against Its Nature and on Its Time," *Capital & Class* 34, no. 2 (2010): 257–276.

32 Warren Weaver, "The Mathematics of Communication," *Scientific American* 181, no. 1 (1949), 12; William Cronon, *Nature's Metropolis: Chicago and the Great West* (W. W. Norton, 2009).

33 Turners Falls Lumber Company Records, Series II. Unbound material, 1872–1908, Box 3, f. 4 Columbia, Colebrook land, 1889–1897, Box 3, f. 3 Papers re: land, 1889–1897; Box 3, f. 8 Contracts-Johnson land, 1895, Box 3, f. 4 Columbia, Colebrook land, 1889–1897, "Mucker to Comstock, Colebrook, NH, March 16, 1891" Baker Library Historical Collections, Harvard Business School; Gove, *Log Drives on the Connecticut River*, 197.

34 Turners Falls Lumber Company Records, Series II. Unbound material, 1872–1908, Box 3, f. 3 Papers re: land, 1889–1897, "T. M. Stoughter to S. M. Comstock" March 5, 1892.

35 Erik Reardon, "Managing the River Commons: Fishing and New England's Rural Economy, 1783–1848" (PhD diss., University of Maine–Orono, 2016), 142–145, 136–137; James R. Sedell, F. N. Leone, and W. S. Duval, "Water Transportation and Storage of Logs," *American Fisheries Society Special Publication* 19 (1991): 328; McMartin, *The Great Forest of the Adirondacks*, 53; MacMahon, *Progress, Stability, and the Struggle for Equality*, 261; Koroleff and Walker, *River Drive of Pulpwood*, 7, 82–83; William C. Osborn, *The Paper Plantation: Ralph Nader's Study Group Report on the Pulp and Paper Industry in Maine* (New York: Grossman Publishers, 1974), 13–14; Neil S. Forkey, "Anglers, Fishers, and the St. Croix River: Conflict in a Canadian-American Borderland, 1867–1900," *Forest & Conservation History* (1993): 181–182; John T. Cumbler, "The Early Making of an Environmental Consciousness: Fish, Fisheries Commissions and the Connecticut River," *Environmental History Review* 15, no. 4 (1991): 73–91; Horowitz, *The Transformation of American Law*, 116; Steinberg, *Nature Incorporated*, 172–175.

36 Osborn, *The Paper Plantation*, 21–23; D. R. Warren, W. S. Keeton, H. A. Bechtold, and C. E. Kraft, "Forest-Stream Interactions in Eastern Old-Growth Forests" in *Ecology and Recovery of Eastern Old-Growth Forests*, ed. Andrew M. Barton and William S. Keeton (Washington, DC: Island Press, 2018); Koroleff and Walker, *River Drive of Pulpwood*, xiii, 8, 149; Geller, "Log Driving on the West Branch of the Penobscot River," 26, 117; MacMahon, *Progress, Stability, and the Struggle for Equality*, 265.

4. The Winter Workscape

1 US Census Bureau, Federal Census, 1910, 1880, Herbert Emery Robinson, Island Falls, Aroostook, Maine, accessed August 11, 2014, ancestry.com; World War I, Registration Card #3498 Local Board District No. 1 Aroostook, Holton, ME, April, 18, 1918, Herbert Emery Robinson, accessed August 11, 2014, ancestry.com; US Census Bureau, Federal Census Non-Population Schedules, Production of Agriculture, 1880, Herbert Emery Robinson, Carroll, Penobscot, Maine, accessed August 11, 2014, ancestry.com.

2 Bernard Albert Chandler, "Lumbering in Northern Maine: As Illustrated by an Operation of the Emerson Lumber Company" (Thesis, University of Maine Orono, 1909), 7, 15, 26.

3 James Willard Hurst, *Law and Economic Growth: The Legal History of the Lumber Industry in Wisconsin, 1836–1915* (Cambridge, MA: Harvard University Press, 1964), 145; L. F. Kneipp, "The Technical Forester in National Forest Administration," *Journal of Forestry* 16, no. 2 (1918): 382.

4 "Oil #5: Imagine A World Without Oil," Planet Money, NPR (August 24, 2016); David Edgerton, *Shock of The Old: Technology and Global History Since 1900* (London: Profile Books, 2011), 29; Kenneth Lipartito, "Reassembling the Economic: New Departures in Historical Materialism," *The American Historical Review* 121, no. 1 (2016): 110; Gareth Austin and Kaoru Sugihara, eds., *Labor-Intensive Industrialization in Global History* (London: Routledge, 2013); Masayuki Tanimoto, ed., *The Role of Tradition in Japan's Industrialization: Another Path to Industrialization* (Oxford: Oxford University Press, 2006).

5 R. T. Gheen, "Taught at the Ranger School 1912–1914," *Bulletin: The New York State College of Forestry at Syracuse University: Dedication, Conference, and History: The New York State Ranger School, Wanakena, August 1928, NY,* 2, no. 1 (1929):

54; Edgerton, *Shock of The Old*, 186; Evelyn M. Dinsdale (Evelyn Stokes), "Spatial Patterns of Technological Change: The Lumber Industry of Northern New York," *Economic Geography* 41, no. 3 (1965): 255; Cecil Max Hilton, *Rough Pulpwood Operating in Northwestern Maine, 1935–1940* 45, no. 1 (Orono: University of Maine Press, 1942); Alexander Koroleff, *Pulpwood Cutting: Efficiency of Technique*, no. 630 (Montreal: Woodlands Section, Canadian Pulp and Paper Association, 1941); Alexander Koroleff, *Pulpwood Skidding with Horses: Efficiency of Technique* (Montreal: Woodlands Section, Canadian Pulp and Paper Association, 1943).

6 Ralph Thornton (b. 1885), interviewed by Wayne Bean, 1972, p. 717333, transcript (LLC) (MFC).

7 René Bonnière and Pierre Perrault, *Three Seasons* (Nepean, ON: Crawley Films Limited, 1960).

8 Glenn C. Prescott, and Raymond E. Rendall, "Lumbering in the Dead River Region, Somerset County, Maine," (Ph.D. diss., University of Maine Orono, 1916), 42–46.

9 Thomas G. Andrews, *Killing for Coal: America's Deadliest Labor War* (Cambridge, MA: Harvard University Press, 2008), 125, 150–159, 173, 183, 197.

10 Megan K. Prins, "Winters in America: Cities and Environment, 1870–1930" (PhD diss., University of Arizona, 2015), 19.

11 Andreas Malm, *Fossil Capital: The Rise of Steam-Power and The Roots of Global Warming* (Westminster, MD: Random House, 2016), 161–162.

12 On cruising see: Craig William Kinnear, "Cruising for Pinelands: Knowledge Work in the Wisconsin Lumber Industry, 1870–1900," *Environmental History* 21, no. 1 (2016): 76–99; Hilton, *Rough Pulpwood Operating in Northwestern Maine,* 3; Robert E. Pike, *Tall Trees, Tough Men* (New York: W. W. Norton, 1984), 64–65, 69–70; Chandler, "Lumbering in Northern Maine . . . Emerson Company," 13, 14; R. Boultbee, A. P. Leslie, and J. B. Matthews, "Report of Logging Operation on Limits of the Canoe Lake Lumber Co., Canoe Lake Ont., 1927–1928 (Thesis, University of Maine Orono, 1928), 11, 13; William James Henry Miller, James Plummer Poole, and Harlan Hayes Sweetser, "A Lumbering Report of Work on Squaw Mountain Township, Winter of 1911–1912" (Thesis, University of Maine Orono, 1912), 7; Susan McVetty "Interviews about Dan Murray," 1970, transcript, p. 578008 (LLC) (MFC); David Nathan Rogers, "Lumbering in Northern Maine: A Report Presented to the Department of Forestry of the University of Maine" (Thesis, University of Maine, Orono: 1906), 13; Glenn C. Prescott and Raymond E. Rendall, "Lumbering in the Dead River Region, Somerset County, Maine" (PhD diss., University of Maine Orono, 1916), 12; Lewis Freeman Pike and John N. Jewett "A Report on a Lumbering Operation on Township No. 29, Washington County, Maine (Thesis, University of Maine Orono, 1908), 4; George W. Dulany Jr. (1877–1959), interviewed by Elwood R. Maunder, 1956, transcript, p. 25–25 (FHS) (OHIC); Benjamin Cole interviewed by Larry Gallant, 1972, transcript, p. 720022–23 (LLC) (MFC); George Frederick Eitel (b. 1880) 1950s(?), transcript, p. 10–12, OHI, FHS; Donald MacKenzie (b. 1887) interviewed by Elwood R. Maunder, 1956, transcript, p. 18, OHI, FHS; Susan McVetty "Interviews about Dan Murray," 1970, transcript, p. 578008, LLC (MFC); Prescott and Rendall, "Lumbering in the Dead River Region, Somerset County, Maine," 12; Austin Cary, *A Manual for Northern Woodsmen* (Cambridge, MA: Harvard University Press, 1918), 161; Roy Headley, "Personnel of Forest Service Discussed," *Bulletin: The New York State College of Forestry at Syracuse University: Dedication, Conference, and History: The New York State Ranger School, Wanakena, August 1928, NY* 2, no. 1 (1929): 54.

13 Prescott and Rendall, "Lumbering in the Dead River Region," 7; Miller, Poole, and Sweetser, "A Lumbering Report of Work on Squaw Mountain Township," 2–3; Rogers, "Lumbering in Northern Maine," 7; Chandler, "Lumbering in Northern Maine . . . Emerson Company," 10.

14 Quote in Charlotte Todes, *Labor and Lumber* (New York: International Publishers, 1931), 120.
15 Lorimer, "Eastern White Pine Abundance," 258.
16 Grant Crandall, Sarah J. Starrett, and Douglas L. Parker, "Hiding Behind the Corporate Veil: Employer Abuse of the Corporate Form to Avoid or Deny Workers' Collectively Bargained and Statutory Rights," *West Virginia Law Review* 100 (1997): 558–565.
17 Marc D. Abrams, "Eastern White Pine Versatility in The Presettlement Forest: This Eastern Giant Exhibited Vast Ecological Breadth in The Original Forest but Has Been on the Decline with Subsequent Land-Use Changes," *BioScience* 51, no. 11 (2001): 976.
18 Vernon H. Jensen, *Lumber and Labor* (New York: Farrar & Rinehart, 1945), 120; Rogers, "Lumbering in Northern Maine," 2, 7.
19 Peter J. Marchand, *North Woods: An Inside Look at the Nature of Forests in the Northeast* (Boston: Appalachian Mountain Club, 1987), 103.
20 Alexander M. Koroleff and Ralph Clement Bryant, "The Transportation of Wood in Chutes," *Yale School of Forestry Bulletin* 34 (1932): 14–46.
21 Charles E. Oak, *Annual Report of the Forest Commissioner of the State of Maine* (Augusta, ME: Burleigh & Flynt, 1896), 137; Chandler, "Lumbering in Northern Maine . . . Emerson Company," 9–10; US Census Bureau, Federal Census, 1910, Township 6, Penobscot, Maine, accessed August 11, 2014, ancestry.com; Rogers, "Lumbering in Northern Maine," 9.
22 "Westcott, Arthur and Smith Family" MS-A30, Diary 1902–1905, Vermont Historical Society, Barre, VT.
23 Bernie Weisgerber, "An Ax to Grind: A Practical Ax Manual," USDA Forestry Service, p. 8, accessed June 20, 2009, http://www.fs.fed.us/eng/pubs/pdfpubs/pdf99232823/pdf99232823Pdpi72pt03.pdf Felling Trees continued; Bryant, *Logging: The Principles and General Methods*, 105.
24 Harold K. Hochschild, *Lumberjacks and Rivermen in the Central Adirondacks, 1850–1950* (Blue Mountain Lake, NY: Adirondack Museum, 1962), 49.
25 Chandler, "Lumbering in Northern Maine . . . Emerson Company," 19; Pike, *Tall Trees, Tough Men*, 42; Bryant, *Logging: The Principles and General Methods*, 111; Morris H. Jones, interviewed by John Larson, 1954, transcript, p. 3 (FHS) (OHIC).
26 "Westcott, Arthur and Smith Family" MS-A30, Diary 1902–1905, Vermont Historical Society, Barre, VT; on wages nationally, regionally, and in the logging industry, see: USDA Agriculture Marketing Service, Farm Wage Rates Seasonally Lower, National Agricultural Statistics Service, USDA, January 12, 1940, accessed March 31, 2015, http://usda.mannlib.cornell.edu/MannUsda/viewDocumentInfo.do?documentID=1063; Paul H. Douglas, *Real Wages in the United States, 1890–1926* (Boston: Houghton Mifflin Company, 1930), 41, 130, 177; James H. Blodgett, *Wages of Farm Labor in the United States: Results of Twelve Statistical Investigations, 1866–1902* (Washington, DC: US Department of Agriculture, Bureau of Statistics, 1903), 14; W. C. Sykes to C. H. Sisson, May 1, 1919; C. H. Sisson to W. C. Sykes, May 2, 1919; W. C. Sykes to C. H. Sisson, May 3, 1919, Emporium Forest Company Records Box 13 Adirondack Museum, Blue Mountain Lake, New York; E. L. Stables to Mr. Sykes, Mr. Caflish, and Mr. Turner, November 7, 1912, Emporium Forest Company Records Box 5 Adirondack Museum, Blue Mountain Lake, New York."
27 Madison Adams Thurston, *Prices Paid by Vermont Farmers for Goods and Services and Received by Them for Farm Products, 1790–1940; Wages of Vermont Farm Labor, 1780–1940* (Burlington, VT: Vermont Agricultural Experiment Station, 1944), 98–100.

28 "Westcott, Arthur and Smith Family" MS-A30, Diary 1902–1905; Edward P. Thompson, "Time, Work-Discipline, and Industrial Capitalism," *Past & Present* 38 (1967): 73.

29 Ann Norton Greene, *Horses at Work Harnessing Power in Industrial America* (Cambridge, MA: Harvard University Press, 2008), 28–29; Ralph Clement Bryant, *Logging: The Principles and General Methods of Operation in the United States* (New York: J. Wiley & Sons, 1923), 129, 130, 131; John S Springer, *Forest Life and Forest . . .* (New York: Harper, 1856), 90; Pike, *Tall Trees, Tough Men*, 40, 43, 117; John Sharpe (b. 1881), interviewed by Lillian Shirley, 1970, p. 76, transcript (LLC) (MFC); Edgerton, *Shock of The Old*, 33–34.

30 Frank Carey (b. 1886), interviewed by Rita Swidrowski, 1970, p. 6980064–65, 6980114, transcript (LLC) (MFC); Ernest Kennedy (b. 1889) interviewed by Lillian Shirley, 1970, p. 579065, 579093, transcript (LLC) (MFC); Amos A. Graffte and Octavia Moulton Graffte, "Payroll" box 1 folder 14, Folger Library Special Collection; Fred Alliston Gilbert Papers, "Geo E. Thompson to F. A. Gilbert," June 27, 1911, box 1 folder 8, Raymond H. Fogler Library, University of Maine; Prescott and Rendall, "Lumbering in the Dead River Region," 25; Asa Flagg (b. 1898), interviewed by Rhoda Mitchell, 1970, p. 57557, transcript (LLC) (MFC);Victor Bushey (b. 1900) interviews by Sue Dauphinee, 1972, p. 719022, transcript (LLC) (MFC); Hilton, *Rough Pulpwood*, 45, 46; Prescott and Rendall, "Lumbering in the Dead River Region," 25; Miller, Poole, and Sweetser, "A Lumbering Report of Work on Squaw Mountain Township," 14; Rogers, "Lumbering in Northern Maine," 51; Boultbee, Leslie, and Matthews, "Report of Logging Operation on Limits of the Canoe Lake Lumber Co.," 25; Carlisle and Shatney, "Report on a Logging Operation in Northern Maine," 10.

31 Coe Family Papers, box 8, "E.S. Coe: "Application for permits 1889–91" p. 10, 25, 77, 99; Special Collections, Raymond H. Fogler Library, University of Maine; Raymond J. Smith, Samuel B. Locke, "A Study of the Lumber Industry of Northern Maine" (Thesis, University of Maine Orono, 1908), 14; Carlisle and Shatney, "Report on a Logging Operation in Northern Maine," 11; Rogers, "Lumbering in Northern Maine," 29; Chandler, "Lumbering in Northern Maine . . . Emerson Company," 19–20; Miller, Poole, and Sweetser, "A Lumbering Report of Work on Squaw Mountain Township," 16; Pike and Jewett, "A Report on a Lumbering Operation on Township No. 29," 6; Frank Carey (b. 1886), interviewed by Rita Swidrowski, 1970, p. 698015, transcript (LLC) (MFC); Harry Dyer (b. 1896), interviewed by Jeanne Milton, 1970, p. 568023, 581070, transcript (LLC) (MFC); Ernest Kennedy (b. 1889) interviewed by Lillian Shirley, 1970, p. 579097, transcript (LLC) (MFC); Boultbee, Leslie, and Matthews, "Report of Logging Operation on Limits of the Canoe Lake Lumber Co.," 15.

32 Lee Roberts (b. 1911), interviewed by Linda Hubbard, 1970, p. 571059, transcript (LLC) (MFC).

33 Charles Dayton Woods and Edward Raymond Mansfield, *Studies of the Food of Maine Lumbermen* (Washington, DC: Government Printing Office, 1904), 7, 16, 30; Miller, Poole, and Sweetser, "A Lumbering Report of Work on Squaw Mountain Township," 11; "Contract between Margret McClinton and Emporium," Emporium Forest Company Records Box 2. Adirondack Museum; Barbara Kephart Bird, *Calked Shoes; Life in Adirondack Lumber Camps* (Prospect, NY: Prospect Books, 1952), 47; Peter C. Welsh, *Jacks, Jobbers, and Kings: Logging the Adirondacks, 1850–1950* (Utica, NY: North Country Books, 1995), 46; John G. Franzen, *The Archaeology of the Logging Industry* (Gainesville: University Press of Florida, 2020), 94.

34 Hilton, *Rough Pulpwood*, 4; Pike, *Tall Trees, Tough Men*, 91; Boultbee, Leslie, and Matthews, "Report of Logging Operation," 13; Chandler, "Lumbering in Northern Maine . . . Emerson Company," 14, 13; Pike and Jewett, "A Report on a Lumbering

Operation on Township No. 29," 5; Bryant, *Logging: The Principles and General Methods*, 60, 102; Barbara McMartin, *The Great Forest of the Adirondacks* (Utica, NY: North Country Books, 1994), 57, 59; Harry Dyer (b. 1896), interviewed by Jeanne Milton, 1970, p. 581014, transcript (LLC) (MFC); Miller, Poole, and Sweetser, "A Lumbering Report of Work on Squaw Mountain Township," 7, 8; Rogers, "Lumbering in Northern Maine," 14; Prescott and Rendall, "Lumbering in the Dead River Region," 14.

35 On building a camp, see Frederick Burke (b. 1915), interviewed by Norma Coates 1971, transcript, p. 702012, 702022, 702076, 702014 (LLC) (MFC); Boultbee, Leslie, and Matthews, "Report of Logging Operation," 17; Walter Augustus Wyckoff, *The Workers: An Experiment in Reality: The East* (New York: C. Scribner, 1897), 201; Ferris Meigs, "The Santa Clara Lumber Company vol. I," Santa Clara Collection, Adirondack Museum, New York, typeset 1941, 84; Andrew Chase (b. 1888) interviewed by Linda Edgerly, 1971, p. 697043, 697033, transcript (LLC) (MFC); Pike, *Tall Trees, Tough Men*, 75, 90; Carlisle and Shatney, "Report on a Logging Operation in Northern Maine," 8; Prescott and Rendall, "Lumbering in the Dead River Region," 15, 19; Miller, Poole, and Sweetser, "A Lumbering Report of Work on Squaw Mountain Township," 10; Edmund W. Bradwin, *The Bunkhouse Man; A Study of Work and Pay in the Camps of Canada, 1903–1914* (Toronto: University of Toronto Press, 1972), 76, 77, 78, 80 160; Chandler, "Lumbering in Northern Maine . . . Emerson Company," 15; Rogers, "Lumbering in Northern Maine," 17; Asa Flagg (b. 1898), interviewed by Rhoda Mitchell, 1970, p. 575032, 57552, transcript (LLC) (MFC); Carroll C. Noyes interviewed by Lynn MacFarland, 1972, transcript, p. 577053 (LLC) (MFC); John F. Flanagan, "Industrial Conditions in the Maine Woods," *First Biennial Report of the Department of Labor and Industry* (Waterville, ME: Sentinel Publishing Company, 1912), 213; William F. Fox, *A History of the Lumber Industry in the State of New York* (Washington, DC: US Department of Agriculture, Bureau of Forestry, 1902), 62; Henry Conklin, *Through "Poverty's Vale": A Hardscrabble Boyhood in Upstate New York, 1832–1862* (Syracuse, NY: Syracuse University Press, 1974), 102; Harry Dyer (b. 1896), interviewed by Jeanne Milton, 1970, p. 581022, transcript (LLC) (MFC); Ernest Kennedy (b. 1889) interviewed by Lillian Shirley, 1970, p. 579097, transcript (LLC) (MFC); Rogers, "Lumbering in Northern Maine," 17; Bryant, *Logging: The Principles and General Methods*, 63; Hilton, *Rough Pulpwood*, 5.

36 Bradwin, *The Bunkhouse Man*, 80.

37 Prescott and Rendall, "Lumbering in the Dead River Region," 19; Wyckoff, *The Workers . . . The East*, 210; Springer, *Forest Life and Forest Trees*, 71–72; Smith and Locke, "A Study of the Lumber Industry of Northern Maine," 11; Carlisle and Shatney, "Report on a Logging Operation in Northern Maine," 9; Miller, Poole, and Sweetser, "A Lumbering Report of Work on Squaw Mountain Township," 9; Hilton, *Rough Pulpwood*, 7; Harry Dyer (b. 1896), interviewed by Jeanne Milton, 1970, p. 581038, transcript (LLC) (MFC); Pike, *Tall Trees, Tough Men*, 91–92; Asa Flagg (b. 1898), interviewed by Rhoda Mitchell, 1970, p. 579097, 57599, transcript (LLC) (MFC).

38 David N. Borton, "Adirondack Lumbering—The Jessup Operation" (Independent Study, 1965), p. 2, Adirondack Museum, Blue Mountain Lake, NY object number, 2389, MS 65–13; Bird, *Calked Shoes*, 112–113; Bryant, *Logging: The Principles and General Methods*, 63–64; Flanagan, "Industrial Conditions in the Maine Woods," 212.

39 Bradwin, *The Bunkhouse Man*, 76; Leo Poirier (b. 1891), interviews by Bobbie Violette, 1974, transcript, p. 800010 (LLC) (MFC); Carlisle and Shatney, "Report on a Logging Operation in Northern Maine," 10; Pike, *Tall Trees, Tough Men*, 96, 129; Rogers, "Lumbering in Northern Maine," 27.

40 "'haywire, n. and adj.' OED Online, accessed July 30, 2015, http://www.oed.com; Bryant, *Logging: The Principles and General Methods*, 493; Captain A. E. Rowell, "Recollections," *The Brown Bulletin* 2 (August 1921): 3, https://berlinnh historicalsociety.org/wp-content/uploads/2011/02/The_Brown_Bulletin_V3_No2_Aug_1921.pdf.

41 Pike, *Tall Trees, Tough Men*, 91; Springer, *Forest Life and Forest Trees*, 68–69; Prescott and Rendall, "Lumbering in the Dead River Region," 19; William James, Henry Miller, James Plummer Poole, and Harlan Hayes Sweetser, "A Lumbering Report of Work on Squaw Mountain Township, Winter of 1911–1912" (Thesis, University of Maine–Orono, 1912), 11; John Sharpe (b. 1881), interviewed by Lillian Shirley, 1970, p. 63, transcript (LLC) (MFC); Carroll C. Noyes interviewed by Lynn MacFarland, 1972, transcript, p. 577053–54, 577097 (LLC) (MFC); Asa Flagg (b. 1898), interviewed by Rhoda Mitchell, 1970, p. 575012, 575043, 575076, transcript (LLC) (MFC); Frederick Burke (b. 1915), interviewed by Norma Coates (1971), transcript, p. 702046, 702012 (LLC) (MFC); Frank Carey (b. 1886), interviewed by Rita Swidrowski, 1970, p. 698033, transcript (LLC) (MFC); Andrew Chase (b. 1888), interviewed by Linda Edgerly, 1971, p. 6970047, transcript (LLC) (MFC); Russell Nutting (b. 1887), interviews by Lynn MacFarland, 1971, transcript, p. 626032, 626096–97 (LLC) (MFC); Robert Volney (b. 1890), interviewed by Linda Hubbard, 1970, p. 571023, transcript (LLC) (MFC); Bradwin, *The Bunkhouse Man*, 77; Borton, "Adirondack Lumbering—The Jessup Operation" 2, Adirondack Museum, Blue Mountain Lake, NY, object number 2389, MS 65–13; Radforth "The Shantymen," 228.

42 Miller, Poole, and Sweetser, "A Lumbering Report of Work on Squaw Mountain Township," 10; Rogers, "Lumbering in Northern Maine," 19–20. Also see Franzen, *The Archaeology of the Logging Industry*, 160.

43 Lyman Sutton (1867–1956) interviewed by John Larson,1954, transcript, p. 2–3 (FHS) (OHIC); Bradwin, *The Bunkhouse Man*, 51; Pike, *Tall Trees, Tough Men*, 93; Rogers, "Lumbering in Northern Maine," 18; W. T. Turner to G. W. Sykes, August 21, 1919, Emporium Forest Company Records Box 8, Adirondack Museum; Prescott and Rendall, "Lumbering in the Dead River Region," 36.

44 George Thomas Carlisle and Thomas Franklin Shatney, "Report on a Logging Operation in Northern Maine" (Thesis, University of Maine Orono, 1909), 10; Bernard Albert Chandler, "Lumbering in Northern Maine: As Illustrated by an Operation of the Emerson Lumber Company" (Thesis, University of Maine Orono, 1909), 7, 15, 26.

45 Kaoru Sugihara, "Varieties of Industrialization: An Asian Regional Perspective" in *Global Economic History*, ed. Giorgio Riello and Tirthankar Roy (London: Bloomsbury Academic, 2019).

46 Stanley L. Engerman, Claudia Dale Goldin, and National Bureau of Economic Research "Seasonality in Nineteenth Century Labor Markets" (Cambridge, MA: National Bureau of Economic Research, 1991), 29–32.

47 Adams, *Prices Paid by Vermont Farmers*, 85.

48 Hilton, *Rough Pulpwood*, 25; US Department of Labor, *Farm Labor Fact Book* (Washington, DC: US Government Printing Office, 1959), 6–10; William B. Meyer, *Americans and Their Weather* (New York: Oxford University Press, 2014), 67, 118–119; USDA Bureau of Agricultural Economics, Farm Wage Rates Break Sharply From October 1 to January 1, Farm Labor National Agricultural Statistics Service, Agriculture Marketing Service, January 14, 1938, accessed March 31, 2015, http://usda.mannlib.cornell.edu/MannUsda/viewDocumentInfo.do?documentID=1063; Thomas Hubka, *Big House, Little House, Back House, Barn: The Connected Farm Buildings of New England* (Lebanon, NH: University Press of New England, 1984),

145. Some historians have speculated that it was actually this fluctuating seasonal labor market in the Northeast that spurred on the rapid industrialization post-1860; Carville Earle, "The Industrial Revolution as a Response to Cheap Labor and Agricultural Seasonality, 1790–1860: A Reexamination of the Habakkuk Thesis," in *Geographical Inquiry and American Historical Problems*, ed. Carville Earle (Palo Alto, CA: Stanford University Press, 1992), 176.

49 Asa Flagg (b. 1898), interviewed by Rhoda Mitchell, 1970, p. 575066, transcript (LLC) (MFC); Walker Family Diaries, 1828–1893, vol. 8, Daniel Walker Diary 1873, March 15, March 29, April 11, June 7, June 10–12, Maine Historical Society, Portland, Maine; Andrew Chase (b. 1888) interviewed by Linda Edgerly, 1971, p. 69725, transcript (LLC) (MFC); Ernest Kennedy (b. 1889) interviewed by Lillian Shirley, 1970, p. 57946, 57947, transcript (LLC) (MFC); Andrew Chase (b. 1888) interviewed by Linda Edgerly, 1971, p. 69719, transcript (LLC) (MFC).

50 Bryant, *Logging: The Principles and General Methods*, 109, 111; Springer, *Forest Life and Forest Trees*, 98; Stewart Edward White, *The Blazed Trail* (New York: McClure, [1902] 1907), 12; Boultbee, Leslie, and Matthews, "Report of Logging Operation on Limits of the Canoe Lake Lumber Co.," 31; Stephen C. Harper, Laura L. Falk, and Edward W. Rankin, *The Northern Forest Lands Study of New England and New York: A Report to the Congress of the United States on the Recent Changes in Landownership and Land Use in the Northern Forest of Maine, New Hampshire, New York and Vermont* (Rutland, VT: Forest Service, US Department of Agriculture, 1990), 102; Fox, *A History of the Lumber Industry in the State of New York*, 78; McMartin, *Great Forest of the Adirondacks*, 58; Miller, Poole, and Sweetser, "A Lumbering Report of Work on Squaw Mountain Township," 17; David Nathan Rogers, "Lumbering in Northern Maine: A Report Presented to the Department of Forestry of the University of Maine" (Thesis, University of Maine, Orono: 1906), 30; Flanagan, "Industrial Conditions in the Maine Woods," 213.

51 Welsh, *Jacks, Jobbers and Kings*, 27, 29; Pike, *Tall Trees, Tough Men*, 17, 16, 19; Ronald Jager, "Tool and Symbol: The Success of the Double-Bitted Axe in North America," *Technology and Culture* 40, no. 4 (1999): 844; Weisgerber, "An Ax to Grind," 8; Prescott and Rendall, "Lumbering in the Dead River Region," 32, 30; Carroll C. Noyes interviewed by Lynn MacFarland, 1972, transcript, p. 577035–36 (LLC) (MFC); Boultbee, Leslie, and Matthews, "Report of Logging Operation," 29; Koroleff, *Pulpwood Cutting*, 43–44; Andrew Mason Prouty, *More Deadly Than War!: Pacific Coast Logging, 1827–1981* (New York: Garland, 1985), 82; Jensen, *Lumber and Labor*, 134; Robert Volney (b. 1890), interviewed by Linda Hubbard, 1970, p. 571034–36, transcript (LLC) (MFC).

52 Pike, *Tall Trees, Tough Men*, 20, 102; Geraldine Tidd Scott, *Isaac Simpson's World: The Collected Works of an Itinerant Photographer* (Falmouth, ME: Kennebec River Press, 1990), 119; Prescott and Rendall, "Lumbering in the Dead River Region," 32; Boultbee, Leslie, and Matthews, "Report of Logging Operation," 30; Bryant, *Logging: The Principles and General Methods*, 102, 106.

53 Boultbee, Leslie, and Matthews, "Report of Logging Operation," 31). Hilton, *Rough Pulpwood*, 129; Welsh, *Jacks, Jobbers and Kings*, 6; Lee J. Vance, "Lumbering in the Adirondacks," *Godey's Magazine* 113, no. 789 (March 1896): 231; Ferris Meigs, *The Santa Clara Lumber Company*, vol. 1 (unpublished manuscript, typeset 1941) Santa Clara Collection, Adirondack Museum, Blue Mountain Lake, New York, 88; Hochschild, *Lumberjacks and Rivermen*, 49; Harvey L. Dunham, *Adirondack French Louie: Early Life in the North Woods* (New York: North Country Books, 1953). 121; Asa Flagg (b. 1898), interviewed by Rhoda Mitchell, 1970, p. 57586, transcript (LLC) (MFC); Harry Dyer (b. 1896), interviewed by Jeanne Milton, 1970, p. 581017, transcript (LLC) (MFC).

54 Daniel J. Leathers and Barbara L. Luff, "Characteristics of Snow Cover Duration Across the Northeast United States of America," *International Journal of Climatology* 17, no. 14 (1997): 1535; William Cronon, *Changes in the Land: Indians, Colonists, and the Ecology of New England* (New York: Hill and Wang, 1983), 123; Jerry Jenkins and Andy Keal, *The Adirondack Atlas: A Geographic Portrait of the Adirondack Park* (Syracuse, NY: Syracuse University Press, 2004), 9; Welsh, *Jacks, Jobbers and Kings*, 3; Meyer, *Americans and Their Weather*, 35.

55 A. Koroleff, J. F. Walker, and D. R. Stevens, "Pulpwood Hauling with Horse and Sleigh: Efficiency of Technique," *Woodlands Section Index/Canadian Pulp and Paper Association*, no. 706 (1947): 4.

56 Chandler, "Lumbering in Northern Maine . . . Emerson Company," 14, 18.

57 John Sharpe (b. 1881), interviewed by Lillian Shirley, 1970, p. 22, transcript (LLC) (MFC); "Snow at Last, Loggers Rejoice: Heavy Fall Up North Calls Back Discharged Woodsmen a Freak Winter," *Bangor Daily News*, January 26, 1915.

58 "Snow at Last, Loggers Rejoice: Heavy Fall Up North Calls Back Discharged Woodsmen a Freak Winter," *Bangor Daily News*, January 26, 1915. Also see, "Moriah" *Ticonderoga Sentinel*, January 11, 1912; "Country Events," *The Lake Placid News*, January 10, 1919; "Lumbering at a Standstill," *The Lake Placid News*, January 10, 1919; "Local Department," *The Malone Farmer*, January 31, 1906; "Lumberman Want More Snow Fall," *The Tupper Lake Herald*, January 31, 1919; "Lumbering in North Woods: Lack of Snow This Season Handicaps Operation—Will Result in Heavy Lumbering Next Year—Rivers Free from Logs," *Chateaugay Record and Franklin County Democrat*, June 6, 1913; "Snow Aids Adirondack Lumbering Operations," *Essex County Republican*, January 23, 1920.

59 Quote from Meyer, *Americans and Their Weather*, 6.

60 Koroleff, *Pulpwood Cutting*, 90–91.

61 Gerald Averill, *Ridge Runner; The Story of a Maine Woodsman* (Philadelphia: J. B. Lippincott, 1948), 89; Pike, *Tall Trees, Tough Men*, 103; Frank Carey (b. 1886), interviewed by Rita Swidrowski, 1970, p. 69837, transcript (LLC) (MFC); Meyer, *Americans and Their Weather*, 6.

62 Boultbee, Leslie, and Matthews, "Report of Logging Operation," 32; Bryant, *Logging: The Principles and General Methods*, 124–125; Smith and Locke, "A Study of the Lumber Industry of Northern Maine," 15; Pike and Jewett, "A Report on a Lumbering Operation on Township No. 29," 6; Welsh, *Jacks, Jobbers and Kings*, 6.

63 Fox, *History of the Lumber Industry*, 36.

64 Boultbee, Leslie, and Matthews, "Report of Logging Operation," 33; Fox, *History of the Lumber Industry*, 36; Hochschild, *Lumberjacks and Rivermen*, 53; Chandler, "Lumbering in Northern Maine . . . Emerson Company," 20; Prescott and Rendall, "Lumbering in the Dead River Region," 38; Rogers, "Lumbering in Northern Maine," 34; Wilson, *The Hill Country of Northern New England*, 128.

65 Bryant, *Logging: The Principles and General Methods*, 138; Hilton, *Rough Pulpwood*, 54; Koroleff, *Pulpwood Cutting*, 13; "The Lincoln and Idella Toothaker Letters, 1890–1892," November 19, 1891, John Toothaker to Lincoln.

66 Chandler, "Lumbering in Northern Maine . . . Emerson Company," 20; Hilton, *Rough Pulpwood*, 26–27, 54; Rogers, "Lumbering in Northern Maine," 42.

67 Prescott and Rendall, "Lumbering in the Dead River Region," 34; Boultbee, Leslie, and Matthews, "Report of Logging Operation," 33, 25, 37; Flanagan, "Industrial Conditions in the Maine Woods," 214; Scott, *Isaac Simpson's World*, 127; Smith and Locke, "A Study of the Lumber Industry of Northern Maine," 15; Rogers, "Lumbering in Northern Maine," 35; Miller, Poole, and Sweetser, "A Lumbering Report of Work on Squaw Mountain Township," 17, 18; Boultbee, Leslie, and

Matthews, "Report of Logging Operation," 33; Bryant, *Logging: The Principles and General Methods*, 140, 174, 175.

68 Bryant, *Logging: The Principles and General Methods*, 126; Hilton, *Rough Pulpwood*, 37; Miller, Poole, and Sweetser, "A Lumbering Report of Work on Squaw Mountain Township," 19; Meigs, *Santa Clara Lumber Company*, 48–49; Bradwin, *The Bunkhouse Man*, 122; White, *The Blazed Trail*, 311; Stephen Ballew, *"Suthin": It's the Opposite of Nothin': An Oral History of Grover Morrison's Woods Operation at Little Musquash Lake, 1945–1947* (Orono, ME: Northeast Folklore Society, 1978), 53–54.

69 Peter J. Marchand, *Life in The Cold: An Introduction to Winter Ecology* (Chicago: University Press of New England, 2014), 44, 24–28.

70 Marchand, *Life in The Cold*, 36, 30.

71 Boultbee, Leslie, and Matthews, "Report of Logging Operation," 9; J. L. Turner to Shepard Cary, Fort Kent, ME, April 2, 1857, Shepard Cary papers, box 1, folder 12, Maine Historical Society, Portland, Maine; Springer, *Forest Life and Forest Trees*, 88–89; Marchand, *Life in The Cold*, 31.

72 Bharat Bhushan, *Introduction to Tribology* (Hoboken, NJ: John Wiley & Sons, 2013), 1–4.

73 Marchand, *Life in The Cold*, 28–29.

74 Bryant, *Logging: the Principles and General Methods*, 169; Bird, *Calked Shoes*, 46, 55–56; Williams, *Americans and Their Forests*, 208–209; Harry Dyer (b. 1896), interviewed by Jeanne Milton, 1970, p. 568027, 568028, transcript (LLC) (MFC); Bradwin, *The Bunkhouse Man*, 163; Prescott and Rendall, "Lumbering in the Dead River Region," 44; Fox, *History of the Lumber Industry*, 32; Hochschild, *Lumberjacks and Rivermen*, 60–61; Ian Walter Radforth, *Bushworkers and Bosses: Logging in Northern Ontario, 1900–1980* (Toronto: University of Toronto Press, 1987), 60; Flanagan, "Industrial Conditions in the Maine Woods," 217; Benjamin Cole interviewed by Larry Gallant, 1972, transcript, p. 720021 (LLC) (MFC); Frank Carey (b. 1886), interviewed by Rita Swidrowski, 1970, p. 6980115, transcript (LLC) (MFC); Ernest Kennedy (b. 1889) interviewed by Lillian Shirley, 1970, p. 579062–63, transcript (LLC) (MFC); John Sharpe (b. 1881), interviewed by Lillian Shirley, 1970, p. 22, 99,79, transcript (LLC) (MFC); Hilton, *Rough Pulpwood*, 42; Koroleff and Bryant, *The Transportation of Wood in Chutes*, 36–37.

75 Ballew, *"Suthin": It's the Opposite of Nothin'*, 53; Leathers and Luff, "Characteristics of Snow Cover," 1545.

76 Koroleff, Walker, and Stevens, "Pulpwood Hauling with Horse and Sleigh," 6.

77 Hilton, *Rough Pulpwood*, 54; Bryant, *Logging: The Principles and General Methods*, 169–172; Bird, *Calked Shoes*, 76; Boultbee, Leslie, and Matthews, "Report of Logging Operation," 9, 25, 34; Miller, Poole, and Sweetser, "A Lumbering Report of Work on Squaw Mountain Township," 20; Juvenal, "Lumbering in the Adirondacks," *Forest and Stream* 67, no. 24 (December 1906): 939; Asa Flagg (b. 1898), interviewed by Rhoda Mitchell, 1970, p. 57597, transcript (LLC) (MFC); Ballew, *"Suthin": It's the Opposite of Nothin'*, 53; Fred Cottrell, *Energy and Society: The Relation between Energy, Social Changes, and Economic Development* (New York: McGraw-Hill, 1955), 259.

78 Bryant, *Logging: The Principles and General Methods*, 167, 168; Frederick Burke (b. 1915) interviewed by Norma Coates (1971), transcript, p. 702016 (LLC) (MFC); Miller, Poole, and Sweetser, "A Lumbering Report of Work on Squaw Mountain Township," 20; Flanagan, "Industrial Conditions in the Maine Woods," 216; Prescott and Rendall, "Lumbering in the Dead River Region," 50; Chandler, "Lumbering in Northern Maine . . . Emerson Company," 19; Nora A. Vagnarelli, "A History of Lumbering in the Ausable Valley (1800–1900)" (Thesis, Cornell University, 1946), 35; Harry Dyer (b. 1896), interviewed by Jeanne Milton, 1970, p. 581048, transcript (LLC) (MFC); Hochschild, *Lumberjacks and Rivermen*, 60.

79 Vagnarelli, "A History of Lumbering in the Ausable Valley," 35; Bill Gove, *Logging Railroads of the Adirondacks* (Syracuse, NY: Syracuse University Press, 2006), 47; Miller, Poole, and Sweetser, "A Lumbering Report of Work on Squaw Mountain Township," 20; Chandler, "Lumbering in Northern Maine . . . Emerson Company," 21; Bryant, *Logging: The Principles and General Methods*, 177.

80 Hochschild, *Lumberjacks and Rivermen*, 60–61; Pike and Jewett, "A Report on a Lumbering Operation on Township No. 29," 8; Hilton, *Rough Pulpwood*, 37, 39–41; Williams, *Americans and Their Forests*, 211; Bryant, *Logging: The Principles and General Methods*, 168; Miller, Poole, and Sweetser, "A Lumbering Report of Work on Squaw Mountain Township," 20.

81 Bryant, *Logging: The Principles and General Methods*, 176.

82 Pike, *Tall Trees, Tough Men*, 77; Hilton, *Rough Pulpwood*, 24; Boultbee, Leslie, and Matthews, "Report of Logging Operation," 27; Bryant, *Logging: The Principles and General Methods*, 166, 176; Rogers, "Lumbering in Northern Maine," 33, 35, 38; Prescott and Rendall, "Lumbering in the Dead River Region," 32, 40; McMartin, *Great Forest of the Adirondacks*, 156; Maitland C. DeSormo, *The Heydays of the Adirondacks* (Burlington, VT: The George Little Press, 1974), 206; Chandler, "Lumbering in Northern Maine . . . Emerson Company," 19; John Sharpe (b. 1881), interviewed by Lillian Shirley, 1970, p. 77, 98, transcript (LLC) (MFC); Russell Nutting (b.1887) interviews by Lynn MacFarland, 1971, transcript, p. 6260102 (LLC) (MFC); Oak, *Annual Report of the Forest Commissioner of the State of Maine*, 137; "Inventory of personal property sold by McCoy & Son to Emporium Lumber Co." Emporium Forest Company Records Box 2 Adirondack Museum.

83 Springer, *Forest Life and Forest Trees*, 104; Hochschild, *Lumberjacks and Rivermen*, 60; Bill Lennon, *Barienger Brakes* (pamphlet in a special series), Adirondack Museum, New York; Meigs, *Santa Clara Lumber Company*, 91; Bryant, *Logging: The Principles and General Methods*, 164–165, 176–177; Ernest Kennedy (b. 1889), interviewed by Lillian Shirley, 1970, p. 579067, transcript (LLC) (MFC); Erroll "John" Haley (b. 1898) interviewed by Stephen Richard, 1980, transcript, p. 1384011 (LLC) (MFC).

84 Bryant, *Logging: The Principles and General Methods*, 139; Smith and Locke, "A Study of the Lumber Industry of Northern Maine," 17; "Loggers Are Busy," *Bangor Daily Commercial*, March 8, 1915.

85 Ballew, *"Suthin": It's the Opposite of Nothin'*, 56; William Boyd and Michael Watts, "Agro-Industrial Just-In-Time: The Chicken Industry and Postwar American Capitalism" in *Globalizing Food: Agrarian Questions and Global Restructuring*, ed. David Goodman and Michael Watts (London: Routledge, 1997), 194–195.

86 Smith and Locke, "A Study of the Lumber Industry of Northern Maine," 20; Carlisle and Shatney, "Report on a Logging Operation in Northern Maine," 13; Rogers, "Lumbering in Northern Maine," 40; Bradwin, *The Bunkhouse Man*, 162; Thompson, "Time, Work-Discipline, and Industrial Capitalism," 56–97; Franzen, *The Archaeology of the Logging Industry*, 64–65; Jager, "Tool and Symbol," 833–860.

87 Deborah Cowen, *The Deadly Life of Logistics: Mapping the Violence of Global Trade* (Minneapolis: University of Minnesota Press, 2014), 93; David Besanko, David Dranove, Mark Shanley, and Scott Schaefer, *Economics of Strategy* (Hoboken, NJ: John Wiley & Sons, 2009), 98.

88 Erroll "John" Haley (b. 1898) interviewed by Stephen Richard, 1980, transcript, p. 1384122 (LLC) (MFC); Harry Dyer (b. 1896), interviewed by Jeanne Milton, 1970, p. 581049, transcript (LLC) (MFC); Bryant, *Logging: The Principles and General Methods*, 134; Asa Flagg (b. 1898), interviewed by Rhoda Mitchell, 1970, p. 575095, transcript (LLC) (MFC); Félix Albert, *Immigrant Odyssey: A French Canadian Habitant in New England—A Bilingual Edition of Histoire D'un Enfant Pauvre* (Orono:

University of Maine Press, 1991), 94; René Bonnière and Pierre Perrault, *Three Seasons* (Nepean, ON: Crawley Films Limited, 1960).

89 Hilton, *Rough Pulpwood*, 46–49; "The Lincoln and Idella Toothaker Letters, 1890–1892," January 4, 1891, Minnie E. Pillsbury to Lincoln.

90 Asa Flagg (b. 1898), interviewed by Rhoda Mitchell, 1970, p. 575022–23, transcript (LLC) (MFC); also see, Chandler, "Lumbering in Northern Maine . . . Emerson Company," 21.

91 Flanagan, "Industrial Conditions in the Maine Woods," 214; Pike, *Tall Trees, Tough Men*, 105–106, 112; Ernest Kennedy (b. 1889) interviewed by Lillian Shirley, 1970, p. 579058, transcript (LLC) (MFC); Jensen, *Lumber and Labor*, 127; Bird, *Calked Shoes*, 111; Frank A. Reed, *Lumberjack Sky Pilot* (New York: North Country Books, 1965), 63; Hochschild, *Lumberjacks and Rivermen*, 6; Fox, *History of the Lumber Industry*, 18; Dunham, *Adirondack French Louie*, 138; Gove, *Logging Railroads of the Adirondacks*, 48–49.

92 Vaclav Smil, *Energy and Civilization: A History* (Cambridge, MA: MIT Press, 2017), 75, 146.

93 Albert, *Immigrant Odyssey*, 72; Hilton, *Rough Pulpwood*, 17–18; Smith and Locke, "A Study of the Lumber Industry of Northern Maine," 13; Prescott and Rendall, "Lumbering in the Dead River Region," 25; Boultbee, Leslie, and Matthews, "Report of Logging Operation" 25; Ernest Kennedy (b. 1889) interviewed by Lillian Shirley, 1970, p. 57968, transcript (LLC) (MFC); Bryant, *Logging: The Principles and General Methods*, 529; Others estimate between 14 and 26 pounds of fodder per cord of wood landed. Russell Nutting (b. 1887) interviews by Lynn MacFarland, 1971, transcript, p. 626103 (LLC) (MFC); Frank Carey (b. 1886), interviewed by Rita Swidrowski, 1970, p. 6980066, transcript (LLC) (MFC).

94 Wirt Mineau (b. 1878) interviewed by Helen McCann White, 1955, p. 4, OHI, FHS; Also see, Miller, Poole, and Sweetser, "A Lumbering Report of Work on Squaw Mountain Township," 21, 83; Smith and Locke, "A Study of the Lumber Industry of Northern Maine," 17; Hilton, *Rough Pulpwood*, 57, 25.

95 The Lincoln and Idella Toothaker Letters, 1890–1892," March 8, 1891, Lincoln to Ida.

96 Robert Volney (b. 1890), interviewed by Linda Hubbard, 1970, p. 571048, transcript (LLC) (MFC); Asa Flagg (b. 1898), interviewed by Rhoda Mitchell, 1970, p. 575030, transcript (LLC) (MFC).

97 Grover Cleveland Field, Clyde Willard, Lester Cole, and Raymond Olmstead interviewed by Dorothy Bodwell, 1970, p. 561006, transcript (LLC) (MFC); Frank Carey (b. 1886), interviewed by Rita Swidrowski, 1970, p. 698013, transcript (LLC) (MFC); Reed, *Lumberjack Sky Pilot*, 47; White, *The Blazed Trail*, 57.

98 Bryant, *Logging: The Principles and General Methods*, 178, 180; Miller, Poole, and Sweetser, "A Lumbering Report of Work on Squaw Mountain Township," 14; Karl Marx, *Capital: A Critique of Political Economy*. (Harmondsworth, UK: Penguin, 1990), 134, 304.

99 Ralph Thornton (b. 1885), interviewed by Wayne Bean, 1972, p. 717471, transcript (LLC) (MFC).

100 Ballew, *"Suthin": It's the Opposite of Nothin'*, 57.

101 Hilton, *Rough Pulpwood*, 25, 28, 127–128; Jensen, *Lumber and Labor*, 128; Flanagan, "Industrial Conditions in the Maine Woods," 207.

102 Frank Carey (b. 1886), interviewed by Rita Swidrowski, 1970, p. 6980106, transcript (LLC) (MFC); Springer, *Forest Life and Forest Trees*, 82; W. L. Sykes to D. H. Dorr, February 3, 1919. Emporium Forest Company Records Box 13 Adirondack Museum; Charles Scontras, "Organized Labor and Labor Politics in Maine, 1880–1890" 68, no. 14, University of Maine Press (1966): 81; Charles

Scontras, *Organized Labor in Maine: Twentieth Century Origins, Bureau of Labor Education of the Continuing Education Division* (Orono: University of Maine, 1985), 94.

103 On work hours see, Roy Higby, *A Man from the Past* (New York: Big Moose Publishing, 1974), 7; "The Lincoln and Idella Toothaker Letters, 1890–1892," March 22 1891, Lincoln to Ida; Pike, *Tall Trees, Tough Men*, 121; Fox, *History of the Lumber Industry*, 69; Dunham, *Adirondack French Louie*, 138; Hochschild, *Lumberjacks and Rivermen*, 62; Grover Cleveland Field, Clyde Willard, Lester Cole, and Raymond Olmstead interviewed by Dorothy Bodwell, 1970, p. 561005–6, transcript (LLC) (MFC); Bradwin, *The Bunkhouse Man*, 163; John Sharpe (b. 1881), interviewed by Lillian Shirley, 1970, p. 12, transcript (LLC) (MFC); Asa Flagg (b. 1898), interviewed by Rhoda Mitchell, 1970, p. 575034, transcript (LLC) (MFC); Chandler, "Lumbering in Northern Maine . . . Emerson Company," 21; Harry Dyer (b. 1896), interviewed by Jeanne Milton, 1970, p. 581024568025, transcript (LLC) (MFC); Robert Volney (b. 1890), interviewed by Linda Hubbard, 1970, p. 571059, transcript (LLC) (MFC); Russell Nutting (b.1887), interviewed by Lynn MacFarland, 1971, transcript p. 626084 (LLC) (MFC); Leo Poirier (b. 1891) interviewed by Bobbie Violette, 1974, transcript, p. 800012 (LLC) (MFC).

104 "The Lincoln and Idella Toothaker Letters, 1890–1892," January 4, 1891, Lincoln to Ida; March 22, 1891, Lincoln to Ida; Rogers, "Lumbering in Northern Maine," 130; Alan Derickson, *Dangerously Sleepy: Overworked Americans and the Cult of Manly Wakefulness* (Philadelphia: University of Pennsylvania Press, 2013); Benjamin Reiss, *Wild Nights: How Taming Sleep Created Our Restless World* (New York: Basic Books, 2017), 11; Prouty, *More Deadly Than War!*, 277–278; Jensen, *Lumber and Labor*, 130; Arthur F. McEvoy, "Working Environments: An Ecological Approach to Industrial Health and Safety," *Technology and Culture* 36, no. 2 (1995): S161, S166; Arthur F. McEvoy, "The Triangle Shirtwaist Factory Fire of 1911: Social Change, Industrial Accidents, and the Evolution of Common-sense Causality," *Law & Social Inquiry* 20, no. 2 (1995): 630.

105 Ether A. Austin to Luke Usher, January 9, 1892, February 8th, 1892, March 7th, 1892, Luke Usher to Ether A. Austin, December 9th, 1891, Luke Usher Papers, 1891–1898, New York State Library, Manuscripts, box 2, folder 2.

106 Chandler, "Lumbering in Northern Maine . . . Emerson Company," 17; Carroll C. Noyes interviewed by Lynn MacFarland, 1972, transcript, p. 57795 (LLC) (MFC); Prescott and Rendall, "Lumbering in the Dead River Region," 67; Asa Flagg (b. 1898), interviewed by Rhoda Mitchell, 1970, p. 575039, transcript (LLC) (MFC); Harry Dyer (b. 1896), interviewed by Jeanne Milton, 1970, p. 581052, transcript (LLC) (MFC); Pike, *Tall Trees, Tough Men*, 86.

107 Wyckoff, *The Workers . . . The East*, 233, 256–257, 258.

108 Wyckoff, *The Workers . . . The East*, 17.

109 Pike, *Tall Trees, Tough Men*, 85; Harry Dyer (b. 1896), interviewed by Jeanne Milton, 1970, p. 581036, transcript (LLC) (MFC); Ernest Kennedy (b. 1889), interviewed by Lillian Shirley, 1970, p. 579057, transcript (LLC) (MFC); Andrew Chase (b. 1888), interviewed by Linda Edgerly, 1971, p. 697049, transcript (LLC) (MFC); Asa Flagg (b. 1898), interviewed by Rhoda Mitchell, 1970, p. 575039, transcript (LLC) (MFC).

110 Meigs, *Santa Clara Lumber Company*, 119.

111 R. T. Fisher, "Methods of Instruction in The Forest School," *Forest Quarterly* 8 (1910): 12, 15–16; Hugh P. Baker, "Some Needs in Forestry Education," *Journal of Forestry* 10, no. 1 (1912): 49; H. H. Chapman, "The Forest Service and Its Men," *Journal of Forestry* 16, no. 6 (1918): 569; F. Roth, "The School-Trained Forester," *Journal of Forestry*, 16, no. 8 (1918): 856; Kinnear, "Cruising for Pinelands," 78; Ballew, *"Suthin": It's the Opposite of Nothin'*, 52.

112 F. Roth, "The School-Trained Forester," *Journal of Forestry* 16, no. 8 (1918): 856; Kinnear, "Cruising for Pinelands," 78.
113 Quote in Wyckoff, *The Workers . . . The East*, 256–257. Also see, Boultbee, Leslie, and Matthews, "Report of Logging Operation," 26; Smith and Locke, "A Study of the Lumber Industry of Northern Maine," 15–16; Boultbee, Leslie, and Matthews, "Report of Logging Operation," 27; Prescott and Rendall, "Lumbering in the Dead River Region," 41; Rogers, "Lumbering in Northern Maine," 24–25; Bryant, *Logging: The Principles and General Methods*, 122.
114 R. T. Gheen, "Taught at the Ranger School 1912–1914," *Bulletin: The New York State College of Forestry at Syracuse University: Dedication, Conference, and History: The New York State Ranger School, Wanakena, August 1928, NY* 2, no. 1 (1929): 54.
115 Andrews, *Killing for Coal*, 136–137.
116 Johannes Fabian, *Time and the Other: How Anthropology Makes Its Object* (New York: Columbia University Press, 1983), 31.
117 Frank Tobias Higbie, *Indispensable Outcasts: Hobo Workers and Community in the American Midwest, 1880–1930* (Urbana: University of Illinois Press, 2003), 100; Latour and McEvoy, "Working Environments," 150.
118 Edward Baptist, *The Half Has Never Been Told: Slavery and The Making of American Capitalism* (New York: Basic Books, 2014); Edgerton, *The Shock of the Old*, 29–33; Greene, *Horses at Work*.

5. The Body as Cheap Nature

1 Dayton Woods and Edward Raymond Mansfield, *Studies of the Food of Maine Lumbermen* (Washington, DC: Government Printing Office, 1904), 17, 30, 59, 36–37.
2 Christopher C. Sellers, *Hazards of the Job: From Industrial Disease to Environmental Health Science* (Chapel Hill: University of North Carolina Press, 1997).
3 Quoted in Ian Walter Radforth, *Bushworkers and Bosses: Logging in Northern Ontario, 1900–1980* (Toronto: University of Toronto Press, 1987), 78, 87.
4 J. M. Tuttle, "The Minnesota Pineries," *Harper's New Monthly Magazine* 36, no. 214 (March 1868): 414.
5 Gregory Clark, *A Farewell to Alms: A Brief Economic History of The World* (Princeton, NJ: Princeton University Press, 2008).
6 "The People's Food—A Great National Inquiry: Professor W. O. Atwater and His Work," *The Review of Reviews* XIII, no. 77 (1896): 580; Helen Zoe Veit, *Modern Food, Moral Food: Self-Control, Science, and the Rise of Modern American Eating in the Early Twentieth Century* (Chapel Hill: The University of North Carolina Press, 2013).
7 Nick Cullather, *The Hungry World: America's Cold War Battle against Poverty in Asia* (Cambridge, MA: Harvard University Press, 2013), 16. Labor and the body have become an important topic of discussion in both environmental history and labor history, but few have considered the importance of food as an industrial fuel. Neil M. Maher, "The Body Counts: Tracking the Human Body through Environmental History" in *A Companion to American Environmental History*, ed. Douglas Cazaux Sackman (Chichester, UK: Wiley-Blackwell, 2010); Neil M. Maher, *Nature's New Deal: The Civilian Conservation Corps and the Roots of the American Environmental Movement* (Oxford: Oxford University Press, 2008), 13, 54, 84. 34; Ava Baron and Eileen Boris, "'The Body' as a Useful Category for Working-Class History," *Labor* 4, no. 2 (2007): 23–43. The idea of making the body the focus of history is synonymous with the call among labor and environmental historians to more fully integrate the two subfields, see Stefania Barca, "Laboring the Earth: Transnational Reflections on the Environmental History of Work," *Environmental*

History 19, no. 1 (2014): 3–27; Richard White, "Are You an Environmentalist or Do You Work for a Living?," in *Uncommon Ground: Rethinking the Human Place in Nature*, ed. William Cronon (New York: W. W. Norton & Company, 1996); Gunther Peck, "The Nature of Labor: Fault Lines and Common Ground in Environmental and Labor History," *Environmental History* 11, no. 2 (2006): 213; Thomas G. Andrews, *Killing for Coal: America's Deadliest Labor War* (Cambridge, MA: Harvard University Press, 2008); John Field, *Working Men's Bodies: Work Camps in Britain, 1880–1940* (Manchester, UK: Manchester University Press, 2013), 5.

8 Christopher Sellers, "Thoreau's Body: Towards an Embodied Environmental History," *Environmental History* 4, no. 4 (1999).

9 Notice the absence of discussion of the biological importance of food and digestion in the special issue of *Environmental History* on food. Robert N. Chester III, Nicholas Mink, Jane Dusselier, Nancy Shoemaker, "Having Our Cake and Eating It Too: Food's Place in Environmental History, a Forum," *Environmental History* 14, no. 2 (2009): 309–339; Douglas Sackman, "Food," in *A Companion to American Environmental History*, ed. Douglas Cazaux Sackman (Chichester, UK: Wiley-Blackwell, 2010), 531–532.

10 Les Beldo, "Metabolic Labor: Broiler Chickens and the Exploitation of Vitality," *Environmental Humanities* 9, no. 1 (2017): 108.

11 Joel Isaac Seidman, *The Needle Trades* (New York: Farrar & Rhinehart, 1942), 41.

12 Jason W. Moore, "The Rise of Cheap Nature," in *Anthropocene or Capitalocene?: Nature, History, and the Crisis of Capitalism*, ed. Christian Parenti and Jason W. Moore (Oakland, CA: PM Press, 2016), 78–84.

13 Richard William Judd and Patricia A. Judd, *Aroostook: A Century of Logging in Northern Maine* (Orono: University of Maine Press, 1988), 56.

14 Joseph Robert Conlin, *Bacon, Beans, and Galantines: Food and Foodways on the Western Mining Frontier* (Reno: University of Nevada Press, 1986), 14; Joseph R. Conlin, "Old Boy, Did You Get Enough of Pie? A Social History of Food in Logging Camps," *Journal of Forest History* 23, no. 4 (1979): 164–185, 166; Ian Radforth, "The Shantymen" in *Laboring Lives: Work and Workers in Nineteenth-Century Ontario*, ed. Paul Craven (Toronto: University of Toronto Press, 1995), 229.

15 Laura Beam, *A Maine Hamlet* (New York: W. Funk, 1957), 6, 15; Sarah F. McMahon, "'A Comfortable Subsistence': A History of Diet in New England, 1630–1850" (PhD diss., Brandeis University, 1982), 15, 71; Sarah F. McMahon, "'All Things in Their Proper Season': Seasonal Rhythms of Diet in Nineteenth Century New England," *Agricultural History* 63, no. 2 (1989): 144–145.

16 State of Maine, Department of Agriculture, *Sixth Annual Report of the Secretary of the Maine Board of Agriculture, 1861* (Augusta, ME: Stevens & Sayward, 1861), 344; John F. Flanagan, "Industrial Conditions in the Maine Woods," *First Biennial Report of the Department of Labor and Industry* (Waterville, ME: Sentinel Publishing Company, 1912): 210–211.

17 Wilber Atwater, "The Potential Energy of Food, the Chemistry and Economy of Food," *Century* 34 (1887): 405; Chamberlain Farm, Chamberlain Farm to A. Palmer . . . [account January 29—March 9 1850], Chamberlain Farm collection, Maine Historical Society, Portland, Maine.

18 Woods and Mansfield, *Studies of the Food of Maine Lumbermen*, 53, 17–29, 60.

19 Conlin, *Bacon, Beans, and Galantines*, 24–25; Richard James Hooker, *Food and Drink in America: A History* (Indianapolis, IN: Bobbs-Merrill Company, 1981), 223; McMahon, "'A Comfortable Subsistence'" [dissertation], 216; Sarah F. McMahon, "A Comfortable Subsistence: The Changing Composition of Diet in Rural New England, 1620–1840," *The William and Mary Quarterly* 42, no. 1 (1985): 47; Lyman Sutton (b. 1867), interviewed by John Larson, 1954, p. 17, transcript (OHI) (FHS); John G.

Franzen, *The Archaeology of the Logging Industry* (Gainesville: University Press of Florida, 2020), 175; "The Lincoln and Idella Toothaker Letters, 1890–1892," March 28, 1891, Lincoln to Ida, Property of Becky Ellis Martineau and the Rangeley Lakes Region Logging Museum, Rangeley, Maine, http://rlrlm.org.

20 Joshua Specht, *Red Meat Republic: A Hoof-to-Table History of How Beef Changed America* (Princeton, NJ: Princeton University Press, 2019); Catherine Leonard Turner, *How The Other Half Ate: A History of Working-Class Meals at the Turn of the Century* (Berkeley: University of California Press, 2014), 31; Dean B. Bennett, *The Wilderness from Chamberlain Farm: A Story of Hope for the American Wild* (Washington, DC: Island Press/Shearwater Books, 2001), 88–89; Gerald E. Morris, Richard D. Kelly, and Ronald F. Banks, *The Maine Bicentennial Atlas: An Historical Survey* (Maine Historical Society, 1976), 30–31; Bill Gove, *Logging Railroads of New Hampshire's North Country* (Littleton, NH: Bondcliff Books, 2010), vii; Jerry Jenkins and Andy Keal, *The Adirondack Atlas: A Geographic Portrait of the Adirondack Park* (Syracuse, NY: Syracuse University Press, 2004), 88–89; Judd and Judd, *Aroostook*, 145; Woods and Mansfield, *Studies of the Food of Maine Lumbermen*, 7.

21 Anne C. Wilson, *Waste Not, Want Not: Food Preservation in Britain from Early Times to the Present Day* (Edinburgh, UK: Edinburgh University Press, 1991), 128; Hooker, *Food and Drink in America*, 214; Beam, *A Maine Hamlet*, 64; Wirt Mineau (b. 1878), interviewed by Helen McCann White, 1955, p. 5 (OHI) (FHS); Kathryn Taylor Morse, *The Nature of Gold: An Environmental History of the Klondike Gold Rush* (Seattle, WA: University of Washington Press, 2003), 140; Anna Zeide and Darra Goldstein, *Canned: The Rise and Fall of Consumer Confidence in the American Food Industry* (Berkeley: University of California Press, 2018).

22 Franzen, *The Archaeology of the Logging Industry*, 123; Veit, *Modern Food, Moral Food*.

23 Turner, *How the Other Half Ate*; Conlin, "Old Boy, Did You Get Enough of Pie?," 167–68; John Sharpe (b. 1881), interviewed by Shirley Lillian, 1970, p. 621029, transcript (LLC) (MFC); James Shea interviewed by David Currier, 1970, p. 7–8, transcript (LLC) (MFC).

24 Béatrice Craig, *Backwoods Consumers and Homespun Capitalists: The Rise of a Market Culture in Eastern Canada* (Toronto: University of Toronto Press, 2009), 6, 173, 176; Julian D. Boyd, "The Nature of the American Diet," *The Journal of Pediatrics* 12, no. 2 (1938): 252; Ellis L. Kirkpatrick and Daisy D. Williamson, "Living Conditions and Family Living in Farm Homes of Merrimack County, New Hampshire: A Preliminary Report," Mimeo, DC: USDA, BAE [DFPRL], and the University of New Hampshire, Agriculture Extension Service cooperating, [NAL v. 63] (1926), p. 8.

25 Robert Dirks, "Diet and Nutrition in Poor and Minority Communities in the United States 100 Years Ago," *Annual Review of Nutrition* 23, no. 1 (2003), 95; also see, McMahon "'All Things in Their Proper Season,'" 130, 144–145; Turner, *How the Other Half Ate*, 13.

26 Harvey A. Levenstein, *Revolution at the Table: The Transformation of the American Diet* (New York: Oxford University Press, 1988), 29, 178–179; McMahon, "'A Comfortable Subsistence,'" 157; Beam, *A Maine Hamlet*, 15.

27 John Sharpe (b. 1881), interviewed by Lillian Shirley, 1970, p. 621036, transcript (LLC) (MFC).

28 Beam, *A Maine Hamlet*, 75. Also see, Levenstein, *Revolution at the Table*, 25, 175–76, 178; Boyd, "The Nature of the American Diet," 250; Elaine N. McIntosh, *American Food Habits in Historical Perspective* (Westport, CT: Praeger, 1995), 110; 176; Béatrice Craig, "Agriculture and the Lumberman's Frontier in the Upper St. John Valley, 1800–70," *Journal of Forest History* 32, no. 3 (1988): 129, 136.

29 "The Future of Rural New England," *Atlantic Monthly* 80 (1897): 75–76.

30 Charles O. Paullin, *Atlas of the Historical Geography of the United States*, ed. John K. Wright (Washington, DC: Carnegie Institution, 1932), digital edition edited by Robert K. Nelson et al., 2013. http://dsl.richmond.edu/historicalatlas/Plate 146N-Q.

31 Richard William Judd, *Common Lands, Common People: The Origins of Conservation in Northern New England* (Cambridge, MA: Harvard University Press, 1997), 61–62; Craig, *Backwoods Consumers*, 165–179; Judd, *Second Nature*, 114.

32 Levenstein, *Revolution at the Table*, 30; Dirks, "Diet and Nutrition," 88; Alvan F. Sanborn, "The Future of Rural New England," *Atlantic* 80 (1897): 80; Judd, *Common Lands, Common People*, 60–61,64–65; Levenstein, *Revolution at the Table*, 179, 181; Julian D. Boyd, "The Nature of the American Diet," *The Journal of Pediatrics* 12, no. 2 (1938): 252; Megan J. Elias, *Food in the United States, 1890–1945* (Santa Barbara, CA: Greenwood Press/ABC-CLIO, 2009), 6; Richard Osborn Cummings, *The American and His Food; A History of Food Habits in the United States* (Chicago: The University of Chicago Press, 1941), 172.

33 Harold F. Wilson, *The Hill Country of Northern New England: Its Social and Economic History, 1790–1930* (New York: Columbia University Press, 1936), 373–374.

34 Karl Jacoby, *Crimes against Nature: Squatters, Poachers, Thieves, and the Hidden History of American Conservation* (Berkeley: University of California Press, 2005), 53; Judd, *Common Lands, Common People*, 60.

35 Alice Ross, "Health and Diet in 19th-Century America: A Food Historian's Point of View," *Historical Archaeology* 27, no. 2 (1993): 50; Levenstein, *Revolution at the Table*, 203; Roger Horowitz, *Putting Meat on the American Table: Taste, Technology, Transformation* (Baltimore: Johns Hopkins University Press, 2006), 16; Dora L. Costa and Richard H. Steckel, *Long-Term Trends in Health, Welfare, and Economic Growth in the United States* (Chicago: University of Chicago Press, 2008), 63; Dora L. Costa, "Height, Wealth, And Disease Among the Native-Born in the Rural, Antebellum North," *Social Science History* 17, no. 3 (1993): 364–365; Scott Alan Carson, "Weight and Economic Development: Current Net Nutrition in The Late 19th- and Early 20th-Century United States," *Biodemography and Social Biology* 65, no. 2 (2019): 23.

36 It is unclear if these people were charged for food, but oral histories suggest they weren't. Woods and Mansfield, *Studies of the Food of Maine Lumbermen*, 17, 21, 24, 29; "The Lincoln and Idella Toothaker Letters, 1890–1892," Lincoln Toothaker to Idella Toothaker, December 27, 1890; March 22, 1891; Arnold Hall (b. 1892), interviewed by William Bonsall, 1970, p. 580056, transcript (LLC) (MFC); James Shea, interviewed by David Currier, 1970, p. 7–8, transcript (LLC) (MFC).

37 Charlotte Todes, *Labor and Lumber* (New York: International Publishers, 1931), 203; Thomas R. Cox, *The Lumberman's Frontier: Three Centuries of Land Use, Society, and Change in America's Forests* (Corvallis: Oregon State University Press, 2010), 125–126; Judd and Judd, *Aroostook*, 13, 103, 146, 173, 183; Radforth, *Bushworkers and Bosses*, 6, 107; Flanagan, "Industrial Conditions in the Maine Woods," 220.

38 Thurston Madison Adams, *Prices Paid by Vermont Farmers for Goods and Services and Received by Them for Farm Products, 1790–1940; Wages of Vermont Farm Labor, 1780–1940* (Burlington, VT: Free Printing Co., 1944), 96–97.

39 Anna Zeide and Darra Goldstein, *Canned: The Rise and Fall of Consumer Confidence in the American Food Industry* (Berkeley: University of California Press, 2018), 1, 13.

40 Frank Tobias Higbie, *Indispensable Outcasts: Hobo Workers and Community in the American Midwest, 1880–1930* (Urbana: University of Illinois Press, 2003), 39, 208; Walter Augustus Wyckoff, *A Day with a Tramp, and Other Days* (New York: C. Scribner's Sons, 1901), 21; Todd DePastino, *Citizen Hobo: How a Century of Homelessness Shaped America* (Chicago: University of Chicago Press, 2010), 68; Nels

Anderson and Raffaele Rauty, *On Hobos and Homelessness* (Chicago: University of Chicago Press, 1998), 47, 80, 114; Nels Anderson, *The American Hobo: An Autobiography* (Leiden: Brill, 1975), 61, 62, 68, 79, 97, 135.

41 Walter Augustus Wyckoff, *The Workers: An Experiment in Reality: The East* (New York: C. Scribner, 1897), quote on page 12. Also see 56, 12, 212, 49, 51, 181, 226.

42 Quoted in Harvey A. Levenstein, *Fear of Food: A History of Why We Worry about What We Eat* (Chicago: The University of Chicago Press, 2012), 50; on immigrants' improved diet in America, see Levenstein, *Revolution at the Table*, 7–8, 15, 219, 101–102; Trevon D. Logan, "Nutrition and Well-Being in the Late Nineteenth Century," *The Journal of Economic History* 66, no. 2 (2006): abstract; Dirks, "Diet and Nutrition," 94; Conlin, *Bacon, Beans, and Galantines*, 9–10; Cummings, *The American and His Food*, 89; Woods and Mansfield, *Studies of the Food of Maine Lumbermen*, 30–34; Gunther Peck, *Reinventing Free Labor: Padrones and Immigrant Workers in the North American West, 1880–1930* (Cambridge: Cambridge University Press, 2000), 28, 35, 132.

43 Elliott Robert Barkan, "French Canadians," in *Harvard Encyclopedia of American Ethnic Groups*, ed. Stephan Thernstrom (Cambridge, MA: Belknap Press, 1980), 392; Gerard J. Brault, *The French Canadian Heritage in New England* (Lebanon, NH: University Press of New England, 1986), 52–53; Gary Gerstle, *Working-Class Americanism: The Politics of Labor in a Textile City, 1914–1960* (Cambridge: Cambridge University Press, 1989), 21; Bruno Ramirez and Yves Otis, *Crossing the 49th Parallel: Migration from Canada to the United States, 1900–1930* (Ithaca, NY: Cornell University Press, 2001), 1; Flanagan, "Industrial Conditions in the Maine Woods," 220; Woods and Mansfield, *Studies of the Food of Maine Lumbermen*, 13; Frank Lewis and Marvin McInnis, "The Efficiency of the French Canadian Farmer in the Nineteenth Century," *The Journal of Economic History* 40, no. 3 (1980): 497–499.

44 John Irvine Little, *Nationalism, Capitalism and Colonization in Nineteenth-Century Québec: The Upper St. Francis District* (Kingston, ON: McGill-Queen's University Press, 1989), 3; Yves Roby, "The Economic Evolution of Québec and the Emigrant (1850–1929)," in *Steeples and Smokestacks: A Collection of Essays on the Franco-American Experience in New England*, ed. Claire Quintal (Worcester, MA: Institut Francais of Assumption College, 1996), 7–8, 11–13; Bruno Ramirez, *On the Move: French Canadian and Italian Migrants in the North Atlantic Economy, 1860–1914* (Toronto: McClelland & Stewart, 1991); 46–47; John Irvine Little, *Crofters and Habitants: Settler Society, Economy, and Culture in a Québec Township, 1848–1881* (Montreal: McGill-Queen's University Press, 1991), 136, 143.

45 Dirks, "Diet and Nutrition," 91; Also see Levenstein, *Revolution at the Table*, 26, 101; Iris Saunders Podea, "Québec to 'Little Canada': The Coming of the French Canadians to New England in the Nineteenth Century," *The New England Quarterly* 23, no. 3 (1950): 367, 376.

46 Atwater, "What the Coming Man Will Eat," 497.

47 Woods and Mansfield, *Studies of the Food of Maine Lumbermen*, 36–37.

48 Cummings, *The American and His Food*, 125–128; Veit, *Modern Food, Moral Food*.

49 Quote in Cummings, *The American and His Food*, 128; also see Levenstein, *Revolution at the Table*, 46–47; Turner, *How the Other Half Ate*, 26; Nick Cullather, *The Hungry World*, 18–19.

50 Woods and Mansfield, *Studies of the Food of Maine Lumbermen*, 3.

51 Cummings, *The American and His Food*, 127.

52 Quote in Levenstein, *Revolution at the Table*, 57; also see Veit, *Modern Food, Moral Food*; Horowitz, *Putting Meat on the American Table*, 57; Cummings, *The American and His Food*, 130–131; Dirks, "Diet and Nutrition," 83.

53 Quote in Daggett, *The Birth of Energy: Fossil Fuels, Thermodynamics, and the Politics of Work* (Durham, NC: Duke University Press, 2019), 167–168; also see James L. Hargrove, "History of The Calorie in Nutrition," *The Journal of Nutrition* 136, no. 12 (2006): 2957–2961.
54 Cullather, *The Hungry World*, 12, 19.
55 Atwater, "What the Coming Man Will Eat," 497–498.
56 "The People's Food—A Great National Inquiry: Professor W. O. Atwater and His Work," *The Review of Reviews* XIII, no. 77 (1896): 581.
57 Atwater, "The Potential Energy of Food," 403, 398.
58 Veit, *Modern Food, Moral Food*; Moore, "The Rise of Cheap Nature," 90; Daggett, *The Birth of Energy*, 85–86, 90; John Bellamy Foster, Brett Clark, and Richard York, *The Ecological Rift: Capitalism's War on the Earth* (NYU Press, 2011), 228.
59 Woods and Mansfield, *Studies of the Food of Maine Lumbermen*, 13, 36, 84.
60 Woods and Mansfield, *Studies of the Food of Maine Lumbermen*, 30, 59; M. J. Karvonen and Osmo Turpeinen, "Consumption and Selection of Food in Competitive Lumber Work," *Journal of Applied Physiology* 6, no.10 (1954): 609.
61 Cullather, *The Hungry World: America's Cold War Battle against Poverty in Asia*, 28; Carson, "Weight and Economic Development," 28.
62 Woods and Mansfield, *Studies of the Food of Maine Lumbermen*, 17.
63 "A Tenderfoot at Hamlin's: Adventures of A 'City Feller' in a Maine Logging Camp," *Lewiston Journal: Illustrated Magazine* (January 13–17, 1906).
64 Woods and Mansfield, *Studies of the Food of Maine Lumbermen*, 35, 53, 17–29, 60, 30, 33, 59.
65 Woods and Mansfield, *Studies of the Food of Maine Lumbermen*, 8.
66 Evelyn M. Dinsdale (Evelyn Stokes), "Spatial Patterns of Technological Change: The Lumber Industry of Northern New York," *Economic Geography* 41, no. 3 (1965): 252–274; Peter C. Welsh, *Jacks, Jobbers and Kings* (New York: North Country Books, 1995), 27; Radforth, *Bushworkers and Bosses*, 26.
67 Alexander Koroleff, *Pulpwood Cutting: Efficiency of Technique* (Montreal: Woodlands Section, Canadian Pulp and Paper Association, 1941), 22; William James Henry Miller, James Plummer Poole, and Harlan Hayes Sweetser, "A Lumbering Report of Work on Squaw Mountain Township, Winter of 1911–1912" (Thesis, University of Maine–Orono, 1912), 17.
68 R. Passmore and J. V. G. A. Durnin, "Human Energy Expenditure," *Physiological Reviews* 35, no. 4 (1955): 813; Conlin, "Old Boy, Did You Get Enough of Pie," 184–187.
69 W. L. Sykes to D. H. Dorr, February 3, 1919. Emporium Forest Company Records Box 13 Adirondack Museum; Asa Flagg (b. 1898), interviewed by Rhoda Mitchell, 1970, p. 5750013, 57500134, transcript (LLC) (MFC); Arnold Hall (b. 1892), interviewed by William Bonsall, 1970, p. 580021, transcript (LLC) (MFC); Robert Volney (b. 1890), interviewed by Linda Hubbard, 1970, p. 571022, transcript (LLC) (MFC); Ernest Kennedy (b. 1889), interviewed by Lillian Shirley, 1970, p. 5790044, transcript (LLC) (MFC); Flanagan, "Industrial Conditions in the Maine Woods," 207.
70 Karvonen and Turpeinen, "Consumption and Selection of Food in Competitive Lumber Work," 610.
71 Daniel Raff, "The Puzzling Profusion of Compensation Systems in the Interwar Automobile Industry," in *Coordination and Information: Historical Perspectives on the Organization of Enterprise*, ed. Naomi R. Lamoreaux and Daniel Raff (Chicago: University of Chicago Press, 2007), 14.
72 Michael Hillard and Jonathan P. Goldstein, "Cutting off the Canadians: Nativism and the Fate of the Maine Woodman's Association, 1970–1981," *Labor* 5, no. 3 (2008): 70–71.

73 Quoted in Radforth, *Bushworkers and Bosses*, 55, 75, 76.

74 Harry Dyer (b. 1896), interviewed by Jeanne Milton, 1970, p. 581017, transcript (LLC) (MFC).

75 Bradwin, *The Bunkhouse Man; A Study of Work and Pay in the Camps of Canada, 1903–1914* (Toronto: University of Toronto Press, 1972), 120–125, 199; William C. Osborn, *The Paper Plantation; Ralph Nader's Study Group Report on the Pulp and Paper Industry in Maine* (New York: Grossman Publishers, 1974), 138.

76 Harold K. Hochschild, *Lumberjacks and Rivermen in the Central Adirondacks, 1850–1950* (Blue Mountain Lake, NY: Adirondack Museum, 1962), 26.

77 Woods and Mansfield, *Studies of the Food of Maine Lumbermen*, 33.

78 Woods and Mansfield, *Studies of the Food of Maine Lumbermen*, 13, 33, 59.

79 Julius Joel (b. 1876), interviewed by John Larson, 1953, p. 3–4, transcript, OHI, FHS; "The Lincoln and Idella Toothaker Letters, 1890–1892," Lincoln Toothaker to Idella Toothaker, March 28, 1891.

80 Woods and Mansfield, *Studies of the Food of Maine Lumbermen*, 33, 34, 59; Nils Peter Vilhelm Lundgren, "The Physiological Effects of Time Schedule Work on Lumber-Workers," 27–28; National Research Council (US), *Subcommittee on the Tenth Edition of the Recommended Dietary Allowances: Recommended Dietary Allowances: 10th Edition* (Washington, DC: National Academies Press, 1989); Protein and Amino Acids; RDA information found at "Nutrition for Everyone: Protein" Center for Disease Control and Prevention, accessed October 13, 2013, http://www.cdc.gov/nutrition/everyone/basics/protein.html#How%20much%20protein.

81 Karvonen and Turpeinen, "Consumption and Selection of Food in Competitive Lumber Work," 602; Kenneth J. Carpenter, "Proteins" in *The Cambridge World History of Food*, ed. Kenneth F. Kiple and Kriemhild Conee Ornelas (Cambridge: Cambridge University Press, 2000); Logan, "Food, Nutrition, and Substitution," 540.

82 Woods and Mansfield, *Studies of the Food of Maine Lumbermen*, 53; Kenneth F. Kiple and Virginia Himmelsteib King, *Another Dimension to the Black Diaspora: Diet, Disease, and Racism* (Cambridge: Cambridge University Press, 1981), 94.

83 Quote in William B. Laughead (b. 1885), interviewed by W. H. Hutchinson, September 17 and 18, 1957, p. 48–49, transcript (OHI) (FHS). Also see Karvonen and Turpeinen, "Consumption and Selection of Food in Competitive Lumber Work," 610; Wyckoff, *The Workers . . . the East*, 216.

84 H. P. F. Peters, W. R. De Vries, G. Vanberge-Henegouwen, and L. M. A. Akkermans, "Potential Benefits and Hazards of Physical Activity and Exercise on the Gastrointestinal Tract," *Gut* 48, no. 3 (2001): 435–439; Karvonen and Turpeinen, "Consumption and Selection of Food in Competitive Lumber Work," 603–604, 610; Radforth, *Bushworkers and Bosses*, 42.

85 Frederick Burke (b. 1915) interviewed by Norma Coates (1971), transcript, p. 702118 (LLC) (MFC); another example in Hochschild, *Lumberjacks and Rivermen*, 26.

86 Quote in Beam, *A Maine Hamlet*, 54; Wyckoff, *The Workers . . . the East*, 137; Hillard, "Cutting off the Canadians," 70–71.

87 The Journal of Dr. Donald Eyre Bowen, 1941, Magalloway Lumber Camp Physician," 36–39, exhibit edited by Donald and Peggy Bowen, 1995. Property of the Rangeley Lakes Region Logging Museum, Rangeley, Maine, http://rlrlm.org; Conlin, "Old Boy, Did You Get Enough of Pie," 178–179; Carroll C. Noyes (b. 1890), interviewed by Lynn MacFarland, 1970, p. 621116, transcript (LLC) (MFC); Frank A. Reed, *Lumberjack Sky Pilot* (New York 1965), 59; Ferris Meigs, *The Santa Clara Lumber Company*, vol. 1 (unpublished manuscript, typeset 1941), Santa Clara Collection, Adirondack Museum, Blue Mountain Lake, New York, 86; Prouty, "More Deadly than War," 160; Radforth, *Bushworkers and Bosses*, 96–97; Flanagan, "Industrial

Conditions in the Maine Woods," 212; Fannie Hardy Eckstorm and Mary Winslow Smyth, *Minstrelsy of Maine: Folk-Songs and Ballads of the Woods and the Coast* (Boston: Houghton Mifflin, 1927), 165; Barbara Kephart Bird, *Calked Shoes; Life in Adirondack Lumber Camps* (Prospect, NY: Prospect Books, 1952), 53; Conlin, "Old Boy, Did You Get Enough of Pie," 178–179.

88 The Dechene Family (Adirondack lumbering family) in communication with the author, September 2010.

89 Wyckoff, *The Workers . . . the East*, 49; "A Tenderfoot at Hamlin's."

90 Woods and Mansfield, *Studies of the Food of Maine Lumbermen*, 7, 16, 30.

91 Radforth, *Bushworkers and Bosses*, 38–40, 98, 101; Samuel Schrager, "Migratory Lumberjack: A Portrait of Michigan Bill Stowell," *Forest and Conservation History* 35, no. 1 (January 1991): 4–15; Peck, *Reinventing Free Labor*, 11, 51; Grover Swett, interviewed by Florence Ireland, 1970, transcript (LLC) (MFC); Flanagan, "Industrial Conditions in the Maine Woods," 224–226; Franzen, *The Archaeology of the Logging Industry*, 114, 140.

92 *The Rumford Citizen*, vol. 2, no. 27 (January 16, 1908); also see Franzen, *The Archaeology of the Logging Industry*, 114.

93 These numbers are all calculated without the costs of provisions during the river drive. Woods and Mansfield, *Studies of the Food of Maine Lumbermen*, 7, 16, 30; Conlin, "Old Boy, Did You Get Enough of Pie," 183–184.

94 Using the average amount of food eaten by each man in each study (5.822, 4.578, 2.626, and 5.621 pounds a day), not counting food waste, it is possible to calculate how much the freight costs were for food for each man for each day based on a 26-day work month. Woods and Mansfield wrote that the camp was located near Lake Onawa with the closest railway station, the Onawa station, 15 miles to the south. They also mention the food was purchased in Bangor. Freight on the Bangor and Aroostook and the Canadian Pacific was an average of 1.343 and 0.48 cents per ton per mile, respectively, during the years of the studies. The shipment from Bangor had to travel 49.3 miles north on the Bangor and Aroostook line and 14 miles west on the Canadian Pacific. That means it cost roughly \$0.037 to transport one pound of food.

The food also had to be toted into camp and according to the study there was one man who made regular trips to the train station, who made \$1.08 a day or \$28.08 a month. There was also one cook working at \$30 a month, and although the study doesn't say how many cookees, or assistant chefs, there were, it suggests there were at least two. Assuming there were two cookees, working for \$26 a month, I divided the wages of the tote man and the cooking team by the number of men in the studies to get the amount that the company spent on this aspect of preparation and transport and added to this the cost per pound of food transported by train. I did this for all four diet studies to get \$0.307 per man per day for food transportation and preparation. This does not include the cost of the depreciation of the horses for making the trips to the station regularly. Omer Lavallée, *Canadian Pacific to the East: The International of Maine Division* (Ottawa, ON: Bytown Railway Society, 2007), front cover image; "The Short Line and its Connections, 1919"; Jerry Angier and Herb Cleaves, *Bangor and Aroostook, the Maine Railroad* (Littleton, MA: Flying Yankee Enterprises, 1987), 26; *Annual Report of the Railroad Commissioners of the State of Maine* (Augusta, ME: Burleigh & Flynt, 1905), 17.

95 Miller et al., "A Lumbering Report of Work on Squaw Mountain Township," 14.

96 Judd and Judd, *Aroostook*, 112; William Freeman Fox, *A History of the Lumber Industry in the State of New York* (US Department of Agriculture, Bureau of Forestry, 1902), 69; Meigs, *Santa Clara Lumber Company*, 56; Lee J. Vance, "Lumbering in

the Adirondacks," *Goody's Magazine* 113, no. 789 (March 1896): 231; W. C. Sykes to C. H. Sisson, May 1, 1919; C. H. Sisson to W. C. Sykes, May 2, 1919; W. C. Sykes to C. H. Sisson, May 3, 1919, Emporium Forest Company Records Box 13 Adirondack Museum, Blue Mountain Lake, New York; E. L. Stables to Mr. Sykes, Mr. Caflish and Mr. Turner, November 7, 1912, Emporium Forest Company Records Box 5 Adirondack Museum, Blue Mountain Lake, New York; David C. Smith, *A History of Lumbering in Maine, 1861–1960* (Orono: University of Maine Press, 1972), 21; Radforth, *Bushworkers and Bosses*, 28; Radforth, "The Shantymen," 249; Flanagan, "Industrial Conditions in the Maine Woods."

97 Turner, *How the Other Half Ate.*

98 Paul H. Douglas, *Real Wages in the United States, 1890–1926* (Boston: Houghton Mifflin, 1930), 19–42, 130, 177; James H. Blodgett, *Wages of Farm Labor in the United States: Results of Twelve Statistical Investigations, 1866–1902* (Washington, DC: US Department of Agriculture, Bureau of Statistics, 1903), 14; Adams, *Prices Paid by Vermont Farmers*, 89.

99 Woods and Mansfield, *Studies of the Food of Maine Lumbermen*, 32.

100 Moore, "The Rise of Cheap Nature," 88.

6. The Lumberjack Problem

1 Frederick Burke (b. 1915), interviewed by Norma Coates, 1971, transcript, p. 702114, 702010, 702103, 702026 (LLC) (MFC).

2 Andrew Chase (b. 1888), interviewed by Linda Edgerly, 1971, p. 697001, transcript (LLC) (MFC); Wirt Mineau (b. 1878), interviewed by Helen McCann White, 1955, p. 6 (FHS) (OHIC); Frank Carey (b. 1886), interviewed by Rita Swidrowski, 1970, p. 6980106, transcript (LLC) (MFC).

3 Walter Augustus Wyckoff, *The Workers: An Experiment in Reality: The East* (New York: C. Scribner, 1897), 181, 267.

4 Edmund W. Bradwin, *The Bunkhouse Man: A Study of Work and Pay in the Camps of Canada, 1903–1914* (Toronto: University of Toronto Press, 1972), vii, 179; Rolf Knight, *Work Camps and Company Towns in Canada and the US: An Annotated Bibliography* (Vancouver, BC: New Star Books, 1975).

5 E. P. Thompson, *The Making of the English Working-Class* (New York: Pantheon Books, 1964), 9–10; Robert J. Steinfeld, *Coercion, Contract, and Free Labor in the Nineteenth Century* (Cambridge: Cambridge University Press, 2001), 3, 18; Scott A. Sandage, *Born Losers: A History of Failure in America* (Harvard University Press, 2005), 64, 67.

6 Louis Hyman, *Borrow: The American Way of Debt* (New York: Vintage Books, 2012), 10–11.

7 John R. Commons, *Races and Immigrants in America* (New York: The MacMillan Co., 1907), 138.

8 Lawrence B. Glickman, *A Living Wage: American Workers and the Making of Consumer Society* (Ithaca, NY: Cornell University, 1997).

9 Stan J. Liebowitz and Stephen E. Margolis, "Path Dependence," in *Encyclopedia of Law and Economics*, vol. 1, ed. Boudewijn Bouckaert, Gerrit De Geest and Charles F. Nagel (Cheltenham, UK: Edward Elgar Publishing, 1999), 982–983.

10 Juliana Mansvelt, *Geographies of Consumption* (London: SAGE, 2005), 11; Jo Guldi, "What Is the Spatial Turn?" and "The Spatial Turn in History," *Spatial Humanities, A Project of the Institute for Enabling Geospatial Scholarship* (blog), accessed June 29, 2015, http://spatial.scholarslab.org/spatial-turn/what-is-the-spatial-turn/; Richard White, "What is Spatial History" in Ryan Delaney, "Backend Visualizations: Tools for Helping the Research Process," *The Spatial History Project* (2009): 22

pars, August 30, 2009, accessed June 29, 2015, http://www.stanford.edu/group/spatialhistory/cgi-bin/site/pub.php?id=11; Frank Tobias Higbie; *Indispensable Outcasts: Hobo Workers and Community in the American Midwest, 1880–1930* (Urbana: University of Illinois Press, 2003), 208.

11 Joseph Parker Bursk, *Seasonal Variations in Employment in Manufacturing Industries: A Statistical Study Based on Census Data* (Philadelphia: University of Pennsylvania Press, 1931), 2; John Koren and Henry Walcott Farnam, *Economic Aspects of the Liquor Problem* (Boston: Houghton Mifflin, 1899), 321, 183; John Koren, *Alcohol and Society* (New York: H. Holt, 1916), 45; Kenneth L. Kusmer, *Down and Out, on the Road: The Homeless in American History* (New York: Oxford University Press, 2001); Tim Cresswell, *The Tramp in America* (London: Reaktion, 2001).

12 Robert Suits, "Hoboes, Wheat, and Climate Precarity, 1870–1922," *Agricultural History* 97, no. 1 (2023): 1–47.

13 Higbie, *Indispensable Outcasts*, 14–15, 19, 30, 34, 76, 100.

14 Norman S. Hayner, "Taming the Lumberjack," *American Sociological Review* 10, no. 6 (1945): 219, 225.

15 Ian Radforth, "The Shantymen" in *Laboring Lives: Work and Workers in Nineteenth-Century Ontario*, ed. Paul Craven (University of Toronto Press, 1995), 208; Robert E. Pike, *Tall Trees, Tough Men* (New York: W. W. Norton, 1984), 55; United States Senate, *Report of the Select Committee on Immigration and Naturalization: And Testimony Taken by the Committee on Immigration of the Senate and the Select Committee on Immigration and Naturalization of the House of Representatives Under Concurrent Resolution of March 12, 1890* (Washington, DC: Government Printing Office, 1891), 324.

16 "Congress of All Nations Maine's Lumber Camps," *Bangor Daily News*, April 17, 1913.

17 Bradwin, *The Bunkhouse Man*, x, 156; Gunther Peck, *Reinventing Free Labor: Padrones and Immigrant Workers in the North American West, 1880–1930* (Cambridge: Cambridge University Press, 2000), 74; Vernon H. Jensen, *Lumber and Labor* (New York: Farrar & Rinehart, 1945), 77; Glenn C. Prescott and Raymond E. Rendall, "Lumbering in the Dead River Region, Somerset County, Maine" (PhD diss., University of Maine Orono, 1916), 26, 65; David Nathan Rogers, "Lumbering in Northern Maine," 25; Robert Volney (b. 1890), interviewed by Linda Hubbard, 1970, p. 571043, transcript (LLC) (MFC); John Sharpe (b. 1881), interviewed by Lillian Shirley, 1970, p. 59, transcript (LLC) (MFC); Robert Volney (b. 1890), interviewed by Linda Hubbard, 1970, p. 571048, transcript (LLC) (MFC); Harry Dyer (b. 1896), interviewed by Jeanne Milton, 1970, p. 568034, transcript (LLC) (MFC); Higbie, *Indispensable Outcasts*, 123–127.

18 Gerald Averill, *Ridge Runner: The Story of a Maine Woodsman* (Philadelphia: J. B. Lippincott, 1948), 94.

19 "The Lincoln and Idella Toothaker Letters, 1890–1892," March 15, 1891, Lincoln to Ida, Property of Becky Ellis Martineau and the Rangeley Lakes Region Logging Museum, Rangeley, Maine, http://rlrlm.org; also see Higbie, *Indispensable Outcasts*, 48–49.

20 Fannie Hardy Eckstorm, *The Penobscot Man* (Somersworth, NH: New Hampshire Publishing, 1972), 53, 163.

21 Barbara Kephart Bird, *Calked Shoes; Life in Adirondack Lumber Camps* (Prospect, NY: Prospect Books, 1952), 6.

22 The interviewer's notes are in parentheses. Arnold Hall (b. 1892), interviewed by William Bonsall, 1970, transcript, 580035 (LLC) (MFC).

23 John Sharpe (b. 1881), interviewed by Lillian Shirley, 1970, p. 121, transcript (LLC) (MFC).

24 Erroll "John" Haley (b. 1898) interviewed by Stephen Richard, 1980, transcript, p. 1384125 (LLC) (MFC); *The Malone Farmer*, May 13, 1914, p. 3.

25 George Chauncey, *Gay New York: Gender, Urban Culture, and the Makings of the Gay Male World, 1890–1940* (New York: Basic Books, 1994), 61, 82–83; George Chauncey, "Christian Brotherhood or Sexual Perversion? Homosexual Identities and the Construction of Sexual Boundaries in the World War One Era," *Journal of Social History* 19, no. 2 (1985): 189–211; Todd DePastino, *Citizen Hobo: How a Century of Homelessness Shaped America* (Chicago: University of Chicago Press, 2010), 85–91; Bradwin, *The Bunkhouse Man*, 99; Nels Anderson and Raffaele Rauty, *On Hobos and Homelessness* (Chicago: University of Chicago Press, 1999), 115; Higbie, *Indispensable Outcasts*, 123–127.

26 Asa Flagg (b. 1898), interviewed by Rhoda Mitchell, 1970, p. 57599, transcript (LLC) (MFC).

27 Edwin H. Eddy (b. 1863), "Lumber Camps (Recollections)," Maine Historical Society, Portland, Maine, p. 6–7.

28 Averill, *Ridge Runner*, 86; Robert D. Bethke, *Adirondack Voices: Woodsmen and Woods Lore* (Chicago: University of Illinois Press, 1981), 16; Bird, *Calked Shoes*, 112–113.

29 Grover Cleveland Field, Clyde Willard, Lester Cole, and Raymond Olmstead, interviewed by Dorothy Bodwell, 1970, p. 17, transcript (LLC) (MFC).

30 George Chauncey, *Why Marriage?: The History Shaping Today's Debate Over Gay Equality* (New York: Basic Books, 2004), 13; "Local Department," *The Malone Farmer*, September 2, 1925, and also in the same newspaper January 14, 1931; April 28, 1915; February 26, 1936; March, 28 1906; January 10, 1934; and November 24, 1926; untitled, *The Malone Palladium*, July 19, 1877, p. 3; "Five Given Sentence in County Court at Malone," *Chateauguay Record and Franklin County Democrat*, November 1942.

31 Andrew Chase (b. 1888), interviewed by Linda Edgerly, 1971, p. 697008, transcript (LLC) (MFC); Frank Carey (b. 1886), interviewed by Rita Swidrowski, 1970, p. 698105, transcript (LLC) (MFC); Wyckoff, *The Workers . . . the East*, 193; Radforth, "The Shantymen," 230; Higbie, *Indispensable Outcasts*, 179.

32 Susan Lee Johnson, "Bulls, Bears, and Dancing Boys: Race, Gender, and Leisure in the California Gold Rush," and Dee Garceau, "Nomads, Bunkies, Cross-Dressers, and Family Men," *Across the Great Divide: Cultures of Manhood in the American West*, ed. Matthew Basso, Laura McCall, and Dee Garceau (New York: Routledge, 2001); William Benemann, *Workers in Eden: William Drummond Stewart and Same-Sex Desire in the Rocky Mountain Fur Trade* (Lincoln: University of Nebraska Press, 2012); Peter Boag, *Same-Sex Affairs: Constructing and Controlling Homosexuality in the Pacific Northwest* (University of California Press, 2003), 28, 40.

33 Quote from Steven Maynard, "Rough Work and Rugged Men: The Social Construction of Masculinity in Working-Class History," *Labour/Le Travail* 23, no. 23 (1989): 167.

34 Michael Merrill, "Cash Is Good to Eat: Self-Sufficiency and Exchange in the Rural Economy of the United States," *Radical History Review*, no. 13 (1977): 42–71, 53, 54, 58; Béatrice Craig, *Backwoods Consumers and Homespun Capitalists: The Rise of a Market Culture in Eastern Canada* (Toronto: University of Toronto Press, 2009), 128; Allan Kulikoff, *The Agrarian Origins of American Capitalism* (Charlottesville: University Press of Virginia, 1992), 6; Rusty Bittermann, "Farm Households and Wage Labour in the Northeastern Maritimes in the Early 19th Century," *Labour/Le Travail* (1993): 13–45; Christopher Clark, "Household Economy, Market Exchange and the Rise of Capitalism in the Connecticut Valley, 1800–1860," *Journal of Social History* 13, no. 2 (1979): 173; Hyman, *Borrow*, 8.

35 Turner Falls Lumber Company, Series I, bound volumes, v. 14, Notes and bills receivable, 1899–1902, Baker Library Historical Collections. Harvard Business School.

36 Edwin Walter Kemmerer, *Seasonal Variations in the Relative Demand for Money and Capital in the United States: A Statistical Study* (Washington, DC: US Government Printing Office, 1910), 15–18.

37 Rowena Olegario, *A Culture of Credit: Embedding Trust and Transparency in American Business*, Harvard Studies in Business History 50 (Cambridge, MA: Harvard University Press, 2006), 30; Richard White, *Railroaded: The Transcontinentals and the Making of Modern America* (New York: W. W. Norton, 2011), 81; Craig, *Backwoods Consumers*, 11, 21, 125, 135; Hyman, *Borrow*, 26.

38 Hyman, *Borrow*, 11.

39 Bradwin, *The Bunkhouse Man*, 8; Gunther Peck, *Reinventing Free Labor*, 35; Gunther Peck, "Manly Gambles: The Politics of Risk on the Comstock Lode, 1860–1880," *Journal of Social History* (1993): 701–723.

40 "wanigan, n.", OED Online, Oxford University Press: 2014, accessed March 13, 2015, http://www.oed.com; Rogers, "Lumbering in Northern Maine," 19–20; "Inventory of personal property sold by McCoy & Son to Emporium Lumber Co.," Emporium Forest Company Records, Box 2, Adirondack Museum, Blue Mountain Lake, NY; Bradwin, *The Bunkhouse Man*, 49; Raymond J. Smith and Samuel B. Locke, "A Study of the Lumber Industry of Northern Maine" (Thesis, University of Maine Orono, 1908), 8; Prescott and Rendall, "Lumbering in the Dead River Region" 20, 22; Frederick Burke (b. 1915), interviewed by Norma Coates, 1971, transcript, p. 702012 (LLC) (MFC).

41 Smith and Locke, "A Study of the Lumber Industry of Northern Maine," 11; R. Boultbee, A. P. Leslie, and J. B. Matthews, "Report of Logging Operation on Limits of the Canoe Lake Lumber Co., Canoe Lake Ont., 1927–1928 (Thesis, University of Maine Orono, 1928), 23; Frank Carey (b. 1886), interviewed by Rita Swidrowski, 1970, p. 698040, transcript (LLC) (MFC); John Sharpe (b. 1881), interviewed by Lillian Shirley, 1970, p. 6, transcript (LLC) (MFC); Asa Flagg (b. 1898), interviewed by Rhoda Mitchell, 1970, p. 575104, transcript (LLC) (MFC); Asa Flagg (b. 1898), interviewed by Rhoda Mitchell, 1970, p. 575041, transcript (LLC) (MFC).

42 Erroll "John" Haley (b. 1898), interviewed by Stephen Richard, 1980, transcript, p. 1380097 (LLC) (MFC); Geraldine Tidd Scott, *Isaac Simpson's World: The Collected Works of an Itinerant Photographer* (Falmouth, ME: Kennebec River Press, 1990), 65; Harry Dyer (b. 1896), interviewed by Jeanne Milton, 1970, p. 581055, transcript (LLC) (MFC); Bradwin, *The Bunkhouse Man*, 108–109; Wyckoff, *The Workers . . . the East*, 200; "The Lincoln and Idella Toothaker Letters, 1890–1892," Lincoln to Ida, March 15, 1891, Lincoln to Ida, January 18, 1892, Ida to Lincoln, February 4, 1892; Stewart G. McHenry, "The Syrian Movement into Upstate New York," *Ethnicity* 4, no. 6 (1979): 327–345; Amy E. Rowe "A Trace of Arabic in Granite: Lebanese Migration to the Green Mountains, 1890–1940," *Vermont History* 76, no. 2 (2008): 91–129; George Thomas Carlisle and Thomas Franklin Shatney, "Report on a Logging Operation in Northern Maine" (Thesis, University of Maine Orono, 1909), 10.

43 Wendy A. Woloson, *Crap: A History of Cheap Stuff in America* (Chicago: University of Chicago Press, 2020), 4, 17–20.

44 Fannie Hardy Eckstorm and Mary Winslow Smyth, *Minstrelsy of Maine: Folk-Songs and Ballads of the Woods and the Coast* (Boston: Houghton Mifflin, 1927), 142–143.

45 Maria Mackinney-Valentin, "The Lumberjack Shirt: The Fabric and Fabrication of Zeitgeist," *Catwalk: The Journal of Fashion, Beauty, and Style* 1, no. 1 (2012): 7; Victor Bushey (b. 1900), interviews by Sue Dauphinee, 1972, p. 719076, transcript

(LLC) (MFC); Leo Poirier (b. 1891), interviews by Bobbie Violette, 1974, transcript, p. 800010 (LLC) (MFC); Carroll C. Noyes interviewed by Lynn MacFarland, 1972, transcript, p. 577066 (LLC) (MFC); John Sharpe (b. 1881), interviewed by Lillian Shirley, 1970, p. 60, 61, transcript (LLC) (MFC); Andrew Chase (b. 1888), interviewed by Linda Edgerly, 1971, p. 697068, transcript (LLC) (MFC).

46 Craig, *Backwoods Consumers*, 182.

47 Pike, *Tall Trees, Tough Men*, 55.

48 "A French Canadian Home," *New York Times*, January 18, 1880; "The Habitant," *New York Times*, October 18, 1874; "The French Canadians," *All the Year Round: A Weekly Journal* 39, no. 928 (1886): 125–128; Craig, *Backwoods Consumers*, 188; Eckstorm and Smyth, *Minstrelsy of Maine*, 119.

49 Frank Carey (b. 1886), interviewed by Rita Swidrowski, 1970, p. 6980068–69, transcript (LLC) (MFC); Robert Volney (b. 1890), interviewed by Linda Hubbard, 1970, p. 571043–44, 571053, 571066, transcript (LLC) (MFC); Fred E. Johnson (b. ????) interviews by Paul Gauvin, 1971, p. 639006, transcript (LLC) (MFC); Pike, *Tall Trees, Tough Men*, 57–58, 81.

50 "The Shanty Boys Ragged Out," *Commercial Advertiser*, March 13, 1895, p. 3, image 3.

51 Robert Volney and Lee Roberts (b. 1890), interviewed by Linda Hubbard, 1970, p. 571022, transcript (LLC) (MFC).

52 Leslie, Boultbee, and Matthews, "Report of Logging Operation on Limits of the Canoe Lake Lumber Co.," 23; Frederick Burke (b. 1915), interviewed by Norma Coates, 1971, transcript, p. 702012 (LLC) (MFC); Maggie Orr O'Neill (b. 1872), interviewed by Helen McCann White, 1955, transcript, p. 4 (FHS) (OHIC); Asa Flagg (b. 1898), interviewed by Rhoda Mitchell, 1970, p. 575108, transcript (LLC) (MFC); Andrew Chase (b. 1888), interviewed by Linda Edgerly, 1971, p. 697069, transcript (LLC) (MFC); Cecil Max Hilton, *Rough Pulpwood Operating in Northwestern Maine, 1935–1940* (Orono: University of Maine Press, 1942), 121–122.

53 Stewart H. Holbrook, *Holy Old Mackinaw: A Natural History of the American Lumberjack* (New York: Macmillan, 1956); Robert E. Walls, "The Making of the American Logger: Traditional Culture and Public Imagery in the Realm of the Bunyanesque" (PhD diss., Indiana University, 1997), 145, 405; "mackinaw" in *The Canadian Oxford Dictionary*, edited by Katherine Barber (Oxford University Press, 2004), accessed September 11, 2015, http://www.oxfordreference.com; Victor Bushey (b. 1900), interviews by Sue Dauphinee, 1972, p. 719049–50, 719078–79, transcript (LLC) (MFC); John Sharpe (b. 1881), interviewed by Lillian Shirley, 1970, p. 61, transcript (LLC) (MFC); Carlisle and Shatney, "Report on a Logging Operation in Northern Maine," 9.

54 Harry Dyer (b. 1896), interviewed by Jeanne Milton, 1970, p. 581045, transcript (LLC) (MFC); Prescott and Rendall, "Lumbering in the Dead River Region," 22; John Sharpe (b. 1881), interviewed by Lillian Shirley, 1970, p. 61, transcript (LLC) (MFC).

55 "Inventory of personal property sold by McCoy & Son to Emporium Lumber Co." (no date), Emporium Forest Company Records, Box 2, Adirondack Museum.

56 Benjamin Cole interviewed by Larry Gallant, 1972, transcript, p. 720022 (LLC) (MFC); John Sharpe (b. 1881), interviewed by Lillian Shirley, 1970, p. 62, transcript (LLC) (MFC); Stewart Edward White, *The Blazed Trail* (New York: McClure, [1902] 1907), 46.

57 Asa Flagg (b. 1898), interviewed by Rhoda Mitchell, 1970, p. 575104, transcript (LLC) (MFC); Rogers, "Lumbering in Northern Maine," 20.

58 Quote from Wyckoff, *The Workers . . . the East*, 38; Higbie, *Indispensable Outcasts*, 119.

59 Matthew Warner Osborn, *Rum Maniacs: Alcoholic Insanity in the Early American Republic* (Chicago: The University of Chicago Press, 2014); W. J. Rorabaugh, *The Alcoholic Republic, an American Tradition* (New York: Oxford University Press, 1979),

xi, 11, 141; John S. Springer, *Forest Life and Forest Trees* (New York: Harper, 1856), 151–152; Graeme Wynn, "'Deplorably Dark and Demoralized Lumberers'? Rhetoric and Reality in Early Nineteenth-Century New Brunswick," *Forest & Conservation History* 24, no. 4 (1980): 168–187; Bradwin, *The Bunkhouse Man*, 177; Paul E. Johnson, *A Shopkeeper's Millennium: Society and Revivals in Rochester, New York, 1815–1837* (New York: Hill and Wang, 2004).

60 Rogers, "Lumbering in Northern Maine," 29; John G. Franzen, *The Archaeology of the Logging Industry* (Gainesville: University Press of Florida, 2020), 128–131; Hilton, *Rough Pulpwood*, 121–122.

61 Quoted in Craig, *Backwoods Consumers*, 207; Carlisle and Shatney, "Report on a Logging Operation in Northern Maine," 9; Rogers, "Lumbering in Northern Maine," 20; Miller, Poole, and Sweetser, "A Lumbering Report of Work on Squaw Mountain Township," 12; Andrew Chase (b. 1888), interviewed by Linda Edgerly, 1971, p. 697070, transcript (LLC) (MFC); Andrew Chase (b. 1888), interviewed by Linda Edgerly, 1971, p. 697069, transcript (LLC) (MFC).

62 Hilton, *Rough Pulpwood*, 121.

63 Pike, *Tall Trees, Tough Men*, 121–122; "The French Canadians," *All the Year Round* 39, no. 928 (1886): 127; Lady Jephson, *A Canadian Scrap-Book* (London: M. Russell, 1897), 16; Craig, *Backwoods Consumers*, 144; John Irvine Little, *Crofters and Habitants: Settler Society, Economy, and Culture in a Québec Township, 1848–1881* (Montreal: McGill-Queen's University Press, 1991), 140–141, 154; Pike, *Tall Trees, Tough Men*, 94; Bradwin, *The Bunkhouse Man*, 63; Boultbee, Leslie, and Matthews, " Report of Logging Operation on Limits of the Canoe Lake Lumber Co.," 23.

64 Hilton, *Rough Pulpwood*, 121–122.

65 Alvan F. Sanborn, "The Future of Rural New England," *Atlantic Monthly* 79 (1897): 477–498.

66 Erroll "John" Haley (b. 1898), interviewed by Stephen Richard, 1980, transcript, p. 1380060 (LLC) (MFC); Harvey A. Levenstein, *Revolution at the Table: The Transformation of the American Diet* (New York: Oxford University Press, 1988), 22; Richard Osborn Cummings, *The American and His Food: A History of Food Habits in the United States* (Chicago: The University of Chicago Press, 1941), 169; Martin Bruegel, *Farm, Shop, Landing: The Rise of a Market Society in the Hudson Valley, 1780–1860* (Durham, NC: Duke University Press, 2002), 180–181; Samuel Martínez, *Decency and Excess: Global Aspirations and Material Deprivation on a Caribbean Sugar Plantation* (Boulder, CO: Paradigm, 2007), 208.

67 Pike, *Tall Trees, Tough Men*, 122, 146; Hilton, *Rough Pulpwood*, 121–122; Smith and Locke, "A Study of the Lumber Industry of Northern Maine," 11; Prescott and Rendall, "Lumbering in the Dead River Region," 22; Miller, Poole, and Sweetser, "A Lumbering Report of Work on Squaw Mountain Township," 12; Rogers, "Lumbering in Northern Maine," 19; Thurston Madison Adams, *Prices Paid by Vermont Farmers for Goods and Services and Received by Them for Farm Products, 1790–1940; Wages of Vermont Farm Labor, 1780–1940* (Burlington, VT: Vermont Agricultural Experiment Station, 1944), 27; Bradwin, *The Bunkhouse Man*, 70–71, 190–191.

68 "The Lincoln and Idella Toothaker Letters, 1890–1892," Lincoln to Ida, January 31, 1892.

69 John Clifton Elder, "Peonage in Maine" (A Manuscript Report sent to the Attorney General of the United States), National Archives, Record Group #60, Department of Justice file #50-34-0, 13–21, p. 4; State of Maine, "Third Biennial Report of the Department of Labor and Industry State of Maine" (Waterville, ME: Sentinel Publishing, 1917), 10.

70 Miller, Poole, and Sweetser, "A Lumbering Report of Work on Squaw Mountain Township," 17; Russell Nutting (b. 1887), interviews by Lynn MacFarland, 1971,

transcript, p. 626083 (LLC) (MFC); Radforth "The Shantymen," 247; Eckstorm and Smyth, *Minstrelsy of Maine*, 111–112; Higbie, *Indispensable Outcasts*, 52–53.

71 Elder, "Peonage in Maine," 5–7, 10, 15, 16–17, 21; "Does Peonage Exist in the Maine Lumber Camps?," *Paper Trade Journal* (November, 1915), p. 16; Steinfeld, *Coercion, Contract, and Free Labor*, 279; John F. Flanagan, "Industrial Conditions in the Maine Woods," *First Biennial Report of the Department of Labor and Industry* (Waterville, ME: Sentinel Publishing, 1912), 225; "May Repel Law Protecting Lumbermen," *Paper: A Weekly Technical Journal for Paper and Pulp Mills*, vol. 20 (New York: Paper, Inc., 1910); Commons, *Races and Immigrants in America*, 138–139; Maine, "Third Biennial Report of the Department of Labor and Industry State of Maine," 10–11. Also see, Jason L. Newton, "'These French Canadian of the Woods are Half-Wild Folk': Wilderness, Whiteness, and Work in North America, 1840–1955," *Labour/Le Travail* 77, no. 1 (2016): 145–146; Charles Andrew Scontras, *Organized Labor in Maine: Twentieth Century Origins* (Bureau of Labor Education of the Continuing Education Division, University of Maine, 1985), 97.

72 Benjamin Cole interviewed by Larry Gallant, 1972, transcript, p. 720011 (LLC) (MFC); Leo Poirier (b. 1891), interviews by Bobbie Violette, 1974, transcript, p. 800012 (LLC) (MFC); Radforth "The Shantymen," 250–251; John Sharpe (b. 1881), interviewed by Lillian Shirley, 1970, p. 6, transcript (LLC) (MFC); Asa Flagg (b. 1898), interviewed by Rhoda Mitchell, 1970, p. 575104, transcript (LLC) (MFC); Craig, *Backwoods Consumers*, 130; Bradwin, *The Bunkhouse Man*, 183.

73 John Sharpe (b. 1881), interviewed by Lillian Shirley, 1970, p. 47, transcript (LLC) (MFC).

74 Prescott and Rendall, "Lumbering in the Dead River Region," 29.

75 Erroll "John" Haley (b. 1898), interviewed by Stephen Richard, 1980, transcript, p. 1384033 (LLC) (MFC); Bradwin, *The Bunkhouse Man*, 71; Asa Flagg (b. 1898), interviewed by Rhoda Mitchell, 1970, p. 575104, transcript (LLC) (MFC); 32 US Congress, Importation of Canadian Bonded Labor, 84th Congress, 1st Session, 1955, Hearings before the Subcommittee on Labor of the Committee on Labor and Public Welfare on S. Res. 98, A Resolution to Authorize a Study of the Policy and Practice of the United States with Respect to Permitting Bonded Laborers from Canada to Enter and Work in the United States, 32.

76 Scontras, "Labor Day 2007: Pausing to Reflect on Images of Maine Labor One Hundred Years Ago," 7.

77 Félix Albert, *Immigrant Odyssey: A French Canadian Habitant in New England—A Bilingual Edition of Histoire D'un Enfant Pauvre* (Orono: University of Maine Press, 1991), 68–69, 95–97; Bradwin, *The Bunkhouse Man*, 126; Richard W. Judd and Patricia A. Judd, *Aroostook: A Century of Logging in Northern Maine* (Orono: University of Maine Press, 1988), 192; Higbie, *Indispensable Outcasts*, 53–54.

78 Charles Scontras, *Labor in Maine: Building the Arsenal of Democracy and Resisting Reaction at Home, 1939–1952* (Maine Bureau of Labor Education, 2006), 324.

79 Judd and Judd, *Aroostook*, 61; Craig, *Backwoods Consumers*, 87, 119, 123–126, 130.

80 Asa Flagg (b. 1898), interviewed by Rhoda Mitchell, 1970, p. 5750013, 57500134, transcript (LLC) (MFC). Also see Rogers, "Lumbering in Northern Maine," 50; Bradwin, *The Bunkhouse Man*, 183.

81 Harry Dyer (b. 1896), interviewed by Jeanne Milton, 1970, p. 581014, transcript (LLC) (MFC); also see Peck, *Reinventing Free Labor*, 71.

82 Albert, *Immigrant Odyssey*, 70–72.

83 William P. Dillingham et al., Abstracts of *Reports of the Immigration Commission: With Conclusions and Recommendations and Views of the Minority* (Washington, DC: Government Printing Office, 1911), 447–448.

84 Steinfeld, *Coercion, Contract, and Free Labor*, 318–320; William E. Forbath, *Law and the Shaping of the American Labor Movement* (Cambridge, MA: Harvard University Press, 1991), 154–155.

85 Harry Dyer (b. 1896), interviewed by Jeanne Milton, 1970, p. 568029, transcript (LLC) (MFC); Bradwin, *The Bunkhouse Man*, 163. On bosses also see Peck, *Reinventing Free Labor*, 148; Miller, Poole, and Sweetser, "A Lumbering Report of Work on Squaw Mountain Township," 14; Arnold Hall (b. 1892), interviewed by William Bonsall, 1970, transcript, p. 58042 (LLC) (MFC); Russell Nutting (b.1887), interviews by Lynn MacFarland, 1971, transcript, p. 626110 (LLC) (MFC); Harry Dyer (b. 1896), interviewed by Jeanne Milton, 1970, p. 581021, 581096, transcript (LLC) (MFC); Pike, *Tall Trees, Tough Men*, 84; Prescott and Rendall, "Lumbering in the Dead River Region," 29; Frank Carey (b. 1886), interviewed by Rita Swidrowski, 1970, p. 6980106, transcript (LLC) (MFC); Carroll C. Noyes interviewed by Lynn MacFarland, 1972, transcript, p. 577077 (LLC) (MFC).

86 Wyckoff, *The Workers . . . the East*, 236.

87 Bradwin, *The Bunkhouse Man*, 202–203; Osborn, *The Paper Plantation*; Michael G. Hillard, *Shredding Paper: The Rise and Fall of Maine's Mighty Paper Industry* (Ithaca, NY: ILR Press, 2020), 144–147.

88 Hayner, "Taming the Lumberjack," 217, 219, 224, 225.

89 Stewart H. Holbrook, *Yankee Loggers: A Recollection of Woodsmen, Cooks, and River Drivers* (New York: International Paper Co., 1961), 11; "Here and There in Northern New York," *Plattsburgh Republican*, April 23, 1947.

90 Stewart Edward White, *The Riverman* (New York: The McClure Company, 1908), 4.

91 Averill, *Ridge Runner*, 93; Walls, "The Making of the American Logger," 145; Pike, *Tall Trees, Tough Men*, 19.

92 Eckstorm, *The Penobscot Man*, 156–158.

93 Adams, *Prices Paid by Vermont Farmers*, 37; Benjamin Cole interviewed by Larry Gallant, 1972, transcript, p. 720022 (LLC) (MFC); Bird, *Calked Shoes*, 3–4, 116; William R. Marleau, *Big Moose Station* (New York: Marleau Family Press, 1986), 290.

94 Marleau, *Big Moose Station*, 331–332.

95 Elliott J. Gorn, "Gouge and Bite, Pull Hair and Scratch": The Social Significance of Fighting in the Southern Backcountry," *The American Historical Review* 90, no. 1 (February 1985): 21–22; For other accounts of poxing see Averill, *Ridge Runner*, 93–94; and Pike, *Tall Trees, Tough Men*; Walls, "The Making of the American Logger," 243–244; Radforth, "The Shantymen," 255–256; "Turner Falls and Vicinity," *Turner Falls Reporter*, August 13, 1883; "Distressing Rudeness," *Turner Falls Reporter*, September 22, 1897; "Turner Falls and Vicinity," *Turner Falls Reporter*, September 3, 1879; "Canton," *The Adirondack News*, March 28, 1903.

96 Nutting (b. 1887), interviews by Lynn MacFarland, 1971, transcript, p. 626034, 626091 (LLC) (MFC); Asa Flagg (b. 1898), interviewed by Rhoda Mitchell, 1970, p. 575079, transcript (LLC) (MFC).

97 Benjamin Cole interviewed by Larry Gallant, 1972, transcript, p. 720011 (LLC) (MFC); Miller, Poole, and Sweetser, "A Lumbering Report of Work on Squaw Mountain Township," 15, 20; Frank Carey (b. 1886), interviewed by Rita Swidrowski, 1970, p. 698044, transcript (LLC) (MFC); Flanagan, "Industrial Conditions in the Maine Woods," 216.

98 Stanley L. Engerman, Claudia Dale Goldin, and National Bureau of Economic Research, *Seasonality in Nineteenth Century Labor Markets* (Cambridge, MA: National Bureau of Economic Research, 1991), http://proxy.library.cornell.edu/login?url=http://www.nber.org/papers/h0020.

99 Lyman Sutton (1867–1956), interviewed by John Larson, 1954, transcript, p. 10 (FHS) (OHIC); Boultbee, Leslie, and Matthews, "Report of Logging Operation on

Limits of the Canoe Lake Lumber Co.," 4; Frank Carey (b. 1886), interviewed by Rita Swidrowski, 1970, p. 698059–61, transcript (LLC) (MFC); Bradwin, *The Bunkhouse Man*, 161; Asa Flagg (b. 1898), interviewed by Rhoda Mitchell, 1970, p. 575066, transcript (LLC) (MFC).

100 Higbie, *Indispensable Outcasts*, 48–49.

101 Introduction, "Ida Toothaker to Lincoln Toothaker, November 19, 1891"; "Lincoln Toothaker to Ida Toothaker, January 12, 1892 Rangeley, Maine"; "The Lincoln and Idella Toothaker Letters, 1890–1892," Property of Becky Ellis Martineau and the Rangeley Lakes Region Logging Museum, Rangeley, Maine, http://rlrlm.org; Averill, *Ridge Runner*, 100–112. Also see, Asa Flagg (b. 1898), interviewed by Rhoda Mitchell, 1970, p. 575106, 575066, transcript (LLC) (MFC).

102 Harry Dyer (b. 1896), interviewed by Jeanne Milton, 1970, p. 581069, transcript (LLC) (MFC). Also see Frederick Burke (b. 1915), interviewed by Norma Coates, 1971, transcript, p. 702089 (LLC) (MFC); Asa Flagg (b. 1898), interviewed by Rhoda Mitchell, 1970, p. 575042, transcript (LLC) (MFC).

103 Judith Fingard, "The Winter's Tale: The Seasonal Contours of Pre-industrial Poverty in British North America, 1815–1860," *Historical Papers/Communications Historiques* 9, no. 1 (1974): 86; Rorabaugh, *The Alcoholic Republic*, 141–142; Wynn, "'Deplorably Dark and Demoralized Lumberers,'" 169; Springer, *Forest Life and Forest Trees*, 149–150; Theodore Steinberg, *Down to Earth Nature's Role in American History* (Oxford: Oxford University Press, 2002), 58; Walls, "The Making of the American Logger," 252; Anthony Rotundo, *American Manhood* (New York: Basic Books, 1993), 170.

104 Koren and Farnam, *Economic Aspects of The Liquor Problem*, 27; Rorabaugh, *The Alcoholic Republic*, 128–132, 159–160; Bruegel, *Farm, Shop, Landing*, 161; Bradwin, *The Bunkhouse Man*, 77–78, 89.

105 "Three Arrested for Public Intoxication," *Tupper Lake Free Press*, October 23, 1941; "Local News Items," *Adirondack News*, August 5, 1911; W. C. Sykes to G. W. West, not dated; Emporium Forest Company Records Box 15, Adirondack Museum; Susan McVetty, "Interviews about Dan Murray," 1970, transcript, p. 578005 (LLC) (MFC); *Plattsburgh Republican*, March 26, 1881, p. 1; "Local Brevities," *Watertown Re-Union*, October 5, 1904, p. 8; *The Malone Farmer*, April 14, 1915, p. 7; "A Murderer's Rambles," *Norwood News*, September 25, 1888, p. 1; "Adirondack Lumberjack Arrested in Glens Falls," *Essex County Republican*, September 24, 1920, p. 8,"; "In Justice Court," *Courier and Freeman*, October 27, 1915, p. 2; "In Justice Court," *Courier and Freeman*, November 26, 1913, p. 1; "Local Brevities," *Watertown Re-union*, October 16, 1901, p. 6; "Local Department," *The Malone Farmer*, February 6, 1907, p. 5.

106 Averill, *Ridge Runner*, 100–112.

107 Wyckoff, *The Workers . . . the East*, 217; Bradwin, *The Bunkhouse Man*, 124, 182–183.

108 Asa Flagg (b. 1898), interviewed by Rhoda Mitchell, 1970, p. 578013, transcript (LLC) (MFC); Walls, "The Making of the American Logger," 247, 255; Wyckoff, *The Workers . . . the East*, 247; Margot Canaday, *The Straight State: Sexuality and Citizenship in Twentieth-Century America* (Princeton, NJ: Princeton University Press, 2009), 123–124.

109 Hayner, "Taming the Lumberjack," 219.

110 Prescott and Rendall, "Lumbering in the Dead River Region," 68; *Potsdam Junction Commercial Advertiser*, March 13, 1895, p. 3. Also see Bradwin, *The Bunkhouse Man*, 159.

111 "Turner Falls and Vicinity," *Turner Falls Reporter*, July 27, 1887; "Turner Falls and Vicinity," *Turner Falls Reporter*, September 3, 1879. Also see Benjamin Cole

interviewed by Larry Gallant, 1972, transcript, p. 720049–50 (LLC) (MFC); Bird, *Calked Shoes*, 39.

112 Ernest Kennedy (b. 1889), interviewed by Lillian Shirley, 1970, p. 23, transcript (LLC) (MFC); Martínez, *Decency and Excess*, 140.

113 Bradwin, *The Bunkhouse Man*, 137. Also see, Walls, "The Making of the American Logger," 251–252; Frederick Burke (b. 1915), interviewed by Norma Coates, 1971, transcript, p. 702089–26 (LLC) (MFC).

114 Quoted in Walls, "The Making of the American Logger," 249; Trudy Irene Scee, *Rogues, Rascals, and Other Villainous Mainers* (Camden, ME: Down East Books, 2014), 88–90; Radforth, "The Shantymen," 247–248.

115 "An Oasis Apparent," *Bangor Daily Commercial*, March 27, 1908, 5; "Joy Trip Strewn with Greenbacks," *Bangor Daily News*, June 11, 1910. Also see, Bradwin, *The Bunkhouse Man*, 182, 137; Frederick Burke (b. 1915), interviewed by Norma Coates, 1971, transcript, p. 702026 (LLC) (MFC).

116 Radforth, "The Shantymen" 235; also see, Higbie, *Indispensable Outcasts*, 14–15.

117 Quoted in Wyckoff, *The Workers . . . the East*, 254; Susanna Barrows and Robin Room, *Drinking: Behavior and Belief in Modern History* (Berkeley: University of California Press, 1991), 12; Paul Michel Taillon, "'What We Want Is Good, Sober Men:' Masculinity, Respectability, and Temperance in The Railroad Brotherhoods, c. 1870–1910." *Journal of Social History* 36, no. 2 (2002): 319–338.

118 Frederick Burke (b. 1915), interviewed by Norma Coates, 1971, transcript, p. 702042, 702088 (LLC) (MFC); Andrew Chase (b. 1888), interviewed by Linda Edgerly, 1971, p. 697032, transcript (LLC) (MFC); George Frederick Eitel (b. 1880), 1950s (?), transcript, p. 4 (FHS) (OHIC).

119 Miller, Poole, and Sweetser, "A Lumbering Report of Work on Squaw Mountain Township," 17; Bradwin, *The Bunkhouse Man*, 55; Asa Flagg (b. 1898), interviewed by Rhoda Mitchell, 1970, p. 575097, transcript (LLC) (MFC); Pike, *Tall Trees, Tough Men*, 75; Radforth, "The Shantymen," 203; Hutt, "An Adirondack Lumberjack," 15–17.

120 Newton, "'These French Canadian of the Woods are Half-Wild Folk,'" 145; Elder, "Peonage in Maine," 20; Eckstorm and Smyth, *Minstrelsy of Maine*, 142–143.

121 Frederick Burke (b. 1915), interviewed by Norma Coates, 1971, transcript, p. 702011, 702026, 702041–42 (LLC) (MFC); Wyckoff, *The Workers . . . the East*, 181; Frank Carey (b. 1886), interviewed by Rita Swidrowski, 1970, p. 6980109, transcript (LLC) (MFC).

122 Kostas Gounis, "The Manufacture of Dependency: Shelterization Revisited," *New England Journal of Public Policy* 8, no. 1 (1992): 685–692.

123 Frederick Burke (b. 1915), interviewed by Norma Coates, 1971, transcript, p. 702041–42 (LLC) (MFC).

124 Miller, Poole, and Sweetser, "A Lumbering Report of Work on Squaw Mountain Township," 16; Radforth, "The Shantymen," 232; Harry Dyer (b. 1896), interviewed by Jeanne Milton, 1970, p. 581069, transcript (LLC) (MFC); Rogers, "Lumbering in Northern Maine," 29; Wyckoff, *The Workers . . . the East*, 255.

125 Glickman, *A Living Wage*, 80.

126 Frederick Burke (b. 1915), interviewed by Norma Coates, 1971, transcript, p. 702041–42 (LLC) (MFC); also see, Peck, *Reinventing Free Labor*, 66–67; Elder, "Peonage in Maine," 2; Gounis, "The Manufacture of Dependency," 689.

127 US Congress, Importation of Canadian Bonded Labor, 17–18.

128 The Dechene Family (Adirondack lumbering family) in communication with the author, September 2010; Flanagan, "Industrial Conditions in the Maine Woods," 223; also see, John Field, *Working Men's Bodies: Work Camps in Britain, 1880–1940*

(Manchester, UK: Manchester University Press, 2013), 61–64; Barrows and Room, *Drinking*, 275; Bradwin, *The Bunkhouse Man*, 54, 66–67, 75; Frederick Burke (b. 1915), interviewed by Norma Coates 1971, transcript, p. 702042 (LLC) (MFC).

129 Eckstorm and Smyth, *Minstrelsy of Maine*, vii.

130 Eckstorm and Smyth, *Minstrelsy of Maine*, 18; 118–119.

131 Eckstorm and Smyth, *Minstrelsy of Maine*, 140–144; 111–113.

132 Eckstorm and Smyth, *Minstrelsy of Maine*, 140–144.

133 Eckstorm and Smyth, *Minstrelsy of Maine*, 19, 97, 140–144; Other songs that mention similar cycles are "Shanty Boy and the Farmer's Son," 27–28; "The Lumberman's Life," 34–35; "The Logger's Boast," 41–43; "The River-Driver," 61; "Mauling Live Oak," 64–67; "Katahdin Green," 76; "The Lumberman in Town," 96; "The Winter of Seventy-Three," 114–118; "When the Harvest Days Were Ended," 171–172; "The Lumberjack's Exit," 172–174. Also see Pike, *Tall Trees, Tough Men*, "The Ballad of Roaring Bert," 152–153; "When the Drive Comes Down," 160.

134 "From the Files," *Tupper Lake Free Press*, January 29, 1948, p. 3, image 3; "Kill Himself as Climax to Spree, Lumberjack Slits Throat, Dying Instantly," *The Ogdensburg Journal*, January 23, 1914, p. 2, image 2; "Local All Sorts," *The Adirondack News*, October 26, 1895, p. 5, image 5; "Russian Commits Suicide in Springfield VT, Barn," *Essex County Republican*, December 25, 1914, p. 1, image 1; "Miscellaneous Items," *The Adirondack News*, August 15, 1908, p. 3, image 3; "Local Department," *The Malone Farmer*, February 6, 1907, p. 5, image 5; "Suicide in Lumber Camp," *Norwood News*, January 2, 1906, p. 8, image 8; "Lumberman Kills Self at Tupper Lake," *The Adirondack Record*, July 12, 1918, p. 1, image 1; "Horrible Find in the Woods," *Essex County Republican*, July 3, 1925, p. 1, image 1; "Elizabeth Town Authorities Puzzled Over Dead Man's Identity," *The Republican Journal*, February 12, 1924, p. 1, image 1; "Here, There and Everywhere," *Sullivan County Record*, March 21, 1912, p. 1, image 1; "Out of Town Notes: Glen's Fall," *The Troy Weekly Times*, December 6, 1877, p. 3, image 3; "Neighboring Counties: Washington," *The Plattsburgh Sentinel*, April 13, 1883, p. 8, image 8; "Lumberjack a Suicide," *Courier and Freeman*, March 15, 1922, p. 1, image 1; "Bert Clintsman of Cranberry Lake a Suicide," *Commercial Advertiser*, November 12, 1929, p. 1, image 1; *The Lake Placid News*, March 31, 1950, p. 3, image 3; "Commits Suicide," *The Lake Placid News*, March 31, 1950, p. 3, image 3; "Takes Own Life James Garno Shoots Himself at Lumber Camp," *Courier and Freeman*, January 11, 1928, p. 7, image 7.

135 Centers for Disease Control, Suicides Due to Alcohol and/or Drug Overdose: A Data Brief from the National Violent Death Reporting System (2011), accessed April 28, 2017, https://web.archive.org/web/20150701200635, http://www.cdc.gov:80/violenceprevention/pdf/nvdrs_data_brief-a.pdf; I. Rossow, "Alcohol and Suicide—Beyond the Link at the Individual Level," *Addiction*, 91 no. 10 (1996): 1413–1416; Anne Case and Angus Deaton, *Deaths of Despair and the Future of Capitalism* (Princeton, NJ: Princeton University Press, 2020), 95.

136 Mark Lawrence Schrad, *Smashing the Liquor Machine: A Global History of Prohibition* (Oxford University Press, 2021); Barrows and Robin Room, *Drinking*, 14; Peter Way, *Common Labour: Workers and the Digging of North American Canals, 1780–1860* (Cambridge: Cambridge University Press, 1993), 182–184, 186; Johnson, *A Shopkeeper's Millennium*.

137 Frederick Burke (b. 1915), interviewed by Norma Coates, 1971, transcript, p. 702026 (LLC) (MFC); Craig, *Backwoods Consumers*, 215–216; Martínez, *Decency and Excess*, 130.

138 Wyckoff, *The Workers . . . the East*, 213–214, 220. "The Lincoln and Idella Toothaker Letters, 1890–1892," Lincoln to Ida, March 22, 1891. Also see Rorabaugh, *The Alcoholic Republic*, 149–155.

139 Martínez, *Decency and Excess*, 14–15, 48; Harry Dyer (b. 1896), interviewed by Jeanne Milton, 1970, p. 56831, transcript (LLC) (MFC).

140 Lyman Sutton (1867–1956), interviewed by John Larson, 1954, transcript, p. 16 (FHS) (OHIC); Bradwin, *The Bunkhouse Man*, 79; Harry Dyer (b. 1896), interviewed by Jeanne Milton, 1970, p. 581015, 581065–66, transcript (LLC) (MFC); Wyckoff, *The Workers . . . the East*, 180, 224.

141 Bradwin, *The Bunkhouse Man*, 180; Prescott and Rendall, "Lumbering in the Dead River Region," 67; Wyckoff, *The Workers . . . the East*, 255; Lyman Sutton (1867–1956), interviewed by John Larson, 1954, transcript, p. 19 (FHS) (OHIC).

142 Koren, *Alcohol and Society*, 103–104.

143 Kenneth Carter, *Buzz! Inside the Minds of Thrill-Seekers, Daredevils, and Adrenaline Junkies* (Cambridge: Cambridge University Press, 2019), 5.

144 Wyckoff, *The Workers . . . the East*, 59; Rorabaugh, *The Alcoholic Republic*, 173; Eckstorm, *The Penobscot Man*, 204; Pike, *Tall Trees, Tough Men*, 137; Bradwin, *The Bunkhouse Man*, 207; Carter, *Buzz!*, 59–66; Katherine Leonard Turner, *How the Other Half Ate: A History of Working-Class Meals at the Turn of the Century*, California Studies in Food and Culture (Berkeley: University of California Press, 2014).

145 Martínez, *Decency and Excess*, 162; Alan Bloom, "The Floating Population: Homelessness in Early Chicago, 1833–1871" (PhD diss., Duke University, 2001), 75.

146 Carter, *Buzz!*, 144–145; Erin Fink, "The Taste of Danger: Taste Perception and Food Consumption Interact to Predict the Acquired Capability for Suicide" (PhD diss., Florida State University, 2012); Case and Deaton, *Deaths of Despair*, 96.

147 Johann Hari, *Chasing the Scream: The First and Last Days of the War on Drugs* (New York: Bloomsbury, 2015), 172–175, 179–180; Carl L. Hart, "As with Other Problems, Class Affects Addiction," *New York Times*, March 10, 2014, accessed July 6, 2015, http://www.nytimes.com/roomfordebate/2014/02/10/what-is-addiction/as-with-other-problems-class-affects-addiction; Carl L. Hart, "Deal With the Pain That Leads to the Drug Problem," *New York Times*, March 17, 2014, accessed July 6, 2015, http://www.nytimes.com/roomfordebate/2014/03/17/lowering-the-deadly-cost-of-drug-abuse/deal-with-the-pain-that-leads-to-the-drug-problem.

148 Bruce Dorsey, *Reforming Workers and Women: Gender in the Antebellum City* (Ithaca, NY: Cornell University Press, 2002), 105; Sandage, *Born Losers*, 6–9; Glickman, *A Living Wage*, 38; Bradwin, *The Bunkhouse Man*, 120, 126.

149 White, *The Blazed Trail*, 123–124.

150 Rorabaugh, *The Alcoholic Republic*, 145–146, 161, 176, 244–245.

151 Steinfeld, *Coercion, Contract, and Free Labor*, 284, 313–315; Bloom, "The Floating Population: Homelessness in Early Chicago, 1833–1871," 73; Wyckoff, *The Workers . . . The East*, 181, 267.

152 Case and Deaton, *Deaths of Despair*, 139, 163, 220.

153 Case and Deaton, *Deaths of Despair*, 101.

154 Matt Wray, Cynthia Colen, and Bernice Pescosolido. "The Sociology of Suicide," *Annual Review of Sociology* 37 (2011): 509; Francis Shor, "Masculine Power and Virile Syndicalism: A Gendered Analysis of the IWW in Australia, 1914–1917," *Labour History* 63 (1992): 83–99.

155 Prescott and Rendall, "Lumbering in the Dead River Region," 68.

156 Pike, *Tall Trees, Tough Men*, 61.

157 Walls, "The Making of the American Logger," 61–62, 351; "lumber, n.1," OED Online, September 2021, Oxford University Press, https://www.oed.com/; Jean-Baptiste Michel, Yuan Kui Shen, Aviva Presser Aiden, Adrian Veres, Matthew K. Gray, William Brockman, The Google Books Team, Joseph P. Pickett, Dale Hoiberg, Dan Clancy, Peter Norvig, Jon Orwant, Steven Pinker, Martin A. Nowak, and Erez Lieberman Aiden, "Quantitative Analysis of Culture Using Millions of Digitized

Books. Science," published online ahead of print (2010); Yuri Lin, Jean-Baptiste Michel, Erez Lieberman Aiden, Jon Orwant, William Brockman, and Slav Petrov, "Syntactic Annotations for the Google Books Ngram Corpus," *Proceedings of the 50th Annual Meeting of the Association for Computational Linguistics*, vol. 2: *Demo Papers* (2012).

158 "May Repel Law Protecting Lumbermen," *Paper: A Weekly Technical Journal for Paper and Pulp Mills*, vol. 20 (New York: Paper, Inc., 1910); Eckstorm and Smyth, *Minstrelsy of Maine*, 174; Radforth, "The Shantymen," 204; Benton MacKaye; "Some Social Aspects of Forest Management, Journal of Forestry," 16, no. 2 (1918): 210; Hayner, "Taming the Lumberjack," 217–225.

7. Half-Wild Folk

1 William Robinson Brown, *Our Forest Heritage: A History of Forestry and Recreation in New Hampshire* (Concord: New Hampshire Historical Society, 1958), 187, 241, 317; "Big Business," *The Brown Bulletin* 3, no. 6 (Jan. 1955): 4–6, https://berlinnhhistoricalsociety.org/wp-content/uploads/2011/06/The_Brown_Bulletin_V3_No6_Feb_1955; James Elliott Defebaugh, *History of the Lumber Industry of America* (Chicago: American Lumberman, 1906), 70.

2 Edward H. Elwell, *Aroostook: With Some Account of the Excursions Thither of the Editors of Maine, in the Years 1858 and 1878, and of the Colony of Swedes, Settled in the Town of New Sweden* (Portland, ME: Transcript Print, 1878), 37.

3 "First Annual Conference of the Woods Department [Brown Company]," Berlin and Coös County Historical Society (1903), 47, 43.

4 Edmund W. Bradwin, *The Bunkhouse Man: A Study of Work and Pay in the Camps of Canada, 1903–1914* (Toronto: University of Toronto Press, [1928] 1972), 95–96.

5 Michael Stamm, *Dead Tree Media: Manufacturing the Newspaper in Twentieth-Century North America* (Baltimore: Johns Hopkins University Press, 2018), 179.

6 Stephen J. Hornsby, Richard William Judd, and Michael J. Hermann, *Historical Atlas of Maine* (Orono: University of Maine Press, 2015), plate 42; Yves Roby, "The Economic Evolution of Québec and the Emigrant (1850–1929)," in *Steeples and Smokestacks: A Collection of Essays on the Franco-American Experience in New England*, ed. Claire Quintal (Worcester, MA: Assumption College, Institut Francais, 1996), 7; Marcus Lee Hansen and John Bartlet Brebner, *The Mingling of the Canadian and American Peoples*, vol. 1 (New Haven, CT: Yale University Press, 1940), 180–181; Gerard J. Brault, *The French Canadian Heritage in New England* (Hanover, NH: University Press of New England, 1986), 53.

7 United States Senate, *Report of the Select Committee on Immigration and Naturalization: And Testimony Taken by the Committee on Immigration of the Senate and the Select Committee on Immigration and Naturalization of the House of Representatives Under Concurrent Resolution of March 12, 1890* (Washington, DC: Government Printing Office, 1891), 324.

8 Ralph Dominic Vicero, "Immigration of French Canadians to New England, 1840–1900: A Geographic Analysis" (PhD diss., University of Wisconsin—Madison, 1968), 347.

9 Charles A. Scontras, *Two Decades of Organized Labor and Labor Politics in Maine, 1880–1900* (Orono, ME: Bureau of Labor Education of the Continuing Education Division, University of Maine, 1969), 21–22.

10 Ferris Meigs, "The Santa Clara Lumber Company vol. I," Santa Clara Collection, Adirondack Museum, New York, typeset 1941, 113–114.

11 Fred Alliston Gilbert Papers, "F. A. Gilbert to G. Schenck, December 20, 1925," box 7, Correspondence, 1924–1925 Special Collections, Raymond H. Fogler

Library, University of Maine; Meigs, "The Santa Clara Lumber Company," 113–114; William F. Fox, *A History of the Lumber Industry in the State of New York* (Washington, DC: US Department of Agriculture, Bureau of Forestry, 1902); John F. Flanagan, "Industrial Conditions in the Maine Woods," *First Biennial Report of the Department of Labor and Industry* (Waterville, ME: Sentinel Publishing Company, 1912), 219, 223–226.

12 Ashley Johnson Bavery, *Bootlegged Aliens: Immigration Politics on America's Northern Border* (Philadelphia: University of Pennsylvania Press, 2020), 33.

13 Ashley Johnson Bavery, "Militarizing the Northern Border: State Violence and the Formation of the US Border Patrol," *The Journal of American History* 109, no. 2 (2022), https://doi.org/10.1093/jahist/jaac239, 369.

14 W. C. Sykes to C. H. Sisson, May 1, 1919; C. H. Sisson to W. C. Sykes, May 2, 1919; W. C. Sykes to C. H. Sisson, May 3, 1919, box 13; E. L. Stables to Mr. Sykes, Mr. Caflish and Mr. Turner, November 7, 1912, box 5, Emporium Forest Company Records, AdkM.

15 Bill Parenteau, "Bonded Labor: Canadian Woods Workers in the Maine Pulpwood Industry, 1940–55," *Forest & Conservation History* 37, no. 3 (1993): 113–115; US Congress, Importation of Canadian Bonded Labor, 84th Congress, 1st Session, 1955, Hearings before the Subcommittee on Labor of the Committee on Labor and Public Welfare on S. Res. 98, A Resolution to Authorize a Study of the Policy and Practice of the United States with Respect to Permitting Bonded Laborers from Canada to Enter and Work in the United States, 155, 56; William P. Dillingham et al., *Abstracts of Reports of the Immigration Commission: With Conclusions and Recommendations and Views of the Minority* (Washington, DC: Government Printing Office, 1911), 447–448.

16 Arnold Hall (b. 1892), interview by William Bonsall, 1970, p. 580038, transcript (LLC) (MFC); Flanagan, "Industrial Conditions in the Maine Woods," 220; "Among the Woodcutters," *Chateaugay Record*, May 11, 1883; also see Herman Feldman and Bruno Lasker, *Racial Factors in American Industry* (New York: Harper & Brothers, 1931), 156–159.

17 Quote from Daylanne K. English, *Unnatural Selections: Eugenics in American Modernism and the Harlem Renaissance* (Chapel Hill: University of North Carolina Press, 2004), 1, 33.

18 Ann G. Winfield, *Eugenics and Education in America: Institutionalized Racism and the Implications of History, Ideology, and Memory* (New York: Peter Lang, 2007), 70.

19 James C. Mohr, "Academic Turmoil and Public Opinion: The Ross Case at Stanford," *Pacific Historical Review* 39, no. 1 (1970): 39–61.

20 Edward Alsworth Ross, *Foundations of Sociology* (New York: Macmillan Company, 1905), 377; John R. Commons, *Races and Immigrants in America* (New York: Macmillan, 1907), 127.

21 Daniel E. Bender, *American Abyss: Savagery and Civilization in the Age of Industry* (Ithaca, NY: Cornell University Press, 2009); Paul R. D. Lawrie, *Forging a Laboring Race: The African American Worker in the Progressive Imagination* (New York: New York University Press, 2016), 4; Gloria Marshall, "Racial Classifications: Popular and Scientific"; Elspeth H. Brown, "Racialising the Virile Body: Eadweard Muybridge's Locomotion Studies 1883–1887," *Gender & History* 17, no. 3 (2005), https://doi.org/10.1111/j.0953-5233.2005.00399.x, 642; Carl N. Degler, *In Search of Human Nature: The Decline and Revival of Darwinism in American Social Thought* (New York: Oxford University Press, 1992), 48; Matthew Frye Jacobson, *Whiteness of a Different Color: European Immigrants and the Alchemy of Race* (Cambridge, MA: Harvard University Press, 1998), 88; Nell Irvin Painter, *The History of White People* (New York: W. W. Norton, 2010), 252; Thomas F. Gossett, *Race: The History of an Idea*

in America (Dallas, TX: Southern Methodist University Press, 1963); Reginald Horsman, *Race and Manifest Destiny: The Origins of American Racial Anglo-Saxonism* (Cambridge, MA: Harvard University Press, 1981), 137–138, 156–157; Nancy Stepan Leys and Sander L. Gilman, "Appropriating the Idioms of Science: The Rejection of Scientific Racism," in *The "Racial" Economy of Science: Toward a Democratic Future, Race, Gender, and Science*, ed. Sandra Harding (Bloomington: Indiana University Press, 1993), 175.

22 Elizabeth Esch and David Roediger, "Scientific Management, Racist Science, and Race Management," in *Against Labor: How the US Employers Organized to Defeat Union Activism*, ed. Rosemary Feurer and Chad Pearson (Chicago: University of Illinois Press, 2017).

23 William P. Dillingham et al., *Immigrants in Industries: Part 21; Diversified Industries*, vol. 2 (Washington, DC: Government Printing Office, 1911), 342; Bradwin, *The Bunkhouse Man*, 110; also see Feldman and Lasker, *Racial Factors in American Industry*, 116.

24 Gunther Peck, *Reinventing Free Labor: Padrones and Immigrant Workers in the North American West, 1880–1930* (Cambridge: Cambridge University Press, 2000), 166–169.

25 Lucy E. Salyer, *Laws Harsh as Tigers: Chinese Immigrants and the Shaping of Modern Immigration Law* (Chapel Hill: University of North Carolina Press, 1995), 12, 18; Vincent J. Cannato, *American Passage: The History of Ellis Island* (New York: Harper, 2009), 6, 11; Margot Canaday, *The Straight State: Sexuality and Citizenship in Twentieth-Century America* (Princeton, NJ: Princeton University Press, 2009), 39, 95; Mae M. Ngai, *Impossible Subjects: Illegal Aliens and the Making of Modern America* (Princeton, NJ: Princeton University Press, 2004), 77; Peck, *Reinventing Free Labor*, 167; Jacobson, *Whiteness of a Different Color*, 8–9, 69, 78.

26 Robert DeCourcy Ward, "National Eugenics in Relation to Immigration," *The North American Review* 192, no. 656 (1910): 61; Mae M. Ngai, "Oscar Handlin and Immigration Policy Reform in the 1950s and 1960s," *Journal of American Ethnic History* 32, no. 3 (Spring 2013): 64; Aristide R. Zolberg, *A Nation by Design: Immigration Policy in the Fashioning of America* (Cambridge, MA: Harvard University Press, 2009), 6–7; John Higham, *Strangers in the Land: Patterns of American Nativism, 1860–1925* (New York: Atheneum, 1963); Robert F. Zeidel, *Immigrants, Progressives, and Exclusion Politics: The Dillingham Commission, 1900–1927* (DeKalb: Northern Illinois University Press, 2004), 5.

27 Matthew Frye Jacobson, *Barbarian Virtues: The United States Encounters Foreign Peoples at Home and Abroad, 1876–1917* (New York: Hill and Wang, 2001), 97; Peck, *Reinventing Free Labor*, 18, 166, 169–170; Jacobson, *Whiteness of a Different Color*, 31; Horsman, *Race and Manifest Destiny*, 253; Lawrence B. Glickman, *A Living Wage: American Workers and the Making of Consumer Society* (Ithaca, NY: Cornell University, 1997), 25; Joyce Appleby, "Commercial Farming and the 'Agrarian Myth' in the Early Republic," *Journal of American History* 68, no. 4 (1982): 833–849; Rossell Dave, "Tended Images: Verbal and Visual Idolatry of Rural Life in America, 1800–1850," *New York History* 69, no. 4 (1988): 425–440; Gary Gerstle, *American Crucible: Race and Nation in the Twentieth Century* (Princeton, NJ: Princeton University Press, 2017), 16, 46–47; Brenna Bhandar, *Colonial Lives of Property: Law, Land, and Racial Regimes of Ownership* (Durham, NC: Duke University Press, 2018).

28 Paul Outka, *Race and Nature from Transcendentalism to the Harlem Renaissance* (New York: Palgrave Macmillan, 2008), 3, 31–33, 154; James Belich, *Replenishing the Earth: The Settler Revolution and the Rise of the Anglo-World, 1783–1939* (Oxford: Oxford University Press, 2009); Peck, *Reinventing Free Labor*, 169; David R. Roediger, *Working toward Whiteness: How America's Immigrants Became White: The Strange Journey from Ellis Island to the Suburbs* (New York: Basic Books, 2005), 13.

29 Jacobson, *Barbarian Virtues*, 111.

30 Tara Watson and Kalee Thompson, *The Border Within: The Economics of Immigration in an Age of Fear* (Chicago: University of Chicago Press, 2022), 19–20.

31 Jason W. Moore, *Capitalism in the Web of Life: Ecology and the Accumulation of Capital* (New York: Verso Books, 2015), 53; Jacobson, *Barbarian Virtues*, 111; quoted in Ian Walter Radforth, *Bushworkers and Bosses: Logging in Northern Ontario, 1900–1980* (Toronto: University of Toronto Press, 1987), 78, 87.

32 Julie Greene, "Rethinking the Boundaries of Class: Labor History and Theories of Class and Capitalism," *Labor* 18, no. 2 (2021): 102.

33 Christian G. De Vito, "Labour Flexibility and Labour Precariousness as Conceptual Tools for the Historical Study of the Interactions between Labour Relations" in *On the Road to Global Labour History: A Festschrift for Marcel van der Linden*, ed. Karl Heinz Roth, Ben Lewis, and Marcel van der Linden (Leiden: Brill, 2018), 226; Verónica Martínez-Matsuda, "For Labor and Democracy: The Farm Security Administration's Competing Visions for Farm Workers' Socioeconomic Reform and Civil Rights in the 1940s," *Journal of American History* 106, no. 2 (2019): 340; Peck, *Reinventing Free Labor*, 16–18; Deborah Cohen, *Braceros: Migrant Citizens and Transnational Subjects in the United States and Mexico* (Chapel Hill: University of North Carolina Press, 2010); Jacobson, *Whiteness of a Different Color*; 31; Doug Sackman, *Orange Empire: California and the Fruits of Eden* (Berkeley: University of California Press, 2005), 128; David Gutiérrez, *Walls and Mirrors: Mexican Americans, Mexican Immigrants, and the Politics of Ethnicity* (Berkeley: University of California Press, 1995), 48.

34 Ngai, *Impossible Subjects*, 13.

35 US Congress, Importation of Canadian Bonded Labor, 11.

36 David Vermette, *A Distinct Alien Race: The Untold Story of Franco-Americans, Industrialization, Immigration, Religious Strife* (Montreal: Baraka Books, 2018); Stacy Warner Maddern, "Bonded Labor and Migration, United States" in *The Encyclopedia of Global Human Migration*, ed. Immanuel Ness (Chichester, UK: Wiley-Blackwell, 2013), 3; Fred Alliston Gilbert Papers, F. A. Gilbert to G. Schenck, December 20, 1925, box 7, Correspondence, 1924–1925 Special Collections, Raymond H. Fogler Library, University of Maine; United States; *Report of the Select Committee on Immigration and Naturalization*, 322–325; US Congress, Importation of Canadian Bonded Labor, 56.

37 Horsman, *Race and Manifest Destiny*, 159, 301.

38 Adam Gaudry and Darryl Leroux, "White Settler Revisionism and Making Métis Everywhere: The Evocation of Métissage in Québec and Nova Scotia," *Critical Ethnic Studies* 3, no. 1 (2017): 120; Fulmer Mood and Frederick J. Turner, "An Unfamiliar Essay by Frederick J. Turner," *Minnesota History* 18, no. 4 (1937): 393; Bolton Valencčius, *The Health of the Country: How American Settlers Understood Themselves and Their Land* (New York: Basic Books, 2002), 250; Frederic Gregory Mather, "On the Boundary Line," *Harper's New Monthly Magazine* (1874): 338.

39 Wayne Franklin, *James Fenimore Cooper: The Early Years* (New Haven, CT: Yale University Press, 2007), xxix; James Fenimore Cooper, *The Deerslayer* (New York: Dodd, Mead, [1841] 1952), 23, 41; James Fenimore Cooper, *The Pathfinder* (New York: Dodd, Mead, [1840] 1953), 164; Henry David Thoreau, *A Yankee in Canada with Anti-Slavery Reform Papers* (Boston: Ticknor and Fields, 1866), 60, 61. Also see Charles Hallock, "Aroostook and the Madawaska," *The Harper's Monthly* 20 (October 1863): 695; Zadok Cramer, *The Navigator* (Pittsburgh, PA: Cramer & Spear, [1801] 1824), 44, 254, 388.

40 Parkman, quoted in Edward Watts, *In This Remote Country: French Colonial Culture in the Anglo-American Imagination, 1780–1860* (Chapel Hill, NC: University of North Carolina Press, 2006), 72.

41 Richard White, *The Middle Ground: Indians, Empires, and Republics in the Great Lakes Region, 1650–1815* (Cambridge: Cambridge University Press, 1991), 60–75, 316; Peter Cook, "Onontio Gives Birth: How the French in Canada Became Fathers to their Indigenous Allies, 1645–1673," *Canadian Historical Review* 96, no. 2 (2015): 165–193; Carolyn Podruchny, *Making the Voyageur World: Travelers and Traders in the North American Fur Trade* (Lincoln: University of Nebraska Press, 2007), 1, 2, 71, 98.

42 William P. Dillingham et al., *Dictionary of Races or Peoples* (Washington, DC: Government Printing Office, 1911), 29; Jean Charlemagne Bracq, *The Evolution of French Canada* (New York: Macmillan, 1924), 206; Madison Grant, *The Conquest of a Continent; or, The Expansion of Races in America* (New York: C. Scribner's Sons, 1933), 310–311; Horsman, *Race and Manifest Destiny*, 183, 216, 240, 241, 272; Raymund A. Paredes, "The Mexican Image in American Travel Literature, 1831–1869," *New Mexico Historical Review* 52, no. 1 (1977): 5–29.

43 Thoreau, *Yankee in Canada*, 62; also see, Mood and Turner, "An Unfamiliar Essay," 395; Watts, *In This Remote Country*, 37; Konrad Gross, "The Voyageurs: Images of Canada's Archetypal Frontiersmen," in *A Talent(ed) Digger: Creations, Cameos, and Essays in Honour of Anna Rutherford*, ed. Hena Maes-Jelinek, Gordon Collier, Geoffrey V. Davis, and Anna Rutherford (Amsterdam: Rodopi, 1996), 411–422; Béatrice Craig and Maxime Dagenais, *The Land in Between: The Upper St. John Valley, Prehistory to World War I* (Gardiner, NY: Tilbury House, 2009), 48.

44 Quoted in Watts, *In This Remote Country*, 15, 8–9; Thoreau, *Yankee in Canada*, 62; see also Zadok Cramer, *The Navigator*; Jacobson, *Whiteness of a Different Color*, 218; Horsman, *Race and Manifest Destiny*, 156, 198, 200, 230, 291.

45 John Irving Little, *Nationalism, Capitalism and Colonization in Nineteenth-Century Québec, the Upper St. Francis District* (Kingston, ON: McGill-Queen's University Press, 1989), 5; Elliott Robert Barkan, "French Canadians," *Harvard Encyclopedia of American Ethnic Groups*, ed. Stephan Thernstrom (Cambridge, MA: Belknap Press, 1980), 391, 401; Brault, *The French Canadian Heritage*, 34, 158; Bruno Ramirez, *On the Move: French Canadian and Italian Migrants in the North Atlantic Economy, 1860–1914* (Toronto: McClelland & Stewart, 1991), 81–84.

46 Louis Hémon, *Maria Chapdelaine*, trans. W. H. Blake (Toronto: MacMillan, 1921), 45, 46.

47 Paul Socken, "Maria Chapdelaine," in *The Oxford Companion to Canadian Literature*, ed. Eugene Benson and William Toye (Oxford: Oxford University Press, 1997), accessed August 2, 2014, http://site.ebrary.com/id/10334814.

48 Brigitte Lane, "Three Major Witnesses of Franco-American Folklore in New England: Honore Beaugrand, Adelard Lambert, and Romeo Berthiaume," in *Steeples and Smokestacks*, ed. Claire Quintal, 416–417. Another example is Frank Oliver Call, *The Spell of French Canada* (Boston: L. C. Page, 1926), 247, 205, 227.

49 William Henry Drummond, *The Voyageur and Other Poems* (New York: G. P. Putnam's Sons, 1905) v; Gerald Noonan, "Drummond, William Henry," in *The Oxford Companion to Canadian Literature*, ed. Eugene Benson and William Toye (Oxford: Oxford University Press, 1997), accessed August 27, 2014, http://site.ebrary.com/id/10334814.

50 Jules Tessier "Menaud, maître-draveur," in *The Oxford Companion to Canadian Literature*, ed. Eugene Benson and William Toye (Oxford: Oxford University Press, 1997), accessed August 28, 2014, http://site.ebrary.com/id/10334814. Also see Little, *Nationalism, Capitalism and Colonization*, 9; Armand Chartier, "Towards a History of Franco-American Literature: Some Considerations," in *Steeples and Smokestacks*, ed. Claire Quintal, 295–306; Richard S. Sorrell, "'History as a Novel, the Novel as History': Ethnicity and the Franco American English Landguar Novel," in *Steeples and Smokestacks*, ed. Claire Quintal, 361. Other authors are

Gilbert Parker, Cornelius Krieghoff, George Boucher, Rosarie Dion-Levesque, Reine Malouin, Camille Lessard, Jacque Durcharme, and Felix Albert.

51 Jack London, *The Call of the Wild* (New York: Macmillan, 1963), 17.

52 Stewart Edward White, *The Blazed Trail* (NY: McClure, [1902] 1907), 13, 41, 46; Jon Tuska and Vicki Piekarski, *Encyclopedia of Frontier and Western Fiction* (New York: McGraw-Hill, 1983), 252–253; Richard H. Dillon, "White, Stewart Edward," *American National Biography Online*, accessed March 9, 2014, http://www.anb.org/articles/16/16-01754.html; Max J. Herzberg, *The Reader's Encyclopedia of American Literature* (New York: Crowell, 1962), 241–242; "Stewart Edward White," Internet Movie Database, accessed June 20, 2014, http://www.imdb.com/name/nm0925481; "Holman Francis Day," Internet Movie Database, accessed June 20, 2014, http://www.imdb.com/name/nm0206425/?ref_=fn_al_nm_1.

53 Watts, *In This Remote Country*, 123; David C. Smith, "Virgin Timber: The Maine Woods as a Locale for Juvenile Fiction" in *A Handful of Spice; A Miscellany of Maine Literature and History*, ed. Richard S. Sprague (Orono: University of Maine Press, 1968), 194–196. See Sara Bassett Ware, *The Story of Lumber* (Philadelphia: The Penn Publishing Company, 1912); Levi Parker Wyman, *The Golden Boys among the Lumberjacks* (New York: A. L. Burt, 192?); Stephen W. Meader, *Lumberjack* (San Francisco: Harcourt, Brace, 1934); Captain Charles A. J. Farrar, *Through the Winds: A Record of Sport and Adventure in the Forests of New Hampshire and Maine* (Boston, MA: Estes and Lauriat, 1892); Frank Gee Patchin, *The Pony Rider Boys in New England: Or, An Exciting Quest in the Maine Wilderness* (Philadelphia: H. Altemus, 1924).

54 Jacobson, *Barbarian Virtues*, 50–51, 145. Also see Johannes Fabian, *Time and the Other: How Anthropology Makes Its Object* (New York: Columbia University Press, 1983), 31; Jacobson, *Whiteness of a Different Color*, 6, 48, 70; John S. Haller, *Outcasts from Evolution; Scientific Attitudes of Racial Inferiority, 1859–1900* (Urbana: University of Illinois Press, 1971); Roediger, *Working Toward Whiteness*, 7–8, 37; Painter, *The History of White People*, x; Ngai, *Impossible Subjects*, 33; Peck, *Reinventing Free Labor*, 169.

55 Roediger, *Working Towards Whiteness*, 68; Degler, *In Search of Human Nature*, 20–21, 65; Linda Nash, "Finishing Nature: Harmonizing Bodies and Environments in Late Nineteenth-Century California," *Environmental History* 8, no. 1 (2003), https://doi.org/10.2307/3985971, 23, 28; Stephen Jay Gould, "American Polygeny and Craniometry before Darwin," in *The "Racial" Economy of Science*, ed. Sandra Harding, 90; Ibram X. Kendi, *Stamped from the Beginning: The Definitive History of Racist Ideas in America* (New York: Nation Books, 2016), 3; Colm Lavery, "Situating Eugenics: Robert DeCourcy Ward and the Immigration Restriction League of Boston," *Journal of Historical Geography* 53 (2016), https://doi.org/10.1016/j.jhg.2016.05.015; Robert V. Rohli and Gregory D. Bierly, "The Lost Legacy of Robert DeCourcy Ward in American Geographical Climatology," *Progress in Physical Geography* 35, no. 4 (2011): 547–564; Robert DeCourcy Ward, *Climate: Considered Especially in Relation to Man* (New York: G. P. Putnam's Sons, 1918), 281; Daniel E. Bender, *American Abyss: Savagery and Civilization in the Age of Industry* (Ithaca, NY: Cornell University Press, 2011), 58; Lawrie, *Forging a Laboring Race*, 146–147; Feldman and Lasker, *Racial Factors in American Industry*, 54.

56 Quoted in Jacobson, *Barbarian Virtues*, 112.

57 Dillingham et al., *Abstracts of Reports of the Immigration Commission*, 555.

58 Richard William Judd, *Common Lands, Common People: The Origins of Conservation in Northern New England* (Cambridge, MA: Harvard University Press, 1997); Karl Jacoby, *Crimes against Nature: Squatters, Poachers, Thieves, and the Hidden History of American Conservation* (Berkeley: University of California Press, 2014); William

Cronon, *Changes in the Land: Indians, Colonists, and the Ecology of New England* (New York: Hill and Wang, 1983); Charles Sellers, *The Market Revolution: Jacksonian America, 1815–1846* (New York: Oxford University Press, 1994), 5–12.

59 Gilman M. Ostrander, "Turner and the Germ Theory," *Agricultural History* (1958): 259; Gail Bederman, *Manliness & Civilization: A Cultural History of Gender and Race in the United States, 1880–1917* (Chicago: University of Chicago Press, 1995), 25.

60 Quote in Dillingham et al., *Immigrants in Industries: Part 24; Recent Immigrants in Agriculture*, vol. 1 (Washington, DC: Government Printing Office, 1911), 424. Also see, Jacobson, *Barbarian Virtues*, 112, 145, 171; Jacobson, *Whiteness of a Different Color*, 7, 71; Adam Kuper, *The Reinvention of Primitive Society: Transformations of a Myth* (London: Routledge, 2005); Horsman, *Race and Manifest Destiny*, 113–114; Ostrander, "Turner and the Germ Theory," 259; Peter Novick, *That Noble Dream: The "Objectivity Question" and the American Historical Profession* (Cambridge: Cambridge University Press, 1988), 81, 457; Horsman, *Race and Manifest Destiny*, 43; Bederman, *Manliness & Civilization*, 25; Bronwen J. Cohen, "Nativism and Western Myth: The Influence of Nativist Ideas on the American Self-Image," *Journal of American Studies* 8, no. 1 (1974): 28–29; Patricia Nelson Limerick, *The Legacy of Conquest: The Unbroken Past of the American West* (New York: W. W. Norton, 1987).

61 Madison Grant, *The Passing of the Great Race or the Racial Basis of European History* (New York: Charles Scribner's Sons, 1916), 227–228; Robert DeCourcy Ward, "The Agricultural Distribution of Immigrants," *Popular Science* 66 (1904): 169; also see Feldman and Lasker, *Racial Factors in American Industry*, 49.

62 Feldman and Lasker, *Racial Factors in American Industry*, 49–50. Also see Lawrie, *Forging a Laboring Race*, 62.

63 Frederick Jackson Turner, *The Frontier in American History* (Project Gutenberg, [1920] 2007), 37, accessed November 22, 2021, https://www.gutenberg.org/files/22994/22994-h/22994-h.htm; also see, Feldman and Lasker, *Racial Factors in American Industry*, 49, 53; Degler, *In Search of Human Nature*, 69; Edward Alsworth Ross, *Social Control: A Survey of the Foundations of Order* (New York: The Macmillan Company, 1910), 17; Jacobson, *Whiteness of a Different Color*, 72; Peck, *Reinventing Free Labor*, 166–169; Dillingham et al., *Immigrants in Industries: Part 24; Recent Immigrants in Agriculture*, vol. 2, 175; Turner, *The Frontier in American History*, 37; Horsman, *Race and Manifest Destiny*, 72; Alexandra Minna Stern, *Eugenic Nation: Faults and Frontiers of Better Breeding in Modern America* (Berkeley: University of California Press, 2005), 133.

64 Commons, *Races and Immigrants in America*, 128, 129.

65 Feldman and Lasker, *Racial Factors in American Industry*, 116–117.

66 Bradwin, *The Bunkhouse Man*, 98.

67 Edward Alsworth Ross, *The Old World in the New* (New York: Century, 1914), 21; Theodore Roosevelt, *The Strenuous Life: Essays and Addresses* (New York: Charles Scribner's Sons, 1906), 242.

68 Quoted in Ostrander, "Turner and the Germ Theory," 258. Also see, William P. Dillingham et al., *Reports of The Immigration Commission: Changes in Bodily Form of Descendants of Immigrants* (Washington, DC: Government Printing Office, 1911), 5, 72, 75; Degler, *In Search of Human Nature*, 63–64; Painter, *The History of White People*, 238.

69 Turner, *The Frontier in American History*, 154; Cohen, "Nativism and Western Myth," 25; Dillingham et al., *Abstracts of Reports of the Immigration Commission*, 547–549, 551; Jacobson, *Whiteness of a Different Color*, 47; Lawrie, *Forging a Laboring Race*, 151.

70 Ross, *The Old World in the New*, 82, 73–74, 52. Also see Dillingham et al., *Immigrants in Industries: Part 24; Recent Immigrants in Agriculture*, vol. 1 (Washington, DC:

Government Printing Office, 1911), 424; Cohen, "Nativism and Western Myth," 37; Painter, *The History of White People*, 251–252.

71 Novick, *That Noble Dream*, 90; Horsman, *Race and Manifest Destiny*, 34, 66, 68, 69; Gilbert F. LaFreniere, *The Decline of Nature: Environmental History and the Western Worldview* (Bethesda, MD: Academica Press, 2007), 55–56; Ostrander, "Turner and the Germ Theory," 260; Painter, *The History of White People*, 17–18, 27.

72 George P. Marsh, *Man and Nature or, Physical Geography as Modified by Human Action* (Project Gutenberg, [1864] 2011), http://www.gutenberg.org/ebooks/37957, 6, 7, 49, 279; also see Horsman, *Race and Manifest Destiny*, 181; LaFreniere, *The Decline of Nature*, 55–57; Ross, *The Old World in the New*, 203.

73 Dillingham et al., *Dictionary of Races or Peoples*, 81–82; Ross, *The Old World in the New*, 97; also see, Cohen, "Nativism and Western Myth," 31.

74 Dillingham et al., *Dictionary of Races or Peoples*, 74; Commons, *Races and Immigrants in America*, 133; Shari Rabin, *Jews on the Frontier: Religion and Mobility in Nineteenth-Century America* (New York: NYU Press, 2017).

75 Quote in Ross, *The Old World in the New*, 146, 289, 209, 290, 145; Jacob Riis, *How the Other Half Lives: Studies among the Tenements of New York* (New York: Charles Scribner's Sons, 1890), 48, 101; also see Dillingham et al., *Dictionary of Races or Peoples*, 75; Ross, *Social Control*; Robert D. Ward, "The Immigration Problem: Its Present Status and Its Relation to the American Race of the Future," *Carities* 12, no. 6 (1904): 148; Ava F. Kahn, "American West, New York Jewish," in *Jewish Life in the American West: Perspectives on Migration, Settlement, and Community*, ed. Ava F. Kahn (Los Angeles: Autry Museum of Western Heritage in association with University of Washington Press, Seattle, 2002), 37.

76 Roediger, *Working Toward Whiteness*, 44; Ross, *The Old World in the New*, 120; Dillingham et al., *Dictionary of Races or Peoples*, 104.

77 Painter, *The History of White People*, 289.

78 Degler, *In Search of Human Nature*, 51; Painter, *The History of White People*, 100–101, 232; Watts, *In This Remote Country*, 9, 24; John Davidson, "The Growth of the French Canadian Race in America," *Annals of the American Academy of Political and Social Science* 8 (1896): 20; Dillingham et al., *Dictionary of Races or Peoples*, 28–31; Bradwin, *The Bunkhouse Man*, 92–95; Jacobson, *Whiteness of a Different Color*, 45, 162.

79 Dillingham et al., *Abstracts of Reports of the Immigration Commission*, 543, 595; *Immigrants in Industries: Part 24; Recent Immigrants in Agriculture*, vol. 2, 555, 96, 212.

80 Dillingham et al., *Immigrants in Industries: Part 24; Recent Immigrants in Agriculture*, vol. 2, 145, 175, 190, 213, 265, 346, 262; Dillingham et al., *Dictionary of Races or Peoples*, 104.

81 Dillingham et al., *Abstracts of Reports of the Immigration Commission*, 561, 565, 574; Dillingham et al., *Immigrants in Industries: Part 24; Recent Immigrants in Agriculture*, vol. 1, 41–42, 399, 431, 205–206, 211–212, 406–408, 372; also see Ross, *The Old World in the New*, 97, 102; Dillingham et al., *Dictionary of Races or Peoples*, 82; Peck, *Reinventing Free Labor*, 169; Cohen, "Nativism and Western Myth," 31.

82 Dillingham et al., *Abstracts of Reports of the Immigration Commission*, 565; Ross, *The Old World in the New*, 102.

83 Dillingham et al., *Immigrants in Industries, Part 24, Recent Immigrants in Agriculture*, vol. 1, 414.

84 Dillingham et al., *Immigrants in Industries, Part 24, Recent Immigrants in Agriculture*, vol. 1, 41–42; also see Ross, *The Old World in the New*, 103; Elliott Robert Barkan, *From All Points: America's Immigrant West, 1870s–1952* (Bloomington: Indiana University Press, 2007), 185.

85 Dillingham et al., *Immigrants in Industries, Part 24, Recent Immigrants in Agriculture*, vol. 2, 146–148, 93, 143.

86 Dillingham et al., *Abstracts of Reports of the Immigration Commission*, 479; Dillingham et al., *Immigrants in Industries, Part 24, Recent Immigrants in Agriculture*, vol. 2, 93, 143–147; also see Ross, *The Old World in the New*, 145, 289.

87 Dillingham et al., *Immigrants in Industries, Part 24, Recent Immigrants in Agriculture*, vol. 2, 265, 346; Dillingham et al., *Abstracts of Reports of the Immigration Commission*, 586–587; Dillingham et al., *Abstracts of Reports of the Immigration Commission*, 586.

88 George Monroe Grant, ed., *French Canadian Life and Character: With Historical and Descriptive Sketches of the Scenery and Life in Québec, Montreal, Ottawa, and Surrounding Country* (Chicago: A. Belford, 1899), 73–75.

89 Gerald Morgan, "The French Canadian Problem: From an American Standpoint," *The North American Review* 205, 734 (1917): 79; Grant, *French Canadian Life and Character*, 12, 73. Also see Anders Larson, "Franco-Americans and the International Paper Company Strike of 1910," *Maine History* 33, no. 1 (1993): 42–43; Tyler Cline, "'A Dragon, Bog-Spawned, Is Now Stretched O'er This Land': The Ku Klux Klan's Patriotic-Protestantism in the Northeastern Borderlands during the 1920s and 1930s," *Histoire Sociale* 52, no. 106 (2019), 306; Elin L. Anderson, *We Americans: A Study of Cleavage in an American City* (Cambridge, MA: Harvard University Press, 1937); Call, *The Spell of French Canada*, 311, 225; Brault, *The French Canadian Heritage*, 27, 28; Mather, "On the Boundary Line," 338; "Some Traditional Beliefs of the French Canadians," *All the Year Round: A Weekly Journal* 3, no. 282 (1894): 484–485; Barkan, *From All Points: America's Immigrant West*, 185; Watts, *In This Remote Country*, 3, 9; Mood and Turner, "An Unfamiliar Essay," 393, 397; Ross, *The Old World in the New*, 13, 71, 82; Ostrander, "Turner and the Germ Theory," 28, 206; Craig and Dagenais, *The Land in Between*, 298, 327–337; Elwell, *Aroostook*, 25.

90 Larson, "Franco-Americans and the International Paper Company Strike"; Scontras, *Two Decades of Organized Labor*, 51–52.

91 Grant, ed., *French Canadian Life and Character*, 22; Bradwin, *The Bunkhouse Man*, 95.

92 Larson, "Franco-Americans and the International Paper Company Strike of 1910"; Gerstel, *Working-Class Americanism*.

93 Watts, *In This Remote Country*, 61; Craig, *Backwoods Consumers*, 41, 148.

94 Mather, "On the Boundary Line," 337–339; Mood and Turner, "An Unfamiliar Essay," 397.

95 Massachusetts Bureau of Statistics of Labor, *Twelfth Annual Report* (Boston: 1881), 469; Commons, *Races and Immigrants in America*, 98; Grant, *The Passing of the Great Race*, 81. Also see Morgan, "The French Canadian Problem," 77–80; Outka, *Race and Nature*, 3.

96 "Lumbering Operations in the Adirondacks," *The Watertown Re-Union*, March 9, 1904.

97 Elisa Elisabeth Andrea Sance, "Language, Identity, and Citizenship: Politics of Education in Madawaska, 1842–1920" (PhD diss., University of Maine, 2020), 162–163.

98 Nancy L. Gallagher, *Breeding Better Vermonters: The Eugenics Project in the Green Mountain State* (Hanover, NH: University Press of New England, 1999), 39–40, 154–159; Cline, "'A Dragon, Bog-Spawned,'" 309; Mark Paul Richard, "'This Is Not a Catholic Nation': The Ku Klux Klan Confronts Franco-Americans in Maine," *New England Quarterly* 82, no. 2 (2009): 296–297.

99 Bradwin, *The Bunkhouse Man*, 163; Robert E. Pike, *Tall Trees, Tough Men* (New York: W. W. Norton, 1967), 57; White, *The Blazed Trail*, 218–219; Wyckoff, *The Workers*, 236; "Telephones after Murder," *Chateaugay Record and Franklin County Democrat*, June 5, 1908.

100 Robert Howard and Rodney Ford, "From the Jumping Frenchmen of Maine to Posttraumatic Stress Disorder: The Startle Response in Neuropsychiatry," *Psychological Medicine* 22 (1992): 700, 702; George Beard, "Remarks upon 'Jumpers or Jumping Frenchmen,'" *The Journal of Nervous and Mental Diseases* 5 (1878): 526; Marie-Hélène Sainte-Hilaire, Jean-Marc Sainte-Hilaire, and Luc Granger, "Jumping Frenchmen of Maine," *Neurology* 36 (1986): 1269–1271; George M. Beard, "Experiments with the 'Jumpers' or 'Jumping Frenchmen' of Maine," *Journal of Nervous and Mental Disease* 7 (1880): 487–490.

101 English, *Unnatural Selections*, 177, 182; Jacobson, *Whiteness of a Different Color*, 95–96, 98–99.

102 Brigitte Lane, "Three Major Witness of Franco-American Folklore in New England," in *Steeples and Smokestacks*, ed. Claire Quintal, 416; Robert Redfield, *Peasant Society and Culture: An Anthropological Approach to Civilization* (Chicago: University of Chicago Press, 1956), 25–29, 116, 144; Horace Miner, *St. Denis, a French Canadian Parish* (Chicago: University of Chicago Press, 1963), 20, 158–159; Everett C. Hughes, *French Canada in Transition* (Chicago: University of Chicago Press, 1943), 2; Marlene Shore, *The Science of Social Redemption: McGill, the Chicago School, and the Origins of Social Research in Canada* (Toronto: University of Toronto Press, 1987), 253–260.

103 United States Wage and Hour and Public Contracts Divisions, Small Logging Operations: Data Pertinent to an Evaluation of the 13(a)(15) Exemption of the Fair Labor Standards Act (Washington, DC: 1964); Richard Carlson, "The Small Firm Exemption and the Single Employer Doctrine in Employment Discrimination Law," *St. John's Law Review* 80, no. 4 (2006); Brian Callaci, "Control Without Responsibility: The Legal Creation of Franchising, 1960–1980," *Enterprise & Society* 22, no. 1 (2021), https://doi.org/10.1017/eso.2019.58, 158.

104 Farm Production Forest Products Program, Magazine Publishers Association, and Periodical Publishers National Committee, *Timber Is a Crop* (New York: Periodical Publishers National Committee, 1950); Gerald Mayer, "Child Labor in America: History, Policy, and Legislative Issues" (Library of Congress, Congressional Research Service, 2013), 8.

105 Larry DeWitt, "The Decision to Exclude Agricultural and Domestic Workers from the 1935 Social Security Act," *Social Security Bulletin* 70 (2010): 49, 52, 53, 57–58; Canaday, *The Straight State*; Kati L. Griffith, "The Fair Labor Standards Act at 80: Everything Old Is New Again," *Cornell Law Review* 104, no. 3 (2019); Birchard E. Wyatt, William H. Wandel, and William Lytle Schurz, *The Social Security Act in Operation: A Practical Guide to the Federal and Federal-State Social Security Programs* (Washington, DC: Graphic Arts Press, 1937), microform 92.

106 Quoted in Parenteau, "Bonded Labor," 115.

107 US Congress, Importation of Canadian Bonded Labor, 46, 49, 26, 152.

108 US Congress, Importation of Canadian Bonded Labor, 49.

109 US Congress, Importation of Canadian Bonded Labor, 51, 125, 100.

110 US Congress, Importation of Canadian Bonded Labor, 55, 2, 21, 29; Brown Company Records, Brown Company Management v. Mv14, Program for Special Meeting of Board of Directors to Be Held in New York, September 12, 1955," New Hampshire Historical Society.

111 US Congress, Importation of Canadian Bonded Labor, 16, 111.

112 Brown Company Records, Brown Company Management v. Mv14, Program for Special Meeting of Board of Directors to Be Held in New York, September 12, 1955, New Hampshire Historical Society; John B. Allen, *Reflections of Berlin* (Berlin, NH: Berlin City Bank, 1985); "We're Going Places," *The Brown Bulletin* 3, no. 6 (Jan. 1955): 8–9, https://berlinnhhistoricalsociety.org/wp-content/uploads/2011/06/The_Brown_Bulletin_V3_No6_Feb_1955.pdf; "Brown Company and Brown

Corporation Consolidated Results . . ." *The Brown Bulletin* 3, no. 9 (April 1955): 2, https://berlinnhhistoricalsociety.org/wp-content/uploads/2011/06/The_Brown_Bulletin_V3_No9_Apr_1955.pdf.

113 US Congress, Importation of Canadian Bonded Labor, 25.

114 On this history, see Félix Albert, *Immigrant Odyssey: A French Canadian Habitant in New England—A Bilingual Edition of Histoire D'un Enfant Pauvre* (Orono: University of Maine Press, 1991), 34–37, 40, 56; Richard William Judd and Patricia A. Judd, *Aroostook: A Century of Logging in Northern Maine* (Orono: University of Maine Press, 1988), 194–195; Bruno Ramirez and Yves Otis, *Crossing the 49th Parallel: Migration from Canada to the United States, 1900–1930* (Ithaca, NY: Cornell University Press, 2001), 5, 8, 63, 11–12, 16; Vicero, "Immigration of French Canadians to New England," 70, 197–198, 214; Little, *Nationalism, Capitalism and Colonization*, 7, 16, 31–35, 47, xii–xiii, 81, 83, 89; John Irvine Little, *Crofters and Habitants: Settler Society, Economy, and Culture in a Québec Township, 1848–1881* (McGill-Queen's Press-MQUP, 1991), 47, 72, 154, 149, 154; Brault, *The French Canadian Heritage*, 34, 158; Ramirez, *On the Move*, 47, 77–79; Bradwin, *The Bunkhouse Man*, 95.

115 US Congress, Importation of Canadian Bonded Labor, 105.

116 Jason W. Moore, "The Rise of Cheap Nature" in *Anthropocene or Capitalocene?: Nature, History, and The Crisis of Capitalism*, ed. Christian Parenti and Jason W. Moore (Oakland, CA: PM Press, 2016), 87.

117 Jacobson, *Whiteness of a Different Color*, 18–19; Zolberg, *A Nation by Design*, 3, 7; Cannato, *American Passage*, 9; Ngai, *Impossible Subjects*, 165.

118 Michael Hillard and Jonathan Goldstein, "Cutting off the Canadians: Nativism and the Fate of the Maine Woodman's Association, 1970–1981," *Labor* 5, no. 3 (2008): 67–89; William C. Osborn, *The Paper Plantation: Ralph Nader's Study Group Report on the Pulp and Paper Industry in Maine* (New York: Grossman Publishers, 1974), 159–163; Josh Keefe, "Maine Senate President: Feds Failing to Protect US Logging Jobs from Canadian Competition," Maine Public (2020).

Epilogue

1 "Adirondack Park Land Use Classification Statistics," March 20, 2018, https://apa.ny.gov/gis/stats/colc201803.htm; Adirondack Council, *Vision 2050: Fulfilling the Promise of the Adirondack Park* (Elizabethtown, NY: Adirondack Council, 2021), ix; David R. Foster, *Wildlands and Woodlands, Farmlands and Communities: Broadening the Vision for New England* (Cambridge, MA: Harvard University Press, 2017), 12; Mark J. Ducey, John S. Gunn, and Andrew A. Whitman, "Late-Successional and Old-Growth Forests in the Northeastern United States: Structure, Dynamics, and Prospects for Restoration," *Forests* 4, no. 4 (2013): 1073.

2 Brian Mann, "Disarray in Adirondack Environmental Community, Defeat on Tupper Resort," *North Country Public Radio*, accessed January 1, 2015, https://www.northcountrypublicradio.org/news/story/19181/20120124/disarray-in-adirondack-environmental-community-defeat-on-tupper-resort; Megan Plete Postol, "As White Lake Quarry Application Moves Forward, Opposition Grows," *Adirondack Explorer*, September 10, 2021, https://www.adirondackexplorer.org/stories/as-white-lake-quarry-application-moves-forward-opposition-grows; Gwendolyn Craig, "2021 Explored: Snowmobile Trails/Tree Cutting," December 26, 2021, https://www.adirondackexplorer.org/stories/2021-explored-snowmobile-trails-tree-cutting.

3 Barbara McMartin, *The Great Forest of the Adirondacks* (New York: North Country Books, 1994), 102; Jonathan D. Anzalone, *Battles of the North Country: Wilderness Politics and Recreational Development in the Adirondack State Park, 1920–1980* (Amherst: University of Massachusetts Press, 2018), 16.

4 Michael G. Hillard, *Shredding Paper: The Rise and Fall of Maine's Mighty Paper Industry* (Ithaca, NY: ILR Press, 2020).

5 Andreas Malm, *Fossil Capital: The Rise of Steam-Power and The Roots of Global Warming* (Westminster, MD: Random House, 2016).

6 Stephanie Kaza, "Ethical Tension in the Northern Forest," in *The Future of the Northern Forest*, ed. Christopher McGrory Klyza and Stephen C. Trombulak (Middlebury, VT: Middlebury College Press, 1994), 74.

7 US Congress, Importation of Canadian Bonded Labor, 84th Congress, 1st Session, 1955, Hearings before the Subcommittee on Labor of the Committee on Labor and Public Welfare on S. Res. 98, A Resolution to Authorize a Study of the Policy and Practice of the United States with Respect to Permitting Bonded Laborers from Canada to Enter and Work in the United States, 5–7; Harold K. Hochschild, *Township 34* (Blue Mountain Lake, NY: Adirondack Museum, c. 1962–1980), 45.

8 Henry David Thoreau and Jeffrey S. Cramer, *The Maine Woods: A Fully Annotated Edition* (New Haven, CT: Yale University Press, 2010), 116, 143, 8.

9 Bayard O. Wheeler, "Lumber and Labor by Vernon H. Jensen," *Pacific Historical Review* 14, no. 3 (September 1945): 353; Charles A. Scontras, *Collective Efforts among Maine Workers: Beginnings and Foundations, 1820–1880* (Orono: Bureau of Labor Education, University of Maine, 1994), 108.

10 William R. Marleau, *Big Moose Station* (New York: Marleau Family Press, 1986), 334; Robert D. Bethke, *Adirondack Voices: Woodsmen and Woods Lore* (Urbana: University of Illinois Press, 1981), 31.

11 Edmund W. Bradwin, *The Bunkhouse Man: A Study of Work and Pay in the Camps of Canada, 1903–1914* (Toronto: University of Toronto Press, [1928] 1972), 163.

12 Cramer and Thoreau, *The Maine Woods*, 143; Roderick Frazier Nash, *Wilderness and the American Mind* (New Haven, CT: Yale University Press, 2014), 91; Graeme Wynn, "'Deplorably Dark and Demoralized Lumberers'? Rhetoric and Reality in Early Nineteenth-Century New Brunswick," *Forest & Conservation History* 24, no. 4 (1980): 169.

13 The following is a list of some other popular Adirondack local logging histories: Barbara K. Bird, *Calked Shoes* (Prospect, NY: Prospect Books, 1952); Maitland C. DeSormo, *The Heydays of the Adirondacks* (Burlington, VT: The George Little Press, 1974); Harold K. Hochschild, *Lumberjacks and Rivermen in the Central Adirondacks, 1850–1950* (New York: Adirondack Museum, 1962); Marleau, *Big Moose Station*; Roy Higby, *A Man from the Past* (New York: Big Moose Publishing, 1974); Harvey L. Dunham, *Adirondack French Louie: Early Life in the North Woods* (Utica, NY: North Country Books, 1953); Holbrook, *Yankee Logger*; Frank A. Reed, *Lumberjack Sky Pilot* (Utica, NY: North Country Books, 1965); Peter C. Welsh, *Jacks, Jobbers and Kings* (Utica, NY: North Country Books, 1995); Louis J. Simmons, *Mostly Spruce and Hemlock* (Saranac Lake, NY: Hungry Bear Publishing, 1979).

14 "Golff-Nelson to Host 'Mostly Spruce and Hemlock' Reading Marathon," *Adirondack Daily Enterprise*, accessed December 13, 2010, http://www.adirondackdailyenterprise.com/page/content.detail/id/514967/Goff-Nelson-to-host—Mostly-Spruce-and-Hemlock—reading-marathon.html.

15 Laura E. Tam and Andrea Bruce Woodall, *At Home in the Northern Forest: Reflections on a Region's Identity* (Concord, NH: Northern Forest Center, 2001), 67.

16 Jay Field, "Tech Firm Opening Waterville Office, Hopes to Employ 200," Maine Public Broadcasting (December 9, 2015), accessed July 6, 2016, http://news.mpbn.net/post/tech-firm-opening-waterville-office-hopes-employ-200#stream/0.

17 Some historians avoid these local histories and advised I do the same. Historians who ignore these sources are simply refusing to historicize them and read them in

context. Avoiding these sources can lead to oversights. When I asked one award-winning historian of consumption in rural North America about the spending sprees described in chapter 6—a favorite topic of folklore, oral history, and local history—I was told that the author knew of no work on the subject that did "not perpetuate a stereotype . . . [and that] it has yet to be proven that loggers went on wild spending sprees." By using local history alongside more conventional sources, I found that the spending sprees not only happened, but they were crucial to class formation and an important force that embedded workers into seasonal cycles of the forest.

18 Philip G. Terrie, *Contested Terrain: A New History of Nature and People in the Adirondacks* (Blue Mountain Lake, NY: Adirondack Museum, 1997), xx–xxi.

19 Harper, Falk, and Rankin, *The Northern Forest Lands Study*, 37.

INDEX

Illustrations are indicated by *italics*. Maps are indicated by *italics* followed by *m*. Tables are indicated by *italics* followed by *t*.